W9-ADZ-095

DRAFTING LEGAL DOCUMENTS:

Principles and Practices

Second Edition

By

Barbara Child
Director of Legal Drafting
University of Florida

AMERICAN CASEBOOK SERIES®

WEST GROUP

A THOMSON COMPANY

ST. PAUL, MINN., 1992

American Casebook Series, and the West Group symbol
are registered trademarks used herein under license.

COPYRIGHT © 1988 WEST PUBLISHING CO.
COPYRIGHT © 1992 By WEST PUBLISHING CO.
                610 Opperman Drive
                P.O. Box 64526
                St. Paul, MN 55164–0526
                1–800–328–9352

ISBN 0–314–00325–8

TEXT IS PRINTED ON 10% POST
CONSUMER RECYCLED PAPER

∞

7th Reprint — 2004

In loving memory of
Galen Keller Lewis
and
Gail Atkinson Palmarini
Who inspired the best in everyone they knew.

*

Preface to the Second Edition

This edition reflects the evolution over the past four years of our Legal Drafting Program at the University of Florida College of Law. The book now has three parts: Part One on drafting in litigation practice, Part Two on drafting in the practice of preventive law, and Part Three on drafting processes applicable to drafting any legal document. Part Three covers clients and documents as resources, flexible (vague and general) language, ambiguity, definitions, and style. Part Three is intended to serve as a process manual to use while working on any document covered in Part One or Part Two.

Many of the changes in this edition result from the suggestions of students who used the first edition as their drafting text. They wanted more attention to litigation. They wanted more complete documents. They wanted more examples of what to do instead of lots of examples of what not to do. Finally, in our course evaluations, they have told us that among our most helpful teaching methods are checklists. Therefore, this edition features: (1) annotated sample documents which, although not perfect, are designed to show good drafting rather than poor, and (2) both document checklists and skills checklists. This edition, like the first, treats drafting skills as largely transferable from one document to another.

The subtitle of the book has changed to "Principles and Practices" from "Materials and Problems." This edition, like the first, contains materials; however, unlike the first, it distinguishes between "exercises," which focus on analysis and usually involve little or no drafting, and "drafting assignments," which usually involve drafting an entire document. Part One focuses on assignments for drafting complaints, motions, and answers. Part Two focuses on assignments for drafting contracts, public and private legislation, and wills.

This edition includes many more drafting assignments and exercises than are feasible to use in one semester. The variety is intended to give options for people who prefer different approaches. The multiplicity is intended to make the book usable over a period of time without necessarily re-using assignments.

Every day I have worked on this edition I have become more aware of the many contributions of those who teach or have taught in the Florida program with me: Margaret Emanuel, Alison Gerencser, Lynn McGilvray-Saltzman, Linda Morton, Betsy Ruff, and Anne Rutledge. Each has brought a wealth of ideas, new perspectives, and a different approach to our work. I thank them all for everything they have done for the drafting program, this book, and me.

Special thanks to Maggie for the outspoken maximalism of her glosses on the first edition, for her fact patterns, and for her thoughtful commentary on an earlier draft of Chapter 6; to Alison for her valuable contributions to the substance of Chapters 2 and 5; to Lynn for her thoughtful commentary on an earlier draft of nearly the entire manuscript, with particular attention to students' needs; to Linda for her outspoken minimalism and her gusto, which remain in spirit long after she has moved to California; to Betsy for her incisive analysis of drafting assignments, for her fact patterns, and for her storehouse of superb teaching documents; and to Anne for her insightful and merciless editing, especially of an earlier draft of Part One and Chapter 11.

I also wish to thank friends and colleagues elsewhere who have shared ideas and materials generously, including Ralph Brill, Susan Brody, Scott Burnham, Peter Butt, Charles Calleros, John Dernbach, Robert Dick, Michael Gerber, George Gopen, Grayfred Gray, Thomas Haggard, Hollis Hurd, Joseph Kimble, Richard Neumann, Donald Revell, Marjorie Rombauer, and Thomas Stipanowich. Special thanks to Joe Kimble, who has given me valuable suggestions based on his experience teaching from the first edition.

I thank all my own students who have shared their efforts, their willingness to experiment, their commitment to become expert drafters, their intelligence, and their pleasure in learning. Their work is here on every page, for they have shown me what they needed to have explained or demonstrated, and what went without saying. Special thanks to Regina DeIulio for permission to adapt her declaration of restrictions and covenants for a subdivision as the sample private legislation in Chapter 5.

I thank my secretary Carol Velasquez for all her assistance in preparing the manuscript and for her patience and good nature.

Whatever mistakes or weaknesses remain are mine alone.

I also wish to thank Alan Morris, who continues to encourage me in my writing, even though he wishes I would write a novel instead.

Finally, I wish to express once more my deep gratitude to Reed Dickerson. Through his writing about legal drafting and through his encouragement of my work, he changed the course of my professional life.

BARBARA CHILD

Gainesville, Florida
February, 1992

Summary of Contents

*

Table of Contents

Table of Cases

The principal cases are in bold type. Cases cited or discussed in the text are roman type. References are to pages. Cases cited in principal cases and within other quoted materials are not included.

*

DRAFTING LEGAL DOCUMENTS:

Principles and Practices

Second Edition

*

Introduction

LEGAL DRAFTING: A PREVIEW OF THE COURSE

I. PURPOSE OF THE COURSE

The purpose of a course in legal drafting is to engage you in the practical drafting experience that will form a major part of your work as a lawyer: preparing documents that effectuate clients' intentions while planning to avoid potential legal problems. In law practice, lawyers address specific disputes and also prevent disputes by designing documents to make clear to people what their rights and responsibilities are.

As drafters, lawyers not only litigate; they also seek to avoid litigation. In litigation practice, they draft pleadings, motions, interrogatories, jury instructions, settlement agreements, and orders, among other documents. In practice that seeks to avoid litigation, they draft contracts, public and private legislation, wills, trusts, and other planning documents. In an ordinary office practice, a lawyer is likely in the space of a month or a year to draft everything from a purchase and sale agreement to a lease with a purchase option, or from by-laws for a corporation to a proposed local ordinance on some matter of interest to a client. Thus a legal drafting course focuses on the lawyer's roles as litigator and as planner, problem-solver, and preventer of trouble. Legal drafting has been described as "preventive law" by Reed Dickerson, author of the classic treatise on drafting, *The Fundamentals of Legal Drafting.*[1]

II. THE FOCUSES OF THE COURSE

A. THE FOCUS ON SKILLS

1. *Skills Involved in Drafting*

A legal drafting course focuses on the following skills:

- Analyzing documents critically.

---

1. (2d ed. 1986).

1

- Analyzing a body of facts for missing information and conceptual overlaps or gaps.
- Making appropriate use of forms.
- Arranging material systematically in whole documents, sections of documents, and individual provisions.
- Articulating meaning clearly and concisely with extraordinary attention to internal consistency and to degrees of generality or particularity.
- Using flexible language as an advocate's tool.
- Avoiding inadvertent ambiguity.
- Defining terms and naming concepts.
- Creating a readable style.

2. The Skills as Elements of Strategy

Legal drafting skills are strategic, not simply the technical skills of grammar and word usage. These strategic skills involve not only finding the right word but also producing the right concept, just as the process of writing not only reflects thought but also gives it shape.[2] Thus the study of drafting is not so much about the techniques of manipulating language as it is about the process of shaping solutions to conceptual problems.[3] Moreover, the study of drafting should help you learn to exercise sound judgment about what works in real situations involving clients with practical problems, concerns, goals, and limits.

One legal educator describes the lawyer as "at once the architect and the builder of human relationships."[4] To do this work, you need legal training in the use of linguistic tools and conceptual materials "and their capacity to bear loads and withstand stresses."[5] You also need to develop a working knowledge of human nature and business practices as well as problem-solving skills and effective use of language. All these are necessary for a lawyer to evaluate plans and the documents embodying those plans for appropriate attention to contingencies and avoidance of the risks that ambiguity can cause.[6]

B. THE FOCUS ON AUDIENCE

1. Drafting for Litigation and to Avoid It

A legal drafting course also focuses special attention on the audience of users of legal documents. On the one hand, you draft for the trial counsel and judge as potential users; on the other hand, you hope by good drafting to prevent litigation altogether. The first job, therefore, is to draft documents that communicate clearly to your own client.

---

2. Id. at 354.

3. Id. at 5–6.

4. Cavers, Legal Education and Lawyer–Made Law, 54 W.Va.L.Rev. 177, 180 (1952).

5. Id.

6. Id.

This job becomes further complicated when the client is more than one person, as when you draft a partnership agreement for a set of partners or a trust agreement and companion wills for a husband and wife. In such circumstances, you need to be aware of how the joint clients communicate with each other and whether they have a common understanding of the document in question.

2. *Drafting for Users With Different Degrees of Understanding*

A document is likely to be used by people with different degrees of understanding. Some will fully understand technical terms or legal terms of art. Others will not understand them at all. Furthermore, it is one thing to assess your own client or clients; it is another to speculate about other parties who will use the document but whose identity may be unknown, to say nothing of the identity of their present or future counsel. Some private documents such as corporate by-laws or sets of regulations have as their audience whole communities of users, who may be as numerous as the users of some public legislation.

3. *Drafting for Different Uses*

In addition, you may intend to use a document in a number of ways. For example, you may draft a lease for an individual who wants to rent one single-family dwelling for one year. That lease will not work for another client who owns an apartment complex. As soon as you begin to view the lease as a form, the number of possible contingencies increases. If the client owns several apartment complexes, the further increased possible contingencies dictate still more flexibility. If you specialize in real estate practice and anticipate producing a form lease for use by many clients, the document needs to be even more flexible. At some point the document may not be able to tolerate any further variety. Then it is time to reconceptualize the problems and produce multiple documents.

4. *Drafting for Users With Different Points of View*

Different users of the same document will approach it from different points of view. One may look to it for protection. Another may be chiefly interested in escaping its coverage. A constant challenge is drafting for the "reader in bad faith." In other words, you need to make meaning so clear that a reader who would prefer another meaning cannot support it.

If a document is one that a court is likely to construe strictly against the drafter—such as a consumer contract—then explicit language is more necessary than in contracts between businesses or in other documents that courts commonly construe by looking at the internal context to resolve doubtful matters.[7]

7. Dickerson, above note 1, at 46.

5. *Drafting for Reference Use*

Writers are used to assuming that readers read material straight through, from beginning to end. However, many legal documents are used for reference. The tenant suddenly wants to know what to do when the landlord fails to repair the steps. The dissident stockholder reads up on voting rights and proxies in time for the annual meeting. Thus legal documents require special organization to make individual provisions easy to find and also sometimes easy to amend.[8]

III. THE ROLES OF THE LAWYER AND THE CLIENT IN MAKING POLICY

A. THE NATURE OF "POLICY"

The lawyer as drafter needs to develop skills particularly well when dealing with clients in the clients' role as policy makers. "Policy" here refers to any plan or rule that a client wishes to legislate or propose for agreement in a legal document. Thus government legislators are not the only ones who make policy. A landlord makes policy when providing in a lease how security deposits may be used or specifying tenants' duties to maintain the property. Likewise a testator makes policy when providing in a will who will administer the estate or who will take the remainder. In other words, much of the substantive content of every legislative or contractual document may be policy.

Many clients have only a rough idea of what they want to accomplish. Others have a detailed, even rigidly formed, idea but little appreciation of its ramifications. The lawyer is often in a better position than the client to anticipate problems of administering or enforcing a policy. The client may ask the lawyer merely to put the client's ideas on paper in "proper legal form." But the process of drafting involves a great deal more than that.

Even though the lawyer cannot ethically take over the client's decision-making rights and responsibilities, the lawyer can and should advise the client and participate in refining policy. For example, you might have as a client a landlord who wants to incorporate into a lease the policy that tenants cannot have waterbeds. When preparing to draft the lease, you have a duty first to discover whether the state has a statute such as the following one.

> **83.535 Flotation bedding system; restrictions on use.**—No landlord may prohibit a tenant from using a flotation bedding system in a dwelling unit, provided the flotation bedding system does not violate applicable building codes. The landlord may

---

8. See R. Dick, Legal Drafting 8–10 (2d ed. 1985); C. Felsenfeld and A. Siegel, Writing Contracts in Plain English 86–91 (1981), both in part summarized here. See also Conard, New Ways to Write Laws, 56 Yale L.J. 458, 469–81 (1947).

require the tenant to carry in the tenant's name flotation insurance as is standard in the industry in an amount deemed reasonable to protect the tenant and owner against personal injury and property damage to the dwelling units. In any case, the policy shall carry a loss payable clause to the owner of the building.

If there is such a statute, your next duty is to investigate the applicable building codes and then advise the client about the legislative restrictions. You should not merely leave out the waterbed provision. Neither should you go ahead and include a provision for flotation insurance without first consulting the client. At the very least, the client may have something to say about whether to spell out in the lease the amount of insurance that reasonably protects against property damage to the dwelling unit.

In short, lawyers as drafters are obligated to investigate and advise and not to make policy on their own initiative when no one is looking. The most successful drafting occurs when lawyer and client are true collaborators, each contributing particular kinds of expertise and neither viewing their relationship in terms of the power of one over the other. Thus, for successful collaboration, you must be an investigator and thinker as well as a writer.

B. THE STAGES OF COLLABORATION

1. Investigating Stage

In the investigating stage, you learn about the client's objectives and the relevant factual and legal background.

2. Thinking Stage

In the thinking stage, you refine those objectives into concepts and decide how broad or narrow the concepts ought to be as well as how they ought to be arranged. At this stage, the interaction between lawyer and client is critical. If you have earned the client's confidence and respect, you can influence policy in major ways and sometimes can serve as an agent for changes of wide-ranging significance.

3. Writing Stage

Finally, in the writing stage you compose a document that clearly communicates the client's wishes. If this final stage is successful, you and the client together achieve a refined understanding of the original objectives. The drafting process ultimately expresses these refined concepts.[9]

9. For a more detailed introduction to the discipline of legal drafting and its relationship to both substantive policy-making and communication, see Dickerson, above note 1, at 1–50; Dick, above note 8, at 1–10, both in part summarized here.

*

Part One

DRAFTING IN LITIGATION PRACTICE: INTRODUCTION TO THE DOCUMENTS *

I. PLEADINGS AND MOTIONS DISTINGUISHED

Pleadings are documents in which parties to a legal action (a) allege facts to set out causes of action or claims for relief and (b) respond with admissions and defenses, the latter in the form of denials and affirmative defenses. The pleadings in an action establish what issues the action has to resolve.

In contrast to pleadings, motions are applications to the court for orders. The orders may resolve some or all of the issues in an action. In other words, a granted motion may result in a final judgment, or it may only affect the course of the continuing action.

II. PLEADINGS REQUESTING AFFIRMATIVE RELIEF

In most jurisdictions, the pleadings requesting affirmative relief are: complaint, petition, counterclaim, cross-claim, and third party complaint. The process of amending pleadings results in pleadings called amended complaint, second amended complaint, etc.

III. DEFENSIVE PLEADINGS

A. ANSWER

Most jurisdictions provide for an answer to the following pleadings: complaint, petition, counterclaim, cross-claim, and third party complaint.

* Pleadings and motions are the litigation documents covered in this book. For discussion of discovery documents, see W. Schwartzer and L. Pasahow, Civil Discovery: A Guide to Efficient Practice (1989); D. Suplee and D. Donaldson, The Deposition Handbook: Strategies, Tactics and Mechanics (1988). For discussion of jury instructions, see Symposium: Making Jury Instructions Comprehensible, 8 U. Bridgeport L.Rev. (No. 2, 1987).

A defendant's counterclaim against the plaintiff seeks affirmative relief based on a cause of action. A counterclaim is thus distinguished from a defense, which seeks to defeat a cause of action by denial or avoidance. In turn, the plaintiff's answer to a counterclaim responds to the allegations in the counterclaim only; it does not deny the denials in the defendant's answer.

B. REPLY

A reply is commonly authorized only to avoid affirmative defenses in an answer or third party answer. The plaintiff avoids an affirmative defense by pleading new matter that provides a legal excuse or exception. In other words, a reply pleads an affirmative defense to an affirmative defense. It does not deny allegations. For example, the plaintiff may avoid the defense of release if the defendant made fraudulent misrepresentations to induce the plaintiff to sign the release. This avoidance by pleading new matter differs from denying having signed the release.

IV. CONTENTS AND STRUCTURE OF THE BODY OF PLEADINGS AND MOTIONS

The contents and structure of the body of complaints, motions, and answers are treated in Chapters 1, 2, and 3 respectively. The chapters refer generally to common rules of civil procedure and statutes related to drafting pleadings and motions. For exact compliance with the statutes and rules applicable in the jurisdiction where you plan to file a pleading or motion, consult that jurisdiction's statutes and rules as well as cases construing them.

V. FORMALITIES BEFORE AND AFTER THE BODY

A. CAPTION

Both pleadings and motions begin with a caption. Rules commonly require in the caption:

• The name of the court, including the jurisdiction it serves, for example: "The Eighth Judicial Circuit Court in and for Alachua County, Florida" or "United States District Court in and for the Northern District of Ohio."

• The court file number, which is supplied by the court clerk at the time of filing the complaint or other initial pleading.

• The name of the first party on each side, and all additional parties if it is the initial pleading; for subsequent pleadings, "*et al.*" ("and others") conventionally follows the name of the first party on each side.

- The nature of the pleading, including identification of the party filing the pleading if there are multiple parties on the filing party's side, for example: "Defendant Jane Doe's Counterclaim" or "Plaintiff John Roe's Amended Complaint."

B. ATTORNEY'S SIGNATURE

Rules commonly require that every pleading and motion of a represented party be signed by an attorney of record. The paper must also state the attorney's name, address with zip code, and phone number with area code. In some jurisdictions, a rule of judicial administration also requires the attorney's state Bar license number.

It is no longer common to require pleadings to be verified or accompanied by affidavit, except in circumstances specified by statute or rule, such as a required poverty affidavit for exemption from filing fees or a required verification of a motion to strike a sham pleading.

In general, the attorney's signature certifies that the attorney has read the pleading and believes there is good ground to support it. Federal Rule of Civil Procedure 11 specifies, in addition, that the signature certifies "that to the best of the signer's knowledge, information, and belief formed after reasonable inquiry [the pleading, motion, or other paper] is well grounded in fact and is warranted by existing law or a good faith argument for the extension, modification, or reversal of existing law, and that it is not interposed for any improper purpose, such as to harass or to cause unnecessary delay or needless increase in the cost of litigation." Rule 11 provides for sanctions for signing in violation of the rule.

C. CERTIFICATE OF SERVICE

A certificate of service must appear on each pleading or motion after the initial pleading, *including on an amended complaint,* but *not* on the initial pleading. Initial pleadings are served by the court. All other pleadings and motions are served, usually by regular United States mail or else by hand delivery, by the attorney or party filing them. If there are multiple parties on a side, the filing attorney or party must serve a copy on *all* other parties, including one's co-plaintiffs or co-defendants. If a party is represented by an attorney, service is made on the attorney rather than the party. The certificate of service identifies each person being served as attorney or party and gives that person's address where served.

Chapter 1

COMPLAINTS

Table of Sections

I. USING OFFICIAL AND UNOFFICIAL PLEADING FORMS

A. STANDARDIZED OFFICIAL PLEADING FORMS

The federal and state civil procedure rules make some of the work of drafting pleadings essentially a matter of following formal requirements. In jurisdictions operating on the theory that the purpose of pleadings is merely to give notice to the opposing party, drafting pleadings becomes largely a matter of filling out a form authorized or even provided by the court. For example, some mandatory California Judicial Council forms are standardized to the extent that one form serves as the complaint for the whole range of personal injury, property damage, and wrongful death actions. The attorney merely chooses which boxes to check and picks which cause-of-action form to attach. In a jurisdiction with such forms, the actual task of drafting pleadings becomes limited to matters of nonroutine complexity. Here is a sampling of California's forms.[1]

---

1. Reprinted from West's 1987 Annotated California Codes Judicial Council Forms 32–34, 38, with permission of the West Publishing Company.

10

WEST'S 1987 ANN.CALIF. CODES JUDICIAL COUNCIL FORMS

ATTORNEY OR PARTY WITHOUT ATTORNEY (NAME AND ADDRESS) TELEPHONE	FOR COURT USE ONLY
ATTORNEY FOR (NAME)	
Insert name of court, judicial district or branch court, if any, and post office and street address	
PLAINTIFF	
DEFENDANT	
☐ DOES 1 TO _____	

COMPLAINT—Personal Injury, Property Damage, Wrongful Death	CASE NUMBER

☐ MOTOR VEHICLE   ☐ OTHER *(specify):*
     ☐ Property Damage   ☐ Wrongful Death
     ☐ Personal Injury ☐ Other Damages *(specify):*	

1 This pleading, including attachments and exhibits, consists of the following number of pages.

2 a Each plaintiff named above is a competent adult
    ☐ **Except** plaintiff *(name).*
        ☐ a corporation qualified to do business in California
        ☐ an unincorporated entity *(describe)*
        ☐ a public entity *(describe)*
        ☐ a minor   ☐ an adult
            ☐ for whom a guardian or conservator of the estate or a guardian ad litem has been appointed
            ☐ other *(specify):*
        ☐ other *(specify)*

    ☐ **Except** plaintiff *(name).*
        ☐ a corporation qualified to do business in California
        ☐ an unincorporated entity *(describe).*
        ☐ a public entity *(describe):*
        ☐ a minor   ☐ an adult
            ☐ for whom a guardian or conservator of the estate or a guardian ad litem has been appointed
            ☐ other *(specify):*
        ☐ other *(specify)*

   b ☐ Plaintiff *(name).*
        is doing business under the fictitious name of *(specify):*

        and has complied with the fictitious business name laws.
   c. ☐ Information about additional plaintiffs who are not competent adults is shown in Complaint—
        Attachment 2c.   (Continued)

Form Approved by the
Judicial Council of California
Effective January 1, 1982
Rule 982 1(1)
      **COMPLAINT—Personal Injury, Property Damage,
Wrongful Death**   CCP 425 12
                                                     (E146)

SHORT TITLE	CASE NUMBER

COMPLAINT—Personal Injury, Property Damage, Wrongful Death   Page two

3. a. Each defendant named above is a natural person
   ☐ **Except** defendant *(name):*   ☐ **Except** defendant *(name)*

   ☐ a business organization, form unknown   ☐ a business organization, form unknown
   ☐ a corporation   ☐ a corporation
   ☐ an unincorporated entity *(describe):*   ☐ an unincorporated entity *(describe):*

   ☐ a public entity *(describe)*   ☐ a public entity *(describe)*

   ☐ other *(specify):*   ☐ other *(specify):*

   ☐ **Except** defendant *(name):*   ☐ **Except** defendant *(name):*

   ☐ a business organization, form unknown   ☐ a business organization, form unknown
   ☐ a corporation   ☐ a corporation
   ☐ an unincorporated entity *(describe):*   ☐ an unincorporated entity *(describe).*

   ☐ a public entity *(describe)*   ☐ a public entity *(describe).*

   ☐ other *(specify)*   ☐ other *(specify)*

   b. The true names and capacities of defendants sued as Does are unknown to plaintiff

   c. ☐ Information about additional defendants who are not natural persons is contained in Complaint—
      Attachment 3c.
   d. ☐ Defendants who are joined pursuant to Code of Civil Procedure section 382 are *(names)*.

4. ☐ Plaintiff is required to comply with a claims statute, and
   a ☐ plaintiff has complied with applicable claims statutes, **or**
   b ☐ plaintiff is excused from complying because *(specify)*

5. This court is the proper court because
   ☐ at least one defendant now resides in its jurisdictional area.
   ☐ the principal place of business of a corporation or unincorporated association is in its jurisdictional area
   ☐ injury to person or damage to personal property occurred in its jurisdictional area
   ☐ other *(specify):*

6. ☐ The following paragraphs of this complaint are alleged on information and belief *(specify paragraph numbers):*

(Continued)

SHORT TITLE	CASE NUMBER

COMPLAINT—Personal Injury, Property Damage, Wrongful Death (Continued)   Page three

7 ☐ The damages claimed for wrongful death and the relationships of plaintiff to the deceased are ☐ listed in Complaint—Attachment 7 ☐ as follows.

8. Plaintiff has suffered
     ☐ wage loss   ☐ loss of use of property
     ☐ hospital and medical expenses   ☐ general damage
     ☐ property damage   ☐ loss of earning capacity
     ☐ other damage *(specify)*:

9. Relief sought in this complaint is within the jurisdiction of this court

10. PLAINTIFF PRAYS
     For judgment for costs of suit, for such relief as is fair, just, and equitable, and for
     ☐ compensatory damages
         ☐ **(Superior Court)** according to proof

         ☐ **(Municipal and Justice Court)** in the amount of $
     ☐ other *(specify)*:

11 The following causes of action are attached and the statements above apply to each *(Each complaint must have one or more causes of action attached)*
     ☐ Motor Vehicle
     ☐ General Negligence
     ☐ Intentional Tort
     ☐ Products Liability
     ☐ Premises Liability
     ☐ Other *(specify)*:

                 _____   _____
                    (Type or print name)   (Signature of plaintiff or attorney)

Rule 982 1(1) (cont d)   **COMPLAINT**—Personal Injury, Property Damage,   Page three
                                           Wrongful Death (Continued)   CCP 425 12
                                                                      [E148]

SHORT TITLE:	CASE NUMBER

_____ .. **CAUSE OF ACTION—Premises Liability**   **Page**
    (number)

ATTACHMENT TO ☐ Complaint   ☐ Cross-Complaint

(Use a separate cause of action form for each cause of action.)

Prem.L-1. Plaintiff *(name)*:
    alleges the acts of defendants were the legal (proximate) cause of damages to plaintiff.
    On *(date)*:   plaintiff was injured on the following premises in the following

    fashion *(description of premises and circumstances of injury)*:

Prem.L-2   ☐ **Count One—Negligence** The defendants who negligently owned, maintained, managed and operated
    the described premises were *(names)*:

    ☐ Does   to

Prem.L-3.   ☐ **Count Two—Willful Failure to Warn** [Civil Code section 846] The defendant owners who willfully
    or maliciously failed to guard or warn against a dangerous condition, use, structure, or activity were
    (names):

    ☐ Does .   to
    Plaintiff, a recreational user, was ☐ an invited guest ☐ a paying guest

Prem.L-4.   ☐ **Count Three—Dangerous Condition of Public Property** The defendants who owned public property
    on which a dangerous condition existed were *(names)*

    ☐ Does   to
    a. ☐ The defendant public entity had ☐ actual ☐ constructive notice of the existence of the
    dangerous condition in sufficient time prior to the injury to have corrected it.
    b. ☐ The condition was created by employees of the defendant public entity.

Prem.L-5. a. ☐ **Allegations about Other Defendants** The defendants who were the agents and employees of the
    other defendants and acted within the scope of the agency were *(names)*:

    ☐ Does __ __ ___ to _ . _____
    b ☐ The defendants who are liable to plaintiffs for other reasons and the reasons for their liability are
    ☐ described in attachment Prem.L-5.b ☐ as follows *(names)*:

Form Approved by the
Judicial Council of California
Effective January 1, 1982
Rule 982 1(5)   **CAUSE OF ACTION—Premises Liability**   CCP 425 12
    [E152]

B. PRIVATELY PUBLISHED FORM BOOKS

    A great many privately published form books provide what purport to be model pleadings for use in a given jurisdiction even though they are not authorized by any court. An attorney should not routinely rely on them with confidence. They are of uneven quality. Many are written in an obsolete style, and some are based on obsolete law as well. Although some do provide the basis for legally sufficient pleadings, the attorney using them bears the burden of testing them against the applicable civil rules as well as other statutory and common law.

C. COURT–APPROVED MODEL FORMS

On the other hand, some states have model pleading forms approved by the state supreme court or other official body. These are not pieces of paper to be ripped off a pad and filed with check marks in boxes. Attorneys are not required to use them. In fact, attorneys are expected to adapt the forms to the facts in a particular case. Nonetheless, some of these forms address quite specific situations, such as a plaintiff burned in a nightclub or a plaintiff injured because a defendant failed to keep a hallway lighted. In any event, attorneys may use court-approved forms with confidence that pleadings based on them are legally sufficient under the state's civil procedure rules, assuming, of course, that appropriate matter is inserted in the blanks.

Following are conversion and replevin complaint forms approved by the Florida Supreme Court.

FORM 1.939

CONVERSION

COMPLAINT

1   Plaintiff, A.B., sues defendant, C.D., and alleges:

2   1. This is an action for damages that (insert jurisdictional
3 amount).

4   2. On or about _____, 19__, defendant converted to his own
5 use (insert description of property converted) that was then the
6 property of plaintiff of the value of $_____.

7   WHEREFORE plaintiff demands judgment for damages against
8 defendant.

FORM 1.937

REPLEVIN

COMPLAINT

1   Plaintiff, A.B., sues defendant, C.D., and alleges:

2   1. This is an action to recover possession of personal property
3 in _____ County, Florida.

4   2. The description of the property is:

5   (list property)

6 To the best of plaintiff's knowledge, information and belief, the
7 value of the property is $_____.

8   3. Plaintiff is entitled to the possession of the property under a
9 security agreement dated _____, 19__, a copy of the agreement
10 being attached.

11   4. To plaintiff's best knowledge, information and belief, the
12 property is located at _____.

13   5. The property is wrongfully detained by defendant. Defen-
14 dant came into possession of the property by (describe method of
15 possession). To plaintiff's best knowledge, information and belief,
16 defendant detains the property because (give reasons).

17   6. The property has not been taken for any tax, assessment or
18 fine pursuant to law.

19   7. The property has not been taken under an execution or
20 attachment against plaintiff's property.

21   WHEREFORE plaintiff demands judgment for possession of the
22 property.

NOTE: Paragraph 3 must be modified if the right to possession arose in another manner. Allegations and a demand for damages, if appropriate, can be added to the form.

Exercise 1.1

Court-approved forms can be especially helpful for drafting a complaint based on a statutory cause of action. Study the excerpts below from the statutes upon which the replevin form above is based. What statutory sections give rise to what paragraphs in the complaint form? To what extent does the complaint form exactly track the statutory language?

78.01 Right of replevin.—Any person whose personal property is wrongfully detained by any other person or officer may have a writ of replevin to recover said personal property and any damages sustained by reason of the wrongful taking or detention as herein provided. Notice of lis pendens to charge third persons with knowledge of plaintiff's claim on the property may be recorded.

78.03 Venue and jurisdiction.—The action shall be brought in the court in the county where the property is which has jurisdiction of the value of the property sought to be replevied. When property consists of separate articles, the value of any one of which is within the jurisdiction, the plaintiff shall not divide the property to give jurisdiction to the lower court to enable plaintiff to bring separate actions therefor.

78.045 Writ; court order required.—No clerk of court shall issue a writ of replevin prior to final judgment unless there has been filed with the clerk of court an order authorizing the issuance of such writ of replevin.

78.055 Complaint; requirements.—To obtain an order authorizing the issuance of a writ of replevin prior to final judgment, the plaintiff shall first file with the clerk of the court a complaint reciting and showing the following information:

(1) A description of the claimed property that is sufficient to make possible its identification and a statement, to the best knowledge, information, and belief of the plaintiff of the value of such property and its location.

(2) A statement that the plaintiff is the owner of the claimed property or is entitled to possession of it, describing the source of such title or right. If the plaintiff's interest in such property is based on a written instrument, a copy of said instrument must be attached to the complaint.

(3) A statement that the property is wrongfully detained by the defendant, the means by which the defendant came into possession thereof, and the cause of such detention according to the best knowledge, information, and belief of the plaintiff.

(4) A statement that the claimed property has not been taken for a tax, assessment, or fine pursuant to law.

(5) A statement that the property has not been taken under an execution or attachment against the property of the plaintiff or, if so taken, that it is by law exempt from such taking, setting forth a reference to the exemption law relied upon.

78.065 Order to show causes; contents.—

(1) The court without delay shall examine the complaint filed; and, if on the basis of the complaint and further showing of the plaintiff in support of it the court finds that the defendant has waived in accordance with § 78.075 his right to be notified and heard, the court shall promptly issue an order authorizing the clerk of the court to issue a writ of replevin.

(2) If, upon examination of the complaint filed and on further showing of the plaintiff in support of it, the court finds that the defendant has not waived in accordance with § 78.075 his right to be notified and heard, the court shall promptly issue an order directed to defendant to show cause why the claimed property should not be taken from the possession of the defendant and delivered to plaintiff.   *   *   *

78.068 Prejudgment writ of replevin.—

(1) A prejudgment writ of replevin may be issued and the property seized delivered forthwith to the petitioners when the nature of the claim and the amount thereof, if any, and the ground relied upon for the issuance of writ clearly appear from specific facts shown by the verified petition or by separate affidavit of the petitioner.

(2) This prejudgment writ of replevin may issue if the court finds, pursuant to subsection (1), that the defendant is engaging in, or is about to engage in, conduct that may place the claimed property in danger of destruction, concealment, waste, removal from the state, removal from the jurisdiction of the court, or transfer to an innocent purchaser during the pendency of the action or that the defendant has failed to make payment as agreed.

(3) The petitioner must post bond in the amount of twice the value of the goods subject to the writ or twice the balance remaining due and owing, whichever is lesser as determined by the court, as security for the payment of damages the defendant may sustain when the writ is obtained wrongfully.

78.075 Order to show cause; waiver.—The right to be heard provided in §§ 78.065 and 78.067 is waived if the defendant, after receiving a show-cause order, engages in any conduct that clearly shows that he wants to forgo his right to be heard on that order. The defendant's failure to appear at the hearing duly scheduled on the order to show cause presumptively constitutes conduct that clearly shows that he wants to forgo his right to be so heard. If the defendant, after service of the order to show cause, sends or delivers to the plaintiff or the court issuing the order to show cause a writing prepared by anyone but signed by the defendant after service of the order to show cause, indicating in any language that the defendant does not want to be heard on the show-cause order, the defendant shall be presumed to have waived his right to be heard. For this purpose, a writing containing the following language is sufficient, "I, (name of the defendant), am aware that I have the right and opportunity to be heard on a show-cause order that has been served upon me concerning the right of plaintiff to obtain a writ of replevin authorizing the appropriate officer of the court to take (describe property) from my possession prior to final judgment against me. I hereby state that I do not want to be heard on this matter and that I expressly waive my right to be heard. I understand that the effect of my signing this paper probably will be a court order authorizing the issuance of a writ of replevin directing an officer of the court to take possession of the property described above prior to final judgment against me with respect to the claim under which the property is taken."

——————

II. ANNOTATED SAMPLE COMPLAINT

Following is a complaint based on the replevin and conversion forms above.

1   **IN THE COUNTY COURT IN AND FOR ALACHUA**
2   **COUNTY, FLORIDA**

3   LESLIE WOROB,

4   Plaintiff,

5   vs.

6   JANICE ANDREWS,

7   Defendant.

CIVIL ACTION

Case No.: 92–000–CA
Division: J

8   **COMPLAINT FOR REPLEVIN AND DAMAGES**

9   Plaintiff, LESLIE WOROB, sues Defendant, JANICE AN-
10 DREWS, and says:

Lines 1–8   • These lines make up the caption.

Lines 3–7   • If there were more than one plaintiff or defendant, the names of all of them would be given here in the initial pleading. In all subsequent papers filed in the action, including any amended complaints, "*et al.*" ("and others") would substitute for all the names on a side after the first name. Note that there is no period after "*et*" because it is not an abbreviation; a period appears after "*al.*" because it is the abbreviation for "*alia.*" The names of the parties together with their designations as Plaintiff and Defendant are sometimes called the "style" of the action.

Line 5   • The case number is supplied by the court clerk when the action is filed.

Line 8   • In some jurisdictions, it is sufficient to name the pleading "Complaint," "Petition," etc. Others require the further designation of relief sought, as given here.

Lines 9–10   • This is the introductory clause. It specifies who sues whom, by name and party designation ("Plaintiff" and "Defendant"). In this action, there is only one party on each side; therefore, it is convenient to refer to them throughout as Plaintiff and Defendant.

• If there were multiple parties, it would be appropriate here to establish short forms by which to refer to them throughout. Short forms may be last names of individuals, abbreviations for corporations or organizations, or references to parties' legal status. For example:

JANE DOE ("DOE")

AMALGAMATED TECHNICAL SERVICES, INC. ("ATS")

DUNN, ULLMAN, & MALCOLM, P.A. ("DUNN")

ROGER ROE ("LANDLORD")

If you are inclined to use initials, beware of their potential for unfortunate acronyms. Your clients at Dunn, Ullman & Malcolm might be less than pleased to see themselves referred to throughout a complaint as "DUM."

• Notice how simply the short form is established. All you need is the term you plan to use. Put it in quotation marks, and put parenthesis around them. You do not need the legalese: "hereinafter referred to as. . . ."

• If you establish short forms, use them consistently throughout. It is sloppy drafting to establish a short form and then go on to call a party by full name or by party designation, or worse yet, sometimes by one name and sometimes by another.

11   COUNT 1. REPLEVIN

12   1. This is an action pursuant to F.S. 78.01 et seq. to recover
13 possession of personal property in Alachua County, Florida.

14   2. The description of the property is:

• A helpful practice, especially when there are multiple parties called by name rather than by party designation, is to use all-capital letters for party names throughout. This makes it easy to scan a long pleading for all references to a given party.

• The introductory clause provides a grammatical foundation for the allegations to follow. In pleadings, as in other legal documents, captions or headings are not technically part of the text. Therefore, the drafter needs to express all of the content in complete sentences in the text of the pleading, not rely on the caption to express who sues whom.

• Note the plain language in this contemporary court-approved introductory clause, which replaces the obsolete legalese: "Now comes the above-named Plaintiff, LESLIE WOROB, by and through David S. King, her attorney of record, and shows unto this honorable court. . . ."

• The first line of the introductory clause is indented, but this short paragraph is not numbered.

Line 11   • In a one-count complaint, that count is not headed. In a multi-count complaint, like this one, it is helpful to head each count as well as number it. The headings may refer to relief sought, as here, or to separate transactions giving rise to separate causes of action, or to separate defendants. Beware, however, of limiting your options unnecessarily though a narrow heading that hems a set of facts into one theory of recovery. Later you may want to relate those facts to a different theory.

• An alternative organizational scheme would precede the first count with a series of numbered paragraphs headed "Common Allegations" to give the reader the factual background for all counts at once. Then each count would incorporate those paragraphs by reference, for example: "Plaintiff incorporates by reference paragraphs 1–7" or "Plaintiff realleges paragraphs 1 through 7."

Lines 12–56   • These lines are the body of the complaint. They contain the allegations
and 68–72 regarding the circumstances of the case, expressed as ultimate facts rather than in evidentiary detail or in legal conclusions.

• The body is divided into one continuous sequence of numbered paragraphs throughout the complaint regardless of how many counts there are and regardless of interruptions for unnumbered paragraphs making demands for judgment and relief, as in lines 57–66.

Lines 12–13   • The first numbered paragraph establishes the nature of the action and in this case establishes venue according to the governing statute. Generally, the plaintiff need not establish venue; it is up to the defendant to raise improper venue.

• Since this cause of action is based on statute, it is appropriate here to cite that statute. The citation would be even more important if the statute were obscure or not frequently litigated in the court where the action is filed.

Lines 14–21   • Here jurisdiction is established by establishing the value of the property as within the range appropriate to be litigated in the county court. Since conventionally jurisdiction, not venue, is the first element to be covered in the body of a complaint, it might have been better for the court form to have

Item	Estimated Value
1 Automobile: 1985 Mercury Cougar	$2,300
1 Console Color Television	500
1 Stereo and Speakers	150
Record and Tape Collection	4,000

To the best of Plaintiff's knowledge, information, and belief, the total value of the property is $6,950.

3. Plaintiff is the owner of the property, having purchased all of it, and is entitled to possession of it. A copy of the certificate of title to the 1985 Mercury Cougar automobile is attached as Exhibit "A." Copies of the bills of sale for the console color television set and the stereo and speakers are attached as Exhibits "B" and "C."

4. In early October 1991, Plaintiff and Defendant made an agreement for Plaintiff to store the property at the home of Defendant, and Plaintiff delivered the property to Defendant's garage for storage.

5. In late October 1991, Plaintiff and Defendant agreed that Plaintiff would live in Defendant's home, and Plaintiff moved in and paid rent to Defendant at the agreed rate of $30 per week through December 31, 1991.

6. On December 31, 1991, Defendant, without provocation and without just cause, refused Plaintiff entry to Defendant's home and denied Plaintiff access to Plaintiff's property.

---

paragraph 1 include the description of the property. It is entirely acceptable for one paragraph to consist of more than one sentence.

Lines 14–21 • The subject of this action is property; therefore, that property is identified first, in a paragraph restricted to that function.

Lines 16–21 • Note that amounts of money are rounded off to the nearest dollar. It is needless to write "$2,300.00," instead of "$2,300." In some contexts, however, it may be necessary to write "$2,300.72." It is also needless to write out "Two Thousand Three Hundred Dollars," although some drafters do so as a safeguard against easily missed typographical errors in figures.

Lines 22–26 • It is important to establish the status of each party before moving into a narrative of what happened that gave rise to the action. It helps to introduce each party in a separately numbered paragraph, rather than introducing multiple parties in the same paragraph.

• The plaintiff's status in this action depends on her relation to the property. That status is established next, in a paragraph uncluttered by any reference to the defendant.

Lines 23–26 • These lines illustrate incorporating other documents by reference. Note that once incorporated, the documents are not quoted because they have become part of the complaint.

Lines 27–30 • The defendant is identified last, in a separately numbered paragraph, in terms of her relation to the property and to the plaintiff.

Line 27 • Here begins the narrative in the past tense of what happened that gave rise to the action. Note that establishing the status of the parties in relation to each other generally precedes the narrative, although in this complaint, paragraph 4 both identifies the defendant and introduces the narrative.

38   7. To Plaintiff's best knowledge, information, and belief, the
39 property is located at Defendant's residence at 241 79th Terrace,
40 Gainesville, Alachua County, Florida.

41   8. Plaintiff has made repeated demands to Defendant that she
42 deliver or release the property to Plaintiff, but Defendant has failed
43 and refuses to comply.

44   9. Defendant wrongfully detains the property, with the inten-
45 tion to sell it to pay for damage Defendant wrongly claims Plaintiff
46 caused to Defendant's home. Defendant expressed this to Plaintiff
47 in a letter dated March 9, 1992.

48   10. Plaintiff's property has not been taken for any tax, assess-
49 ment, or fine pursuant to law.

50   11. Plaintiff's property has not been taken under an execution
51 or attachment against Plaintiff's property.

52   12. While Plaintiff has accumulated a certain amount of per-
53 sonal property during her life, much of which is presently in
54 Defendant's possession, Plaintiff has no liquid assets with which to
55 post bond for a Prejudgment Writ of Replevin as required by F.S.
56 78.068(3).

57   WHEREFORE, Plaintiff, LESLIE WOROB, demands that this
58 court:

59   A. Enter judgment for possession of the property;

60   B. Waive the posting of bond by plaintiff as required by F.S.
61 78.068(3); and

Lines 57–66   • The demand for judgment and relief is separate from the body, which has
expressed the allegations on which the demand is based. Therefore, the
demand is not a numbered paragraph.

• By convention, the demand is introduced by "WHEREFORE." Itself a
hold-over from the days of legalese, this convention may soon fall away. It
may persist longer than much legalese, however, because the clause itself is
commonly called "the WHEREFORE clause."

• In some jurisdictions, it is conventional to "pray for" relief or to "request"
it rather than making demands. The choice among these terms also may
reflect the style of the litigator as one who wants the image of playing
hardball or one who values gracious collegiality within the legal profession.
Keep in mind that pleadings are addressed to the court, not directly to one's
adversary.

• The several elements of this demand are presented in tabulated form,
lettered "A" through "C," with "C" subdivided into "(1)" and "(2)." The parts
are presented in parallel sentence construction. This is a useful device to aid
clarity and emphasis, and to avoid ambiguity.

• Just as numbering paragraphs in the complaint makes it easy to refer to
a specific allegation in later court papers or in correspondence about the
action, so also lettered or numbered tabulation of the parallel parts of a
sentence makes it easy to refer later to a specific part.

• Here citations to specific authority for each of the various forms of relief
sought may be more helpful to the judge than the broad citation to the
replevin statutes in the jurisdictional statement.

62   C. (1) Issue an order authorizing the clerk of the court to issue
63 a writ of replevin as authorized by F.S. 78.065(1) and F.S.
64 78.068(1); or in the alternative,

65   (2) Issue Defendant, JANICE ANDREWS, an order to show
66 cause pursuant to F.S. 78.065(2).

67 <center>COUNT 2. DAMAGES</center>

68   13. This is an action for damages that exceed $2,500 but do not
69 exceed $10,000.

70   14. On or about December 31, 1991, Defendant converted to
71 her own use Plaintiff's personal property described in paragraph 2,
72 which Plaintiff realleges.

73   WHEREFORE, Plaintiff, LESLIE WOROB, demands judgment
74 for damages against Defendant, JANICE ANDREWS, costs and all
75 other relief this court deems proper.

76 <center>JURY DEMAND</center>

77   Plaintiff demands a jury trial on all issues triable by jury.

- It is a common practice to refer to the parties by name in the demand even if they have been called "Plaintiff" and "Defendant" throughout the body.

- In some multi-count complaints, drafters present only one demand section at the end of the last count. Here the two counts seek not only different but alternative forms of relief; therefore, separate demands are at least easier to follow if not essential.

Lines 68–69 • The second count requires a new jurisdictional statement because the basis of jurisdiction differs from that of the first count.

- This is a typical jurisdictional statement for a damage action, establishing that the amount of damages sought is within the jurisdictional range for the court in question.

- Note that Count 2 begins with paragraph 13, not paragraph 1.

Lines 70–72 • This paragraph incorporates paragraph 2 by reference and eliminates the need to repeat the information in it.

- Given the Supreme Court's minimalist model, the drafter realleges none of the other facts from Count 1. The drafter may be relying nonetheless on the assumption that the reader has in fact read Count 1. If there were no Count 1, the drafter might well see a need to give the reader a fuller impression of the background.

Lines 73–75 • Here is the demand related to the second count. Distinguish "damages" in reference to monetary relief sought from the factual allegation that the plaintiff suffered damage by losing her property.

Lines 76–77 • This is a jury demand in plain language. If the plaintiff demands a jury trial on all issues, the demand can be even shorter: "Plaintiff demands a jury trial."

78

79   DAVID S. KING

80   Attorney for Plaintiff

81   000 E. Main Street

82   Gainesville, Florida 32601

83   (904) 377–555

84   Fla. Bar No. 00000000

85 STATE OF FLORIDA

86 COUNTY OF ALACHUA

87   Before me, on <u>March 23, 1992</u> personally appeared LESLIE
88 WOROB, who was sworn and then said that the allegations con-
89 tained in the above complaint are true.

90

91   LESLIE WOROB

92 Sworn to and subscribed before me <u>March 23, 1992</u>

93 _____

94 Notary Public—State of Florida at Large

95 My commission expires _____, 19__

Lines 79–84   • Beneath the signature of an attorney of record belongs indication of whom the attorney represents, the attorney's full address including zip code, the attorney's phone number including area code, and in some jurisdictions the attorney's Bar registration license number.

Lines 85–95   • These lines illustrate a notarized verification couched in plain language rather than legalese. The verification refers to the "above complaint" rather than the one "hereinabove" or "the above-entitled action." The plaintiff simply "said" rather than "deposed and stated." She said her allegations were "true" rather than "true and correct." Finally, the verification is dated normally rather than "this 23d day of March."

     • The verification is to be signed by the plaintiff herself, not by her attorney. In most jurisdictions verification is no longer routinely required. The governing statute requires it in this action for the plaintiff to be granted a prejudgment writ of replevin without posting bond.

     • Note that the complaint includes no certificate of service. As an initial pleading, it will be served on the defendant by the court, not by the plaintiff's attorney.

Lines 87, 92   • Dates here are filled in on blank lines. When preparing any document with dates that depend on when parties sign, it is wise to leave blanks instead of typing in the dates. Parties sometimes do not sign on the date you think they will, or even on the date you are sure they will.

Exercise 1.2

On the following pages are three sample (not model) versions of the same complaint.[2] Compare and evaluate them on the following matters: clarity, completeness, compliance with procedural principles and practices, and choice of language.

Read the three versions with the following considerations in mind:

1. Version 1 is a "minimalist" complaint. Evaluate it particularly for what is missing.

2. Version 2 illustrates the organization of a multi-count complaint beginning with the first count. Version 3 illustrates the organization beginning with common allegations. Determine whether one is easier to follow than the other.

3. What does Version 2 include that is missing from Version 1?

4. Version 3 is a "maximalist" complaint. What does it include that is missing from Version 2?

5. Is any one of the versions best, or do you find some qualities to emulate and some to avoid in each?

SAMPLE COMPLAINT: VERSION 1

1   IN THE _____ COURT OF _____ COUNTY, _____

2 GEORGE BRYANT,

3   Plaintiff,

4 v.

5 MARIE JARDON, d.b.a.

6   Chez Marie,

7   Defendant.

         Case No. _____

8   COMPLAINT

9   Plaintiff alleges:

10   COUNT 1

11   I

12   Plaintiff George Bryant is a resident of _____, _____.
13 Defendant Marie Jardon owns and operates Chez Marie, a restau-
14 rant located in _____, _____.

---

2. Versions 1, 2, and 3 of this complaint are adapted from C. Calleros, Legal Method and Writing 292–98 (1990). Copy- right © 1990 by Charles R. Calleros. Adapted by permission of the author.

15   II

16   Bryant worked for Jardon as a waiter at Chez Marie from
17 August 16, 1990 to September 28, 1991.

18   III

19   At the time of his discharge on September 28, 1991, Bryant had
20 an employment contract with Chez Marie that imposed substantive
21 and procedural restrictions upon Jardon's right to terminate Bry-
22 ant's employment.

23   IV

24   Acting through her agent, Mario Prieto, Jardon discharged
25 Bryant September 28, 1991, in breach of her employment contract
26 with Bryant.

27   V

28   As a result of Jardon's breach of contract, Bryant has suffered
29 lost wages and other damages.

30   COUNT 2

31   VI

32   Bryant realleges and incorporates paragraphs I–V above.

33   VII

34   Acting through her agent, Jardon maliciously and unlawfully
35 discharged Bryant for reasons that violate public policy, causing
36 Bryant lost wages and other injuries.

37   Bryant therefore requests judgment granting the following re-
38 lief: an order reinstating Bryant to his position as waiter at Chez
39 Marie; an award of compensatory and punitive damages; an award
40 of costs and attorney's fees; and other appropriate relief.

41   by _____
42   Thomas Sanchez
43   Simpson, Sanchez & Summers
44   303 North Central Avenue
45   _____, _____
46   Attorneys for Plaintiff
47   (___) ____–_____

SAMPLE COMPLAINT: VERSION 2

1   _____ COURT

2   _____ COUNTY, _____

3 GEORGE BRYANT,	
4 Plaintiff,	DIVISION: _____
5 v.	
6 MARIE JARDON, d.b.a.	No: _____
7 Chez Marie,	
8 Defendant.	

9   COMPLAINT

10   Plaintiff, George Bryant, sues Defendant, Marie Jardon, and
11 says:

COUNT I, BREACH OF CONTRACT

13   1. This is an action for damages that exceed $10,000.

14   2. Plaintiff worked for Defendant as a waiter at Chez Marie
15 from August 16, 1990, to September 28, 1991. Mario Prieto acted as
16 the maitre d' and supervisor of waiters at Chez Marie during
17 Plaintiff's employment at Chez Marie. In all the events alleged
18 below, Prieto acted on behalf of Defendant.

19   3. At the time of his discharge on September 28, 1991, Plain-
20 tiff had an employment contract with Chez Marie that included the
21 terms of an "Employee Handbook." Plaintiff foreseeably relied to
22 his detriment on promises contained in the Handbook.

23   4. The Employee Handbook contains promises of job security,
24 including promises that (i) Defendant will not discharge any waiter
25 except for inadequate performance and (ii) any waiter recommended
26 for discharge has the right to meet with Defendant and Prieto to
27 persuade them that the waiter should not be discharged. The
28 Handbook also provides that Defendant will make the final determi-
29 nation in the event of disagreement between Prieto and Defendant
30 on a discharge matter. The material portions of the Handbook are
31 attached as Exhibit "A" and incorporated by reference.

32   5. At all times during his employment at Chez Marie, Plaintiff
33 performed his job in a manner that met the highest standards at
34 Chez Marie. Despite the adequacy of Plaintiff's performance, Prieto
35 discharged Plaintiff September 28, 1991. Although Plaintiff imme-
36 diately requested a meeting with Prieto and Defendant to discuss
37 the discharge, both Prieto and Defendant refused to convene such a
38 meeting.

39   6. As a result of Plaintiff's breach of promises in the Hand-
40 book, Plaintiff has suffered lost wages and other damages.

41   7. Defendant's breach of promises in the Handbook constitutes
42 a breach of her employment contract with Plaintiff and has created
43 an injustice that can be avoided only by enforcing the promises.

COUNT II, WRONGFUL DISCHARGE

44

45   8. Plaintiff realleges and incorporates paragraphs 1–6 above.

46   9. In discharging Plaintiff, Prieto was motivated by malice, by
47 an invidiously discriminatory intent, and by concerns unrelated to
48 the successful operation of Chez Marie. Defendant's termination of
49 Plaintiff's employment therefore violated public policy.

50   Plaintiff therefore requests judgment granting the following
51 relief: (1) an order reinstating Plaintiff to his position as waiter at
52 Chez Marie; (2) an award of compensatory damages in an amount to
53 be set at trial, but not less than $50,000, (3) an award of punitive
54 damages in an amount to be set at trial; (4) an award of costs and
55 attorney's fees; (5) and such other relief as the court deems appro-
56 priate.

JURY DEMAND

57

58   Plaintiff demands trial by jury.

59   Simpson, Sanchez & Summers
60   303 North Central Avenue
61   ————————————, ————
62   Attorneys for Plaintiff
63   (___) ____—_____
64   by _____
65   Thomas Sanchez
66   Bar No. _____

SAMPLE COMPLAINT: VERSION 3

1   IN THE _____ COURT OF THE STATE OF _____ IN
2   AND FOR THE COUNTY OF _____

3 GEORGE BRYANT,	
4 Plaintiff,	
5 v.	CIVIL ACTION
6 MARIE JARDON, d.b.a.	CASE NO:
7 Chez Marie, and	DIVISION:
8 MARIO PRIETO,	
9 Defendants.	

10   COMPLAINT FOR DAMAGES AND INJUNCTIVE RELIEF

11   Plaintiff GEORGE BRYANT (BRYANT), by and through his
12 attorneys, Simpson, Sanchez and Summers, sues Defendants MARIE
13 JARDON, d.b.a. CHEZ MARIE (JARDON) and MARIO PRIETO
14 (PRIETO), and alleges the following:

15   COMMON ALLEGATIONS

16   1. This is an action for injunctive relief and for compensatory
17 damages exceeding $10,000. This court has original jurisdiction
18 pursuant to [citation to statute].

19   2. BRYANT is a resident of _____, _____. JARDON owns
20 and operates CHEZ MARIE, a restaurant located in _____,
21 _____. PRIETO acted as the maitre d' and supervisor of waiters
22 at CHEZ MARIE during Bryant's employment at CHEZ MARIE.
23 All material events alleged below took place in _____ County,
24 _____.

25   3. BRYANT worked for JARDON and PRIETO as a waiter at
26 CHEZ MARIE from August 16, 1990, to September 28, 1991. In all
27 the events alleged below, PRIETO acted on his own behalf as well as
28 on behalf of JARDON.

29   COUNT I
30   FIRST CAUSE OF ACTION
31   (Breach of Contract)

32   4. On January 1, 1991, JARDON and PRIETO modified BRY-
33 ANT'S employment contract to include promises of job security
34 contained in the terms of an "Employee Handbook" and in oral
35 assurance.

36   5. Among other things, the Employee Handbook contains the
37 following promises of job security: (i) JARDON and PRIETO will
38 not discharge any waiter except for inadequate performance, and (ii)
39 any waiter recommended for discharge has the right to meet with
40 JARDON and PRIETO to persuade them that the waiter should not
41 be discharged. The Handbook also provides that JARDON will
42 make the final determination in the event of disagreement between
43 JARDON and PRIETO on a discharge matter. (A copy of the text of
44 excerpts of the Handbook is attached hereto as Exhibit "A" and
45 incorporated herein by this reference).

46   6. At all times during his employment at CHEZ MARIE,
47 BRYANT performed his job in a manner that met the highest
48 standards at CHEZ MARIE. Despite the adequacy of BRYANT's
49 performance, JARDON and PRIETO discharged BRYANT Septem-
50 ber 28, 1991. Although BRYANT immediately requested a meeting
51 with JARDON and PRIETO to discuss the discharge, JARDON and
52 PRIETO refused to convene such a meeting.

53   7. As a result of JARDON and PRIETO's breach of contract,
54 BRYANT has suffered lost wages and other incidental and conse-
55 quential losses.

56   8. BRYANT has been required to retain an attorney for the
57 purpose of bringing this suit and is obligated to pay a reasonable fee
58 for this attorney's services.

59   WHEREFORE, Plaintiff, GEORGE BRYANT, demands judg-
60 ment against Defendants, MARIE JARDON, d.b.a. CHEZ MARIE,
61 and MARIO PRIETO, granting the following relief:

62   (1) an order reinstating BRYANT to his former position at
63 CHEZ MARIE;

64   (2) an award of compensatory damages for all consequential
65 and incidental losses in excess of $10,000 plus interest;

66   (3) an award of costs and attorney's fees; and

67   (4) such other relief as the court deems appropriate.

68   COUNT II
69   SECOND CAUSE OF ACTION
70   (Promissory Estoppel)

71   9. BRYANT realleges paragraphs 1 through 3 and 8 above as
72 if fully alleged in this count and incorporates them herein by this
73 reference.

74   10. On January 1, 1991, JARDON and PRIETO gave BRYANT
75 promises of job security by making oral assurances and by distribut-
76 ing the Employee Handbook. BRYANT relied to his detriment on
77 those promises by performing extraordinary services and by
78 forebearing from taking other job opportunities. That reliance was
79 reasonably foreseeable by JARDON and PRIETO.

80   11. JARDON and PRIETO's termination of BRYANT's em-
81 ployment on September 28, 1991, constituted a breach of their
82 promises of job security and has created an injustice that can be
83 avoided only by enforcing the promises.

84   WHEREFORE, Plaintiff, GEORGE BRYANT demands judg-
85 ment against Defendants, MARIE JARDON, d.b.a. CHEZ MARIE,
86 and MARIO PRIETO, granting the following relief:

87   (1) an order reinstating BRYANT to his former position at
88 CHEZ MARIE;

89   (2) an award of compensatory damages for all consequential
90 and incidental losses in excess of $10,000 plus interest;

91   (3) an award of costs and attorney's fees; and

92   (4) such other relief as the court deems appropriate.

COUNT III
THIRD CAUSE OF ACTION
(Wrongful Discharge)

12. BRYANT realleges paragraphs 1–3, 6, and 8 above as if fully alleged in this count and incorporates them herein by this reference.

13. JARDON and PRIETO maliciously discharged BRYANT because of his sexual orientation and because BRYANT's exemplary performance made PRIETO jealous. Those reasons for discharge are arbitrary and unfair, reflect bad faith and violate public policy.

WHEREFORE Plaintiff, GEORGE BRYANT, demands judgment against Defendants MARIE JARDON, d.b.a. CHEZ MARIE, and MARIO PRIETO, granting the following relief;

(1) an order reinstating Plaintiff to his position as waiter at Chez Marie;

(2) an award of compensatory damages in an amount to be set at trial;

(3) an award of punitive damages in an amount to be set at trial;

(4) an award of costs and attorney's fees; and

(5) such other relief as the court deems appropriate.

DEMAND FOR JURY TRIAL

Plaintiff demands trial by jury as to all issues triable by jury in this cause.

RESPECTFULLY
SUBMITTED:

Simpson, Sanchez and Summers
303 North Central Avenue
_____, _____
Attorneys for Plaintiff
(___) ___—_____
by _____
     Thomas Sanchez
Bar No. _____

III. THE BODY OF PLEADINGS REQUESTING AFFIRMATIVE RELIEF

A. REQUIRED ELEMENTS OF THE COMPLAINT OR OTHER INITIAL PLEADING

1. Jurisdiction

The pleading begins with a short and plain statement of the grounds for jurisdiction, which in an action at law commonly requires a good faith allegation of the amount in controversy. Some jurisdictions require alleging a particular amount; others require alleging a range, for example: "This is an action for damages exceeding $2,500 but not exceeding $10,000." If the cause of action arises under a statute, the statute should be mentioned in the jurisdictional statement.

Most jurisdictions do not require pleading venue affirmatively, although it is fairly common practice to do so. Technically, the plaintiff lays venue by naming the county in the court designation in the caption. The burden is on the defendant to allege and prove improper venue.

2. Cause of Action or Statement of Claim

The general purpose of the initial pleading is to establish the right to initiate judicial proceedings.

In most state courts today, this right is established by stating a "cause of action," language inherited from Section 120 of New York's 1848 Field Code, the source of what is known as "Code pleading." Each cause of action has elements, which are determined by substantive law: statute, common law, or both.

Pleading a cause of action is accomplished by alleging ultimate facts, as distinguished from both conclusions of law and evidentiary facts.

In the federal courts, Federal Rule of Civil Procedure 8(a) requires "a statement of the claim showing that the pleader is entitled to relief." This language is indicative of simplified "notice pleading."

3. Demand for Judgment for Relief

The pleader may demand several types of relief, either cumulatively or alternatively. Distinguish the demand for damages (monetary relief) from the allegation that the plaintiff has suffered damage (injury). Stating that the plaintiff has suffered damage is a factual allegation, which is one of the elements of a cause of action. The demand for damages is a required part of the initial pleading in a damage action; it is not an element of the cause of action.

B. PLEADING SPECIAL MATTERS

Several special matters are commonly addressed by rules of civil procedure, although resolved differently from one jurisdiction to another. Therefore, it is important to see the applicable rules on these matters: capacity of a party; fraud or mistake; condition of mind; condition precedent; official document or act; judgment, decree, or decision; time and place; general and special damages; and punitive damages.

IV. DRAFTING FACTUAL ALLEGATIONS AS A MATTER OF STRATEGY

A. SUBSTANTIATING A CAUSE OF ACTION, NOT MERELY TELLING A STORY

1. *Linking Facts to Elements*

Even if an approved form is available, you still need to tailor the complaint to the particular case at hand. The major task is composing the "short and plain" statements of the ultimate facts required to plead a cause of action or claim. There are some technical differences between a "cause of action," and a "claim for relief." [3] However, in any court, the drafter's contribution to effective pleadings lies mainly in those short and plain statements of facts.

The main thing to remember is that pleadings serve to raise issues for trial. Issues cannot be raised through discovery. Thus each count in a complaint must state a cause of action. It is wise to avoid any temptation merely to view the body of the complaint as a narrative of events that happened. Instead you should first make a list of the elements of the cause of action and then decide what facts establish each element. Only with these preliminary checklists at hand are you ready to begin drafting allegations. When the first draft is done, you can then test it against your checklist to make sure you have substantiated each element.

2. *General Plan for Organizing Allegations*

Here is a general plan for organizing allegations to substantiate a cause of action:

• Who is the plaintiff? Tenant, shareholder of a corporation, buyer, etc.? In other words, what legal status gives the plaintiff the right that is at issue in this action?

• Who is the defendant? Landlord, president of a corporation, seller, etc.? In other words, what legal status gives the defendant a duty that is at issue in this action?

---

3. See Fed.R.Civ.P. 8(a) and (e).

• What did the defendant do or not do that violated the plaintiff's right or breached the defendant's duty? Be sure to allege proximate cause if that is an element of your cause of action.

• How was the plaintiff injured by what the defendant did or did not do? This question is most often left unanswered by inexperienced drafters. Remember that the demand for relief does not substitute for a factual allegation of injury or loss.

According to one theory about pleadings strategy, it is fruitless for plaintiffs to strive to trap defendants into admissions because defendants are almost certain to admit only innocuous facts that do not lead to liability. Under this theory, the only thing for a complaint to do is state a cause of action in terms minimally sufficient to survive a motion to dismiss. However, to the extent that you wish to try using your complaints to strategic advantage, it helps to be adept at some techniques.

B. USING THE COMPLAINT AS A DISCOVERY TOOL

1. Narrow and Precise Allegations

In a complaint the idea is not to complicate or exaggerate, because the effect is to make the job of proving the plaintiff's case harder. It is better to say that the defendant "slapped the plaintiff in the mouth" than to say that the defendant "assaulted, battered, struck, bruised, and wounded the plaintiff." Faced with such a list in a complaint, the defendant can easily respond evasively.

> A well-drawn complaint can serve as a method of discovery; an allegation drawn in narrow and precise language may compel an admission from defendant who could deny the charge, had it been made in general terms. By thus requiring the defendant to reveal in his answer exactly what his position is, the issues may be considerably narrowed, resulting in saving of time at the trial and often serving to open the door to advantageous settlement. Conversely, counsel for defendant can often improve his tactical position if he finds that he can surprise his adversary by denying a carelessly phrased allegation, (thus suggesting the existence of serious questions of fact).[4]

Using the complaint strategically for discovery purposes also involves choosing language to suggest to opposing counsel that you have a strong case. You can force defendants either to admit something or to deny it in such specific terms as to reveal the theory of their case. Thus you want to avoid the general and vague language that is easy for defendants to deny generally.

> The test for the scope of discovery is relevancy to the subject matter of the action. The pleadings establish the subject matter of the action. Consequently the pleadings set the broad limits for discovery. A case involving a "disgruntled distributor" shows how important this can be in practice.

4. F. Cooper, Writing in Law Practice 183 (1963).

The distributor had fallen down on the job. Neither the carrot nor the stick approach seemed to do much good. Finally the manufacturer gave up and canceled the distributorship. The distributor lashed back with an anti-trust action. And he planted a bomb in his complaint. He alleged a lot of history—when the defendant company was formed, how it grew through mergers, certain landmarks in its career, and so forth.

A complaint like this would give plaintiff a field day with discovery * * * start[ing] with the deposition of the chairman of the board and work[ing] * * * down.

Defendant moved to strike this archeological material. The motion took work, a lot of work really, considering the antipathy of the courts to this kind of motion. But the work paid off. The court granted the motion.

For many a defendant, a broad complaint is the opening gun in a campaign of harassment by discovery. * * * Of course it can work the other way too * * *.

* * * [T]he differences between abuse and legitimate use [of discovery] is a matter of degree; and either way, how the pleadings are couched matters a great deal. Other things being equal, if you have more to lose than gain by broad discovery you should try to set limits to discovery.[5]

---

2. *Facts One at a Time*

If several allegations appear together in the same sentence, it is tempting for the defendant to deny the lot generally. In other words, if the plaintiff says that the defendant "owned, operated, managed, and controlled" a store, there are four separate allegations. The defendant who only has a 99–year lease may deny the sentence as a whole. Compound sentences are generally dangerous, for example, a sentence saying that "the defendant did . . ., and the defendant did. . . ." or one saying that "Defendant A did . . ., and Defendant B did. . . ." Lists of synonyms joined by the conjunction "and" are equally dangerous. Also, the internal inconsistency of "and/or" is worth avoiding.

Defendants are obligated under federal and typical state pleading rules to respond to a pleading "in good faith," denying only those parts of allegations that they intend to deny and admitting the rest. However, sometimes defendants do not abide by this rule, and judges have been reluctant to impose sanctions on them. Thus it is up to the pleader to frame allegation that prevent an evasive reply.

5. G. Vetter, Successful Civil Litigation: How to Win Your Case Before You Enter the Courtroom 35–36 (1977). Copyright © 1977. Reprinted from Successful Civil Litigation by George Vetter by permission of the publisher, Prentice Hall, a division of Simon & Schuster, Englewood Cliffs, N.J.

Exercise 1.3

Compare the following approaches to separating allegations. Which is most likely to force admissions from the defendant? What other considerations would cause you to choose or reject each approach?

Approach A

7. Defendant negligently maintained the outside stairway by not replacing non-slip strips on several of the stairs, allowing leaves to collect on the stairway, and not removing broken glass located at the bottom of the stairway.

Approach B

7. Defendant negligently maintained the stairs by (a) failing to repair missing treads designed to prevent falls, (b) failing to remove wet leaves from the stairs, and (c) failing to remove broken glass at the bottom of the stairs.

Approach C

7. Defendant negligently maintained the stairs leading to Wilbert Hall.

8. Defendant negligently maintained the entryway to Wilbert Hall.

9. Defendant negligently repaired or failed to repair the stairs leading to Wilbert Hall.

10. Defendant allowed leaves to collect on the stairs leading to Wilbert Hall.

11. Defendant allowed broken glass to remain on the entryway to Wilbert Hall.

12. Defendant failed to repair or replace a missing tread on the stairs leading to Wilbert Hall.

Approach D

7. Defendant negligently maintained the stairs on the property by failing to maintain rubber treads on each stair so that Plaintiff fell on the stairs.

8. Defendant negligently maintained the stairs by allowing wet leaves to accumulate on the stairs so that Plaintiff fell on the stairs.

Approach E

8. On January 5, 1992, Plaintiff fell down the stairs.

9. At the time of Plaintiff's fall:

    a. some of the rubber treads were missing from the wooden stairs;

    b.   wet leaves were located on the wooden stairs; and

    c.   broken glass lay at the bottom of the wooden stairs.

---

3. *Facts Rather Than Conclusions*

Whenever possible, use objective words. For example, in many states if plaintiff says that defendant physician "acted negligently," that is stating a legal conclusion. In some states, however, alleging that someone was negligent is considered alleging an ultimate fact rather than drawing a legal conclusion. Whether regarded as fact or conclusion, the statement is in subjective language, and thus it is easy for the defendant to deny. It is more difficult to deny if the plaintiff specifies that the defendant "left a surgical clamp in the plaintiff's stomach."

In a state where the plaintiff is obligated to mention negligence itself as the ultimate fact, you might allege in one sentence that the physician did not remove the clamp and in a separate follow-up sentence that the failure constituted negligence. If the defendant is pressed to admit the objective factual allegation, the plaintiff is well on the way to substantiating the subjective conclusion as well.

On the other hand, subjective allegations may often stand alone if no more information is available at the time of pleading. Hence, the plaintiff may successfully allege merely that the defendant negligently operated or maintained a motor vehicle so that it collided with the plaintiff's motor vehicle.

4. *Graphic Favorable Facts and Abstract Unfavorable Ones*

The value of objectivity does not remove your ability to choose words with attention to their positive or negative connotations. Language full of sensory appeal can make favorable facts memorable. Abstract language can shut down the reader's brain as it passes over unfavorable facts. Remember that the judge as well as the defendant's attorney will read what you write. You can use factual allegations in a complaint just as strategically as you do the statement of facts in a brief to create an impression.

> For example, suppose you are litigating the closing of a plant and [you want to convey that] the closing is total and permanent. * * *
>
> The company didn't just close the plant * * *. It let the furnaces die and the bricks crumble, it unbolted and sold the machines, it boarded up the windows and let the lot go to weeds. "Let the lot go to weeds." Doesn't that immediately conjure up the image of a vacant lot in an abandoned neighborhood? Doesn't it import finality and despair? * * *
>
> The opposite technique applies to unfavorable facts. Feel free to be as abstract, general and impersonal about them as you care to. Here's an unfavorable fact if you're representing an individual who

was discharged for behavior problems: "Disciplinary sanctions were imposed with respect to certain conduct which was deemed improper in the circumstances." That sentence makes no impression whatsoever. "Sanctions" are abstract. "Imposing" anything is impersonal. To "deem" something "improper" is admirably general and thus forgettable. Best of all, both verbs are in the passive voice, which gives no indication of anybody actually doing anything. * * *

Writing creates an impression apart from the literal meaning of the sentences. Compare these two: "Plaintiff was Miss Ajax Company and attended a number of functions in that capacity" versus "Plaintiff was chosen to represent Ajax Company as Miss Ajax Company in numerous official relations with the press and public." The first sentence contains only colorless words like "attend". Anyone can "attend" anything; it bespeaks no brains or personality or initiative. The second sentence uses the words "chosen" (sounds as if somebody deliberately reviewed her abilities or whatever and judged them superior to those of all other candidates), "represent" (no one allows himself to be represented by anyone in whom he has less than full confidence), "official" (this was no accident, nor is it minor), "relations" (successful personal relations are an important facet of corporate life), and "press and public" (she really was subjected to close scrutiny and all the lessons of dealing with the public). If you read a whole statement which is laced with words which reverberate with favorable connotations, you will likely take away a highly favorable impression of the subject being discussed, and vice versa.[6]

C. DRAFTING SHORT AND PLAIN STATEMENTS

1. Dismissal for Violation of Plain Statement Rules

Cases have been dismissed for violations of the rules requiring plain statements.[7] The irate court opinions dismissing the complaints or affirming their dismissal refer most commonly to prolixity and redundancy. Sometimes, however, the dismissed complaints have suffered from additional flaws of argumentative and conclusory paragraphs,[8] evidentiary statements,[9] extraneous matter,[10] and failure to make clear whether amended pleadings supersede previous versions or are to be read in conjunction with them.[11] Such dismissals are typically without prejudice. Yet filing an amended complaint is itself

6. H. Hurd, Writing for Lawyers 85–87 (1982). Copyright © 1982 by Hollis T. Hurd; published by Journal Broadcasting & Communications, P.O. Box 3084, Pittsburgh, Pa. 15230. Reprinted by permission of the author.

7. See, e.g., Gordon v. Green, 602 F.2d 743, 747, cases cited at 746 (5th Cir.1979).

8. See, e.g., Benner v. Philadelphia Musical Society, Local 77, of American Federation of Musicians, 32 F.R.D. 197, 198 (E.D. Pa.1963).

9. See, e.g., Johnson v. Hunger, 266 F.Supp. 590, 591 (S.D.N.Y.1967).

10. See, e.g., Carrigan v. California State Legislature, 263 F.2d 560, 566 (9th Cir.1959), cert. denied 359 U.S. 980, 79 S.Ct. 901 (1959); Silver v. Queen's Hospital, 53 F.R.D. 223 (D.Hawaii 1971).

11. See, e.g., Gordon v. Green, 602 F.2d at 745.

an expensive and time-consuming exercise that is not likely to please your client, the plaintiff.

2. The Preference for Plain Language

The movement from traditional common law and code pleadings to contemporary notice pleadings has fostered a preference for drafting in lay terms with minimal use of legal terms of art and a growing tendency to reject archaic legalese.

> Once an instrument of power, legalese no longer carries clout. It is considered a limp club, or worse: a pathetic attempt to display the accoutrements of classy breeding, like wearing a fedora or spats. Once an instrument of meticulous administration of the courts, legalese in court papers today is a symbol of red tape and inefficiency. The judges who know about good writing suspect that beneath your legalese lurks linguistic, and perhaps legal, incompetence.
>
> *   *   *
>
> [T]he courts have discovered a useful fact. Most lawsuit papers— complaints, answers, motions, notices, and so on—do not need to be complicated at all, because they do not really *say* anything. Rather, they *do* things, and the things they do are routine. These papers amount to what the linguists call speech acts ("performatives," in the linguists' own jargon), which make things happen, rather than communicate their content.[12]

A kind of folklore haunts the legal profession perpetuating a myth that judges prefer legalese and that the lawyer who does not use it will be laughed out of court. This myth is beginning to be exposed as such.

> The first systematic research on judges' language preferences was a 1985 California study.[13] "By statistically significant margins, [appellate judges and their research attorneys] rated * * * passages in legalese to be substantively weaker and less persuasive than the plain English versions [of the same passages]."[14] Also, to a significant extent, the respondents supposed that the writers of legalese did not come from prestigious law firms.[15]
>
> A 1987 survey of the language preferences of Michigan judges and lawyers indicated strong preferences for plain English rather than legalese.[16]
>
> *   *   *
>
> The [results of the same survey in] Florida * * * were strikingly similar to those in Michigan. * * * The Michigan judges preferred plain English in 85% of their responses [17] (1% fewer than the Florida

---

12. Benson, Plain English Comes To Court, 13 Litigation 21, 21 (No. 1, Fall 1986). Copyright © 1986 American Bar Association. Reprinted with permission. All rights reserved.

13. See Benson and Kessler, Legalese v. Plain English: An Empirical Study of Persuasion and Credibility in Appellate Brief Writing, 20 Loy.L.A.L.Rev. 301 (1987).

14. Id. at 301.

15. Id. at 314.

16. Harrington and Kimble, Survey: Plain English Wins Every Which Way, 66 Mich.B.J. 1024, 1024 (1987). See the survey itself at p. 395.

17. Id. at 1026.

judges * * *). The same survey was sent to * * * Louisiana judges * * * [who] preferred plain English in 82% of their responses.[18] In a different survey of the California Bar in 1987, 91% of the respondents said legal documents needed to be simpler.[19]

The survey results are good news for everyone who wants to shed legalese but fears plain English will not sound professional.[20]

————

Judges who appreciate good writing are inclined to reward it. A senior partner in a Santa Monica, California, firm tells the results of the firm's having hired an expert in English to edit all papers that leave the office:

> It is not an uncommon experience for us to appear for motions, have the judge indicate a predisposition to the view expressed by our papers, sit through a colloquy between judge and adversary lawyer, and depart without having said anything but our name for the record and thank you at the end.[21]

3. Examples of Conversion From Legalese to Plain Language

Getting rid of legalese goes a long way to make pleadings concise and clear. For example, it is sufficient to refer to the plaintiff and defendant throughout as "plaintiff" and "defendant" or as "Smith" and "Jones," short forms established in the introductory clause. There is no need to refer to "plaintiff Smith" or "Smith, the plaintiff herein," or "Jones, the above-mentioned defendant." If two or more parties have the same last name, first names can serve to distinguish them.

The same principle applies to identifying things, places, and the like. It is sufficient to refer to "the property" or "the lease" without reciting "the hereinabove-described lease" or even "the said lease." If only one lease is involved, "said" does not help identify it. If more than one lease is involved, to avoid potential ambiguity, they ought to be identified as "the 1986 lease" and "the 1987 lease" or "the house lease" and "the apartment lease" or even "lease 1" and "lease 2."

An obsession with "said" is one of the surest symptoms of a drafter afflicted with legalese. The drafter wants to create precision, but the method backfires. If you substitute an unobtrusive "the" for "said" throughout the following excerpt from a complaint, you can see that it is just as clear, probably more so without all the background noise that "said" creates by drawing attention to itself.

18. Prokop, Jr. Simply Tell It To the Judge (unpublished manuscript on file in this author's office at the University of Florida College of Law).

19. Abrahamson, Lawyers' Toughest Case May be With the Language, L.A. Times, Sept. 4, 1989, at 1.

20. Child, Language Preferences of Judges and Lawyers: A Florida Survey, 64 Fla.B.J. 32, 32–33 (No. 2, Feb.1990). Copyright © 1990 by The Florida Bar. Reprinted by permission of the publisher.

21. Fadem, Legalese as Legal Does: Lawyers Clean Up Their Act, Prosecutor's Brief 14 (Jan.–Feb. 1979).

[B]eginning at a point on said railroad track about a half mile or more north of a point opposite said curve in said highway, large quantities of highly volatile coal were unnecessarily thrown into the firebox of said locomotive and upon the fire contained therein, thereby preventing proper combustion of said coal, resulting in great clouds of dense smoke being emitted from the smokestack of said locomotive * * *. [Defendant] knew said smoke would fall upon and cover said curve in said highway when said engine reached a point on said railroad tracks opposite said curve, unless said smoke was checked in the meantime.[22]

D. TRACKING LANGUAGE FROM GOVERNING LAW

Sometimes it is necessary to keep language that is not entirely plain and simple. If an action is brought under a statute, for example, it is crucial to frame the complaint in the exact language prescribed by the statute. Sometimes it is crucial to use exact language from a case. When you do that, you do not need to use quotation marks or cite your authority in the complaint. That would amount to showing your hand unnecessarily.

For example, assume you want to establish that the defendant is a studio under the following regulatory definition.

"Studio" means a facility or its branches where an individual patron can obtain instruction, training, or assistance by contract for the following: physical culture, body building, exercising, reducing, figure development, dancing or any other such similar skill.

If you can get the defendant to admit in its answer that at one of its branches individual patrons can obtain training by contract for exercising, then you have eliminated the need to prove later that defendant is a studio. Successful tracking of statutory language often depends on picking out the most innocuous terms from a long series. Just be sure that the ones you pick do indeed apply.

Exercise 1.4

Your client fell on the tile floor near the swimming pool in the apartment complex where she is a tenant. When you draft your complaint, what language might you want to borrow from the following opinion, assuming it governs in your jurisdiction? Remember that you are drafting a complaint, not an opinion. You want the facts, not the conclusions. Remember too not to anticipate defenses.

22. Button v. Pennsylvania R.R., 115 Ind.App. 210, 213–14, 57 N.E.2d 444, 445 (1944). For further discussion of how to draft lawsuit papers without legalese, see Alterman, Plain and Accurate Style in Lawsuit Papers, 62 Mich.B.J. 964 (1983). In addition to pleadings, Alterman discusses motions, notices, affidavits, orders, briefs, stipulations, and correspondence. This article has been expanded into a book, Plain and Accurate Style in Court Papers (1987). For outspoken commentary on a variety of stylistic matters applicable to both pleadings and other legal documents, see McElhaney, A Style Sheet for *Litigation*, 1 Scribes J. of Legal Writing 63 (1990); Trawick, Form as Well as Substance, 49 Fla.B.J. 437 (1975).

BUFORD, JUSTICE.

We affirm the judgment in favor of plaintiff in a tort action wherein it was alleged as follows:

1. On or about April 8, 1951, at approximately 1:00 A.M., the defendant was possessed of, in control of, and had the responsibility and duty of maintaining the safe condition of a certain breezeway situated just west of the swimming pool located at Karen Club Apartments.

2. The defendant negligently allowed the floor which was constructed with terrazzo to be in a slick and slippery and therefore in an unsafe condition, after knowledge by the defendant of this condition.

3. The defendant negligently failed to warn the plaintiff of the known danger and unsafe condition of the floor of the breezeway, which slick and slippery condition was not observable to tenants of the Karen Club Apartments using the breezeway.

4. The negligent acts caused the plaintiff to fall while she was lawfully walking upon and using the breezeway.

5. As a proximate result thereof, plaintiff was seriously and permanently injured.

We hold that the complaint stated a cause of action. Whether the proof established as true the allegations of the complaint was a question for the jury to determine.

———

V. CHECKLIST FOR DRAFTING COMPLAINTS

Caption

1. Is the name of the court phrased accurately and concisely?

2. Is space provided for the case number?

3. Are the parties' names accurate? Are they properly labeled as plaintiff and defendant?

4. Is there proper indication if a party is a corporation or is representative for another?

5. Is the name of the pleading given, including the relief sought if the jurisdiction requires it?

Introductory Clause

6. Is this clause appropriately unnumbered?

7. Are appropriate short forms established here if at all for later references to the parties?

8. Are excess information and factual allegations properly excluded?

Jurisdictional Statement

9. Is this the first numbered paragraph?

10. In a damage action, is the appropriate monetary range given for the court named in the caption?

11. Is a particular amount of damages specified only if the jurisdiction requires it?

12. Is any governing statute indicated?

Allegations Identifying Parties

13. Is each party introduced and identified in a separate paragraph?

14. Is each party's status established as to rights or duties at issue in the action?

Allegations about the Cause of Action

15. Are allegations couched in short and plain terms?

16. Are allegations sufficiently separated, but not overly so?

17. Are favorable facts presented precisely and graphically?

18. Are unfavorable facts presented generally and abstractly?

19. Are ultimate facts presented rather than evidentiary facts or conclusions of law?

20. Does the tone of the allegations sound objective and matter-of-fact rather than argumentative?

21. Are allegations about dates, times, distances, and the like presented flexibly (for example, "on or about May 4") to avoid proof problems?

22. Are facts alleged to substantiate each element of the cause of action?

23. Are facts pleaded particularly on matters dictated by applicable rules, such as special damages, fraud, mistake, etc.?

24. To lay a foundation if you plan to demand attorney's fees, do you allege that the defendant's breach of duty caused the plaintiff to hire and become obligated to pay an attorney?

25. Do you take care not to anticipate defenses?

26. Are your paragraphs purposefully in either logical or chronological order?

27. Do you sensibly but not excessively rely on any court approved form?

28. Do you track appropriate language from any governing statute or case?

29. If any document forms the foundation for your cause of action, is it attached, incorporated by reference, and not quoted more than is necessary to establish how it relates to the cause of action?

Organization of Multiple Counts

30. Is each count numbered and given a heading?

31. Are all allegations numbered consecutively throughout the complaint instead of returning to paragraph 1 at the beginning of the second and any additional counts?

32. Are any common allegations realleged at the beginning of the second and any additional counts?

33. Are allegations from one count realleged in another only if they are germane to it?

34. Is jurisdiction established either in an opening common allegation or within each count?

35. Is the complaint divided into separate counts only to the extent that the division reflects different transactions or occurrences? Only to the extent that the division facilitates clear presentation?

Demands

36. Is the "WHEREFORE" clause appropriately unnumbered?

37. Do you refrain from specifying a monetary amount for general damages unless the jurisdiction requires it?

38. Is the relief you demand an available remedy for the cause of action you have established?

39. Do you demand punitive damages only if they are authorized?

40. Do you demand attorney's fees only if they are authorized?

41. Do you include a jury demand if it is appropriate?

42. In a multi-count complaint, do you present demands either all at once after all counts or else at the end of each count?

Signature

43. Is the attorney's address given with zip code?

44. Is the attorney's phone number given with area code?

45. Is the attorney's Bar registration number given if the jurisdiction requires it?

46. Is a firm's name given if it is appropriate?

47. Is it clear what party or parties the attorney represents?

Extras

48. Is verification omitted unless required?

49. Is a certificate of service omitted unless the complaint is an amended complaint?

Across-the-Board Checks

50. Are the parties referred to consistently throughout? By short forms if they were established in introductory clause? In all-capital letters if that would aid reference in a long complaint with multiple parties?

51. Do you refer consistently to other people, places, things, or concepts throughout?

52. Do you use past tense consistently for narrative of what happened?

53. Are all allegations in paragraphs numbered consecutively throughout, with no inadvertently missing or duplicated numbers?

54. Have you taken care throughout to refer to multiple parties with plural pronouns and to indicate which one of multiple plaintiffs or defendants is intended by reference in the singular to "Plaintiff" or "Defendant"?

55. Is "it" used to refer to a corporation or other organization rather than "he" or "they"?

56. Is the complaint couched in plain language rather than archaic legalese?

57. Will someone who knows nothing about the case, the judge, for example, find the complaint easy to follow?

———

Exercise 1.5

Evaluate the following slip-and-fall form complaint based on the drafting principles in this chapter.

Name
1/2

COMPLAINT

1   Plaintiff, A.B., sues defendant, C.D., and alleges:

2   1. This is an action for damages that (insert jurisdictional
3 amount).

4   2. On _____, 19__, defendant was the owner and in posses-
5 sion of a building at _____ in _____, _____, that was used as
6 a (describe use).

7   3. At that time and place plaintiff went on the property to
8 (state purpose).

9   4. Defendant negligently maintained (describe item) on the
10   property by (describe negligence or dangerous condition) so that
11   plaintiff fell on the property.

12   5. The negligent condition was known to defendant or had
13   existed for a sufficient length of time so that defendant should have
14   known of it.

15   6. As a result plaintiff was injured in and about his body and
16   extremities, suffered pain therefrom, incurred medical expense in
17   the treatment of the injuries, suffered physical handicap and his
18   working ability was impaired; the injuries are either permanent or
19   continuing in nature and plaintiff will suffer the losses and impair-
20   ment in the future.

21   WHEREFORE plaintiff demands judgment for damages against
22   defendant.

Exercise 1.6

Below is an account of an interview with an injured plaintiff,
Kathryn Faybo. Below that account is a complaint drafted on her
behalf modeled on the above slip-and-fall form. Evaluate the complaint.

Facts for Faybo Complaint

Kathryn Faybo fell and was injured in a drugstore on last August 1
or 2. She is not sure of the date but says she was in the store on
Friday. The incident happened at Crown Drugstore, 700 W. Main
Street in this city. She slipped in a puddle of soap or some other
substance that had been left on the floor.

Faybo went to Crown to take advantage of a sale. She had with
her her five year old daughter, Rachel, and her four year old son, Walt.
She arrived at Crown at around 2:00 p.m. She soon noticed a large
puddle of congealed pale pink goo on the floor near the center of the
cosmetics aisle. She did not notice any broken glass or other container.
She thinks the aisle may have been seven or eight feet wide, but she is
not positive. She says the puddle was large enough that she could not
get down the aisle with a cart without going through it.

Faybo shopped awhile for bargains. She then decided to buy some
toys for her children. She took Rachel and Walt to the lunch counter,
bought them each a hot dog, and told them to wait there for her. She
noticed that the puddle in the cosmetic aisle still had not been cleaned
up. She thinks this must have been "right around 3:00."

Faybo spent about 15 or 20 minutes buying toys. While she was
waiting in the check-out line, the manager rushed up to her and told
her she would have to take "those two brats" out of the store. Apparently her children had become bored waiting for her and had diverted

themselves by wandering up and down until they found the puddle. There they decided to play by skidding around in the accumulated goo. An employee saw them and ordered them to stop, which startled Walt and caused him to skid into a rack of sun visors, toppling it over and falling down on top of it. His mother fell when she took off running to see about her child and skidded in the film of goo about midway down the aisle. She slipped and broke her wrist and hip. Her wrist is in a cast. She has had hip surgery and will be bedridden for an indefinite period.

Faybo is a divorced woman whose husband has been unreliable in paying alimony and child support. She relies for her income on her job waiting tables in a local restaurant. According to her, the surgeon has said that it may be a very long time before she is able to walk normally, and there is some concern that she may be permanently crippled.

Faybo wants to sue Crown Drugstore. She says that the mess on the floor was there for two and a half hours, at least an hour before she came into the store and an hour and a half afterward. Crown Drugstore, Inc. is a family-owned close corporation. The building is owned by one of the shareholders, William Carr.

Faybo Complaint for Evaluation

COMPLAINT

1   Plaintiff, Kathryn Faybo, sues defendant, Crown Drug Store,
2 and alleges:

3   1. This is an action for damages.

4   2. On the 2d day of August, 19__, defendant was the proprietor
5 of and operated a retail drug store, pharmacy, and variety store at
6 No. 700, W. Main Street, in the city of _____, _____ County,
7 where it offered for sale over-the-counter medicines, prescriptions,
8 and sundries and solicited the entrance and patronage of the public.

9   3. Defendant kept the floor of said store waxed and polished,
10 and on the date aforesaid certain cosmetics and soap products had
11 fallen from a counter or otherwise had been allowed by defendant to
12 be upon the floor of an aisle, 8 feet wide, in which customers were
13 invited to walk, and said products were allowed by defendant to
14 remain on the floor thereof for a period of 2½ hours prior to the
15 accident hereinafter described.

16   4. On the aforesaid date plaintiff at the invitation of defendant
17 entered said store and walked along the aisle to view the merchan-
18 dise therein, and by reason of and in direct consequence of the
19 negligence and carelessness of defendant in allowing said products
20 to be and remain on the floor of the aisle aforesaid, plaintiff while
21 proceeding in a reasonably safe and prudent manner stepped upon

22 some of said products and was thereby caused to slip and fall
23 violently to the floor.

24   5. Plaintiff suffered bodily injury and resulting pain and suf-
25 fering, disability, disfigurement, mental anguish, loss of capacity for
26 the enjoyment of life, expense of hospitalization, medical and nurs-
27 ing care and treatment, loss of earnings, loss of ability to earn
28 money, and aggravation of a previously existing condition. The
29 losses are either permanent or continuing and plaintiff will suffer
30 the losses in the future.

31   6. Said injuries were not in any way due to contributory
32 negligence on the part of plaintiff.

33   WHEREFORE, Plaintiff demands judgment against defendant.

VI. DRAFTING ASSIGNMENTS

Drafting Assignment 1.A—Negligence Complaint

Draft a complaint on behalf of Kathryn Faybo.

Drafting Assignment 1.B—Negligence Complaint

Your client is Kim Lohman, a medical student at the local University Medical School. Last Tuesday, Lohman accompanied her friend
Tony Raiford, a law student, to the second floor of Wilbert Hall, a law
school annex, where Raiford had an appointment to discuss his law
review note with a drafting instructor. The appointment was at 4:30
p.m., and they arrived on time. The secretary told Lohman that she
could have a seat in the hall to wait. At 5:00 the secretary left, and
then there was no one on the second floor except Lohman, Raiford, and
the instructor. Lohman does not know the name of the instructor or of
the secretary.

Suddenly Lohman heard screeching tires and then a crash below on
S.W. Second Avenue. Instinctively she jumped up and ran to see what
had happened. The door was open to an office at the front of the
building, with windows facing the street. Lohman ran into that office
to look outside.

The telephone in that office had been set on a computer table
across the room from the wall outlet. The telephone cord dangled
between the desk and the table. As Lohman went behind the desk to
look out the window, she tripped over the cord and fell. When she
tried to get up, she discovered that she could not move her right arm.

The instructor called an ambulance, and Raiford rode with Lohman
to the hospital. It turned out that her arm was broken. Also, there
was a deep gash in her hand that required seven stitches. She received
the gash from a pair of scissors that had been sitting on the edge of the

desk. When she bumped into the desk as she fell, the scissors slipped to the floor, and she landed on one of the blades.

Now Lohman's right arm is in a cast and her hand bandaged. Her physician is not yet willing to predict when she will recover full use of the hand. In any event, she is presently unable to perform many of the tasks required of her as a medical student taking laboratory courses. So far her medical bills amount to $665.47.

Lohman wants you to file an action on her behalf. Draft the complaint.

Drafting Assignment 1.C—Negligence Complaint

It was a dark and rainy night when your client Ferris Franklin, a freshman at the local community college, tripped and fell on the stairs outside his fiancee's apartment at Creekside Apartments. The address of Creekside is 1013 S.W. Creekside Terrace. Franklin's fall took place last Friday.

According to Franklin, he and several friends had been partying at the First Street Bar and Grill. At about 1:00 a.m., Franklin and his fiancee, Christina Miliori, drove back to her place.

On the way home, they became embroiled in an argument and were still arguing when he walked her up the outside stairs. The fight continued outside her door. Finally one of her downstairs neighbors stuck his head outside the door and yelled that if they did not shut up, he would call the police. Franklin screamed at the neighbor to shut up, and the neighbor invited him to come downstairs and say that. At that point, Franklin turned and ran toward the stairs, bellowing about what he had in mind to do to the neighbor.

Unfortunately, the spotlight outside the apartment complex was not working, and the area around the stairs was dark. Franklin skidded on some wet leaves that had accumulated on the top step. As he was falling, he caught hold of the metal railing to try to stop himself, but it turned out to be rusted through. He wound up falling sideways from the second story to the ground below, where he landed in some rose bushes. The results were two broken ribs, a compound fracture of the tibia, and serious lacerations, including a badly scratched cornea.

Franklin wants to sue. He has had medical expenses of over $3000 already and expects to have further surgery on his eye. He is unable to attend school for at least this semester, and very possibly will have to be out for the entire year.

Creekside Apartments is a sole proprietorship, owned by Chris Dewey, who lives at 400 W. First Street. Miliori sends her rent there. She says that when maintenance is done around the apartments, the people who do it come in a truck with "A–1 Maintenance and Management Services, Inc." written on the sides.

Draft a complaint on Franklin's behalf.

Drafting Assignment 1.D—Consumer Complaint

Your client Margie Driscoll says she decided to join an exclusive local health studio called Quantum Physiques, Inc. ("QP") last May after talking to its employee Pat Bachman. QP is located at 473 Vine Street. Bachman's position there is called fitness counselor. Driscoll paid $400 when she joined on May 20. She tried to cancel, but QP refused to honor her request or refund any money.

Driscoll was attracted to QP by a full-page ad in the local paper on May 15. The ad stated:

> Quantum Physiques is a premier full-service luxury health studio offering Stepmasters, Treadmills, Hi-speed Bicycles, full range of Challenger Body Building and Sculpting Equipment and Free Weights along with an Olympic-sized Heated Indoor Pool and over 35 classes a week in Aerobics, Tae Kwon Do, and T'Ai Ch'i—A Complete Program designed to meet all of your fitness needs.

When Driscoll went to see the place, she was disappointed to discover that the pool was not in fact Olympic-sized. Also, there were no Challenger machines, although there was a weight room with free weights and stationary bicycles, which is still all they have. But Bachman told Driscoll on May 20 that they were going to get Challenger machines "before the end of the month."

Bachman wanted to know what Driscoll's "fitness goals" were. She wanted to lose 25 pounds and try to get in better shape. Bachman assured her that if she joined, Bachman herself would serve as Driscoll's fitness counselor and would help her monitor her weight-loss program.

Driscoll used to work at a Challenger club in another city, and she says that when she mentioned that to Bachman, Bachman told her she might be able to "get in on the ground floor as a trainer" as soon as they got the machines. Bachman pointed out that such work could lighten the financial burden of membership in QP.

Driscoll was interested. The other thing that persuaded her to join was the discount Bachman offered. She told Driscoll that she could join for $200, which would give her a six-month membership. But if she paid $400, she could get the special deal of a VIP lifetime member with an annual renewal fee of only $50.

Driscoll paid the $400 and signed a contract. Still there has been no sign of Challenger machines. She asked Bachman about them several times. Bachman finally said that QP will be getting Ultimatic machines instead, insisting that there is no significant difference between Challenger and Ultimatic.

Driscoll finally called QP and talked to the manager, Ray Rossi. Rossi said they had speculated about getting Challenger equipment but decided it was not economically possible until they had more members. He suggested that Driscoll try to recruit some of her friends to sign up. Driscoll said she wanted to quit. Rossi told her that after several months of membership, it was too late to get any of her money back. He suggested instead that Driscoll get involved in QP's upcoming racquetball tournament.

Driscoll wants you to get her money back and anything else she can get. The QP contract that she signed follows. Draft a complaint on her behalf based on the unfair and deceptive trade practices statutes in effect in your state.

QUANTUM PHYSIQUES, INC.

473 Vine Street

City, State 00000

PROMISSORY NOTE

SOURCE: T.V.___ Radio___ N.P. ✔ Member _Margie Driscoll_ Other _____
                                   (Name)   (Specify)

FOR VALUE RECEIVED and in consideration of the extension of membership Privileges as described on the reverse hereof, for the term shown herein, I (or we) promise to pay to the order of Quantum Physiques Inc., together with any assignees hereof or other holder at the office of the holder, the sum of $_____ payable in _____ consecutive monthly installments of _____ each, commencing on _____, _____ on the same day of each succeeding month, plus a final payment of $_____ due on _____, 19___. Upon the default in the payment of any installment, the holder of this note may at its option declare all unpaid installments due hereunder less that portion of such installments representing unearned FINANCE CHARGES, immediately due and payable together with all costs of collection, including reasonable attorney's fees in case this note is collected by or through an attorney at law not a salaried employee of the holder, and for the payment of court costs. The makers and endorsers of this note severally waive presentment hereof for payment, protest and notice of non-payment of court costs. The holder may extend or postpone payment without notice discharging the undersigned.

If any monthly installment stipulated herein is not paid on or before ten (10) days after the due date hereof, the undersigned jointly and severally promises to pay to the order of the holder hereof a sum calculated at the rate of 5% of such defaulted installment or $5.00, whichever is less.

Any unpaid balance may be paid at any time, without penalty, and on prepayment, any unearned FINANCE CHARGES of $1.00 or more will be refunded based on the Rule of 78's. The amount of such refund shall represent at least as great a proportion of the finance charge after first deducting therefrom an acquisition cost of fifteen dollars as the sum of the monthly balances beginning one month after prepayment is made, bears to the sum of all monthly balances under the schedule of payment in the contract. Where the amount of such refund credit is less than $1.00 no refund credit need be made.

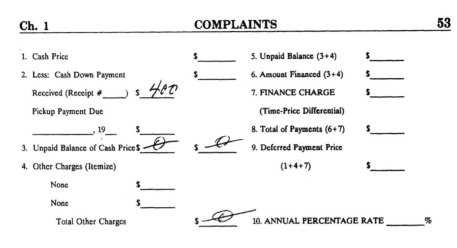

1. Cash Price $_____   5. Unpaid Balance (3+4) $_____

2. Less: Cash Down Payment $_____   6. Amount Financed (3+4) $_____

    Received (Receipt #____) $ *400*   7. FINANCE CHARGE $_____

    Pickup Payment Due   (Time-Price Differential)

    _____, 19__ $_____   8. Total of Payments (6+7) $_____

3. Unpaid Balance of Cash Price $ *0* $ *0*   9. Deferred Payment Price

4. Other Charges (Itemize)   (1+4+7) $_____

       None $_____

       None $_____

       Total Other Charges $ *0*   10. ANNUAL PERCENTAGE RATE _____ %

NOTICE TO THE BUYER

DO NOT SIGN THIS CONTRACT BEFORE YOU READ IT OR IF IT CONTAINS ANY BLANK SPACES. THE PAYMENT OBLIGATION OF MEMBER HEREUNDER MAY BE ASSIGNED BY QUANTUM PHYSIQUES, INC. TO ANY BANK OR FINANCE COMPANY.

YOU ARE ENTITLED TO AN EXACT COPY OF THE CONTRACT YOU SIGN.

THIS CONTRACT OR NOTE IS FOR FUTURE CONSUMER SERVICES AND PUTS ALL ASSIGNEES ON NOTICE OF THE CONSUMER'S STATUTORY RIGHT TO CANCEL.

WITNESS_____   I ACKNOWLEDGE RECEIPT OF A FILLED

                                 IN SIGNED COPY OF CONTRACT AT TIME

WITNESS_____   OF EXECUTION

                                 Margie Driscoll

Approved and accepted for Quantum   (Obligor's Signature)

Physiques, Inc.

by *P. Bachman*

    Authorized Agent

                                 (Member's Address)

                                 _____

                                 (Additional Obligor's Signature)

READ CAREFULLY AND SIGN

1.   I hereby represent to Quantum Physiques Inc., that I am desirous of purchasing a membership in Quantum Physiques Inc. and I agree to pay for such membership as set forth in the above note which I have signed. I further agree to use the Quantum Physiques, Inc. facilities in accordance with the rules and regulations printed on the reverse side hereof. The term of the membership shall be _____*12*_____ months and shall commence on_____*5-20*_____.

2.   I understand that I have signed an installment promissory note. My failure to use the Quantum Physiques Inc. membership and utilize programs and facilities does not relieve me of my liability for payment, regardless of circumstances, and my membership is absolutely non-transferable, non-assignable, non-refundable, and non-cancellable except as stated in paragraph 3 below. I UNDERSTAND THAT THIS CONTRACT COMPRISES THE ENTIRE AGREEMENT PERTAINING TO MEMBERSHIP AND NO OTHER AGREEMENT OF ANY KIND, VERBAL UNDERSTANDING OR PROMISE WHATSOEVER WILL BE RECOGNIZED OR BE BINDING UPON QUANTUM PHYSIQUES, INC.

3.   Consumer's right of cancellation--You may cancel this contract without penalty or obligation within 3 business days from the above date. You may cancel this contract if upon doctor's orders you cannot physically receive the services due to total and permanent disability. You may also cancel this contract if services cease to be offered as stated in the contract. If you cancel this contract for either of these reasons, the seller, Quantum Physiques, Inc., may keep only a portion of the tuition or contract price. You may notify the seller of your intention to cancel by notice to Quantum Physiques, Inc.

Type of membership:_____*VIP life*_____

Annual Renewal fee:_____*50*_____

NOTICE

ANY HOLDER OF THIS CONSUMER CREDIT CONTRACT IS SUBJECT TO ALL CLAIMS AND DEFENSES WHICH THE DEBTOR COULD ASSERT AGAINST THE SELLER OF GOODS OR SERVICES OBTAINED PURSUANT HERETO OR WITH THE PROCEEDS HEREOF. RECOVERY HEREUNDER BY THE DEBTOR SHALL NOT EXCEED AMOUNTS PAID BY THE DEBTOR HEREUNDER.

_____

Drafting Assignment 1.E—Consumer Complaint

Your client Allen Burns, a second year law student at the local University, has had three successful semesters. His studies have been at the expense of his social life, however. After a summer of clerking, he decided it was time to find a wife and settle down.

He decided to investigate dating services. He learned about Custom Companions from a classified ad in the paper that read:

Looking for that special someone? Call Gwen—Custom Companions 555–5555. Professionals only.

Burns called. Gwen Blanding said Custom Companions had a membership of over 500 professionals in the area and had been in business over 15 years. He asked what she meant by "professionals." She said, "Right now I've got an architect, an engineer, and a psychologist I could fix you up with. I have the nicest woman, another lawyer who—"

Burns interrupted and explained that he was not interested in meeting lawyers or law students. Discretion was of utmost importance. She assured him she was "absolutely discreet" and that before a first meeting she gave out only first names, telephone numbers, and a basic thumbnail sketch. She contacted both parties, gave them the necessary information, and then left it up to them whether to meet.

Blanding told Burns that she worked out of her home. They arranged to meet at the Coffee Break Restaurant two weeks ago on Saturday morning. At this meeting, Burns filled out an application and signed it as well as a contract. He was uneasy about the whole thing, but he paid $600 for a one-year membership, relying on the right of cancellation that he knew about from his study of law.

At this point Blanding gave him four index cards with full names, home and business phones, and other information. This alarmed Burns, who reminded her that she was not to give his full name to anyone. She assured him that she did that only with the consent of clients.

As soon as Burns got home, he received a call from a woman who said she had a degree in cosmetology and was attending night classes in computer science. Burns called the social psychologist. She said she had not been in the dating service for over two years. The architect also said she was no longer in the service.

Sunday night Burns received a call from a woman who was a local lawyer and who asked for him by his full name. Burns was furious. As soon as he hung up, he called Blanding and told her she had breached his right of confidentiality. He wanted out.

Blanding apologized, told him she misunderstood and thought it was only law students he wanted to avoid, and assured him she would not give out his full name again. She begged him to reconsider his wish to cancel and gave him five more names to call.

He called them that night. The "chemist" was a lab technician with two children. The teacher was married. The office manager was apparently intoxicated when he called and said she had recently been fired. The social worker was "into meditation and consciousness-focusing" and in the market for a "really conscious individual." The director of a social action agency advised Burns to get out of his contract. She told him that Blanding would work hard for him for about a week and then let him down with nothing further.

Burns called Blanding Monday morning and told her he was cancelling. He even said she could keep $100 of his money for the work she had done for him. She said he could not cancel, that she had not done anything deceptive or unfair and that she was not giving him any money back. Monday night, Burns wrote Blanding the following letter.

Dear Gwen:

This is to notify you that I am cancelling our contract, according to the state statutes which give consumers the right to cancel consumer contracts within three days of signing. Please refund my money in full immediately.

[signed] Allen Burns

Burns' first problem was finding out where to send the letter since there was no address printed on the contract or the application. He called her Monday night, but she was not there. He left a message on her answering machine. She did not call him back until Tuesday night. She said that since she worked out of her home she did not give out her address. She told him he could write to her c/o Landis Construction Company, 44 N.E. Main Street.

He mailed the letter by certified mail on Wednesday morning. On Saturday he received a letter from her accusing him of engaging in deceptive and unethical conduct in signing a contract that he intended to cancel after accepting the benefits. She refused to refund his money and said she was going to sue him for attorney's fees. She emphasized the point that she had not received his letter within three days of signing the contract.

Burns has come to you for help. He is so furious that he does not care any more about confidentiality. He just wants his money back. Also, as he puts it, he would like to "stop this woman from ripping any more people off."

Following are the application and contract he signed. Draft a complaint on his behalf based on the unfair and deceptive trade practices statutes in effect in your state.

———

CUSTOM COMPANIONS DATING SERVICE

NAME _Allen Burns_   AGE _27_

ADDRESS _1002 Portage St._
      (Street)   (City)   (State & Zip)

HOME PHONE _555-0000_   WORK PHONE _____

1. Have you ever had: drug, alcohol, health, or mental problems? if yes, please explain below.
    _NO_

2. Have you ever been arrested? If yes, please explain below.
    _NO_

3. Please provide the following information:
Weight _180_   Height _6'_   Hair Color _Brown_

4. EMPLOYMENT_____ ANNUAL INCOME_____

5. EDUCATION/CAREER GOALS _Law Student / J.D._

6. What are your major interests or "hobbies"?
    biking, Movies, Jazz

7. Describe your "philosophy of life." _Trust Everybody + cut the cards._

8. What are you looking for in a companion?
RELIGIOUS PREFERENCES_____   RACE____ AGE _Under 30_

INCOME _28 to 30,000_   EDUCATION _College_

I CERTIFY THAT THE ABOVE INFORMATION IS TRUE AND CORRECT.

SIGNED _Allen Burns_

DATE_____

CUSTOM COMPANIONS DATING SERVICE

NAME _Allen Burns_   AGE _27_

TELEPHONE: HOME _555-0000_

               WORK _____

ADDRESS: STREET _1002 Portage St._

               APT. NO. _____   CITY _____

               STATE _____   ZIP _____

For and in consideration of my payment of $ _600_ to *CUSTOM COMPANIONS DATING SERVICE, CUSTOM COMPANIONS* promises to arrange for me to meet other members of the service. I understand that *CUSTOM COMPANIONS* makes no promises or warranties respecting the conduct of its members and that it does not guarantee compatibility or qualities of its members. I understand that *CUSTOM COMPANIONS* relies on representations of its members respecting personal qualities. *CUSTOM COMPANIONS* is not responsible for the conduct or safety of members, but promises only to arrange meetings between compatible members based on information supplied in the membership application and interview.

SIGNED _Allen Burns_

SIGNED _Gwen Blanding_

DATE _____

I HAVE CAREFULLY READ THE ABOVE, AND I UNDERSTAND THAT CUSTOM COMPANIONS DOES NOT AGREE TO ACT AS AN INSURER.

[initials]_____

Chapter 2

MOTIONS

Table of Sections

I. MOTIONS AS APPLICATIONS FOR ORDERS

In contrast to pleadings, a motion is an application to the court for an order with respect to a pending action. The number and kind of motions available to a defendant who has been served with a complaint are in a sense limited only by the defense attorney's imagination. The facts may suggest motions to make. The statutes that are the basis for the cause of action may suggest motions. The governing rules of procedure are the most fruitful source of motions.

II. RESPONDING TO A COMPLAINT BY MOTION

A. REQUIRED ELEMENTS

Rules commonly require that motions (1) state particularly their grounds, including the substantial matters of law intended to be argued, and (2) state what order or other relief the maker seeks.

B. DEFENSES THAT MAY BE MADE BY MOTION

Federal Rule of Civil Procedure 12 and common state rules patterned after it provide in particular for several defenses directed to defects in the plaintiff's initial pleading. The defendant is free to assert these defenses either by motion before pleading or in an answer. Motions asserting these defenses are available in addition to others attacking procedural matters such as jurisdiction, venue, process, service of process, and joinder.

III. COMMON DEFENSE MOTIONS BEFORE PLEADING

A. MOTION TO DISMISS

Federal Rule of Civil Procedure 12(b)6 authorizes the motion "to dismiss for failure of the pleading to state a claim upon which relief can be granted"; common state rules refer to failure to state a cause of action. In some code states this motion is still referred to as a demurrer.

B. MOTION FOR MORE DEFINITE STATEMENT

Federal Rule of Civil Procedure 12(e) and state rules mirroring it authorize the motion "for a more definite statement." This motion should not be mistaken for a broad discovery device. Instead it seeks clarification of allegations so ambiguous or vague that the moving party cannot reasonably frame a responsive pleading.

- An ambiguous allegation may mean one thing, or it may mean another. In other words, it squints between two meanings, either of which alone would be definite.

- A vague allegation leaves out critical information. For example, it does not say whether a certain contract is oral or written; or it does not say which of several related contracts is its subject.

The motion should specify the defects and details needed to frame a responsive pleading. How the motion for more definite statement differs from the motion to dismiss is analyzed in *Mitchell v. E–Z Way Towers, Inc.,* explaining how these motions operate in federal practice.

MITCHELL v. E–Z WAY TOWERS, INC.

269 F.2d 126 (5th Cir.1959) (dissent omitted).

E–Z Way [1] is a Tampa, Florida organization engaged in the production, sale and installation of radio and television towers for use in transmitting and receiving broadcasts. The Secretary's complaint for injunction charged E–Z Way with failing to pay the minimum statutory wage for regular and overtime hours, failing to keep records of their employees' wages and hours, and for selling goods manufactured under such conditions in interstate commerce.[2] Fair Labor Standards Act §§ 7, 15(a)(1), 15(a)(2), 15(a)(5), 17, 29 U.S.C.A. § 201 et seq.

1. Both appellees are referred to jointly as E–Z Way. Clarence Jux, a joint appellee in both Nos. 17551 and 17552, is President and Treasurer of both corporations.

2. The Complaint in No. 17551 contained these paragraphs:

"V.

"At all times hereinafter mentioned, defendants employed, and are employing approximately twenty-one (21) employees in and about their said place of business in Tampa, Florida, in the production, sale and distribution of radio and television towers. A substantial portion of the radio and television towers so produced has been, and is being, shipped, delivered, transported, offered for transportation and sold in commerce, and shipped, delivered or sold with knowledge that shipment, delivery or sale thereof in commerce is intended from defendants' said place of business to other states, and thus said employees have been, and are, engaged in the production of goods for commerce within the meaning of the Act.

"VI.

"During the period since July 27, 1956, the defendants repeatedly have violated, and are violating, the provisions of Sections 7 and 15(a)(2) of the Act by employing some of their employees in the production of goods for commerce, as aforesaid, for workweeks longer than forty (40) hours without compensating the said employees for their employment in excess of forty (40) hours in said workweeks at rates of pay not less than one and one-half times the regular rates at which they were employed."

The Complaint in No. 17552 contained these paragraphs:

"V.

"At all times hereinafter mentioned, defendants employed, and are employing, approximately sixteen (16) employees at various points in Florida and in other states in the assembling and erecting of radio and television, which towers are used in transmitting and receiving interstate radio and television broadcasts and constitute integral parts of existing and essential instrumentalities of interstate transmission and communication. Thus said employees have been, and are, engaged in commerce within the meaning of the Act.

"VI.

"During the period since November 3, 1956, the defendants repeatedly have violated, and are violating, the provisions of Sections 6 and 15(a)(2) of the Act by employing some of their employees in commerce, as aforesaid, at rates of pay less than one dollar ($1.00) an hour."

Both contain an identical paragraph VIII, except for dates, as follows:

"VIII.

"Defendants, being subject to the Act and record-keeping requirements thereof, have violated, and are violating the provisions of Sections 11(c) and 15(a)(5) of the Act in that since July 27, 1956 [November 3, 1956 in No. 17552], they have failed to make, keep and preserve adequate and accurate records of their employees and the wages, hours and other conditions and practices of employment maintained by them, as prescribed by the said regulations, in that they failed to show adequately and accurately the hours worked each workday and each workweek by many of their employees."

To this E–Z Way replied with a "Motion for more Definite Statement" [3] requesting particulars as to the employees, weeks, and records involved, and a "Motion to Dismiss" based thereon.[4] This Motion contained two theories: that the Complaint (1) "fails to state a claim" and that it (2) "fails to allege in reasonable detail" the violations charged.

While it appears that both motions were before the Court, it is certain that the Court granted only the Motion to Dismiss for failure to state a claim.[5] Any doubt on that score is eradicated by the Court's action following the Secretary's formal election to stand on the Complaint rather than amend as permitted under the initial order, note 5, supra. As a consequence of this the Court entered a final order of dismissal.[6] This was expressly "on the ground that the Complaint fails

---

3. That in No. 17552, the shorter of the nearly identical two, is typical.

"The Defendants, * * * move this Court to require Plaintiff to furnish them a more definite statement, and allege:

"1. The Complaint is so vague and ambiguous that Defendants cannot reasonably be required to frame a responsive pleading.

"2. The Complaint contains the following defects:

"a) The Complaint fails to allege the specific weeks during which Defendants violated the provisions of the Act.

"b) The Complaint fails to allege the names of the employees concerning whom it is alleged the Defendants failed to keep adequate records.

"c) The Complaint fails to allege in what respect the records of Defendants were inadequate.

"d) The Complaint fails to allege the class of workers concerning whom the Defendants failed to keep adequate records.

"Wherefore, Defendants pray that Plaintiff be required to furnish to Defendants the following details:

"a. the specific weeks during which Defendants are alleged to have violated the provisions of the Act.

"b. the names and addresses of each employee of the Defendants * * * concerning whom it is alleged that Defendants failed to keep adequate records.

"c. the description of the particular records which Plaintiff alleges are inadequate, and in what respect said records are inadequate.

"d. the class of workers and the nature of work performed by the employees of the Defendants concerning whom it is alleged Defendants failed to keep adequate records."

4. The motions to dismiss were identical in both cases:

"The defendants, E–Z Way Towers, Inc., a corporation, and Clarence Jux, move this court to dismiss the Complaint, and allege as follows:

"1. The Complaint fails to state a claim against the Defendants on which relief can be granted.

"2. The Complaint fails to allege in reasonable detail, and in specific terms and by specific acts the manner in which Defendants have violated the Sections of the Act and promulgated regulations, as alleged in the Complaint."

5. "This matter came on for hearing on defendants' motion for more definite statement and motion to dismiss, the parties appearing by their respective counsel, and the court having heard the arguments of counsel and being otherwise sufficiently advised, finds that the complaint fails to allege in reasonable detail and in specific terms and by specific acts the manner in which the defendants have violated the provisions of the Fair Labor Standards Act as alleged in the complaint and thus fails to state a claim against the defendants on which relief can be granted. It is therefore

"Ordered that plaintiff's complaint be, and the same is hereby, dismissed.

"It is further Ordered that plaintiff have sixty (60) days from the date hereof within which to file an amended complaint."

6. "It being made to appear to the court that on the 22nd day of August, 1958, an order was made and entered dismissing plaintiff's complaint with leave to amend, said dismissal being on the ground that the complaint fails to allege in reasonable detail and in specific terms and specific acts the manner in which the defendants have violated the provisions of the Fair Labor

to allege in reasonable detail and in specific terms and specific acts the manner in which the defendants have violated the provisions of the Fair Labor Standards Act and thus fails to state a claim on which relief can be granted, * * *." This was, in turn, the exact language of paragraph 2 of the Motion to Dismiss, note 5, supra.

As an order of dismissal for failure to state a claim it cannot stand. Testing the complaint—as filed and on which the Secretary with propriety claimed a right to stand—it meets the standard so frequently repeated by us and now so recently reiterated in the most positive terms. "In appraising the sufficiency of the complaint we follow, of course, the accepted rule that a complaint should not be dismissed for failure to state a claim unless it appears beyond doubt that the plaintiff can prove no set of facts in support of his claim which would entitle him to relief." Conley v. Gibson, 1957, 355 U.S. 41, 45–46, 78 S.Ct. 99, 102, 2 L.Ed.2d 80.

In this light the complaint charges that (a) defendants have employees who are engaged in interstate commerce, (b) that some employees are required to work in excess of 40 hours per week without being paid statutory overtime, (c) others are paid less than the statutory minimum, and that (d) records are not kept with sufficient accuracy to reflect these facts concerning the employees. If evidence is brought forward showing (a) plus (b), (c), (d), or any one of them, the Fair Labor Standards Act would compel a finding and decree for the Secretary leaving to the Court's informed discretion the scope and nature of the precise relief to be granted. Mitchell v. Hodges Contracting Co., 5 Cir., 1956, 238 F.2d 380.

The defendants, and apparently the Trial Court, have confused the proper function of the motion to dismiss for failure to state a claim, F.R.Civ.P. 12(b), 28 U.S.C.A., and the motion for more definite statement under Rule 12(e). The former allows of no discretion in the usual sense. The complaint is either good or not good. The motion for more definite statement, on the other hand, involves, within the applicable standards of that rule, the exercise of that sound and considered discretion committed unavoidably and properly to the Trial Judge as he presides over the continuous process of adjudication from commencement of the litigation through pleadings, pretrial discovery, trial, submission and decision.

Under 12(e) the Court must determine whether the complaint is such that "a party cannot reasonably be required to frame a responsive pleading." But the fact that a careful Judge, in the exercise of that wise discretion controlled by the prescribed principles of that rule,

Standards Act and thus fails to state a claim on which relief can be granted, and it appearing to the court that plaintiff has given notice to this court and the attorneys for the defendant of his election to stand on the allegations of his original complaint and thereupon refusing to file an amended complaint or to otherwise amend his complaint now on file in said cause, and the court being fully advised, it is hereby

"Ordered, Adjudged and Decreed that this cause be and the same is hereby finally dismissed."

might so conclude does not permit him to dismiss the complaint for failure to state a claim. "It may well be that petitioner's complaint as now drawn is too vague, but that is no ground for dismissing his action. * * *." Glus v. Brooklyn Eastern District Terminal, 1959, 359 U.S. 231, 79 S.Ct. 760, 763, 3 L.Ed.2d 770, 774.

The motion to dismiss, and particularly paragraph 2, note 4, supra, substantially paraphrases like contentions made that " * * * the complaint failed to set forth specific facts to support its general allegations * * * and that * * * dismissal [was] therefore proper," which the Court rejected in Conley v. Gibson, supra, 355 U.S. 41 at page 47, 78 S.Ct. at page 103. To this the Court replied in words which are both authoritative and apt for our case. "The decisive answer to this is that the Federal Rules of Civil Procedure do not require a claimant to set out in detail the facts upon which he bases his claim. To the contrary, all the Rules require is 'a short and plain statement of the claim' that will give * * * notice of what the plaintiff's claim is and the grounds upon which it rests. * * * Such simplified 'notice pleading' is made possible by the liberal opportunity for discovery and the other pretrial procedure established by the Rules to disclose more precisely the basis of both claim and defense and to define more narrowly the disputed facts and issues." Conley v. Gibson, 355 U.S. 41 at pages 47–48, 78 S.Ct. at page 103.

There is more than a mere procedural distinction between the motion to dismiss for failure to state a claim and the motion for more definite statement. The difference is fundamental as this case testifies. If the claim is dismissed because it is too vague or because the plaintiff is unable to supply the details, none of the machinery of discovery whose function it is to ferret out facts and delineate issues before trial can be utilized. On the other hand, with the complaint declared sufficient against a motion to dismiss, the parties, both plaintiff and defendant, are assured both the right fully to exploit the flexible rules of discovery which will disclose in advance of trial what the case is all about and, more important, the full protection of a careful District Judge in the exercise of his wise and considered discretion as the case progresses toward the climax of trial and judgment. And, except for brief periods of 10 or 20 days following the commencement of an action when leave of Court is required, discovery mechanisms of interrogatories, requests for admissions, motions to produce and oral depositions are not contingent upon the state of the pleadings or any necessity for the case to be at formal issue. F.R.Civ.P. 26–37, 28 U.S.C.A.

In addition, by its very nature, a ruling granting or denying a motion for more definite statement is interlocutory in character. It is not appealable as such and must await the final decree with the likely consequence that it will wash out in the trial. If it survives, or if under some unusual circumstances which might make the ruling dispositive and hence open for certification and acceptance as an appealable interlocutory order, 28 U.S.C.A. § 1292(b), or if an obdurate plaintiff suffers a punitive dismissal for failure to comply with an order granting a motion for more definite statement, the party complaining will have the heavy burden of demonstrating an abuse of the Trial Court's discretion.

While Judges Tuttle and Brown agree that, procedurally, questions regarding the defendant's motion for more definite statement are not now before us, they also agree with Judge Hutcheson that if we ignore them nothing of procedural substance will have been accomplished by the present appeal. We therefore deem it appropriate to express the view that the Trial Court should not have granted the order and should it hereafter do so upon remand it would be error.

Appellant joins with appellee in urging that we pass on the correctness of the Trial Court's order on the motion for more definite statement. Not only from the presentation in appellant's brief, but also by reflection on the nature of the complaint before us, we conclude that there is here a matter of real procedural substance that at some stage of the litigation must be resolved.

If an employer is thought by the Secretary of Labor to be violating the wage and hour provisions of the Fair Labor Standards Act, the most effective way in which the employee can be protected is by the obtaining of an injunction; Mitchell v. Lublin McGaughy & Assoc., 1959, 358 U.S. 207, 215, 79 S.Ct. 260, 3 L.Ed.2d 243, quoted by us in Mitchell v. Strickland Transportation Co., Inc., 5 Cir., 1959, 267 F.2d 821, or an early declaration of the question of coverage, records, compliance, etc.

Upon the filing of a suit seeking an injunction, of course, the filing of defensive pleadings is essential to the Trial Court's fair consideration of the motion for preliminary injunction. Moreover, there are doubtless many cases in which, because of its possession of the records of employment and payrolls and knowledge of its own operations, the defendant in the good faith required by the signing and filing of pleadings, F.R.Civ.P. 11, must admit coverage, or violations or both. Upon such admission, of course, the likelihood of the issuing of a preliminary injunction or suitable declaratory order is greatly enhanced. If the time for filing defensive pleadings can be put off, as follows from the filing of a motion for more definite statement, any violations, if such exist, can continue without any effective protection for the employee so much the longer. And in any case, the time of likely trial will be postponed since most trial courts fix dockets on the basis of the case being at issue.

In such a situation it becomes important that great care must be used in passing on a motion for definite statement. In view of the great liberality of F.R.Civ.P. 8, permitting notice pleading, it is clearly the policy of the Rules that Rule 12(e) should not be used to frustrate this policy by lightly requiring a plaintiff to amend his complaint which under Rule 8 is sufficient to withstand a motion to dismiss. It is to be noted that a motion for more definite statement is *not* to be used to assist in getting the facts in preparation for trial as such. Other rules relating to discovery, interrogatories and the like exist for this purpose. Of course, the filing of defensive pleadings is not postponed by proceeding under these other rules.

The Rule provides simply, "If a pleading to which a responsive pleading is permitted is so *vague* or *ambiguous* that a party *cannot reasonably be required to frame a responsive pleading,* he may move * * *." (Emphasis added.) Before the 1948 amendment the Rule was broader in form. It read that a party might "move for a more definite statement or for a bill of particulars of any matter which is not averred with sufficient *definiteness* or *particularity* to enable him properly to prepare his responsive pleading *or to prepare for trial.*" (Emphasis added.)

Reference to the "bill of particulars" and the preparation for trial was left out of the amended Rule. Moreover the words "definiteness" and "particularity" were changed. This was because these matters could be better handled under the discovery rule. As much had been decided by substantially all of the trial courts that had passed on the matter, even before the Rule was amended. See discussion of the history of the Rule and its application in 2 Moore, Federal Practice No. 12.01, p. 2215, and No. 12.17, p. 2278 et seq. (1948), and see 1 Barron & Holtzoff, Federal Practice and Procedure, § 255 (1950, and 1958 Wright Supplement).

There is, of course, a paucity of appellate court cases dealing with this matter because unless a plaintiff stands on his refusal to comply with an order to make a more definite statement and the complaint is thereupon dismissed, no appealable order results. On the other hand, the error in ordering it becomes immaterial after it has been complied with. There are numerous cases in the district courts in which the policy requiring the restricted application of this rule is made clear. See cases cited in the two texts above referred to and see Millsap v. Lotz, D.C.W.D.Mo., 1950, 10 F.R.D. 612; Blane v. Young, D.C.N.D.Ohio, 1950, 10 F.R.D. 524; Granger v. Shouse, D.C.W.D.Mo., 1950, 10 F.R.D. 439.

Now, as to the application of the Rule to the case before us. We have the complete records; we have the complaints, the essential features of which are set out in this opinion; we find no statement or testimony adduced on the hearing on the motion to indicate why the defendants, from their knowledge of their own records and payrolls as well as their operations, would be unable to either admit or deny the allegations concerning coverage and violations. On the record, there is nothing for the Trial Court's discretion to operate on. It is too plain to require elaboration that if the defendants did not in good faith believe that they had violated the act, or that their operations were subject, in whole or in part to the Act, they could say so by denying the allegations in the complaint, and an issue would be drawn. The same would be true if they entertained a genuine doubt whether from uncertainty in the interpretation of the law or the underlying facts as to coverage of one or more employees, or compliance either with record keeping or payment of requisite wages. More especially if they believed they had violated the Act they could say so, and they should be required to do so. As to any specific cases as to which the Secretary contended there was coverage and had been violations which the defendants wished to get further information about, they would have ample opportunity to follow Rules 26–37 for discovery. It was just such detailed evidentiary information which defendants sought in their motions, see note 3, supra (especially par. 2(a), (b) and par. (a),(b) of the prayer). This evidentiary detail was neither a proper part of the complaint under F.R.Civ.P. 8 nor was it needed to frame a response under Rule 12(e).

As a consequence the cause must be reversed and remanded for further and not inconsistent proceedings.

Reversed and remanded.

C. MOTION TO STRIKE

Federal Rule of Civil Procedure 12(f) authorizes the motion to strike "any insufficient defense or any redundant, immaterial, impertinent, or scandalous matter." Some states preserve a separate rule authorizing a motion to strike sham pleadings.

- An insufficient defense is one that does not exist at law, even if the facts alleged to substantiate it are true.

- Redundant material needlessly repeats.

- Immaterial matter does not relate to the issues in the action, or else it needlessly elaborates on material allegations.

- Impertinent matter is likewise irrelevant to the issues.

- Scandalous matter is needlessly accusatory towards a party.

- A sham pleading alleges a valid cause of action but is false in fact. It is the obverse of a frivolous pleading, which is true but alleges no valid cause of action. A motion to strike a sham pleading commonly must be verified or supported by affidavit.

D. MOTION FOR SUMMARY JUDGMENT

The purpose of a summary judgment is to avoid the expense and delay of a trial if there is no real factual dispute. Federal Rule of Civil Procedure 56(c), mirrored in many states, authorizes the motion for summary judgment. The two requisites for granting a summary judgment are the following:

- There must be no genuine issue of material fact.

- One of the parties must be entitled to a judgment as a matter of law based on the undisputed facts. If the record shows a disputed material factual issue, summary judgment must be denied.

In the federal courts summary judgment under Rule 56 has been regarded as a tool for controlling the volume and scope of litigation. In state courts, summary judgments tend to be less frequently granted.

This motion is the only one in the group of motions attacking the adversary's pleading that has the capacity to result in a final judgment in the action rather than merely an order regarding a pleading. Therefore, the moving party bears a heavy burden to succeed in precluding a trial.

> Where * * * cross-examination and assessing the witnesses are important to finding the facts, trial * * * is appropriate. Where the critical facts are within the control and knowledge of one party, summary judgment may not be appropriate either. * * * [W]here the facts are firm, for example as in an action on a contract or a lease or on book account or a note, summary judgment more readily lies.[1]

In deciding a motion for summary judgment, the court may have a number of documents to consider along with the pleadings: depositions, answers to interrogatories, admissions, briefs in support of and in opposition to the motion, and affidavits. In fact, affidavits play such a major role in deciding many motions for summary judgment that summary judgment is sometimes referred to as trial by affidavit instead of trial by jury. Following is a California court's description of the procedure.

> The matter to be determined by the trial court in considering such a motion is whether the defendant (or the plaintiff) has presented any facts which give rise to a triable issue. The court may not pass upon the issue itself. Summary judgment is proper only if the affidavits in support of the moving party would be sufficient to sustain a judgment in his favor and his opponent does not by affidavit show such facts as * * * to present a triable issue. The aim of the procedure is to discover, through the media of affidavits, whether the parties possess evidence requiring the weighing procedures of a trial. * * * [T]he affidavits of the moving party are strictly construed and those of his opponent liberally construed, and doubts as to the propriety of granting the motion should be resolved in favor of the party opposing the motion. Such summary procedure is drastic and should be used with caution so that it does not become a substitute for the open trial method of determining facts.[2]

In general, when a court decides to grant a motion for summary judgment, it may enter:

• Summary judgment for either party, not only the moving party.

1. G. Vetter, Successful Civil Litigation: How to Win Your Case Before You Enter the Courtroom 66 (1977). Copyright © 1977. Reprinted from Successful Civil Litigation by George Vetter by permission of the publisher, Prentice Hall, a division of Simon & Schuster, Englewood Cliffs, N.J.

2. Corwin v. Los Angeles Newspaper Service Bureau, Inc., 4 Cal.3d 842, 851, 94 Cal.Rptr. 785, 790, 484 P.2d 953, 958 (1971). For a discussion of the mechanics of summary judgment and its denial, along with analysis of several illustrative cases, see W. Freedman, The Motion for Summary Judgment, ch. 2, Summary Judgment and Other Preclusive Devices 11 (1989).

- Partial summary judgment, for example, on liability only, leaving other issues for trial.

- Summary judgment for one or more but not all of the parties.

E. MOTION FOR SUMMARY JUDGMENT DISTINGUISHED FROM MOTION TO DISMISS

A motion for summary judgment does not raise the same question of law as that raised by a motion to dismiss for failure to state a cause of action. The motion to dismiss goes to the legal sufficiency of the pleading on its face without inquiry concerning the truth of the allegations. The motion for summary judgment tests the sufficiency of facts to which substantive legal principles are applied. The moving party carries a heavy burden of initially showing the nonexistence of a genuine issue of material fact. Once the moving party does so, the adverse party must show to the contrary to avoid summary judgment. Any doubt concerning the existence of a genuine issue of material fact must be resolved against the moving party.

IV. MOTION STRATEGY

The study of motion practice is much more a study of trial strategy than of drafting strategy. In other words, when the defense attorney determines how to respond to a complaint, the hard questions are about whether to respond with a motion before answering and if so, what orders to seek. The rules commonly prescribe incorporating all motions attacking a pleading into one paper; successive motions attacking a pleading are prohibited. Even if a motion is directed to only one of multiple counts in a complaint, the motion commonly defers answering all counts until the motion has been decided.

The strategic blunder that some inexperienced lawyers make is to focus exclusively on the fact that filing motions can serve to delay the proceedings. What these lawyers forget is that their motions attacking the complaint can result in the plaintiff's amending the complaint, correcting the defects in it, and ultimately improving the plaintiff's case.[3]

In choosing whether to assert a defense by motion or by pleading, you should also keep in mind that raising a defense in a pleading preserves it for trial, while raising it in a motion may mean losing it early in the litigation. Of course, losing some motions leaves you where you started, with nothing seriously lost; losing other motions can amount to losing the case. On the other hand, the potential value of an early settlement may be worth the risk if you can show the

---

3. See F. Cooper, Writing in Law Practice 195 (1963).

plaintiff that you are preparing a major defense for trial and you can expose the plaintiff as having only minimal damages.[4]

Exercise 2.1

Evaluate the sample complaints in Chapter 1 to determine whether each is susceptible to attack by one or more of the following motions: motion to dismiss, motion for more definite statement, motion to strike, or motion for summary judgment. On what grounds would you decide to file one or more of these motions before answering the complaint?

V. DRAFTING THE MOTION

The chief requirements for any motion made other than during a hearing or trial are those expressed in Federal Rule of Civil Procedure 7(b)1:

- It shall be "in writing."
- It shall state its grounds "with particularity."
- It "shall set forth the relief or order sought."

The requirement of stating particular grounds is directly aimed at defeating the former practice of stating motions as broadly and vaguely as possible with the idea of waiting for a hearing to specify what was intended. Thus one might have moved for a more definite statement without even specifying what allegations in the complaint were insufficiently definite for a response. The rules now generally preclude this former practice.

VI. ANNOTATED SAMPLE MOTION TO DISMISS, FOR MORE DEFINITE STATEMENT, AND TO STRIKE

Below is a sample motion to dismiss for failure to state a cause of action and in the alternative for more definite statement and to strike. It demonstrates how one paper may contain motions both for alternative orders and for compatible ones.

---

4. For further discussion of the risk/ return ratio in deciding whether to make a motion, see Vetter, above note 1, at 53–65.

1   SECOND JUDICIAL CIRCUIT COURT

2   LEON COUNTY, FLORIDA

3   NINA ATKINSON,
4   Plaintiff,
                            CASE NO.: 92–999999–CA
5   vs.
6   NEIL LAZAR, *et al.*,   DIVISION: CV–E
7   Defendants.

8   **DEFENDANT MARILYN LEDBURY'S MOTION TO**
9   **DISMISS FOR FAILURE TO STATE A CAUSE OF**
10   **ACTION OR FOR MORE DEFINITE STATEMENT AND**
11   **TO STRIKE**

12   Defendant MARILYN LEDBURY moves for an order dismissing
13   Plaintiff's complaint under Florida Rule of Civil Procedure 1.140(b)
14   (6) for failure to state a cause of action for the following reasons:

15   1. The complaint shows that this action is based on an
16   oral agreement that is not to be performed within one year of
17   its making.

18   2. The complaint does not allege damages resulting from
19   breach of the agreement.

Lines 1–11   • These lines make up the caption.

Line 4   • The drafter can now give the case number, copying it from the complaint, where the court clerk has stamped it.

Line 6   • "*Et al.*" here signifies that there are other defendants. They are all listed by name on the complaint.

Lines 8–11   • The name of the motion specifies who makes it, here clarifying that only one of the multiple defendants makes the motion.

• The name of the motion specifies the orders sought. Note that the name of this motion clarifies what orders are sought in the alternative and what orders are sought in conjunction with each other.

Lines 12–14   • The introductory clause is not numbered, just as it is not in a pleading. In this motion there are actually two introductory clauses. Lines 20–21 introduce the second of the two alternatives.

• The introductory clause repeats the information given in the caption, based on the principle that the caption is not part of the text.

• The introductory clause cites the rule authorizing the first order sought.

Lines 15–19   • The grounds for the order are specified, as required by the rule. Setting forth separate grounds in numbered and tabulated sub-paragraphs makes them easy to read as separate grounds and gives them emphasis.

20 If this motion is denied, Defendant MARILYN LEDBURY
21 moves for two orders as follows:

22   1. Requiring Plaintiff to file a more definite statement
23 under Rule 1.140(e) because paragraph 3 of the complaint is so
24 vague that this Defendant cannot reasonably be required to
25 frame a responsive pleading. In particular, a definite state-
26 ment should be required of the following:

27   a. the date on which the alleged agreement took
28   place;

29   b. the date by which performance of the alleged agree-
30   ment was to be completed; and

31   c. the names of the parties to the alleged agreement.

32   2. Striking paragraph 7 of the complaint, as authorized by
33 Rule 1.140(f), because that paragraph is immaterial, having no
34 bearing on any alleged agreement among the parties. This
35 motion is supported by an accompanying brief.

36   WILLFORD, COIRO & HAROLD

37   By: _____
38   Claudia Coiro
39   1111 Freedom Street
40   Tallahassee, FL 32301
41   (904) 555–5555
42   Fla. Bar No. 000000
43   Attorney for Defendant
44   Marilyn Ledbury

45   CERTIFICATE OF SERVICE

Lines 20–21   • The clause introducing the second alternative does not cite a rule because the second alternative seeks two orders, each of which is authorized by a separate rule.

Lines 22–35   • The authorizing rules are cited instead in the sub-paragraph on each order sought.

Lines 23–25   • Without quotation marks, these lines track the language of the rule that specifies the standard for granting the order.

Lines 27–31   • As prescribed by the order, the motion lists the specific details needed to draft a responsive pleading. These details are set forth in a sentence with internal tabulation for easy reference and for emphasis.

Lines 32–34   • In the second conjunctive part of the second alternative, the rule is cited, language is tracked from it setting forth the standard for the order sought, and the specific ground is expressed.

Lines 36–44   • Signature lines and identification of the signing attorney of record are presented just as they are in a pleading.

Lines 45–51   • This certificate of service demonstrates appropriate phrasing for both mail service and personal service.

46 I certify that I furnished a copy of this motion by U.S. mail to
47 Ronald Ennis, Attorney for Plaintiff, 1112 Gulf Street, Tallahassee,
48 FL 32301, on March 19, 1992; and I personally served a copy by
49 hand delivery to Sara Clemenger, Attorney for Defendant Neil
50 Lazar, 444 Ocean Avenue, Suite 1000, Tallahassee, FL 32302, on
51 March 20, 1992.

52 _____

53 Claudia Coiro

54 Attorney for Defendant

55 Marilyn Ledbury

VII. ANNOTATED SAMPLE MOTION FOR SUMMARY JUDGMENT WITH SUPPORTING AFFIDAVIT

Below is a sample summary judgment motion with a supporting affidavit. The motion demonstrates the option to move for partial summary judgment. It also demonstrates how supporting legal argument can be incorporated into the motion itself rather than presented as a separate supporting brief.

• This certificate of service also illustrates the need to serve a co-defendant represented by another attorney. An unrepresented co-defendant would have to be served as well.

1 IN THE CIRCUIT COURT OF
2 THE FOURTH JUDICIAL
3 CIRCUIT, IN AND FOR
4 DUVAL COUNTY, FLORIDA

5 CASE NO.: 92–00000000–CA
6 DIVISION; CV–L

7 SANTA FE ASSOCIATES,
8 LIMITED,
9 Plaintiff,
10 v.
11 UNITED REALTY INVES-
12 TORS, LIMITED,
13 *et. al.*,
14 Defendants.

DEFENDANTS' MOTION FOR PARTIAL SUMMARY JUDGMENT ON PUNITIVE DAMAGES

15
16

17   Defendants, UNITED REALTY INVESTORS, LIMITED
18 ("UNITED"), ALAN GEORGE & MATTHEW HARRELL, an Illinois
19 general partnership as general partner of UNITED ("GEORGE &
20 HARRELL"), and RIVERFRONT PROPERTY MANAGEMENT
21 CORPORATION ("RIVERFRONT"), move, pursuant to Rule 1.510,
22 Florida Rules of Civil Procedure, for a partial summary judgment in
23 their favor on the grounds that no genuine issue of material fact

---

Lines 1–16   • These lines make up the caption.

Lines 1–4   • Blocking the name of the court in the upper right hand corner of the page is a common alternate to centering it.

Line 5   • The drafter can now give the case number, copying it from the complaint, where the court clerk has stamped it.

Line 13   • "*Et al.*" here signifies that there are other defendants. They are all listed by name on the complaint.

Lines 15–16   • The name of the motion specifies who makes it, here all of the defendants. If only one of multiple defendants were making the motion, the drafter should specify which one.

               • Since this motion is for partial summary judgment only, it is helpful to specify the issue or issues on which the moving parties seek summary judgment, here on punitive damages.

Lines 17–28   • The introductory paragraph functions as the introductory clause of a pleading does. It is not numbered.

Lines 17–21   • The motion begins by establishing short forms for future reference to the multiple defendants, all of whom join in the motion. Putting the names in all-capital letters also establishes that scheme for use throughout to aid a reader in quickly finding all references to a given party.

Lines 21–28   • The motion cites the rule authorizing it and tracks the language that provides the standard for granting the motion: "no genuine issue of materi-

24 remains in this action regarding Plaintiff's demand for punitive
25 damages in Counts I, II, III, IV, and V of the Second Amended
26 Complaint, and that Defendants are entitled to judgment as a
27 matter of law on that issue. The grounds upon which this motion is
28 based and the substantial matters of law to be argued are as follows:

29   1. In Counts I through V of the Second Amended Complaint,
30 Plaintiff has sued Defendants alleging fraud, misrepresentation, or
31 material omission as to representations in connection with the sale
32 of the Santa Fe Apartment Complex, of problems concerning ter-
33 mite infestation, boundaries, and water and sewer system ownership
34 or maintenance.

35   2. Plaintiff has sued RIVERFRONT, which was the manage-
36 ment company in charge of managing the day-to-day operations of
37 Santa Fe Apartment Complex before its sale to Plaintiff.

38   3. Plaintiff has also sued UNITED, a limited partnership
39 which sold the property to Plaintiff. (See Pre-trial Stipulation.)

40   4. Plaintiff has also sued GEORGE & HARRELL, which was
41 the general partner of UNITED. (See Pre-trial Stipulation.)

42   5. GEORGE & HARRELL had no personal involvement in the
43 transaction or knowledge of any problems before the sale concern-
44 ing termite infestation, boundaries, or water and sewer system
45 ownership or maintenance. (See Depositions of Alan George and
46 Matthew Harrell.)

47   6. The persons involved in the sales transaction on behalf of
48 the seller were Rebecca Blankenbaker, an officer of Metro–Ameri-
49 can Investment and Management, who acted as broker and received
50 a commission, Samuel Gruber, a lawyer, and various employees of
51 RIVERFRONT. (See Depositions of Rebecca Blankenbaker and
52 Samuel Gruber, and Plaintiff's Answers to Defendants' First Inter-
53 rogatories to Plaintiff.)

---

al fact" and "entitled to judgment as a matter of law." The motion also
tracks the rule's requirement that it provide the "grounds on which [it] is
based and the substantial matters of law to be argued." Note that the
tracked language is not put in quotation marks in the motion.

Lines 29–98   • The paragraphs setting forth the factual grounds and the matters of law
are numbered.

Lines 31–34   • Note that the language here, which recites the problems at issue, is
repeated verbatim at every later point in the motion where it comes up,
lines 43–45, 56–57, and 60–61. The repetition illustrates the crucial drafting
technique of saying the same thing the same way throughout a document to
prevent a reader from thinking that slightly different phrasings are purposefully intended to refer to different things—and to prevent a reader in
bad faith from so arguing no matter what that reader actually thinks.

Line 39   • Here and throughout, other supporting documents are cited briefly in
parenthetical notes at the end of appropriate paragraphs.

Lines 48, 50   • Note that "Rebecca Blankenbaker" and "Samuel Gruber" are not in all-
capital letters here or in later references. Only the names of parties are in
all-capital letters, not all people mentioned. It would not be wrong, howev-

54 7. There is no evidence or allegation in this case that either
55 Rebecca Blankenbaker or Samuel Gruber had any knowledge of any
56 problems concerning termite infestation, boundaries, or water and
57 sewer system ownership or maintenance. (See Depositions of Rebec-
58 ca Blankenbaker and Samuel Gruber.)

59 8. The only persons who are alleged to have had knowledge of
60 any problems concerning termite infestation, boundaries, or water
61 and sewer system ownership or maintenance were employees of
62 RIVERFRONT. (See Plaintiff's Answer to Defendants' First Inter-
63 rogatories to Plaintiff.)

64 9. Before an employer may be held vicariously liable for puni-
65 tive damages, there must be some fault on the employer's part
66 which foreseeably contributed to the plaintiff's injury. *Mercury*
67 *Motors Express, Inc. v. Smith,* 393 So.2d 545 (Fla.1981).

68 10. The depositions, interrogatories, affidavits and pleadings in
69 this case do not contain any evidence of fault by RIVERFRONT
70 which would render it liable for any alleged misrepresentations or
71 fraudulent non-disclosure by its employees.

72 11. Assuming arguendo that RIVERFRONT was acting as an
73 agent of UNITED in connection with the sales transaction, the
74 pleadings, affidavits, depositions, and interrogatories show no evi-
75 dence of fault of UNITED.

76 12. Assuming arguendo that UNITED was acting as an agent
77 of GEORGE & HARRELL, the pleadings, affidavits, depositions, and
78 interrogatories do not contain any evidence of fault of GEORGE &
79 HARRELL.

80 13. The alleged failure of Defendants to have policies or proce-
81 dures for obtaining information concerning termite infestation and
82 termite damage at Santa Fe Apartment Complex and the alleged
83 negligent treatment for termite infestation, as a matter of law, do
84 not constitute sufficient fault to establish vicarious liability for
85 punitive damages because, among other things, Defendants were
86 under no legal duty to Plaintiff to treat termite infestation or have
87 policies and procedures for obtaining such information; and the
88 case law construing *Mercury Motors* requires evidence that the
89 employer knew or should have known that its agents were engaging
90 in a course of fraudulent conduct likely to harm the plaintiff.
91 *Urling v. Helms Exterminators, Inc.,* 468 So.2d 451 (Fla. 1st DCA
92 1985).

93 14. The pleadings, depositions, affidavits, and interrogatories
94 contain no allegation or evidence that Defendants knew or should
95 have known that their agents were engaging in any course of
96 fraudulent conduct likely to harm Plaintiff. (See Affidavit of Lloyd

---

er, to use all-capital letters for any person or thing that you mentioned often
in a motion or pleading and that you anticipated readers wanting to find
easily.

97 Grant attached as Exhibit "A" and Depositions of Lloyd Grant and
98 Carol Keller.)

99   RIKER, FURMAN, BLOOR & BLOOM

100   By: _____

101   William P. Saffer

102   Florida Bar # 0000000

103   10000 Tenth Union Building

104   P.O. Box 5000

105   Jacksonville, Florida 32201

106   (904) 555-5555

107   Attorney for Defendants

108   CERTIFICATE OF SERVICE

109   I hereby certify that I have hand-delivered a copy of this motion
110 to Susan Romberg, Attorney for Plaintiff, 4000 Central City Build-
111 ing, 8000 City Street, Jacksonville, Florida 32207, today, February
112 24, 1992.

113   _____

114   William P. Saffer

115   Attorney

Lines 99–107   • Signature lines and identification of the signing attorney of record are presented just as they are in a pleading.

Lines 109–112   • Plaintiff's attorney is the only person to be served with a copy of this motion because all of the defendants are represented by the same attorney. If Saffer did not represent them all, he would need to serve this motion also on those he did not represent or their attorneys if they were represented by other attorneys.

EXHIBIT "A"

<u>AFFIDAVIT OF LLOYD GRANT IN SUPPORT OF DEFENDANTS'</u>
<u>MOTION FOR PARTIAL SUMMARY JUDGMENT ON</u>
<u>PUNITIVE DAMAGES</u>

Before me, the undersigned authority, personally appeared LLOYD GRANT, who was sworn and says:

1. I am Lloyd Grant, and I make this affidavit in support of Defendants' motion for partial summary judgment on punitive damages.

2. From 1977 to 1989, I was the Management Vice President of Riverfront Property Management Corporation and had responsibility for management of various regional offices including Florida, which included the Santa Fe Apartment Complex.

3. I have personal knowledge of the facts expressed in this affidavit.

4. Before the sale of the Santa Fe Apartment Complex to Santa Fe Associates, Limited in 1989, I had no knowledge of any problems existing at the time concerning termite infestation or damage, boundary discrepancies, or water and sewer system ownership or maintenance.

Line 1
- Many hurried drafters neglect to label documents as exhibits after they have referred to them as such in the documents to which they are attached. This note is to flag that common problem.

Lines 2–4
- The only part of the caption given in this affidavit is the name of the document. The rest of the caption is not necessary because this affidavit is attached to the fully captioned motion. If it were not attached, it would require a full caption identical to the one on the motion.

- It is helpful to head the affidavit with all the information necessary to link it properly to the other papers in the action, including the affiant's name, especially if there are multiple affidavits in the file.

Lines 5–6
- As in pleadings and motions, the introductory clause is not numbered.

- This introductory clause gets the affidavit underway with a minimum of formality and without the obsolete wordy legalese: "who, being duly sworn, deposes and says."

Lines 7–38
- The text of the sworn statement is set out in numbered paragraphs. If it were very short, it might be set out as one unnumbered paragraph. If it were very long, it might be divided into parts with headings as well as numbered paragraphs for easier use as a reference document.

- Grant's statement is expressed in the first person (using the pronoun "I") in keeping with the tone of a lay person's statement.

- You may want to change style and diction somewhat depending on the level of sophistication of the affiant, to the extent that you know it. Consider the ramifications of having an affiant sign an affidavit drafted in language that is incomprehensible to that person. Explaining it orally may help, but it does not prevent potential problems. Moreover, plain language does not itself convey any lack of sophistication and may help convey the authenticity of the statement.

21   5. At the time of the sale of the Santa Fe Apartment Complex
22 to Santa Fe Associates, Limited in 1989, I had no reason to believe
23 that employees of Riverfront Property Management Corporation
24 had knowledge of any unrepaired termite damage, existing termite
25 infestation, boundary discrepancies or problems concerning water
26 and sewer system ownership or maintenance.

27   6. At the time of the sale of the Santa Fe Apartment Complex
28 to Santa Fe Associates, Limited in 1989, I was not aware of any
29 instances in the past where employees of Riverfront Property Man-
30 agement Corporation made any misrepresentations or failed to
31 disclose matters which they were under a duty to disclose in
32 connection with the sale of properties managed by Riverfront Prop-
33 erty Management Corporation.

34   7. At the time of the sale of the Sante Fe Apartment Complex
35 to Santa Fe Associates, Limited in 1989, I had no reason to believe
36 that any employees of Riverfront Property Management Corpora-
37 tion would engage or were engaging in misrepresentation or fraudu-
38 lent non-disclosures likely to harm Santa Fe Associates, Limited.

39   _____

40   LLOYD GRANT

41 STATE OF FLORIDA
42 COUNTY OF _____

43 Sworn to and subscribed before me on _____, 19__, by LLOYD
44 GRANT.

45   _____

46   Notary Public, State of Florida

47   My Commission Expires:

_____

Exercise 2.2

Just as it is wise to say the same thing the same way throughout one document, it is also wise to do so in related documents. How well

---

Line 38   • The affidavit concludes with the end of Grant's statement. There is no need to add the gratuitous traditional tag line of legalese: "Further affiant sayeth naught."

Line 42   • If you develop a routine form in your office for notarizing, it is wise to leave out the county, if not the state. Affiants often sign affidavits in counties different from the venue of the action.

Line 43   • It is wise to leave blanks for dates, especially dates of signatures. People often sign documents on dates other than when you expect when you draft them.

Line 47   • This affidavit concludes without certificate of service because it is attached to a motion and served with it. If it were not attached, it would require a certificate of service identical to the one on the motion.

does Lloyd Grant's affidavit illustrate each of these principles? First, test multiple references to the same things within the affidavit. Then compare references in the affidavit with those to the same things in the motion to which the affidavit is attached.

———

Exercise 2.3

Compare the writing style and form of the sample motions in this chapter with the writing style and form of some motions recently filed in a court near you.[5] Do you find much variation? On what matters is it important to adopt local style and form? To what extent might you improve on common local style and form?

———

VIII. CHECKLIST FOR DRAFTING MOTIONS

Caption

1. Is the name of the court phrased accurately and concisely?

2. Is the case number included?

3. Are the parties' names accurate? Are they properly labeled as plaintiff and defendant?

4. If there are multiple parties on a side, is only the first one given, with "*et al.*" in place of the others?

5. Is the motion named, including identification of who makes the motion if it is a defense motion and only one of multiple defendants makes it, and including what order or orders are sought?

Introductory Clause

6. Is this paragraph appropriately unnumbered?

7. Are appropriate short forms established here if at all for later reference to the parties?

8. Does this clause appropriately repeat the information from the caption announcing who makes the motion and for what order or orders?

9. Does this clause cite the rule or other authority for the motion? If it is not cited here, is it cited in the body?

---

5. For further suggestions about plain language in motion practice, and especially about its importance in affidavits, see I. Alterman, Motion Practice, ch. 6, Plain and Accurate Style in Court Papers 75 (1987). For full treatment of motion practice in federal courts, including local district court rules and cases cited by circuit, see Shepard's Motions in Federal Court, 3 vols. (2d ed. 1991).

Body

10. Is the body in a series of numbered paragraphs if and only if the length and complexity of the motion warrants separation to facilitate easy reading?

11. Do you state the grounds for the motion with particularity?

12. If you seek an order for more definite statement, do you specify what details you need to be able to frame a responsive pleading?

13. If you seek more than one order, do you clarify whether they are compatible or whether you seek them in the alternative?

14. Do you either incorporate your legal argument into the motion itself or else recite that a brief in support is attached?

15. If you are attaching an affidavit in support of the motion, do you have it labeled as an exhibit and in the motion refer to it as attached and incorporated by reference?

16. If depositions, pre-trial stipulations, or other papers in the court file support your motion, do you cite them at the end of appropriate paragraphs?

Signature

17. Is the attorney's address given with zip code?

18. Is the attorney's phone number given with area code?

19. Is the attorney's Bar registration number given if the jurisdiction requires it?

20. Is the firm's name given if it is appropriate?

21. Is it clear what party or parties the attorney represents?

Certificate of Service

22. Is a certificate of service included?

23. Does it certify service to co-defendants (or co-plaintiffs) as well as the adversary party or parties?

24. Does it show service on unrepresented parties themselves and their addresses where served, and on represented parties' attorneys and their addresses where served?

25. For each person served, does it show whether service was by U.S. mail, hand delivery, or other method?

26. Does it show the date of each service?

27. Is it signed by the person making service? In other words, does it either precede the signature line on the pleading or else have a second signature line following it?

Affidavits

28. If an affidavit is attached to the motion rather than separately filed, does it properly leave out all of the caption other than the name of the affidavit?

29. Does the name of the affidavit indicate who the affiant is and in support of what motion the affiant makes this statement?

30. Is the affidavit labeled with an exhibit number or letter?

31. Does the text of the affidavit begin with an unnumbered introductory clause indicating that the affiant was sworn and made the statement before the authority who will notarize the statement?

32. Is the affidavit couched in sufficiently plain language for the affiant to understand it?

33. Is an appropriate recitation included at the end for the person notarizing the statement, leaving blanks for the county where the statement is signed and the date, unless that information is known with certainty when the affidavit is prepared?

IX. DRAFTING ASSIGNMENTS

Drafting Assignment 2.A—Motion

You represent Chris Dewey, who owns Creekside Apartments, at 1013 S.W. Creekside Terrace in your city. On his behalf, respond by appropriate motion to the complaint below, captioned appropriately for the county court, where it was filed.

COMPLAINT

Plaintiff, Ferris Franklin, sues Defendant, Chris Dewey, and says:

1. This is an action for damages.

2. On August 25, 19__ [last year], Defendant owned or operated Creekside Apartments at 1014 S.W. Creekside Terrace, _____, _____ [your city and state].

3. On August 25, 19__, Plaintiff went onto the premises to take his fiance home.

4. Defendant negligently maintained the stairs on the premises.

5. Plaintiff fell on the stairs.

6. Plaintiff was injured, suffered pain, incurred medical expense, and had his working ability impaired. His injuries are either permanent or continuing.

WHEREFORE, Plaintiff demands judgment against Defendant.

Drafting Assignment 2.B—Motion

As defense counsel, respond by motion to a complaint drafted on behalf of Kathryn Faybo, Kim Lohman, Ferris Franklin, Margie Driscoll, or Allen Burns, as assigned in Chapter 1. The complaint may be one you drafted, one drafted by another student in your class, or one provided by your instructor for this purpose.

Drafting Assignment 2.C—Affidavit

You represent Quantum Physiques, Inc. ("QP"), the health studio sued by Margie Driscoll on facts set forth in Drafting Assignment 1.D. Assume that the complaint includes a count for common law fraudulent misrepresentation, based on statements made to Driscoll by QP's employee Pat Bachman. In that count Driscoll seeks punitive damages. The complaint alleges:

　　1.　that on May 20 of last year Bachman misrepresented to Driscoll:

　　　　a.　that QP would have Challenger exercise machines available for patrons' use before the end of that month; and

　　　　b.　that Driscoll was being offered employment as a trainer as soon as the machines arrived;

　　2.　that Bachman knew these representations were false; and

　　3.　that Driscoll suffered a loss as a result of these misrepresentations.

Assume that there is case law in your state holding:

• Before an employer may be held vicariously liable for punitive damages, there must be some fault on the employer's part which foreseeably contributed to the plaintiff's injury or loss.

• To hold an employer liable for punitive damages, there must be evidence that the employer knew or should have known that its employees or agents were engaging in a course of fraudulent conduct likely to harm the plaintiff.

Assume you are preparing to draft a motion for partial summary judgment on punitive damages in the case (not part of this assignment). Draft an affidavit to attach to the motion. The affiant will be Ray Rossi, the Manager of QP.

You have interviewed Rossi and learned that he had no idea Bachman told anybody anything about Challenger machines. He acknowledged that he considered getting those machines but quickly ruled them out as being too expensive. Moreover, he said, Bachman knew that people who were already employed at QP would do all the training on any machines QP installed.

Rossi said if he had any idea Bachman was making the representations alleged in the complaint, he would have fired her immediately. In fact, after he received the complaint, he questioned her about it. He was not satisfied with her answers, and so then he did fire her.

Chapter 3

ANSWERS

I. RESPONDING TO A COMPLAINT BY ANSWER

If the defendant does not succeed in dismissing a complaint by motion or in having a motion for full summary judgment granted, eventually the time comes to draft an answer. The defendant accomplishes two very different tasks in the answer:

- Responding to the plaintiff's averments or allegations with admissions, denials, and responses of "without knowledge."

- Presenting affirmative defenses.

In addition, as part of the answer, the defendant may present counterclaims against the plaintiff and cross-claims against a co-defendant. Both counterclaims and cross-claims may instead be presented in separate papers.

II. COMPLAINT AND ANNOTATED SAMPLE ANSWER WITH COUNTERCLAIM

Following is a complaint for damages against two defendants, followed in turn by the answer of one of the defendants, which incorporates a counterclaim.

1 IN THE COUNTY COURT
2 COLUMBIA COUNTY, FLORIDA

3 BEST BUY CARS, INC.,
4 a Florida Corporation,
5   Plaintiff,
6 vs.   } CASE NO.
7 MARGARET DONOFREY and
8 HENRY DONOFREY, individ-
9 ually,
10   Defendants.

11 COMPLAINT FOR DAMAGES

12   Plaintiff, BEST BUY CARS, INC., sues Defendants, MAR-
13 GARET DONOFREY and HENRY DONOFREY, individually, and
14 says:

15 COUNT I AGAINST MARGARET DONOFREY

16   1. This is a cause of action for damages in excess of $2,500 but
17 not exceeding $10,000.

18   2. At all times material to this cause of action, Plaintiff has
19 been and is a Florida corporation engaged in the trade of selling
20 automobiles to the public.

21   3. On or about January 21, 1990, Defendant MARGARET
22 DONOFREY was a customer at Plaintiff's place of business for the
23 purpose of purchasing an automobile, a 1989 Alora Supra.

24   4. As partial payment for this automobile, Defendant MAR-
25 GARET DONOFREY offered as trade the automobile she was driv-
26 ing, a 1988 Matsuda A240, subject to security interest of National
27 Motors Financing Corporation.

28   5. Defendant MARGARET DONOFREY falsely represented to
29 Plaintiff, contrary to the title certificate which listed Defendant
30 HENRY DONOFREY as joint owner, that she was the sole owner by
31 way of a court order awarding her sole title in her divorce proceed-
32 ing.

33   6. Defendant MARGARET DONOFREY knew that her repre-
34 sentation was false because she knew that no such court order has
35 ever been issued.

36   7. Defendant MARGARET DONOFREY made the false repre-
37 sentation in order to induce Plaintiff to accept the Matsuda automo-
38 bile as a trade.

39   8. Plaintiff relied on the false representation of Defendant
40 MARGARET DONOFREY and did accept the trade. Pursuant to

41 standard business procedure, Plaintiff paid off the security interest
42 of National Motors Financing Corporation in order that Plaintiff
43 could then obtain full title to the Matsuda automobile.

44   9. As a result of the false representation of Defendant MAR-
45 GARET DONOFREY, Plaintiff now has an actual equitable interest
46 in the Matsuda of $4,147.34, yet no legal title interest in the
47 automobile.

48   10. The false representation of Defendant MARGARET DO-
49 NOFREY was made with knowledge of its falsity, with the pur-
50 poseful intent to deceive Plaintiff, and in reckless disregard and
51 great indifference to the rights of Plaintiff.

52   11. Plaintiff has been required to retain an attorney for the
53 purpose of bringing this suit and is obligated to pay a reasonable fee
54 for this attorney's services.

55   WHEREFORE, Plaintiff demands judgment against Defendant
56 MARGARET DONOFREY for damages and attorney's fees, and
57 demands trial by jury of all issues so triable.

58   COUNT II AGAINST HENRY DONOFREY

59   12. Plaintiff realleges paragraphs 1 through 5, 8, 9, and 11 of
60 this complaint and by this reference makes them part of this count.

61   13. Defendant HENRY DONOFREY has title interest in the
62 Matsuda automobile.

63   14. Defendant HENRY DONOFREY has been unjustly en-
64 riched by Plaintiff's satisfaction of the security interest on the
65 Matsuda automobile, to the detriment of Plaintiff.

66   WHEREFORE, Plaintiff demands judgment against HENRY
67 DONOFREY for compensatory damages of $4,147.34, and demands
68 trial by jury of all issues so triable.

69   POE, WILSON & HIGH
70   Attorneys for Plaintiff
71   9900 South Drive
72   River Springs, FL 32699
73   (904) 555–5555
74   By: _____
75   Fla. Bar No.: _____

1   IN THE COUNTY COURT
2   COLUMBIA COUNTY, FLORIDA

3 BEST BUY CARS, INC.,
4 a Florida Corporation,
5   Plaintiff,
6 vs.   CASE NO. 91–342 CV–L
7 MARGARET   DONOFREY, *et*
8 *al.,*
9   Defendants.

10   <u>ANSWER AND COUNTERCLAIM OF DEFENDANT</u>
11   <u>MARGARET DONOFREY</u>

12   <u>ANSWER</u>

13   Defendant MARGARET DONOFREY answers Plaintiff's com-
14 plaint and says:

15   1. She admits paragraph 1 for jurisdictional purposes only and
16 otherwise denies it insofar as it is applied to her.

17   2. She admits paragraph 2.

18   3. She admits paragraph 3.

19   4. She admits paragraph 4.

20   5. She denies paragraph 5.

21   6. She denies paragraph 6.

Lines 1–11   • These lines make up the caption.

Line 6   • The drafter can now give the case number, copying it from the complaint, where the court clerk has stamped it.

Lines 7–8   • "*Et al.*" here signifies that Margaret Donofrey is not the only defendant. The complete list of names appears on the complaint.

Lines 10–11   • The name of the pleading specifies whose answer it is. If it were the answer of all multiple defendants, it would be sufficient to name the pleading "Defendants' Answer." If there were only one defendant, it would be sufficient to name the pleading "Answer."

Lines 13–14   • The introductory clause is not numbered, just as it is not in a complaint, other pleading, or motion.

Lines 15–35   • The pronoun "she" is a convenient device to clarify throughout Margaret Donofrey's responses that they are hers alone in this action in which one defendant is female and the other male. In any action involving multiple defendants, if one is answering separately, the drafter needs to use some device to clarify the limitation.

        • This answer uses Structure 1 as discussed below in Section III.B of this chapter. See Section III.B for discussion of alternative structures as well.

Lines 15–16   • This paragraph illustrates a cautious response to a jurisdictional statement. In some courts, it is common practice to admit jurisdictional statements without more, and routine denial is not looked upon with favor.

22   7. She denies paragraph 7.

23   8. With respect to paragraph 8, she admits only that Plaintiff
24 accepted the trade. She denies making any false representations
25 and denies that Plaintiff relied on any false representations made
26 by her. She is without knowledge of any payment of security
27 interest by Plaintiff.

28   9. With respect to paragraph 9, she denies making any false
29 representation. She is otherwise without knowledge of paragraph 9.

30   10. She denies paragraph 10.

31   11. She is without knowledge of paragraph 11.

32   12. With respect to paragraph 12, she repeats her response to
33 paragraphs 1 through 5, 8, 9, and 11.

34   13. She denies paragraph 13.

35   14. She denies paragraph 14.

36   FIRST AFFIRMATIVE DEFENSE

37   15. Any amounts paid by Plaintiff to National Motors Financ-
38 ing Corporation were payments made voluntarily, without any legal
39 obligation.

Lines 23–27   • This response is careful to admit specifically. It is also specific about
denial and response of "without knowledge." This is because with part to
deny and part about which to respond "without knowledge," it would not be
appropriate to recite a general denial for the remainder after the specific
admission. Sometimes this structure, using three separate sentences, each of
them specific, may be dangerous. If any information in the plaintiff's paragraph is not expressly covered in one of the defendant's three sentences, that
information may be deemed admitted.

    • Note how the defendant is careful to avoid a negative pregnant, discussed
below in Section III of this chapter. What if the defendant had stated:
"Defendant denies that Plaintiff relied on false representations made by her"?

Lines 32–33   • Inexperienced drafters sometimes inadvertently forget to respond to
reallegation paragraphs in a complaint. Depending on what structure the
drafter has chosen for the answer, leaving out a paragraph can cause a serious
problem if every paragraph from that point on is misnumbered.

Lines 36, 40   • Affirmative defenses are separately headed. Some drafters give them
substantive headings as well as numerical ones. Substantive headings are
more useful in a very long answer with numerous and long affirmative
defenses. In some courts it is common practice to head the opening responses
to the paragraphs in the complaint "First Defense." Then the first affirmative defense is headed "Second Defense," etc.

Line 37   • The first paragraph in the first affirmative defense follows in numerical
sequence after the last response paragraph; it is numbered "15" rather than
"1."

40   SECOND AFFIRMATIVE DEFENSE

41   16. Plaintiff has retained possession of the Matsuda automo-
42 bile and has refused to return it to Defendant MARGARET DO-
43 NOFREY despite demand and proof that she is its sole owner.

44   17. This automobile has diminished in value during the time it
45 has been wrongfully held by Plaintiff.

46   18. Any recovery by Plaintiff should be reduced by the value
47 of the automobile at the time it was initially received by Plaintiff
48 and by an amount equal to the value of the loss of use suffered by
49 Defendant MARGARET DONOFREY, together with interest.

50   COUNTERCLAIM

51   Counterclaimant, MARGARET DONOFREY, counterclaims
52 against Plaintiff, BEST BUY CARS, INC., and says:

53   COUNT I—CONVERSION

54   19. This is an action for damages which exceed $10,000.

55   20. At all material times, Plaintiff was acting through its
56 servants or agents who had the full authority of Plaintiff in their
57 actions.

58   21. Counterclaimant is entitled to relief against Plaintiff upon
59 the following facts:

60   A. Counterclaimant is the owner and is entitled to posses-
61   sion of a 1988 Matsuda A240 automobile, as evidenced by the
62   attached Final Judgment in Dissolution (Exhibit "A") awarding
63   her possession.

64   B. Plaintiff has possession of the automobile, which it has
65   converted to its own use.

66   C. Counterclaimant has demanded return of the automo-
67   bile to her, and despite this demand, Plaintiff has refused to
68   return it.

69   22. As a result of the wrongful acts of Plaintiff:

70   A. Counterclaimant has lost the value of her automobile.

71   B. The value of the automobile has been diminished while
72   it has been detained by Plaintiff.

73   C. Counterclaimant has been deprived of and lost the use
74   of her automobile during this time period.

Lines 50–52   • The counterclaim is separately headed and begins with its own introducto-
                 ry clause in which the party who was the defendant in the answer is now
                 identified by her status as counterclaimant.

75   23. Counterclaimant has had to retain the services of an
76 attorney to represent her in this matter and has incurred the
77 obligation to pay this attorney's reasonable fee.

78   WHEREFORE, Counterclaimant demands judgment against
79 Plaintiff for compensatory and punitive damages, together with
80 costs, interest, and attorney's fees, and demands trial by jury of all
81 issues so triable.

82   COUNT II—REPLEVIN

83   24. Counterclaimant realleges paragraphs 20, 21, and 23.

84   25. This is an action to recover possession of personal property
85 in Columbia County, Florida. To Counterclaimant's best knowl-
86 edge, information, and belief, the Matsuda automobile is located at
87 Plaintiff's sales lot, located at 42 River Road, River Springs, Colum-
88 bia County, Florida.

89   26. To the best of Counterclaimant's knowledge, information,
90 and belief, the total value of the automobile is $4,150.

91   27. Plaintiff received the Matsuda automobile for the purpose
92 of applying its value as a trade-in against a 1989 Alora Supra which
93 was purchased by Counterclaimant from Plaintiff.

94   28. Subsequently, Plaintiff informed Counterclaimant that she
95 could not use the Matsuda as a trade-in and that she had to enter
96 into a new sales contract which provided for no trade-in and a
97 $1,230.02 balloon payment.

98   29. Counterclaimant entered into the subsequent contract, a
99 copy of which is attached (Exhibit "B"). Accordingly, Plaintiff is
100 not entitled to possession of the Matsuda automobile.

101   30. The claimed property, the Matsuda automobile, has not
102 been taken for a tax assessment or a fine pursuant to law.

103   31. The property has not been taken under an execution or
104 attachment against the property of Counterclaimant.

105   WHEREFORE, Counterclaimant requests the Court to issue a
106 judgment for possession of the property and an order authorizing a
107 writ of replevin, together with costs, interest, attorney's fees and
108 such other relief as the court deems proper.

109   <u>CERTIFICATE OF SERVICE</u>

110   I furnished a copy of this answer and counterclaim to _____,
111 Attorney for Plaintiff, 9900 South Drive, River Springs, Florida
112 32699, and a copy to Defendant Henry Donofrey, 1234 Market
113 Street, Gainesville, Florida 32604, by U.S. mail on _____, 19__.

Lines 109–
13
     ● By putting the certificate of service ahead of the signature lines, the
        drafter eliminates the need for a second set of signature lines.

114
115   Ronald L. Harris
116   Attorney for Defendant
117   MARGARET DONOFREY
118   P.O. Box _____
119   Gainesville, FL 32602
120   (904) 555–5555
121   Florida Bar No. _____

III. ADMISSIONS, DENIALS, AND RESPONSES OF "WITHOUT KNOWLEDGE"

A. THE DEFENDANT'S OPTIONS

The defendant's first task in the answer is to respond to each averment or allegation in the complaint. "Averment" is the term used in the federal rules as well as in those of some states. "Allegation" is perhaps the more common state term. Federal Rule of Civil Procedure 8(b) and state rules mirroring it give the defendant three choices of what to say in response to each averment:

- Admit it.

- Deny it.

- State that the answering defendant is without knowledge or information sufficient to form a belief as to its truth.

The third choice operates as a denial. It is often abbreviated to say simply that the defendant is "without knowledge" of the paragraph. This is consistent with common state rules prescribing that, like allegations in a complaint, defenses are to be in "short and plain" terms.

The defendant is obligated in good faith to deny an allegation only in part if part of it is true. In that case, the defendant should specify the true part and deny the rest generally. Any of the plaintiff's allegations not denied are treated as admitted.

B. ALTERNATIVE STRUCTURES FOR RESPONSES

Responses to the paragraphs of the complaint precede any affirmative defenses in the body of the answer. Several structures are common.

Structure 1

Defendant answers Plaintiff's complaint and says:

1. Defendant admits paragraph 1.
2. Defendant admits paragraph 2.
3. Defendant denies paragraph 3.
4. Defendant denies paragraph 4.

5. Defendant admits paragraph 5.

6. Defendant is without knowledge of paragraph 6.

Those who recommend this structure point out that it is absolutely explicit about what the defendant's response is to each paragraph in the complaint. Also, by putting each paragraph of the answer in a complete sentence, the defendant conveys care and deliberateness. Finally, addressing each of the complaint's paragraphs in a separate paragraph makes it easy to set the complaint and the answer side by side to see at a glance each allegation and the defendant's response to it.

Those who criticize this structure regard it as needlessly repetitious.

Structure 2

Defendant answers Plaintiff's complaint and says:

1. Defendant admits paragraphs 1 and 2.

2. Defendant denies paragraphs 3 and 4.

3. Defendant admits paragraph 5.

4. Defendant is without knowledge of paragraph 6.

This structure, like Structure 1, responds to paragraphs in the order in which they appear in the complaint. It achieves some of the conciseness that Structure 1 lacks by joining together in the same response all paragraphs in sequence that receive the same form of response.

The numbering of the defendant's paragraphs in this structure is not the same as the numbering of the paragraphs in the complaint. This variation in the sequence of paragraph numbers can lead to confusion. At the very least, it does not help a reader easily track the complaint while moving through the answer.

Structure 3

Defendant answers Plaintiff's complaint and says:

1. Defendant admits paragraphs 1, 2, and 5.

2. Defendant denies paragraphs 3 and 4.

3. Defendant is without knowledge of paragraph 6.

This structure puts a premium on conciseness by collecting all admissions into one paragraph, doing the same with all denials, and then the same again with all allegations of which the defendant is without knowledge. In other words, using this structure, most answers consist of three paragraphs, aside from responses requiring partial admission and partial denial and aside from affirmative defenses.

The most dangerous feature of this structure is that it makes it easy for the defendant to skip a paragraph from the complaint and never know the difference until it is too late, in other words, until the defendant is deemed to have admitted the missing paragraph.

This structure is also hard on readers, judges as well as adversaries, who cannot easily read through the complaint and track the responses to its paragraphs in sequence.

Structure 4

Defendant answers Plaintiff's complaint and says:

1. Admit.
2. Admit
3. Deny.
4. Deny.
5. Admit.
6. Without knowledge.

Conciseness is not just at a premium here; it rules all. The real virtue of this structure is that it promotes easy tracking of responses in sequence with the allegations to which they respond. Again, aside from allegations requiring partial admission and partial denial, there is no extra verbiage to get in the way.

What this structure lacks is polish. Some readers, including judges, may regard the brusk tone as rude and go on to conclude that the drafter has done a quick job of it, not analyzing the allegations fully enough to determine whether partial admissions and denials might be appropriate.

Moreover, this structure does not use coherent syntax. Literally, it says: Defendant says, "Admit." Who admits? Admits what? Just because the defendant's first paragraph is numbered "1," that does not say expressly that the defendant is admitting paragraph 1 of the complaint. All this information is left to inference. Of course, in a court where this structure is commonly used, you are probably safe in relying on those inferences. It would be risky to use this structure in a court where you have not practiced enough to know what the local customs are.

Structure 5

Answering Plaintiff's complaint, Defendant admits, denies, and otherwise responds to each paragraph in it as follows:

Paragraph	Response
1.	Admits.
2.	Admits.
3.	Denies.

Paragraph	Response
4.	Denies.
5.	Admits.
6.	Is without knowledge.

This structure attempts to avoid the objections to Structure 4. You can judge how successfully you think it does so.

———

Exercise 3.1

Evaluate the strengths and weaknesses of Structures 1 through 5 for presenting responses to allegations in a complaint. Discover whether there is a preferred customary structure in the law offices where you have clerked or in the courts where you plan to practice. Which structure do you prefer and why?

———

Exercise 3.2

In the sample complaint given in Section II of this chapter, assume that the drafter mistakenly numbered paragraph 2 as a paragraph 1 so that there were two paragraphs numbered "1." How would you then draft responses to these first two numbered paragraphs of the complaint?

———

C. TROUBLESOME FORMS OF DENIAL

1. Leaving the Plaintiff to Proofs

To "leave the plaintiff to its proofs" formerly was a common response. It amounted to neither admitting nor denying. Today it is no longer regarded as an option in most courts. In fact, according to the common rule that anything not denied is admitted, this response may be construed as an admission.

2. Presenting the Defendant's Version of an Allegation

A second troublesome form of denial, formerly common, was to set forth the defendant's own version of an allegation and then conclude the sentence: "except as so alleged, defendant denies the allegations of paragraph 4."[1] This kind of denial can be construed as not responding to some particulars in the plaintiff's allegations, which are then deemed admitted.

1. See G. Vetter, Successful Civil Litigation: How to Win Your Case Before You Enter the Courtroom, 44 (1977) (recommending this technique as preferable to wading through a convoluted allegation to admit certain isolated words and phrases and deny others).

3. *Expressing a Negative Pregnant*

When the defendant spells out the terms denied rather than simply denying a given paragraph or sentence number, there is a danger that the negative statement may be construed to deny some particular but admit the general statement containing the particular. This concept of the negative containing a positive is called a "negative pregnant." For example, if the defendant states that he did not lease certain property for 366 days, his statement may be construed to contain the admission that he did lease the property, denying only the number of days.

The case below, *Frank v. Solomon,* demonstrates the difficulty a negative pregnant in an answer can cause, especially if the defendant is not blessed with a judge who understands that modern pleading theory dictates liberally allowing amendments so that technicalities do not defeat the parties' right to have claims decided on their merits.

FRANK v. SOLOMON

94 Ariz. 55, 381 P.2d 591 (1963) (citations omitted).

UDALL, VICE CHIEF JUSTICE.

In the trial below plaintiff, an attorney, was granted judgment on the pleadings for the sum of $8,575. This allegedly represented reasonable attorneys' fee for legal service given the defendant in an earlier action, less a sum already paid. Defendant appeals.

Plaintiff alleged in the complaint, inter alia, that reasonable value of the services rendered for defendant was $8,750 of which $175 had been paid. Defendant answered admitting the payment of $175, denying and admitting certain other specific allegations, and denying that reasonable value of attorneys' fee was $8,750.

The trial commenced, the pleadings were read, the plaintiff waived opening arguments and defendant presented opening argument. Plaintiff's counsel then moved for judgment on the pleadings pursuant to Ariz.R.Civ.P., Rule 12(c), 16 A.R.S., advancing his theory that defendant's denial of the reasonableness of the sum amounted to a negative pregnant. Defendant's counsel moved for leave to amend its answer under authority of Ariz.R.Civ.P., Rule 15(a). Plaintiff's motion was granted and defendant's denied. Defendant appeals from these rulings and asserts four assignments of error the first of which alone we will discuss. He said:

> "The court below erred in not permitting defendant to amend his pleadings * * * in that it prevented the cause from being heard on its merits and was an abuse of the court's discretion."

Upon a review of basic principles of pleading we find this assignment well taken.

The modern Rules of Civil Procedure were intended to promote the administration of justice by removing the technical requirements of common law pleading. [citations] In keeping with this spirit the rule under consideration, Rule 15(a) regarding leave to amend, is couched in language of liberality. It specifically states that "Leave to amend shall be freely given when justice requires." Furthermore, this Court has stated that amendments of pleadings should be allowed with great liberality to the end that every cause of action shall be decided on its merits whenever possible without prejudice to the other party. [citations]

The trial judge's refusal in the case at bar to permit the defendant the privilege to amend his answer to avoid losing a substantial property interest because of an alleged highly technical defect in his answer draws our attention to the wisdom of the above expressed principles. The record before us indicates that defendant, by amending his answer, could have easily remedied any possible ambiguities it may have contained.[2] Defendant is entitled to his day in court, and to have denied him that when his handicap could have been so easily remedied was an abuse of the court's discretion.

Appurtenant to our conclusion regarding the court's refusal to allow an amendment to the answer, but necessarily following it because it was the theory upon which the court grounded its refusal, is a comment on the application of the negative pregnant doctrine to this case. This Court has in the past adhered to that doctrine. [citations]

The term is defined in Black's Law Dictionary, Fourth Edition, page 1183, as follows:

"In pleading, a negative implying also an affirmative. * * * Such a form of negative expression as may imply or carry within it an affirmative. [citations]

" * * * A 'negative pregnant,' is a denial in form, but is in fact an admission, as where the denial in haec verba includes the time and place, which are usually immaterial. [citations]

"A denial in such form as to imply or express an admission of the substantial fact which apparently is controverted; or a denial which, although in the form of a traverse, really admits the important facts contained in the allegation to which it relates. [citations]"

The late Chief Justice Levi Udall in a dissenting opinion to the Wingfoot case, supra, wrote as follows:

"The doctrine of negative pregnant is merely a specific application of the general rule that evasive and dilatory pleadings are defective."

To this interpretation we subscribe, but the general rule is not applicable in the case at bar. Defendant denied simply that $8,750 represented reasonable value of attorneys' fee. There seems in this nothing that is evasive or dilatory. Furthermore, it presents a controversy of a material matter. Such a denial leaves for the trier of facts to deter-

---

2. He would have added the following words immediately after his admission that he had paid $175:

"which is the reasonable value of the services furnished to defendant by the plaintiff, and therefore defendant does not owe plaintiff any further sum for his services alleged herein."

mine if $8,750 is a reasonable sum or, if it is not, what a reasonable sum might be.[3] [citation] It is a classic example of the absurdity of a technical application of the negative pregnant doctrine in that it fashions an honest denial into a sword which when turned upon its artificer brings serious injury upon him.

In this age, as we have stated earlier, pleadings are intended to assure a judgment on the merits of a case rather than to impede such a judgment. Consequently no serious penalty should attach to a denial which contains a negative pregnant where the pleader, in good faith, is seeking to controvert certain allegations. Moore's Federal Practice, 2d Ed., Vol. 2, § 8:24, page 1830. Judgment on the pleadings in this case was a serious penalty imposed on a good faith denial. The trial judge violated the spirit of our modern code pleadings.

Judgment is reversed and a trial ordered.

BERNSTEIN, C. J., and STRUCKMEYER and LOCKWOOD, JJ., concur.

Exercise 3.3

Explain the negative pregnant in *Frank v. Solomon*. What was the defendant's mistake? What does the court suggest he should have done to avoid the mistake? What would you recommend to him? Identify and eliminate the negative pregnants in the following statements:

1. The defendant did not convey the land in fee simple.

2. The defendant did not convey the land on May 1, 1990.

3. The defendant denies that when he vacated the premises on May 1, 1990, there was damage done to the bedroom carpet.

4. The defendant denies that she misrepresented to the plaintiff that the automobile had not been in a collision that damaged its steering mechanism.

D. ADMITTING IN PART AND DENYING IN PART

Federal Rule of Civil Procedure 8(d) and mirroring state rules impose on the defendant a duty in good faith to admit a part of an allegation that is true, rather than denying the whole allegation on the basis that part of it is not true. Practice varies widely in the application of these rules. Rules commonly prevent a defendant from generally denying the entire complaint rather than responding to each allegation separately unless the defendant truly intends to deny every single allegation including the jurisdictional statement. Aside from the general denial, however, there remains the question of how meticulous the defendant should be in ferreting out true parts of an allegation to

3. We note that in the case before us the trial court awarded the exact amount prayed for in the complaint rather than some lesser amount as is called for by proper application of the doctrine. See Wingfoot, supra.

admit. Certainly some lawyers routinely deny nearly everything and do not suffer for it, at least not in some courts.

Nonetheless, the duty remains to deny only in part an allegation that is partly true. That leaves the option of whether to deny specifically and admit the remainder or admit specifically and deny the remainder. How you exercise that option should be guided by the principle that everything not expressly denied is admitted. Therefore, it is wise to admit specifically and deny the remainder generally, not the other way around. Inexperienced drafters tend to err in the direction of admitting too much rather than denying too much. Consider the following allegation and alternative responses:

Allegation

17. Plaintiff entered the contract with Defendant in reliance on Defendant's false and misleading information, representations, and advertisements.

Response 1

17. Defendant denies paragraph 17.

Some lawyers would in good conscience deny the entire paragraph on the theory that it makes only one allegation. If Plaintiff did not enter the contract in reliance on the things listed, then the whole paragraph is false.

Response 2

17. Defendant admits Plaintiff entered the contract with Defendant and denies the remainder of paragraph 17.

This response illustrates the recommended practice of admitting specifically and denying generally.

Response 3

17. Defendant denies paragraph 17, except admitting that Plaintiff entered the contract with Defendant.

This response conveys the same information as Response 2 but makes the denial more emphatic by putting it first.

Response 4

17. Defendant denies that Plaintiff entered the contract in reliance on Defendant's false and misleading information, representations and advertisements, but admits the remainder of paragraph 17.

This is a dangerous response. In attempting to be specific about what is denied, it runs the risk of leaving out some detail that would then be admitted. For example, what if somehow the defendant neglected to include the word "misleading"? Over-particularity is nearly always dangerous in this way. Moreover, the attempt here to be meticulous may inadvertently produce an implicit admission that the defendant did provide false and misleading information, representations, and advertisements. Then all the defendant has left is the issue of whether the plaintiff acted in reliance on them.

One difficulty inherent in the process of admitting in part and denying in part is that the defendant has to construct a response that may involve using some language not in the plaintiff's allegation. The danger is that the defendant's language will go beyond the scope of the plaintiff's allegation.

Here is an allegation from a complaint on behalf of someone who was injured when an exercise treadmill in a health club stopped suddenly without warning, and a response to the paragraph.

Allegation

5. There was no notice on the treadmill Plaintiff used to warn her that it would stop automatically.

Response

5. With respect to paragraph 5, Defendant denies failing to post written notice on the treadmill Plaintiff used. Defendant is without knowledge of whether that notice was still posted on the machine when Plaintiff used it. Defendant admits that such notice was absent at the time of Plaintiff's accident.

This response makes several strategic errors. First, the plaintiff's allegation did not say a word about failing to post notice.

The second and third sentences in the defendant's response seem partly to contradict each other, unless there is some reason to convey that the notice was on the machine when the plaintiff started to use it but fell off (or was removed by somebody?) before the machine stopped. Also, the defendant is complicating the whole matter by distinguishing between time of "use" and time of "accident." The plaintiff's allegation was not about periods of time.

Finally, even though it may be in the defendant's best interest to characterize what happened as an "accident," doing so in an answer is not responsive to an allegation not using that term.

To its credit, however, this response helps the reader by dividing the responses into three separate sentences. The defendant is by no means bound to organize a response paragraph in the same order or in the same number of sentences as the paragraph to which it responds.

Exercise 3.4

In the case of the treadmill that stopped suddenly with no warning, the complaint contained the following:

Paragraph 7

Defendant negligently maintained the treadmill by:

- a.   setting it to stop automatically;
- b.   failing to provide or maintain written notice that it would stop automatically; and
- c.   failing to provide or maintain an audible signal on the machine to warn Plaintiff that it would stop automatically.

———

Evaluate the following responses to paragraph 7. Consider first the order of the various responses. Also consider the degree to which the paragraph admits and denies specifically or generally. Finally, does it make any inadvertent implicit admissions?

Responses to Paragraph 7

Defendant admits setting the treadmill to stop automatically. Defendant is without knowledge of whether there was written notice posted on the treadmill that it would stop automatically. Defendant denies failing to provide a warning buzzer.

———

E. SPECIAL PROBLEMS

1. Responding to the Jurisdictional Statement

Inexperienced drafters often express concern about how to respond to the jurisdictional statement in a complaint. They fear that any admission will amount to an admission of liability, or even liability for a given amount of damages. In some courts, it is customary to admit the jurisdictional statement, and the defendant is not treated as having admitted liability. Careful drafters do, however, sometimes explicitly state that they "admit paragraph 1 for jurisdictional purposes only," or admit that plaintiff has based a claim on the named statute but deny all allegations in the paragraph insofar as they relate to the defendant.

2. Responding to Allegations about a Different Defendant

If there are several named defendants in an action, and if one of them is answering separately, that answer can be somewhat difficult to frame. The difficulty is compounded if the complaint persists in making allegations about more than one defendant together in the same paragraph. Nonetheless, a careful answer will admit or deny each paragraph that refers to multiple defendants "as to this defendant" or "as to Defendant Jones" and consistently add that this defendant is without knowledge as to the other defendants, if that is in fact the case.

One writer suggests a catch-all response for allegations about different defendants:

Counts (or paragraphs) ___ to ___ do not apply to this defendant but insofar as any allegation therein does refer to or may apply to this defendant, denies each and every such allegation.[2]

3. Responding to Legal Conclusions

Plaintiffs are not supposed to allege legal conclusions in complaints, but they sometimes do. Then what is the defendant to do? If the allegation accurately states the law *and does nothing else,* there is probably no harm in admitting it.

For example, consider the following paragraph:

> 8. Section 489.113(2) states: "No person who is not certified or registered shall engage in the business of contracting in this state."

Assuming that the statute by that number does in fact say exactly that, there is probably no harm in the defendant's admitting the paragraph without more. In so doing, the defendant is essentially responding by saying: "So what?"

But the defendant should have a sharp eye out for any defect. At the very least, the defendant should look up the statute to make sure that the number and quotation are accurate. If they are not, there is ground for denial. Maybe the statute says what the plaintiff alleges but more besides. The defendant should beware of slipping onto a slope that will end in an implicit admission.

If there is any doubt, it may be wise to call the plaintiff's bluff by admitting that the statute exists and says what the paragraph says it does but adding that defendant denies the paragraph insofar as it makes any allegation regarding the defendant.

IV. AFFIRMATIVE DEFENSES

A. THE WIDE RANGE OF POSSIBLE DEFENSES

When the defendant has finished responding to every paragraph in the complaint, it is then appropriate to put into the answer additional paragraphs that set forth affirmative defenses. In some respects it makes sense to think of affirmative defenses as more like complaints than like defenses. They were formerly known as "confession and avoidance." In other words, they present new information to excuse the defendant from liability even if all of the plaintiff's allegations are taken as true.

The possibilities for affirmative defenses are almost as unlimited as the possibilities for defense motions. Federal Rule of Civil Procedure 8(c) and state rules mirroring it list 19 defenses that must be raised

2. Id. Copyright © 1977. Reprinted from *Successful Civil Litigation* by George Vetter by permission of the publisher, Prentice Hall, a division of Simon & Schuster, Englewood Cliffs, N.J.

affirmatively: accord and satisfaction, arbitration and award, assumption of the risk, contributory negligence, discharge in bankruptcy, duress, estoppel, failure of consideration, fraud, illegality, injury by fellow servant, laches, license, payment, release, res judicata, statute of frauds, statute of limitations, and waiver. It is not appropriate to raise again affirmative defenses that have already been raised by motion.

Since defenses are matters of substantive law, they may arise out of statutes or regulations pursuant to statutes. They may also arise out of common law. In other words, every new case on a subject carries with it the potential for a new affirmative defense.

B. HOW MUCH DETAIL TO PROVIDE

The source of an affirmative defense should be taken into consideration when deciding how much detail to provide about it in the answer. Technically, each defense is comparable to a cause of action. It has elements. Unless you are in a notice pleading jurisdiction, for the defense to succeed the ultimate facts must be pleaded that make out each element. Viewing the defense this way suggests the need to set it out in a number of paragraphs comparable to those in a complaint. Certainly if the defense is the product of a recent case and thus not well known, its presentation warrants that kind of care.

However, some well established affirmative defenses are commonly presented much more briefly, using only one paragraph for each. Some examples follow:

• Before commencement of this action, Defendant discharged each item of Plaintiff's claim by payment.

• Each cause of action, claim, and item of damages did not accrue within the time prescribed by law for them before this action was brought.

• The sole consideration for the execution and delivery of the promissory note described in paragraph 3 of the complaint was Plaintiff's promise to loan Defendant $500; Plaintiff failed to loan that sum to Defendant.

If officially authorized forms provide bare recitals like these for affirmative defenses, you can rely on them as legally sufficient and may be wise to resist the temptation to say more.

C. STRUCTURE OF AFFIRMATIVE DEFENSES

Affirmative defenses are to be clearly separated both from responses to the individual paragraphs in the complaint and from each other. Common rules refer to separation of defenses in the same way as separation of claims into counts. Here too the purpose of separation is to facilitate clear presentation.

Each affirmative defense is separately headed, "First Affirmative Defense," "Second Affirmative Defense," etc., and some drafters help the reader out even more by providing headings that identify the nature of the defense: "Contributory Negligence," "Accord and Satisfaction," etc. In some courts, it is common to head the responses to the plaintiff's allegations "First Defense," in which case the first affirmative defense is headed "Second Defense."

Regardless of how many affirmative defenses an answer presents or how many paragraphs are used to present each one, the entire answer, including the affirmative defenses and any counterclaims and crossclaims, is presented in one numerical sequence of paragraphs start to finish.

D. SHORT AND PLAIN TERMS

The rules also commonly require "short and plain" terms for defenses.[3] If an answer in a case on appeal is verbose and organized so as to obscure the difference between denials and affirmative defenses, the court's impatience is likely to show in the opinion. Here is an example:

> Some time after the complaint was filed, defendants made their first appearance in court by filing a pleading listing five numbered defenses. Both in form and substance, this pleading resembled a collection of affirmative defenses. It set up matter principally in the nature of avoidance. It could have been construed as an answer, in that each defense referred to a paragraph of the complaint and some of the averments therein were denied, but it was virtually impossible to determine from the whole pleading what position the defendants took with regard to the allegations of the complaint. Plaintiff promptly filed a motion to strike on several grounds * * *. Before this motion was heard, defendants filed an amended pleading containing six defenses, but subject to the same infirmities possessed by their original pleading. A second motion to strike was filed, and * * * the court ordered the entire pleading stricken, with leave to amend within ten days.
>
> There can be no doubt as to the propriety of this ruling. This was a simple lawsuit on a written contract and presented no extraordinary problems of defensive pleading. The defendants had twice had their attention called to the requirements * * *, but their amended pleading was objectionable * * * and subject to being stricken * * *.
>
> * * * The availability of affirmative factual material to be pleaded does not relax the requirement * * * that the pleader shall state his defenses in "short and simple terms" * * *. * * * [I]t is the best practice to confine the body of an answer to simple, categorical admissions or denials, in whole or in part, of the allegations of the complaint paragraph by paragraph * * * and to reserve affirmative defenses or matter in avoidance for separate statement, in numbered paragraphs, following the body of the answer. In this way, the issues become clear, the affirmative defenses can readily be examined for sufficiency, and time is conserved both by counsel and the court.

3. For further suggestions about drafting answers in plain language, see I. Alterman, Answers, ch. 5, Plain and Accurate Style in Court Papers 61 (1987).

In the case at bar, the first two defensive pleadings filed were prolix, did not meet the substance of the complaint, and thoroughly obscured the issues, if any there were.[4]

V. CHECKLIST FOR DRAFTING ANSWERS

Caption

1. Is the name of the court phrased accurately and concisely?

2. Is the case number included?

3. Are the parties' names accurate? Are they properly labeled as plaintiff and defendant?

4. If there are multiple parties on a side, is only the first one given, with *"et al."* in place of the others?

5. Is the answer named, including identification of who is answering if fewer than all of multiple defendants?

6. If this paper includes counterclaims or cross-claims, does the name of the paper say so?

Introductory Clause

7. Is this paragraph appropriately unnumbered?

8. Are appropriate short forms established here if at all for later reference to the parties?

9. Does this clause appropriately repeat the information from the caption announcing who is answering?

Responses to Allegations in the Complaint

10. Are the responses headed "First Defense" if you are going to add affirmative defenses and if separate headings are customary in the court in that instance?

11. Does the answer respond to every single allegation in every single paragraph in the complaint?

12. Does each response expressly admit, deny, or indicate that the defendant is without knowledge of each allegation?

13. Does each response admit whatever part of each allegation that the defendant cannot in good faith deny?

14. Do you adopt a structure for your responses that makes the answer easy to follow? Do you use that structure consistently throughout?

4. Pearson v. Sindelar, 75 So.2d 295, 296–97 (Fla.1954).

15.   Do you admit specifically and generally deny the remainder of a paragraph containing multiple allegations? Or else do you deny specifically on purpose?

16.   Do you avoid negative pregnants by avoiding denials that are over-particular?

17.   When you need to track some language from an allegation in order to show what part of it you are admitting or denying, are you careful to track accurately so as to avoid implicit admissions by failure to respond to an allegation as stated?

18.   Do you avoid presenting your own version of the facts in the plaintiff's paragraphs as a means of denying the plaintiff's version?

19.   If there are multiple defendants and you are answering for only one of them, is that clear throughout the responses, especially to allegations about other defendants only?

20.   Do you respond to legal conclusions carefully enough to avoid being trapped into an unintended admission?

21.   In a multi-count complaint, do you respond appropriately to any reallegation paragraph that begins a count after the first one?

Affirmative Defenses

22.   Is the first affirmative defense headed "Second Defense" if the responses were headed "First Defense"? Is it headed "Affirmative Defense" otherwise, assuming you have only one affirmative defense? Is it headed "First Affirmative Defense" only if you have more than one?

23.   Is the first paragraph of the first affirmative defense numbered in sequence after the last response paragraph, rather than numbered "1"?

24.   Is each affirmative defense separated into multiple paragraphs if and only if that would facilitate easy reading?

25.   Are all of the elements of each affirmative defense covered?

26.   If there is an official form in your jurisdiction for your affirmative defense, do you use it, adapting it appropriately to your facts?

27.   Do you present affirmative defenses in short and plain terms, using somewhat more detail only if a defense is novel or authorized by new case or statutory law rather than well established and grounded in the civil rules?

Counterclaims and Cross–Claims

28.   Are any counterclaims and cross-claims separately headed as such?

29.   Does each begin with a new introductory clause?

30. Does the introductory clause of any counterclaim re-identify the defendant as counterclaimant?

31. Do counterclaims and cross-claims continue the numbering sequence following from the last numbered paragraph in the answer rather than beginning again with paragraph 1?

32. Is the body presented in separately numbered paragraphs and also separated into counts if that separation would facilitate easy reading?

33. Does any counterclaim or cross-claim conclude with an unnumbered demand clause just as in a complaint?

Signature

34. Is the attorney's address given with zip code?

35. Is the attorney's phone number given with area code?

36. Is the attorney's Bar registration number given if the jurisdiction requires it?

37. Is the firm's name given if it is appropriate?

38. Is it clear what party or parties the attorney represents?

Certificate of Service

39. Is a certificate of service included?

40. Does it certify service to co-defendants as well as the plaintiff or plaintiffs?

41. Does it show service on unrepresented parties themselves and their addresses where served, and on represented parties' attorneys and their addresses where served?

42. For each person served, does it show whether service was by U.S. mail, hand delivery, or other method?

43. Does it show the date of each service covered?

44. Is it signed by the person making service? In other words, does it either precede the signature line on the pleading or else have a second signature line following it?

VI.　DRAFTING ASSIGNMENTS

Drafting Assignment 3.A—Answer

You represent Chris Dewey in the action filed against him by Ferris Franklin. For this assignment work from the complaint you drafted on Franklin's behalf for Drafting Assignment 1.C, the complaint drafted by another student in your class, or a complaint provided for this assignment by your instructor.

Both Franklin's former fiance, Christina Miliori, and her neighbor, Joe John Jones, say that Franklin was drunk and that he fell because he was running down the stairs in the dark to start a fight. Miliori says that on the way up to her apartment, he had nearly slipped and fallen on the leaves, and at that time he had been swearing about maintenance and specifically about the lack of proper lighting.

Draft an answer on behalf of Dewey, including any appropriate affirmative defenses.

———

Drafting Assignment 3.B—Answer

You represent Henry Donofrey, one of the co-defendants in the action filed by Best Buy Cars, Inc., the subject of the sample pleadings in Section II of this chapter. Donofrey tells you that he has not seen the Matsuda automobile since his wife left him and drove away in it. You find on file in the court clerk's office a final judgment in dissolution of the Donofreys' marriage, awarding her title to and possession of the automobile. Draft an answer on Henry Donofrey's behalf.

Part Two

DRAFTING IN THE PRACTICE OF PREVENTIVE LAW: INTRODUCTION TO THE DOCUMENTS

I. CONTRACTS, LEGISLATION, AND WILLS AS PLANNING DOCUMENTS

Part Two addresses the drafting principles that apply generally to the documents that lawyers draft as planners in the practice of preventive law. These documents, if well drafted, should prevent litigation rather than fostering it. Although the terminology differs somewhat from one document to another, planning documents tend to have the same essential parts. Contracts, public and private legislation, and wills are covered in Chapters 4, 5, and 6 respectively.

II. THE PARTS OF PLANNING DOCUMENTS

A. TITLE

Every legal document should have a title. A separate title page is not conventional except for a document long enough to warrant a table of contents as well. Title pages and tables of contents are common in contracts that are printed and bound.

B. INTRODUCTION

Just as pleadings and motions have introductory clauses to provide a syntactical foundation for the body of the document, all legal documents have a comparable introduction, which is sometimes a single clause and sometimes several sentences. It declares what is the nature of the document, who is "speaking" through the document, and generally whom the document binds. It is variously called a "commencement," "preamble," or "exordium." Its functions, though essential, are chiefly formal and often in part repetitive of the document's title. Information given in the title needs to be repeated in the introduction since the title is not technically part of the text of the document. The introduction is not an appropriate place to put any of the operational substance of the document.

C. RECITALS

Recitals are statements of information that forms the foundation or background for the document. Recitals are about what has been true before the document's existence, not about what people agree to do or are ordered or directed to do after it comes into existence. Formerly it was conventional to introduce recitals with "WHEREAS," although that convention has generally been replaced by headings such as "Background" or "Findings," depending on the context.

D. DEFINITIONS

A definitions section is appropriate only to define words or phrases that appear in more than one other section of the document. If a word or phrase needing definition is used in only one section, it should be defined there. Definitions are justified only for the following purposes: (1) to define technical words or terms of art that a user of the document is likely not to know; and (2) to stipulate for the purposes of the document definitions that differ from the usual definitions of words in common use. It is conventional to head the section "Definitions" and then to list the defined words in alphabetical order, with each word followed by its definition. A definitions section belongs ahead of the body of the document rather than at the end of it.

Sometimes the process of stipulating definitions includes creating a term to label a concept or collection of items. In a definitions section, created terms appear in the same list alphabetized along with other words being defined.

E. BODY OF THE DOCUMENT

The body of the document contains the operative substance that the document exists to express. Everything else in the document is there to activate this part. It is in the body that the different types of planning documents differ the most from each other. What they have in common are characteristics of form. Regardless of their subjects, the substantive provisions should be divided into sections, each with an informative heading and each heading numbered or lettered. Further division into headed and lettered or numbered subsections may be helpful as well, at least for especially long and complex documents.

F. HOUSEKEEPING PROVISIONS

Usually gathered at the end of planning documents are what are commonly known as the "housekeeping" provisions. They attend to the business of managing the document itself, as distinct from the matters that are its subject. The term "housekeeping" is useful drafting jargon by which to refer to these provisions, but the term "housekeeping" is too informal to use as a heading in a legal document. Some drafters collect these provisions in a section headed "Miscellaneous," but that is not informative. For easy reference, it is better to head each housekeeping provision separately with its own subject.

G. SIGNATURES AND DATES

Legal documents are governed by a variety of formalities regarding the signatures they bear and the dates of those signatures. These formalities often rise to the level of requirements for validity and enforceability.

Chapter 4

CONTRACTS

I. RELATIONAL CONTRACTS DISTINGUISHED FROM TRANSACTIONS

Relational contracts are designed to govern the relations between the parties over an extended period of time. Relational contracts are the most challenging to draft because they require a great deal of thinking ahead, speculating, and trouble-shooting. The "relational theory of contract" was developed by Professor Ian Macneil.[1] Here is Professor Peter Linzer's summary of it:

> Macneil defined contract as "the projection of exchange into the future," and argued that people project exchange by both promissory and non-promissory means. He distinguished "discrete" or "transactional" exchanges (essentially one-shot deals between relative strangers; his example is a tourist paying cash for gasoline on the Jersey Turnpike) from "relational" or "intertwined" dealings (long-term, and involving people who get to know one another and whose futures are bound together by their dealings; examples include employment, long-term supply contracts and marriage). In long term relational dealings

---

1. See The Many Futures of Contracts, 47 S.Cal.L.Rev. 691 (1974); Restatement (Second) of Contracts and Presentiation, 60 Va.L.Rev. 589 (1974).

the parties cannot possibly anticipate every problem; they expect to have to work things out as the months or years go by.

However, "classical" contract law requires that all the terms be expressed (and consented to) at the moment of contracting. To describe this requirement, Macneil resurrected an old, largely forgotten theological term, "presentation." (Innumerable proofreaders have well-meaningly "corrected" this to "presentation.") According to Macneil, presentation may be possible to accomplish and may work fairly well in discrete, one-shot deals, but it clashes with the real needs of the parties in long-term relationships.[2]

The characteristics of an "ideal union contract" as envisioned by LeRoy Marceau suggest the challenges of drafting any relational contract.

    * * * The ideal union contract, while difficult to create, is not difficult to envision. It would have the following characteristics:

    1. When a reader wants to learn what the rule is, on any subject the contract covers, an index or table of contents will quickly refer him to the page the rule is on.

    2. When he turns to the page, he will find a prominent caption showing the place on the page where the rule appears.

    3. Everything that the contract has to say about the subject will be said (or at least referred to) at that place. The reader may be referred to other sections for details, but the rule set forth will be reasonably complete.

    4. The language setting forth the rule will be subject to only one possible interpretation.

    5. It will be so clear-cut that one can easily tell whether it applies to the existing facts. "6. a.m.," for example, is preferable to "dawn."

    6. The rule set forth will accurately state what the parties have agreed on.

    7. The rule will be stated simply enough to be understood by the people who can be expected to use the contract.

    8. The rule will be short enough that those people can grasp it readily, and possibly remember it.

    9. The rule will be adaptable to changing conditions. That is, despite the normal changes that can be expected to occur, the rule will continue to meet the desires of the parties; and will require amendment only when a particularly far-reaching change occurs.

    10. When the rule must be amended, it will be possible to amend it without changing many other parts of the contract.

Notice that the foregoing are characteristics of a *complete* contract rather than of any single isolated provision. Good drafting implies a complete job. There is no way to make one section of a contract adequate if the other sections are to remain nebulous. For a contract is an integrated whole; it is not a mere collection of unrelated provisions. Since each provision will be interpreted in the light of the whole, one cannot hope to draft the provision unless there is a foundation and framework of the contract for him to fit it into. Many a provision which might be a masterpiece if standing alone has become a monstrosity when injected into a contract with which it does not mesh. It follows that one who starts with a nebulous contract cannot hope to transform it into an orderly contract by a series of amendments. To create a masterpiece one must start with a fresh canvas.[3]

II. ANNOTATED SAMPLE CONTRACT

A sample contract follows. It is an employment contract, which is an example of a relational contract.

3. Drafting a Union Contract xxvii-xxviii (1965). Copyright © 1965 by LeRoy Marceau; published by Little, Brown & Co. Reprinted by permission of the author. For a textbook that uses drafting to exemplify the principles of contract law, see S. Burnham, Drafting Contracts (1987); for a textbook that uses as a teaching vehicle the conversion of three old-fashioned documents into plain language, see C. Felsenfeld and A. Siegel, Writing Contracts in Plain English (1981).

1   # EMPLOYMENT CONTRACT

2   Dynatron, Inc., a California Corporation ("Employer"), 300 Celia
3 Avenue, San Francisco, California 94114, and Joyce Shipley ("Em-
4 ployee"), 74 Mountain Lane, Denver, Colorado 80202, enter this
5 contract for the employment of Employee by Employer as an Ac-
6 count Executive. The parties mutually agree as follows:

7   ## *1. Definitions*

Line 1

- The title of the contract expresses its nature. Some titles go even further and include the names of the parties, for example, "Employment Contract Between Dynatron, Inc. and Joyce Shipley" or "Contract for Employment of Joyce Shipley by Dynatron, Inc."

- The words "contract" and "agreement" are usually regarded as synonymous, so that it does not matter particularly whether you choose to call a document one or the other. For polished drafting, it is good to use one or the other consistently. Also, it is possible to make a distinction between the words, calling the document the "contract" and using "agreement" to refer to the parties' meeting of the minds. That distinction prevails in these annotations.

Lines 2–6

- This paragraph, providing the introductory material, is sometimes called the "commencement" or "exordium." "Introductory clause" is not an accurate description of this paragraph since it consists of more than one sentence.

- This paragraph identifies the parties, establishes short forms for reference to them throughout the contract, recites the nature of the contract, and expresses the mutual agreement of the parties to everything that follows in the rest of the contract. The paragraph does not contain any of the terms of the agreement.

- This is the only paragraph in the entire contract that is neither headed nor numbered.

Line 7

- This is the first section heading. The drafter of this contract chose Arabic numerals and bold italics for section headings. It does not matter particularly what scheme you choose as long as you use it consistently throughout the contract. Some drafters avoid Roman numerals, especially if the document has many sections, because Roman numerals are not as easy to read as Arabic numerals.

- The section headings in this contract are all nouns or noun phrases. For polished drafting, it is wise to adopt a plan using headings that are at least generally parallel in syntax. Nouns and noun phrases are the most common. Headings may also be clauses such as:

    1. What Definitions Apply

    2. What Understandings Form the Basis

    3. What The Employer's Obligations Are

Some consumer contracts use questions for headings:

    6. What are Tenant's Duties Regarding Rent?

    7. What are Landlord's Maintenance Duties?

It may be easier to be specific in longer headings. Single nouns as headings tend to be more abstract. However, the more sophisticated the parties about the subject matter of the contract, the more virtue there is in short headings, which may be terms of art within the subject area.

8   "Colorado territory" includes Utah and Wyoming.

9   "Confidential information" means manufacturing, design, mar-
10 keting, financial, operating, servicing and other business informa-
11 tion.

12   "Employment year" means a period of 12 successive calendar
13 months, beginning on the date of this contract or any annual
14 anniversary date.

15 **2. *Background***

• It is common for recitals to precede definitions in a contract. In this one, however, two of the defined terms, "Colorado territory" and "confidential information," are used in the recitals in Section 2. If the definitions stipulated are to apply there, the definitions need to precede Section 2.

Lines 8, 9, 12   • The defined words here are put in quotation marks. That is the most common way to set them apart. You can use some other method, however, such as italics, underlining, or all-capital letters.

Lines 8–14   • The first definition in this collection is a partial one, enlarging the ordinary meaning of "Colorado." Thus the defined term *includes* the two added states. The other two definitions stipulate total meanings. Thus the defined terms *mean* what the drafter stipulates. See Chapter 10 for more on naming and defining.

• The only words defined in this opening collection are used in more than one other section of the contract. Any words needing definition that are used in only one section of the contract are defined there.

• This collection of definitions has no introductory clause. Some drafters prefer to use an introductory clause, such as: "In this contract, the following definitions apply." If you use an introductory clause, put it in the present tense; do not say that the defined words "shall mean" something or other, as though you were ordering them to do it, or as though you were directing the definitions to go into effect at some later time.

Lines 15–33   • Section 2 recites background facts that serve as the basis for the contract. Formerly they would have been set out in a series of clauses beginning "WHEREAS." It is not necessary generally to recite such obvious background facts as the information that the employer has a position to offer and the employee wants and needs a job. As a hangover from old "WHEREAS" days, drafters tend to include more background information than serves their clients.

• Recitals are part of the parties' agreement. The parties are agreeing that what is expressed here is true *and* that it is the basis for the contract. In this contract, drafted, by the employer's attorney, this section is designed to accomplish three things:

(a) encourage the potential employee not to base her application for the position on misrepresentations of her expertise;

(b) protect the employer against hiring someone whose employment would violate a covenant not to compete with a former employer; and

(c) pave the way for the covenant not to compete that appears later in this contract.

• Recitals are ordinarily expressed in a present tense sequence, as are definitions and other statements of policy, such as most housekeeping provisions.

16   Employer operates as a wholesale distributor of computer hard-
17 ware and software in California, Arizona, New Mexico, and Nevada.
18 Employer desires to expand its field of operation to include the
19 Colorado territory.

20   Employee has been employed as an account executive in a
21 similar business, Computer Services, Inc., serving the New England
22 states exclusively since 1980. Computer Services, Inc. has no plans
23 to expand its field of operation to the Colorado territory in the
24 foreseeable future. Employee has moved to Denver, Colorado, desir-
25 ing to engage in business there in her field of expertise as an
26 account executive in the sale of computer hardware and software.
27 The employment of Employee by Employer for this purpose will not
28 cause Employee to violate any covenant by which she is bound not
29 to compete with Computer Services, Inc., or any other former
30 employer. Employee understands that her employment by Employ-
31 er will result in her learning confidential information, which this
32 contract binds her not to reveal or otherwise to use in violation of
33 the covenant not to compete that is a part of this contract.

34 ## 3. *Duration of Employment*

35   Employee will begin her employment on _____, 19__. It will
36 expire at the close of the business day on the last business day of the
37 third employment year unless this contract has been terminated
38 earlier under paragraph 9 of this contract or unless Employer and
39 Employee agree earlier on terms of renewal.

• Section 2 illustrates having more than one paragraph in a section without a subheading for each. The paragraph division here breaks up what might otherwise seem an over-long paragraph. The first paragraph focuses on the employer and the second on the employee. Subheadings emphasizing that division would unnecessarily call attention to how much more the employee is bound by recitals than is the employer.

Line 35   • This line leaves a blank for the date employment is to begin, only because that is a matter for last-minute negotiation, as are the quotas in Section 4.b. In fact, leaving a blank rather than making a term part of the printed text is an invitation to negotiation. At the very least, the blank draws attention to the term that gets filled in. If you do not want a term to be at issue, it is better strategy to print the term the way you want it. If it still gets changed by last-minute negotiation, the contract can be amended before signing, either on an attached sheet or even by handwriting in the margin initialed by both parties.

• This line begins the sections where the parties express their promises to each other about what they will do and not do. They use the ordinary future tense, saying that each "will" do things. They do not use "shall," which carries the connotation of orders and a tone more appropriate to legislation than agreement.

Lines 35–39   • This section establishes a difference in meaning between the contract expiring and terminating. Since those concepts do come up elsewhere in the contract, "expire" and "terminate" might have been added to the list of defined words in Section 1.

40 *4. Scope of Employment*

41   **a. Employee's Duties**

42   Employee will serve as Employer's Account Executive for the
43 Colorado territory. In that capacity she will act as Employer's sales
44 representative responsible for generating product sales to retail
45 stores and distributors in that territory, carrying out those duties
46 that are customary for account executives in the computer sales
47 industry. Employee will devote at least 40 hours each calendar
48 week to her employment duties, excluding time on leave and corpo-
49 rate holidays. She will report regularly to her immediate supervi-
50 sor, the Western Mountain District Manager.

51   **b. Exclusive Right to Territory**

52   Employee will have an exclusive right to sell in the Colorado
53 territory during her first employment year. If her net sales during
54 her first employment year exceed _____, she will retain her
55 exclusive right during her second employment year. If her net sales
56 during her second employment year exceed _____, she will retain
57 her exclusive right during her third employment year.

Lines 41, 51   • These lines are the first two subheadings in the contract. If a section has in it enough material that subheadings would aid quick finding within the section, they are a useful device for readability. It is acceptable to have a subsection with only one sentence in it. It is also entirely acceptable to have more than one paragraph in a section without having subheadings for each of them. For example, see Section 2.

    • Subheadings within one section should be parallel with each other in structure. For polished drafting, subheadings throughout the entire document should be parallel with each other; however, clarity is more important that slavish attention to form on such matters.

    • It is important, however, that the subheadings be presented in a format different from that of the headings. Here subheadings are in bold type and indented, but any scheme is acceptable as long as it consistently reflects the difference between headings and subheadings. A reader should be able to turn a page, see only one heading somewhere on that page, and know at a glance what level of division of the material it represents. Also, using headings and subheadings is a greater aid to readability to the extent that the format involves liberal use of white space on a page.

Line 46–47   • These lines illustrate the value of general language to the drafter who wants to cast a wide net. An inexperienced drafter might try to think of every duty that an account executive might have and list them all. The employee could eventually use that list as justification for not performing some particular duty that the drafter happened to leave out. Also, the employer would like enough flexibility to be able to expand the employee's duties without having to modify the contract.

Line 50   • That same principle of flexibility, especially valuable in long-term relational contracts, is the reason for listing the title of the immediate supervisor but not the person's name. Some drafters would go further and refer to regular reporting to the supervisor without even mentioning the manager's title. After all, a business reorganization could result in a new scheme of position titles.

58 *5.* *Compensation*

59   **a. Salary**

60   Employer will pay Employee an annual salary of $40,000 in
61 equal bi-weekly installments.

62   **b. Commission**

63   Employer will pay Employee a commission based on net sales,
64 which are those for which Employer has received full payment from
65 the customer. Employee's commission will be calculated as follows:

66   (1) One percent for the first employment year.

67   (2) Two percent for the second employment year.

68   (3) Four percent for the third employment year.

69 Commissions will be paid on the first business day of every calendar
70 month based on an accounting computed on the first business day of

---

Lines 58–93   • Sections 5, 6, and 7 illustrate how organization of a contract may sacrifice some of the niceties of logic in the interest of easy use as a reference document. The idea is that a contract is drafted to accommodate the reader who wants to look something up in it rather than one who would read the whole document at once as a piece. Logically, one might argue, the employer's payment of the employee's expenses and benefits are forms of compensation just as salary and commission are. Therefore, Sections 6 and 7 ought to be subsections of Section 5. In a reference document, however, the drafter helps the reader more by using more rather than fewer main headings. The less the reader has to figure out where to look for desired information, the better. This principle applies more forcefully in much longer and more complicated contracts than this one. This shorter, simpler contract is used here to illustrate principles quickly. Also, notice that the drafter here could have used the quick reference principle even more fully by dropping the Section 5 heading and instead having Section 5 on salary and Section 6 on commission.

    • If a section has headed subsections, it needs to have at least two. A whole cannot be divided into one part. When you find yourself inclined to write just one subheading in a section, if the material does not lend itself to division into at least two subsections, the solution may be to rehead the section to focus on whatever aspect of the material your one subheading would have stressed.

    • Technically, there is a logical problem in the subdivision of Section 5. Subsections 5.a and 5.b indicate a division into types of compensation. Subsection 5.c is not about a third type; instead, it relates back to both Subsections 5.a and 5.b. In some settings, this kind of breach of logic receives heavy criticism; in others, it goes unnoticed. Those who justify it do so on the principle that easy reference prevails over logic in reference documents.

Lines 66–68   • The numbering of these lines does not indicate subsections. Instead, the drafter is using tabulated structure within one sentence to emphasize certain material. So that that tabulation is not confused with tabulation for subsections, the drafter uses a different format for the numbers. The same principle provides the rationale for spelling out "one percent," etc., and using the ordinal numbers for the "first" employment year, etc. When one provision involves several conceptually different sets of numbers, it is helpful to establish a different style for each set.

71 the previous calendar month and reflecting net sales for the calen-
72 dar month immediately prior to the accounting.

73   **c. Maximum Compensation**

74   Employee's maximum compensation, consisting of salary and
75 commissions, is limited to $150,000 for the first employment year,
76 $200,000 for the second employment year, and $250,000 for the third
77 employment year.

78 *6. Expenses*

79   "Reasonable expenses" means those incurred in the course of
80 employment which are attributable to meals, hotels, automobile and
81 air transportation, and long distance telephone calls. Employer will
82 reimburse Employee for 80% of reasonable expenses, except that
83 Employer will pay no more than $25 per day as reimbursement for
84 meals. Employer will make reimbursements exclusively based on
85 receipts presented by Employee and monthly itemized expense re-
86 ports.

87 *7. Benefits*

88   Employee will receive the benefits of employment with Employ-
89 er, including annual leave, sick leave, personal leave, corporate
90 holidays, medical insurance, and retirement benefits, all of which
91 are described in Employer's handbook for employees, entitled "Dy-
92 natron and You," which is incorporated by this reference into this
93 contract.

94 *8. Agreement Not to Compete*

95   During Employee's employment by Employer and for 730 days
96 after the expiration of this contract or its earlier termination:

Lines 79–81   • Here is an example of a definition presented as part of the text of the
one section to which it applies. The definition precedes the use of the
defined words.

Lines 81–84   • These lines illustrate the principle of stating a general rule before an
exception to it. Beware, however, of exceptions that turn out to be surprise
endings that significantly alter bodies of terms that precede them. Sometimes you can avoid ambiguity or needless misunderstanding by stating a
limitation first rather than last.

Lines 87–93   • This section illustrates how you can often shorten a contract considerably, and also avoid the danger of contradictions between the contract and
another related document, by incorporating the other document by reference. In this context, unlike litigation documents, it would not be appropriate to label the handbook as an exhibit. It would also probably be somewhat awkward to treat the handbook as physically attached to the contract.

Line 95   • The reference here to 730 days is more precise than most drafters would
use. It is an attempt to avoid the ambiguity of referring to "two years."
The difficulty with the words "year" and "month" is that it is not always
clear whether a year means 12 months starting on January 1 or any 12–
month period; likewise, it is not always clear whether a month means 30

97   (a) Employee will not engage directly or indirectly in any
98   computer sales or service business that competes with Employer
99   in any state where it does business.

100   (b) Employee will use Employer's confidential information
101   only within the scope of her duties as Employee.

102   (c) Employee will not disclose confidential information to
103   third parties not authorized by Employer to receive it.

104 At the expiration or earlier termination of employment, Employee
105 will promptly return to Employer all documents in her possession
106 that contain or relate to confidential information.

107 ### 9. *Termination*

108 ### a. By Employer

109   Employer may terminate this contract before the end of Em-
110 ployee's third employment year for cause after 30 days' written
111 notice to Employee. Cause includes but is not limited to disclosure
112 of confidential information or other violation of this contract, dis-
113 honesty, illegal conduct, neglect of duty, or unavailability for em-
114 ployment by reason of any noncompetition agreement with any
115 previous employer.

116 ### b. By Employee

117   Employee may terminate this contract before the end of Em-
118 ployee's third employment year regardless of cause after 30 days'
119 written notice to Employer's Western Mountain District Manager.

---

days (or 31, or 28, or 29) starting on the first day of a given month or any 30–day period (or 31 day period, etc.).

Lines 97–103   • This is another passage of tabulated material within a sentence. Its three tabulated clauses are structurally parallel. They are lettered because the immediately preceding sequential device is numbering. (Lines 66–68 were numbered because the sequential device immediately preceding them was lettering.) The drafter has adopted the device of parenthesis to distinguish tabulated material within a sentence from the lettering and numbering that signals sections and subsections.

Lines 108, 116   • Note that these subheadings are structurally parallel to each other but not to subheadings elsewhere in the contract. Again, this is a detail that matters greatly to some people and not at all to others.

Lines 109–115   • In this section the definition of "cause" follows its use. Sometimes the nature of the material makes it nearly impossible to define before use. Then the important thing is at least to have no intervening substance.

Lines 110, 118   • These lines illustrate the use of a number of days to avoid ambiguous reference to a "month."

Lines 111–115   • The list of definitions of "cause" may be dangerously specific from the employer's point of view. The phrase "includes but is not limited to" is at least intended to widen the net.

120 *10. Modification*

121   This contract may be modified only by dated written agreement
122 which is signed by Employer's authorized agent and Employee.

123 *11. Governing Law*

124   This contract is governed by California law.

125 DYNATRON, INC.

126 By:

127 _____   _____
128 M.P. Ehlers, General Manager   Joyce Shipley
129 EMPLOYER   EMPLOYEE
130 Date: _____   Date: _____

_____

III. THE INTRODUCTORY PARAGRAPH

A. FORMER AND CONTEMPORARY APPROACHES

The introductory material in a contract conventionally appears in
a paragraph that has no heading and is neither numbered nor lettered.
Formerly, this was often a fragmentary clause, couched in legalese, for
example: "Agreement, made and entered into by and between. . . ."
In contemporary drafting, the introductory material is presented in a
complete sentence, for example: "JANE ROE and JOHN DOE enter
this agreement for. . . ."

B. CONTENT

1. Parties

The introductory paragraph in a contract identifies the parties to
the contract by name, often in all-capital letters. If the parties are all
individuals and there is no question about that, you need not label
them as such. If a party is a corporation or is an individual doing
business as ("d.b.a.") another name, this information should be clear.

_____

Lines 120–124   • Sections 10 and 11 illustrate housekeeping provisions, each with its own
heading, rather than collected under any catch-all heading such as "Miscellaneous."

• Housekeeping provisions, as statements of policy rather than promises
regarding future action, are ordinarily presented in the present tense.

Line 126   • "By:" precedes a signature only when one is signing as representative
for another.

Line 128   • It is always helpful to have the parties' names in type, especially
because many people have illegible handwriting. For the client company, it
is helpful also to include the signing agent's position.

Line 130   • It is important to provide a date line for each signature line. The
parties often do not sign on the same day.

The introductory paragraph is the appropriate place to establish any short form by which you will refer to a party throughout the rest of the contract. A short form may be simply a person's last name, or a key word from a company's name, or even a set of initials. Avoid initials that produce a comical or crude acronym. Remember that your client will not appreciate being referred to as "FAT" or "DUM." Another approach to short forms is to use the parties' contractual roles: ("LANDLORD" and "TENANT"), for example.

It is conventional although not essential to put short forms in quotation marks when they are established: JOHN DOE ("DOE"). The quotation marks are dropped for all subsequent references. It is archaic and uselessly wordy to recite: "JOHN DOE (hereinafter referred to as 'DOE')."

If the introductory paragraph establishes a short form for future reference to a party, the point is to use that short form and nothing else for all future references in the contract to that party. Do not set up a system of short forms and then go on calling parties by their full names.

2. *Nature of the Contract*

The introductory paragraph also re-identifies the nature of the contract, even though the same information appears in the title.

3. *Mutuality of Agreement*

Finally, the introductory paragraph expresses in general language that the parties mutually agree on the terms and conditions expressed specifically later in the contract. The specific promises themselves do not belong here. Also, there is no need for wordy archaic recitations of consideration such as: "In consideration of the mutual covenants herein contained, and other good and valuable consideration, the receipt of which is hereby acknowledged, the parties hereby agree. . . ." If the contract in fact expresses specific promises by each party, it is supported by consideration. If it does not express specific promises, all the general recitations of consideration in the world will not save it.

A common problem in some introductory paragraphs is that they read as if one party makes all the promises and the other will reap all the benefits. One of the values of a well drafted introduction is that once it has expressed the mutual agreement of the parties to all of the following terms, the drafter is spared any need to repeat endlessly throughout the contract that "the seller agrees" to do this and "the buyer agrees" to do that. The point is that the seller and buyer both agree that the seller *will* do certain things and the buyer *will* do others.

Exercise 4.1

Compare the following introductions, focusing on these considerations:

1.   Does each include only the appropriate information?

2.   Does it include all of the appropriate information?

3.   Is it expressed in one or more complete sentences rather than fragments?

4.   Does it quickly help you get your bearings to move into the operative language of the contract?

_____

Introduction 1

This agreement made and entered into this _____ day of _____ 19__, by and between _____ as party of the first part, hereinafter called the "CONTRACTOR" and _____, parties of the second part, hereinafter call the "OWNERS." For and in the consideration of the sum of one dollar (1.00) in hand paid by each of the parties hereto unto the other on or before the ensealing and delivery of these presents receipt whereof is hereby severally acknowledged and in further consideration of the mutual terms, covenants and conditions herein contained, it is agreed:

_____

Introduction 2

_____ Hereinafter known as Tenant, hereby agree(s) to accept joint and several responsibility for payment of the rents herein reserved and faithful performance of the other requirements of this contract. _____, Inc. of _____, _____, its successors, or assigns, hereinafter called Landlord, agree to rent to Tenant the following unit(s), described as _____ and located at _____, City of _____, _____ for a rental term beginning _____ and ending on _____, for the total rent of $_____ payable at $_____ per month without demand or billing on the first day of each month to Landlord at above address or such other address which Landlord may subsequently designate by written notice to Tenant, subject to the conditions and terms below, which are hereby mutually accepted by Tenant and Landlord.

_____

Introduction 3

PARTIES: _____ (Seller) of _____ (Phone) _____ and _____ (Buyer) of _____ (Phone) _____ hereby agree that the Seller shall sell and Buyer shall buy the following real property ("Real Property") and personal property ("Personalty") (collectively "Property") upon the following terms and conditions which IN-

CLUDE the Standards for Real Estate Transactions printed on the reverse or attached ("Standard(s)") and any addendum to this instrument.

Introduction 4

Tenant hereby offers to lease from the Owner the premises situated in the City of _____, County of _____, State of _____, described as _____ and consisting of _____, upon the following TERMS and CONDITIONS:

Exercise 4.2

Introduction 4 above presents a different approach from Introductions 1, 2, and 3. How does it differ? How does this approach affect the way the drafter will need to present the rest of the contract?

Exercise 4.3

Compare the introductory paragraphs in Exercise 4.1 with the one in the sample contract in Section II of this chapter. Then draft an introductory paragraph for a contract for your rental of the place where you presently live. The landlord might be your actual landlord or else one you make up. See if you can draft the entire paragraph in one complete sentence.

IV. RECITALS

You have no doubt seen contracts that get underway with an enormous string of clauses beginning "WHEREAS." Perhaps you have even drafted some of them. That word "WHEREAS" has a way of tempting drafters to add more and more recitals.

The temptation is dangerous. Recitals may seem to be innocuous background statements; however, as expressions of the reasons for the contract, they may be construed as expressions of intent and as premises on which the parties enter the contract.

The more particular the recitals, the more dangerous they are. Particular recitals have been held not only admissible but conclusive evidence of the facts they state.[4] If the parties eventually get into a

---

4. Bruno and Rosenfeld, Wither [sic] Whereas—The Legal Implications of Recitals, July 1988 Mich.B.J. 634, 634–35, citing Detroit Grand Park Corp. v. Turner, 316 Mich. 241, 25 N.W.2d 184 (1946), in which a recital of claims to be "approximately $94,000" precluded proof of interest on the claims.

dispute about the scope of the contract, the recitals may play a major role in resolving the dispute.[5]

Of course, certain recitals may aid your client rather than doing harm. That is the intention of the recitals in the Dynatron sample employment contract in Section II: to keep the potential employee honest and put her on notice about the employer's expectations that served as premises for the contract.

Finally, when you consider putting recitals in a contract, here are some suggestions:

• Before you include a recital, consider its potential as proof of the facts it states.

• Prefer general language if you want the recital not to be binding.

• Prefer specific language if you want the recital to be binding.

• Use a heading for recitals like "Introduction" or "Background" rather than "Premises" or "Reasons for Contract" if you want a set of recitals not to be binding.

• If you truly want to bury recitals, treat them as housekeeping provisions and put them at the end of the contract rather than at its beginning.[6] On the other hand, if your point is to bury them, you might as well leave them out, unless you are trying to mollify the other party by putting them in.

• Do not put any promises in a recital section.

Exercise 4.4

Evaluate the following sets of recitals from construction contracts. How specific or general are they? What facts, if any, might they be held to prove? Do they appear to benefit one party more than another?

Set 1

WHEREAS, Seller is in the business of constructing and selling single family dwelling units; and

WHEREAS, Buyer is desirous of contracting with Seller for the construction and purchase of a single family dwelling unit:

NOW THEREFORE, in consideration of the mutual covenants, conditions, and agreements herein contained, the parties hereby agree as follows:

Set 2

WHEREAS, Owner has or will acquire title to real property located at: _____

----

5. Id. at 634.   6. See generally id. at 634–35.

hereinafter referred to as the Tract; and

WHEREAS, Owner has secured a commitment from _____

hereinafter referred to as the Lender, for a construction and permanent loan to finance the construction for certain improvements on the Tract; and

WHEREAS, the Owner desires to employ the Contractor to construct such improvements on the tract, and the Contractor desires to accept such employment in accordance with the terms, covenants and conditions hereinafter set forth, the parties hereto do covenant and agree:

V. DEFINITIONS

See Chapter 10 for complete coverage of definitions, including attention to whether to provide a definitions section.

VI. THE BODY OF THE CONTRACT

A. PROMISES AND POLICIES

The operative language of a contract expresses the parties' promises (sometimes called "covenants") and the policies they establish for the operation of the contract. To some extent, the difference between promise and policy is a matter of how a provision is phrased rather than the inherent nature of its substantive content. For example, compare the following statements of the same information:

Promise

The tenant will pay rent on or before the first day of each month.

Policy

Rent is due on the first day of each month.

The promise expressly obligates the tenant to do something. The policy does not expressly obligate anybody to do anything. Consider the structural difference between the two sentences. The first is about the tenant. "Tenant" is its subject, and the verb is active. The second sentence is not about any party, and the verb does not express action.

What the policy sentence does is lay a foundation for somebody, the unmentioned landlord, to take action if the tenant does not pay the rent when due. The sentence does not say what action. That may or may not be expressed elsewhere in the contract, depending on whether the landlord wants to use the rental contract as a behavior modification device or not. The landlord may instead want an apparently innocuous contract, knowing that the statutes lurk in the background, providing remedies that do not need to be expressed in the contract to be available.

In short, whether you choose to express terms of a contract as promises or as policies is partly a function of whether you view the contract as a memorandum of polite understandings or a rule book for one of the parties, or even a club. It is not exclusively what you say that matters. It is also how you say it.

Consider this excerpt from a residential lease:

4. LANDLORD'S OBLIGATIONS. Landlord shall:

    a. provide Tenant a unit and appliances in good repair and clean, sanitary, safe and usable condition;

    b. make repairs needed to maintain unit and appliances and premises surrounding unit in usable condition during the rental term;

    c. respect Tenant's right to privacy and lawful, reasonable use of unit without interference; and

    d. not be responsible for the interruption of equipment functioning or of any services or utilities due to circumstances beyond Landlord's reasonable control or for any injury to Tenant's person or other persons on or about the premises.

5. TENANT'S OBLIGATIONS. Tenant shall:

    a. keep unit and appliances in a clean condition;

    b. conform to policies set by Landlord for use and care of general premises with respect to parking, garbage and trash disposal;

    c. not use an improperly wired or unsafe electric appliance or install any unsafe wiring in unit;

    d. attach or hang pictures or other decorative items only to picture moldings or tack strips provided in unit;

    e. keep plumbing clear and free from obstruction;

    f. not make any changes or alterations of structure, equipment or furnishings or unit without written consent obtained in advance from Landlord;

    g. report promptly to Landlord in writing any defects or damages of unit or appliances or any repair needed;

    h. pay for cleaning or repairs necessitated by misuse of unit or appliances;

    i. return unit and appliances to Landlord in clean and sanitary condition and good repair at termination of occupancy; and

    j. ensure that Tenant and Tenant's guests conduct themselves on the premises in a manner that does not unreasonably disturb the neighbors or constitute a breach of the peace.

————

These two sections focus on what the parties will and will not do, or rather on what they "shall" do or not do. Hear the difference in tone. Landlords draft leases; tenants don't. This landlord apparently likes to give orders, so much so that one wonders what the "policies" referred to in Section 5.b of the lease might be. But the landlord has exercised some questionable judgment here. First, setting up two sections in sequence to convey the obligations of each party draws attention to how much longer the tenant's list is than the landlord's. Also, it takes only a glance to discover that one of the four things that the landlord shall do is "not be responsible" for something. In contrast, the negatives in the tenant's list, items 5.c and 5.f, do indeed order the tenant not to do certain things. In any event, there is no question that this lease expresses promises and no question about who promises what.

Now consider the following excerpt from a contract for the sale and purchase of real estate, which expresses more terms as policy statements:

    N. INSPECTION; REPAIR AND MAINTENANCE; Seller represents that, as of ten (10) days prior to closing, the roof and walls do not have any visible evidence of leaks or damage and that the septic tank, pool, all major appliances, heating, cooling, electrical, plumbing systems and machinery are in working condition. Buyer may, at Buyer's expense, have inspection made of said items by an appropriately licensed person dealing in the construction, repair and maintenance thereof and shall report in writing to Seller such items that do not meet the above representations, together with the cost of correcting same, prior to occupancy or not less than ten (10) days prior to closing, whichever occurs first. Unless Buyer reports such deficiencies within said period Buyer shall be deemed to have waived Seller's representations as to deficiencies not reported. In the event repairs or replacements are required, Seller shall pay up to 3% of the purchase price for such repairs or replacements by an appropriately licensed person. However, if the cost for such repairs or replacements exceeds 3% of the purchase price, Buyer or Seller may elect to pay such excess, failing which either party may cancel this Contract. In the event Seller is unable to correct the deficiencies prior to closing, the cost thereof shall be paid into escrow at closing. Seller agrees to provide utilities service for inspections upon reasonable notice. Between the Effective Date and the closing, Seller shall maintain the Property and Personalty including but not limited to the lawn and shrubbery, in the condition herein represented, ordinary wear and tear excepted. Buyer shall be permitted access for inspection of the Property prior to the closing in order to confirm compliance with the foregoing.

————

The quick signals to tell you whether a provision is couched in terms of promise or policy are the subjects and verbs of the sentence. If the subject is one of the parties and the verb an active one in the future tense, the provision probably states a promise. If the subject is a thing or a concept rather than a person and the verb is in the present tense or the passive voice, the provision probably states a policy.

As the excerpt from the real estate contract shows, a section may intertwine policies with promises. The seller's representations are actually recitals. But form contracts for the sale of real estate are usually drafted by representatives of realtors, who in turn represent sellers. Therefore, even though the form gets used by the buyer to make an offer, it is drafted to protect the seller's interests. This inspection section is a case in point. Those seller's representations, which might well serve as the rationale for the buyer being willing to enter the contract, are buried in the small print on the back of the form as "standard" policies for the conduct of the parties between execution of the contract and closing.

Given the choice to draft a provision as promise or as policy, you might want to consider the following:

• The advantage of a promise is that it clearly obligates one of the parties to act or not act. However, it may be disadvantageous to draw attention to that fact.

• The advantage of a policy is that it presents a pattern of behavior for one or more parties as an established way of doing things, as though it is not a matter for negotiation. However, it may be disadvantageous not expressly to obligate anyone to act or not act.

————

Exercise 4.5

Analyze the individual provisions in the Dynatron employment contract in Section II of this chapter. Does it present provisions mainly as promises or policies? Try redrafting a section to recast promises as policies or vice versa. How does the effect of your new version differ from the effect of the old? Would you recommend to the drafter of that contract any significant redrafting to convert promises to policies or vice versa?

————

B. THE DRAFTER AS ARCHITECT

Contracts offer the drafter a greater organizational challenge than most other legal documents. There is great freedom for the drafter to design what goes into the space in a contract between the definitions and recitals at the beginning and the housekeeping provisions at the end. Professor Reed Dickerson has referred to the design of legal documents as "architecture" insofar as the legal architect "must participate in exploring the objectives, sketch the structural framework, fill in the broad surfaces, work out the significant details, and add the aesthetic touches."[7] As architect, you should plan the sections of a contract with attention to three organizational matters: division, classification, and sequence.

C. ORGANIZATIONAL MATTERS

1. *Division*

Division is the process of gathering all the promises and policies into groupings that will serve as sections. Some drafters work best from the abstract or general to the concrete or specific. They may begin by outlining. They decide at the outset how many sections to have and what their headings will be. These are people who set up their file cabinets and manage their computer files by labeling the drawers and creating the directories. Then as each new document comes along, there is a place created to put it. That same process works for them when they begin to draft a document.

Other drafters work best from the concrete or specific to the abstract or general. They begin by putting pieces of paper in piles. Eventually when the piles get top heavy, they buy some file cabinets. On their computers, they create file after file. Only when the hard drive directory becomes so long that they have to scroll and scroll to find a file do they decide it is time to create some sub-directories and move files into them. When these people draft, they do not think about organization at all at first. They start writing provisions. Eventually, they take a look at what they have and begin to move some of it around. After that, divisions begin to emerge, and section headings present themselves. Computers and word processing programs make this work style much more manageable.

a. *Testing Division Schemes*

These descriptions present the extremes, of course. Most of us do not fit completely into either category, although we probably recognize ourselves more fully in one than the other. Also, even the cartographer who makes the road map sometimes makes a wrong turn or decides along the way to try a different route. In any event, whether we organize soon or late, the material needs to be divided. If the division is technically sound, it should meet the following tests:

• The sections (and their headings) should be mutually exclusive.

• Added together, they should equal the whole.

• One consistently applied principle should govern the division throughout.

7. Legislative Drafting 12 (1954).

To illustrate the tests, here is a division that fails all three: dividing a whole called "human beings" into parts called "men," "women," and "American." First, the parts do not exclude each other insofar as Americans include both men and women. Second, the parts do not equal the whole insofar as children as such are not included. Third, the division begins as if governed by sex but then shifts as if governed by nationality.

In some contexts it is important to divide material and label the parts strictly according to these tests. Such strictness does not always work sensibly, however, when dividing a contract into sections. In particular, it often is not fruitful to spend time thinking of some principle of division that can be consistently applied to produce a set of headings for sections. To do so would be to force conceptualization at such an abstract level that it would not help the contract's users. This principle provides the rationale for the division of "compensation" in the Dynatron contract into "salary," "commission," and "maximum compensation," which fails the technical division test. It is important, however, to give thought to how many sections are practical for the contract in question, and also to what sections are long and complicated enough to warrant further division into headed subsections.

b. Headings

It is especially important to give thought to informative headings for the sections and subsections. Courts have been known to refuse to enforce provisions in sections of contracts with headings that do not clearly inform readers of their content. For example, consider this disclaimer of warranty provision from a contract for the sale of an automobile:

> 9. *Factory Warranty:* Any warranty on any new vehicle or used vehicle still subject to a manufacturer's warranty is that made by the manufacturer only. The seller hereby disclaims all warranties, either express or implied, including any implied warranty of merchantability or fitness for a particular purpose.

The heading on this provision was found to be misleading, and thus the provision was ineffective as a seller's attempt to disclaim warranties.[8]

In another case a court refused to enforce a form's imposition of personal liability for hospital charges not covered by insurance because the form was misleadingly headed "Assignment of Insurance Benefits."[9]

Another case involved the section of a medical malpractice insurance policy headed "Procedure of insured in claim or suit." Buried in the section with that heading was a requirement that the insured notify the company "in the event of receiving notice of claim or suit, or any unusual occurrence." Because of the misleading heading, a court

---

8. Blankenship v. Northtown Ford, Inc., 95 Ill.App.3d 303, 306–07, 50 Ill.Dec. 850, 853–54, 420 N.E.2d 167, 170–71 (1981).

9. St. John's Episcopal Hosp. v. McAdoo, 94 Misc.2d 967, 405 N.Y.S.2d 935 (Civ. Ct.1978).

refused to allow the insurance company to disclaim coverage when an insured dentist did not notify the company of a patient's death until after an action had been filed.[10]

Some states have statutes expressly prohibiting misleading headings in insurance contract forms. The Washington state insurance commissioner may disapprove of a form with a misleading heading.[11] In Arkansas [12] and Oklahoma,[13] the commissioner is required to disapprove of such a form.

One way to avoid uninformative headings is to avoid abstract nouns altogether and have headings that are phrases about actions or decisions instead. For example, an insurance policy might give up headings like "Coverage" and "Exclusions" and instead have headings like "What Damaged Property We Insure."

Every heading, whether it heads a section or a subsection, should be numbered or lettered. Otherwise there is no easy way to refer to it unless the entire document is line-numbered, which is not a common practice in contract drafting.

2. *Classification*

Classification is the process of deciding what substance goes under what heading or subheading. The decisions should depend mainly on where users of the document may be expected to look for individual provisions. The main principle of classification is to put closely related provisions together. In practice this principle means:

- Exceptions usually belong with the general rules to which they relate, rather than collected together after all of the general rules.

- Definitions usually belong in the context where the defined words are used, rather than collected together at the beginning, unless the defined words appear in multiple sections.

If there are many exceptions or many definitions, it may be more practical to have separate sections for them to avoid excessive repetition and to make amendment easy. This is a "modular" theory of drafting, more appropriate for legislation than for contracts. It favors what is convenient for the drafter rather than the user, especially if the document is intended as a form to be used for many parties over a long period of time. It also values economy of statement over clarity. However, the result is sometimes a document so heavy with cross-references that it is likely either to confuse or to misinform. If clarity and easy use as a reference document are the primary values, then repetition seems less a flaw and more an aid to understanding.

It may seem logical to expect that final decisions about division are made first and then classification happens as a separate following

---

10. Public Service Mut. Ins. Co. v. Levy, 57 A.D.2d 794, 395 N.Y.S.2d 1 (1st Dept. 1977).

11. West's Rev.Code Wash.Ann. 48.44.020.

12. Arkansas Stats. § 66–3210.

13. 36 Okl.St.Ann. § 3611.

stage. However, in practice, drafters often discover while in the midst of classifying that they need to rethink division. If one section becomes overloaded, it may be worth it to subdivide so that information is not buried. If a section ends up with almost nothing in it, perhaps it should be consolidated with another section. However, all sections need not be of similar length.

3. Sequence

The sequence in which subjects are covered in the contract should also be governed by what makes information easy to find. Here are some principles that sometimes govern the sequence of subjects in contracts:

- Events in the chronological order in which they are expected to happen.
- Ordinary, expected events before extraordinary disasters that you hope will not happen at all.
- Provisions that are more important, from the drafting party's point of view, before less important ones.
- Provisions that favor the other party before those that favor the drafting party, which can be a useful device for wooing a reluctant party.
- Provisions you expect to be referred to frequently before more infrequently used ones.
- Promises requiring action before conditions and policies.
- General rules before exceptions.

Often the easiest order for drafter and user alike is chronological order. It may help to think about what circumstances or events are likely to cause a party to want to look something up in the contract. This approach to sequence is consistent with headings that focus on actions rather than abstractions. It usually results in more sections than an organizational plan based on logical abstractions or on grouping all of each party's rights and duties together.

The possible organizing principles overlap considerably. It would be impossible to put them all to work at once without contradiction. They are, therefore, merely matters for consideration. Moreover, as you draft and redraft, changes are likely to occur in all three of the organizational processes: division, classification, and sequence. No matter what your work style, you can expect the design of a contract to be in flux until the polishing stages of the final draft.

Exercise 4.6

Following are the title and section headings extracted from the body of a residential lease. No subheadings are given for Sections 4.A and 4.B because there were none in the lease. Evaluate the division and sequence of this organization. Can you discern one or more logical principles governing the division? Can you discern one or more organizational principles governing the sequence? Also, evaluate whether the headings are informative. What would you expect to find under each one? Do the headings appear to be of roughly the same weight or breadth, or instead do some seem much narrower than others? Should any heading actually be a subheadings under another heading?

RENTAL AGREEMENT—LEASE

TENANT AGREES AS FOLLOWS:

1. PAYMENT OF RENT
2. UTILITIES, RENT, GLASS, DOORS
3. REPAIRS AND MAINTENANCE
4. LIABILITY AND INJURY
    A.
    B.
5. DAMAGE TO PROPERTY
6. INSPECTION OF PREMISES
7. LAWN AND SHRUBBERY
8. SUBLETTING ASSIGNING
9. USE OF OCCUPANCY
10. TELEVISION AERIALS
11. AGENCY
12. EXPENSE OF ENFORCEMENT

SPECIAL STIPULATIONS

SECURITY DEPOSIT

Exercise 4.7

Following is the entire residential lease. Now evaluate the classification of material under each heading. Is everything under a heading that relates to it? Is the scope of what each heading purports to cover broader or narrower than the material under it? Do you find overlaps or gaps between sections?

RENTAL AGREEMENT—LEASE

Made and entered into this _____ day of _____ 19__ between _____, agent for Landlord, and _____, Tenant, whereby the Landlord agrees to rent to said Tenant the property located and

5 known as _____ in the City of _____, _____, County of
6 _____, State of _____ on the following terms and conditions:
7 Rental Rate _____ per month, to begin on the _____ day of
8 _____ 19__ on a lease basis, term of lease to be _____ months
9 with option to renew on date of termination. Tenant to give
10 Landlord notice of intention not later than 15 days prior to termina-
11 tion date of lease. Landlord reserves the right to adjust the rent at
12 the termination of the original lease and/or upon receipt of notifica-
13 tion of Tenant's intention to extend lease.

14   TENANT AGREES AS FOLLOWS:

15 1. PAYMENT OF RENT—To pay on the due date the monthly
16   rent, in advance, to Agent at _____.

17 2. UTILITIES, RENT, GLASS, DOORS—To pay all utility bills
18   when due, to keep sewerage pipes at said premises clear of
19   obstructions and to replace all broken or missing glass, dam-
20   aged doors or other parts during Tenant's occupancy.

21 3. REPAIRS AND MAINTENANCE—To accept the premises in
22   its present condition; to maintain the premises in good condi-
23   tion and repair, natural wear and tear excepted; to make no
24   alteration to said property without the written consent of the
25   Landlord.

26 4. LIABILITY AND INJURY—To relieve and indemnify Landlord
27   and/or Agent from any liability for:

28   A. Inability for any reason beyond the control of Landlord
29   and/or Agent to deliver possession of this property to said
30   Tenant on the effective rental date above written.

31   B. Damage or injury from any cause whatsoever which may be
32   sustained by Tenant, Tenant's property or any other person
33   for any cause whatsoever.

34 5. DAMAGE TO PROPERTY—To pay all costs for damage caused
35   by Tenant's negligence or lack of care.

36 6. INSPECTION OF PREMISES—To permit the Landlord or his
37   Agent to enter the premises at any reasonable time upon four
38   (4) hours written notice prior thereto, to show the property to
39   prospective purchasers or Tenants, to inspect the premises; also
40   to display on the premises for sale signs and/or rental signs,
41   after due notice of the termination of the tenancy has been
42   given by either party hereto.

43 7. LAWN AND SHRUBBERY—To take proper care of the lawn
44   and shrubbery, including mowing, trimming and weeding. Ten-
45   ant shall not remove any shrubbery without written consent of
46   the Landlord.

47 8. SUBLETTING ASSIGNING—Tenant shall not sublet the whole
48   or any part of the premises, nor assign this agreement, or any

49 interest therein. A violation of this covenant shall constitute a
50 breach of this agreement. Tenant shall forfeit the term, and
51 the Landlord shall have the right to evict Tenant.

52 9. USE OF OCCUPANCY—Tenant is not to put the premises to
53 any use which is illegal or to any use other than that for which
54 it is rented, to-wit, for the use and occupancy as a dwelling by
55 Tenant, and his family, consisting of _____ adults and
56 _____ children. No pets other than _____.

57 10. TELEVISION AERIALS—Tenant shall not be at liberty to erect
58 any television aerial upon the premises hereby rented (leased)
59 without first securing permission from the Landlord.

60 11. AGENCY—Agent may act for Landlord in all matters relating
61 hereto.

62 12. EXPENSE OF ENFORCEMENT—If rent is not received within
63 three (3) days after due, a late charge of $5.00 shall be added.
64 If rent and late charge not paid within fifteen (15) days after
65 rent due, entire rental for remainder of rental period shall be
66 due and payable and Landlord shall have such remedies as are
67 provided by law in such cases. If tenant defaults in payment of
68 rent or in compliance with other provisions of this Agreement
69 and it is necessary to place same in hands of an attorney,
70 Tenant agrees to pay a reasonable attorney's fee and all Court
71 costs.

72 SPECIAL STIPULATIONS

73 SECURITY DEPOSIT $_____, refundable within _____ days
74 after vacating and subject to premises being clean and intact. Any
75 violation of above terms will result in forfeiture of any part of said
76 deposit.

77 _____
78 _____

79 Signed, sealed and delivered in presence of

80 _____   _____ (Seal)

81 _____   _____ (Seal)
82 FOR AGENCY

83 _____ By _____ (Seal)

———

Exercise 4.8

Draft a new set of section headings to reflect how you would
reorganize the lease.

———

D. SPECIAL PROBLEMS IN DRAFTING FORM CONTRACTS

Often when you draft a contract, it is for a client who will use it more than once. The landlord hopes to have lots of tenants. The realtor hopes to make lots of sales. The contractor hopes to build lots of houses. The contract thus needs to be usable in somewhat various situations. Even in this computer age that allows you to add or remove a paragraph with a couple of key strokes, the client may not be able or willing to pay to have a new document prepared for each new set of facts. Thus you may find yourself drafting what amounts to a form contract.

The former approach to form contracts was to draft into them every detail that could conceivably apply. This approach is illustrated in a loan note formerly used by First National City Bank (Figure 1).

It well may be that anyone who drafts a sentence like the first one in that note truly hopes no one will read it. Its purpose is not to get the borrower to promise to act and then act accordingly. Rather its purpose is to establish a policy that the lender can act upon later if necessary. But a borrower who does read the sentence wades through every conceivable detail about all the possible payment plans, not just the one chosen. Worse yet, in this opening sentence, way ahead of security for the loan or prepayment, comes information not only about regular payments but also about fines for late payments, interest, and collection of attorney's fees.

————

When Citibank revised the note, the new one (Figure 2) added headings and lots of tabulation and white space for easier reading. It also converted to a personalized style in which "I" the borrower recite the terms of the loan to "you" the bank. These matters are discussed further in Chapter 11.

Note especially the difference in how the new form deals with the alternatives that were excruciatingly detailed in the old form. In the new form blanks are not used for every specific detail. Remember that blanks invite negotiation if the term in question is controversial. Here there is no problem in using blanks for which of several payment plans the borrower wants to use. But a different principle prevails in the late charge section. The bank, the drafting party, certainly does not want the amount of the late charge to be negotiated. Even the final sentence about 2% or $25 provides a way of determining a sum certain, which is all that matters.

In short, when you are drafting a form, you need to make judicious choices about when to use blanks and when to use general language that leaves your client some options. Your goal is to have a form that is usable as is in as many alternative situations as possible. The client does not want a new document every time, and also wants to have as few amendments as possible before the parties sign a contract and as few modifications as possible afterwards.

Figure 1

FOR 668 REV. 9-74

FIRST NATIONAL CITY BANK
PERSONAL FINANCE DEPARTMENT - NEW YORK
APPLICATION
NUMBER ______________________

ANNUAL PER-
CENTAGE RATE ______________ %

$ ______________________
TOTAL OF PAYMENTS (4) + (7)

PROCEEDS TO BORROWER	(1)	$ ________
PROPERTY INS. PREMIUM	(2)	$ ________
FILING FEE	(3)	$ ________
AMOUNT FINANCED (1) + (2) + (3)	(4)	$ ________
PREPAID FINANCE CHARGE	(5)	$ ________
GROUP CREDIT LIFE INS. PREMIUM	(6)	$ ________
FINANCE CHARGE (5) + (6)	(7)	$ ________

FOR VALUE RECEIVED, the undersigned (jointly and severally) hereby promise(s) to pay to FIRST NATIONAL CITY BANK (the "Bank") at its office at 399 Park Avenue, New York, New York 10022 (i) THE SUM OF

____ ($ ____________) (TOTAL OF PAYMENTS)

( ) IN ________ EQUAL CONSECUTIVE MONTHLY INSTALMENTS OF $ ________ EACH ON THE SAME DAY OF EACH MONTH, COMMENCING ________ DAYS FROM THE DATE THE LOAN IS MADE; OR ( ) IN ________ EQUAL CONSECUTIVE WEEKLY INSTALMENTS OF $ ________ EACH ON THE SAME DAY OF EACH WEEK, COMMENCING NOT EARLIER THAN 5 DAYS NOR LATER THAN 46 DAYS FROM THE DATE THE LOAN IS MADE; OR ( ) IN ________ EQUAL CONSECUTIVE BI-WEEKLY INSTALMENTS OF $ ________ EACH, COMMENCING NOT EARLIER THAN 10 DAYS NOR LATER THAN 46 DAYS FROM THE DATE THE LOAN IS MADE, AND ON THE SAME DAY OF EACH SECOND WEEK THEREAFTER; OR ( ) IN ________ EQUAL CONSECUTIVE SEMI-MONTHLY INSTALMENTS OF $ ________ EACH, COMMENCING NOT EARLIER THAN 10 DAYS NOR LATER THAN 46 DAYS FROM THE DATE THE LOAN IS MADE, AND ON THE SAME DAY OF EACH SEMI-MONTHLY PERIOD THEREAFTER, (ii) A FINE COMPUTED AT THE RATE OF 5¢ PER $1 ON ANY INSTALMENT WHICH HAS BECOME DUE AND REMAINED UNPAID FOR A PERIOD IN EXCESS OF 10 DAYS, PROVIDED (A) IF THE PROCEEDS TO THE BORROWER ARE $10,000 OR LESS, NO SUCH FINE SHALL EXCEED $5 AND THE AGGREGATE OF ALL SUCH FINES SHALL NOT EXCEED THE LESSER OF 2% OF THE AMOUNT OF THIS NOTE OR $25, OR (B) IF THE ANNUAL PERCENTAGE RATE STATED ABOVE IS 7.50% OR LESS, THE LIMITATIONS PROVIDED IN (A) SHALL NOT APPLY AND NO SUCH FINE SHALL EXCEED $25 AND THE AGGREGATE OF ALL SUCH FINES SHALL NOT EXCEED 2% OF THE AMOUNT OF THIS NOTE, AND SUCH FINE(S) SHALL BE DEEMED LIQUIDATED DAMAGES OCCASIONED BY THE LATE PAYMENT(S); (iii) IN THE EVENT OF THIS NOTE MATURING, SUBJECT TO AN ALLOWANCE FOR UNEARNED INTEREST ATTRIBUTABLE TO THE MATURED AMOUNT, INTEREST AT A RATE EQUAL TO 1% PER MONTH AND (iv) IF THIS NOTE IS REFERRED TO AN ATTORNEY FOR COLLECTION, A SUM EQUAL TO ALL COSTS AND EXPENSES THEREOF, INCLUDING AN ATTORNEY'S FEE EQUAL TO 15% OF THE AMOUNT OWING ON THIS NOTE AT THE TIME OF SUCH REFERENCE, FOR NECESSARY COURT COSTS. THE ACCEPTANCE BY THE BANK OF ANY PAYMENT(S) EVEN IF MARKED PAYMENT IN FULL OR SIMILAR WORDING, OR IF MADE AFTER ANY DEFAULT HEREUNDER, SHALL NOT OPERATE TO EXTEND THE TIME OF PAYMENT OF OR TO WAIVE ANY AMOUNT(S) THEN REMAINING UNPAID OR CONSTITUTE A WAIVER OF ANY RIGHTS OF THE BANK HEREUNDER.

P.L. NO. AND DATE LOAN MADE

IN THE EVENT THIS NOTE IS PREPAID IN FULL OR REFINANCED, THE BORROWER SHALL RECEIVE A REFUND OF THE UNEARNED PORTION OF THE PREPAID FINANCE CHARGE COMPUTED IN ACCORDANCE WITH THE RULE OF 78 (THE "SUM OF THE DIGITS" METHOD), PROVIDED THAT THE BANK MAY RETAIN A MINIMUM FINANCE CHARGE OF $10, WHETHER OR NOT EARNED, AND, EXCEPT IN THE CASE OF A REFINANCING, NO REFUND SHALL BE MADE IF IT AMOUNTS TO LESS THAN $1. IN ADDITION, UPON ANY SUCH PREPAYMENT OR REFINANCING, THE BORROWER SHALL RECEIVE A REFUND OF THE CHARGE, IF ANY, FOR GROUP CREDIT LIFE INSURANCE INCLUDED IN THE LOAN EQUAL TO THE UNEARNED PORTION OF THE PREMIUM PAID OR PAYABLE BY THE HOLDER OF THE OBLIGATION (COMPUTED IN ACCORDANCE WITH THE RULE OF 78), PROVIDED THAT NO REFUND SHALL BE MADE OF AMOUNTS LESS THAN $1.

AS COLLATERAL SECURITY FOR THE PAYMENT OF THE INDEBTEDNESS OF THE UNDERSIGNED HEREUNDER AND ALL OTHER INDEBTEDNESS OR LIABILITIES OF THE UNDERSIGNED TO THE BANK, WHETHER JOINT, SEVERAL, ABSOLUTE, CONTINGENT, SECURED, UNSECURED, MATURED OR UNMATURED, UNDER ANY PRESENT OR FUTURE NOTE OR CONTRACT OR AGREEMENT WITH THE BANK (ALL SUCH INDEBTEDNESS AND LIABILITIES BEING HEREINAFTER COLLECTIVELY CALLED THE "OBLIGATIONS"), THE BANK SHALL HAVE, AND IS HEREBY GRANTED, A SECURITY INTEREST AND/OR RIGHT OF SET-OFF IN AND TO (a) ALL MONIES, SECURITIES AND OTHER PROPERTY OF THE UNDERSIGNED NOW OR HEREAFTER ON DEPOSIT WITH OR OTHERWISE HELD BY OR COMING TO THE POSSESSION OR UNDER THE CONTROL OF THE BANK, WHETHER HELD FOR SAFEKEEPING, COLLECTION, TRANSMISSION OR OTHERWISE OR AS CUSTODIAN, INCLUDING THE PROCEEDS THEREOF, AND ANY AND ALL CLAIMS OF THE UNDERSIGNED AGAINST THE BANK, WHETHER NOW OR HEREAFTER EXISTING, AND (b) THE FOLLOWING DESCRIBED PERSONAL PROPERTY (ALL SUCH MONIES, SECURITIES, PROPERTY, PROCEEDS, CLAIMS AND PERSONAL PROPERTY BEING HEREINAFTER COLLECTIVELY CALLED THE "COLLATERAL"): ( ) Motor Vehicle ( ) Boat ( ) Stocks, ( ) Bonds, ( ) Savings, and/or ____
SEE CUSTOMER'S COPY OF SECURITY AGREEMENT(S) OR COLLATERAL RECEIPT(S) RELATIVE TO THIS LOAN FOR FULL DESCRIPTION.

IF THIS NOTE IS SECURED BY A MOTOR VEHICLE, BOAT OR AIRCRAFT, PROPERTY INSURANCE ON THE COLLATERAL IS REQUIRED, AND THE BORROWER MAY OBTAIN THE SAME THROUGH A PERSON OF HIS OWN CHOICE.

IF THIS NOTE IS NOT FULLY SECURED BY THE COLLATERAL SPECIFIED ABOVE, AS FURTHER SECURITY FOR THE PAYMENT OF THIS NOTE, THE BANK HAS TAKEN AN ASSIGNMENT OF 10% OF THE UNDERSIGNED BORROWER'S WAGES IN ACCORDANCE WITH THE WAGE ASSIGNMENT ATTACHED TO THIS NOTE.

In the event of default in the payment of this or any other Obligation or the performance or observance of any term or covenant contained herein or in any note or other contract or agreement evidencing or relating to any Obligation or any Collateral on the Borrower's part to be performed or observed; or the undersigned Borrower shall die; or any of the undersigned become insolvent or make an assignment for the benefit of creditors; or a petition shall be filed by or against any of the undersigned under any provision of the Bankruptcy Act; or any money, securities or property of the undersigned now or hereafter on deposit with or in the possession or under the control of the Bank shall be attached or become subject to distraint proceedings or any order or process of any court; or the Bank shall deem itself to be insecure, then and in any such event, the Bank shall have the right (at its option), without demand or notice of any kind, to declare all or any part of the Obligations to be immediately due and payable, whereupon such Obligations shall become and be immediately due and payable, and the Bank shall have the right to exercise all the rights and remedies available to a secured party upon default under the Uniform Commercial Code (the "Code") in effect in New York at the time, and such other rights and remedies as may otherwise be provided by law. Each of the undersigned agrees (for purposes of the "Code") that written notice of any proposed sale of, or of the Bank's election to retain, Collateral mailed to the undersigned Borrower (who is hereby appointed agent of each of the undersigned for such purpose) by first class mail, postage prepaid, at the address of the undersigned Borrower indicated below three business days prior to such sale or election shall be deemed reasonable notification thereof. The remedies of the Bank hereunder are cumulative and may be exercised concurrently or separately. If any provision of this paragraph shall conflict with any remedial provision contained in any security agreement or collateral receipt covering any Collateral, the provisions of such security agreement or collateral receipt shall control.

Acceptance by the Bank of payments in arrears shall not constitute a waiver of or otherwise affect any acceleration of payment hereunder or other right or remedy exercisable hereunder. No failure or delay on the part of the Bank in exercising, and no failure to file or otherwise perfect or enforce the Bank's security interest in or with respect to any Collateral, shall operate as a waiver of any right or remedy hereunder or release any of the undersigned, and the Obligations of the undersigned may be extended or waived by the Bank, any contract or other agreement evidencing or relating to any Obligation or any Collateral may be amended and any Collateral exchanged, surrendered or otherwise dealt with in accordance with any agreement relative thereto, all without affecting the liability of any of the undersigned. In any litigation (whether or not arising out of or relating to any Obligation or Collateral or other matter connected herewith) in which the Bank and any of the undersigned may be adverse parties, the Bank and each such undersigned hereby waives their respective right to demand trial by jury and, additionally, each such undersigned waives his right to interpose in any such litigation any counterclaim of any nature or description which he may have against the Bank. In addition, the Bank shall not be deemed to have obtained knowledge of any fact or notice with respect to any matter relating to this note or any Collateral unless contained in a written notice mailed, postage prepaid, or personally delivered to the Personal Finance Department of the Bank at its address set forth above. Each of the undersigned, by his signature hereto, hereby waives presentation for payment, demand, notice of non-payment, protest and notice of protest with respect to the indebtedness evidenced by this note, and each such undersigned hereby agrees that this note shall be deemed to have been made under and shall be construed in accordance with the laws of the State of New York.

Each of the undersigned hereby authorizes the Bank to date this note as of the day the loan evidenced hereby is made, to correct patent errors herein and, at its option, to cause the signatures of one or more co-makers to be added without notice to any prior obligor.

RECEIPT OF A COPY OF THIS NOTE, APPROPRIATELY FILLED IN, IS HEREBY ACKNOWLEDGED BY THE BORROWER

	FULL SIGNATURE	COMPLETE ADDRESSES
BORROWER	________________	________________
WIFE OR HUSBAND OF BORROWER AS CO-MAKER	________________	________________
CO-MAKER	________________	________________

Figure 2

Consumer Loan Note   Date_____ 19____

_____

(In this note, the words I, me, mine and my mean each and all of those who signed it. The words you, your and yours mean First National City Bank.)

Terms of Repayment To repay my loan, I promise to pay you _____ Dollars ($_____). I'll pay this sum at one of your branches in _____ uninterrupted _____ installments of $_____ each. Payments will be due _____, starting from the date the loan is made.

Here's the breakdown of my payments:

1. Amount of the Loan $_____
2. Property Insurance Premium $_____
3. Filing Fee for Security Interest $_____
4. Amount Financed (1+2+3) $_____
5. Finance Charge $_____
6. Total of Payments (4+5) $_____

Annual Percentage Rate_____ %

Prepayment of Whole Note Even though I needn't pay more than the fixed installments, I have the right to prepay the whole outstanding amount of this note at any time. If I do, or if this loan is refinanced—that is, replaced by a new note— you will refund the unearned finance charge, figured by the rule of 78—a commonly used formula for figuring rebates on installment loans. However, you can charge a minimum finance charge of $10.

Late Charge If I fall more than 10 days behind in paying an installment, I promise to pay a late charge of 5% of the overdue installment, but no more than $5. However, the sum total of late charges on all installments can't be more than 2% of the total of payments or $25, whichever is less.

Security To protect you if I default on this or any other debt to you, I give you what is known as a security interest in my ○ Motor Vehicle and/or _____ (see the Security Agreement I have given you for a full description of this property), ○ Stocks, ○ Bonds, ○ Savings Account (more fully described in the receipt you gave me today) and any account or other securities of mine coming into your possession.

Insurance I understand I must maintain property insurance on the property covered by the Security Agreement for its full insurable value, but I can buy this insurance through a person of my own choosing.

Default I'll be in default:
1. If I don't pay an installment on time; or
2. If any other creditor tries by legal process to take any money of mine in your possession.

You can then demand immediate payment of the balance of this note, minus the part of the finance charge which hasn't been earned figured by the rule of 78. You will also have other legal rights, for instance, the right to repossess, sell and apply security to the payments under this note and any other debts I may then owe you.

Irregular Payments You can accept late payments or partial payments, even though marked "payment in full", without losing any of your rights under this note.

Delay in Enforcement You can delay enforcing any of your rights under this note without losing them.

Collection Costs If I'm in default under this note and you demand full payment, I agree to pay you interest on the unpaid balance at the rate of 1% per month, after an allowance for the unearned finance charge. If you have to sue me, I also agree to pay your attorney's fees equal to 15% of the amount due, and court costs. But if I defend and the court decides I am right, I understand that you will pay my reasonable attorney's fees and the court costs.

Comakers If I'm signing this note as a comaker, I agree to be equally responsible with the borrower, although you may sue either of us. You don't have to notify me that this note hasn't been paid. You can change the terms of payment and release any security without notifying or releasing me from responsibility on this note.

Copy Received The borrower acknowledges receipt of a completely filled-in copy of this note.

Signatures   Addresses

Borrower:_____   _____
Comaker:_____   _____
Comaker:_____   _____
Comaker:_____   _____

Hot Line If something should happen and you can't pay on time, please call us immediately at (212) 559-3061.

VII. HOUSEKEEPING PROVISIONS

Housekeeping provisions are statements of policy about how the contract itself is going to be administered. In a sense, definitions are housekeeping provisions, and sometimes they are put at the end on that account, although they serve better earlier. Aside from definitions, housekeeping provisions are collected at the end of the contract, preferably each with its own informative heading.

Typical housekeeping provisions attend to such matters as modification, assignment, notice, liquidated damages, the law governing the contract, severability of invalid provisions, and merger of the parties' prior agreements into the contract. Sometimes drafters try to use housekeeping provisions to mop up after sloppy drafting by announcing that headings are for convenience only and are not to be construed as limitations on the paragraphs they head (and so, according to the underlying message, it does not matter if they are uninformative). Or they announce that when the masculine gender is used inappropriately, it means the feminine (and so it does not matter if the drafter cannot figure out how to draft gender-neutral prose). These are not legitimate uses of housekeeping provisions; they are flimsy shields against a court's construing an ambiguous or otherwise poorly drafted contract against the drafter.

Housekeeping provisions are generally the most poorly drafted ones in contracts because drafters tend to rely most heavily on old forms for them. At worst, the archaic language may be unintelligible; at best, it may be construed to mean something different from what the drafter intended.

The real work of drafting housekeeping provisions is to dissect the old form language and convert it as drastically as Citibank converted its loan note so that the end result says clearly what you mean.

Exercise 4.9

Revise the following housekeeping provisions into plain language. Keep in mind that positive statements are easier to follow than negative ones, and also that housekeeping provisions are better stated as policies in the present tense than as promises in the future tense.

Provision 1

INVALIDITY OF CERTAIN PROVISIONS. If any term, covenant, condition, or provision of this Agreement is held by a court of competent jurisdiction to be invalid, void, or unenforceable, the remaining terms, covenants, and provisions shall remain in full force and effect and be in no way affected, impaired, or invalidated.

Provision 2

WARRANTIES, AMENDMENTS AND MODIFICATION. It is mutually understood and agreed that any representation, promise, condition, inducement or warranty, express or implied, not included in writing in this agreement shall not be binding upon any party and that this agreement may not be altered, modified, or otherwise changed at any time except with the written consent of each of the parties hereto, and in the form of an addendum to this agreement.

Provision 3

NO WAIVER. Time is expressly made the essence of each and every term and condition hereof. The failure of LANDLORD to enforce or to insist upon the strict performance of any provision of this Agreement shall not prevent a subsequent act constituting a violation or default from having the force and effect of a violation or default.

Provision 4

Any notice required or permitted under this Agreement shall be in writing and shall be deemed given when delivered personally or three days after being sent by first-class registered or certified mail, return receipt requested, to the party for which intended at its or his address set forth at the beginning of this Agreement or to such other address as either party may hereafter specify by similar notice to the other.

VIII. CHECKLIST FOR DRAFTING CONTRACTS

Title and Introductory Paragraph

1. Does the title express the nature of the contract?

2. Are the parties accurately identified with all names correctly spelled?

3. Are short forms established if they will be used throughout?

4. Is the nature of the contract established?

5. Do the parties express mutual agreement generally to all of the terms in the remainder of the contract?

6. Are specific terms of the agreement appropriately omitted?

7. Is the introductory paragraph an unnumbered and unheaded paragraph consisting of one or more complete sentences rather than fragments?

Definitions

8. If you have a definitions section, does it precede any recitals if words used in the recitals need definition?

9. Do you have a definitions section only if you need to define words that are used in more than one other section of the contract?

10. Do you restrict yourself to stipulative definitions that broaden, narrow, or change ordinary meaning, and to lexical definitions of technical terms or terms of art that a party might not know? Do you avoid other lexical definitions?

11. Do you abide by the conventions for stipulative definitions discussed in Chapter 10?

Recitals

12. Do you recite premises for the contract or other background facts only to the extent that they serve your client?

13. Do you use general language for recitals that you do not want held binding and specific language for those you do want binding?

14. Do you place and head recitals consistently with your wish to make them binding or not?

Organization of Promises and Policies

15. Do you express provisions in the form of promises when you want a given party clearly obligated to act or refrain from acting in the future?

16. Do you express provisions in the form of present policies when you want to make a term not negotiable?

17. Does your division of the body of the contract into sections make it easy to use as a reference document? Is it neither over- nor under-divided and subdivided?

18. Are your section headings informative?

19. Are they stylistically consistent?

20. Is any material buried under a heading where a reader would not likely look for it?

21. Is each heading general enough to cover all of the contents of the section? Is each heading specific enough to avoid covering provisions covered elsewhere?

22. Is the contract free from gaps and overlaps among sections?

23. Is there some evident logical or chronological plan in the sequence of sections?

24. Are related provisions together with no needless cross-references?

Housekeeping Provisions

25. Are housekeeping provisions collected at the end of the contract?

26. Is each one informatively headed rather than the lot gathered under a catch-all heading?

27. Is each one clear and exactly appropriate in the contract rather than merely grafted onto it from an old form?

Format of the Contract

28. Is each section numbered or lettered as well as headed?

29. Are headings and subheadings easily distinguishable from each other and from the text?

30. Do you use all-capital letters only for short headings, not for whole blocks of print?

31. Is there sufficient margin, indenting, and other white space to produce readable pages?

32. Do you leave blanks for dates of signatures and any other dates that may change depending on when the parties sign, or else do you draft flexibly enough to do without specified dates other than signature dates?

33. Do you provide a separate signature line for each individual party?

34. Do you type parties' names under the lines where they will sign?

35. Do you use some device to keep signatures from being severed from the text, such as making sure to have the last few lines of text on the same page as the signatures, or numbering the pages "1 of 3," etc.?

36. If you have referred to other documents as attached and incorporated by reference, are they labeled as "Exhibit A," etc. and in fact attached?

IX. DRAFTING ASSIGNMENTS

Drafting Assignment 4.A—Exculpatory Provision in Contract

Your clients, Buddy and Hazel Wild, doing business as "Wild River Canoes," rent canoes for use on the 15–mile–long Santa Clara River. Along with the canoes, they rent a variety of gear, including paddles, seat cushions, life preservers, canteens, tarps, anchors, and coolers. The Wilds' place is on the river. Renters launch there and have their choices of four different pick-up places along the river depending on how long a trip they want. The Wilds then pick up people and canoes at pre-arranged times and take them back to the starting point.

The river is generally placid, but there are a few shoals where it becomes fast-moving when the water is low. There are woods along the river banks on both sides for most of its length, where wild life abounds. There are a few cabins scattered along the river front, some of which have docks. When the river floods, the docks are out of sight, although most of the cabins are on high banks, above the flood plain.

The Wilds have a simple rental contract form. It has spaces to fill in for the beginning and ending points of the canoe trip; the agreed pick-up time; the number of adults and children in the party; the number of canoes, paddles, life preservers, and other items of gear rented, and the amount paid. The Wilds would like you to draft a paragraph for their contract to keep them from being liable to the renters in case of accident, even if the Wilds' own negligence causes the accident.

You research the law in your state on exculpatory clauses in contracts that attempt to deny an injured party the right to recover damages from the person negligently causing the injury. Here is what you glean from cases:

• Exculpatory provisions are strictly construed against the party they benefit.

• An exculpatory provision that is ambiguous or purports to release a person from liability for intentional, willful, or wanton acts is not enforceable.

• The intention to limit liability for negligence will not be inferred but must be expressed in clear and unequivocal terms.

• An agreement to assume the risk of injury or loss must unambiguously indicate which risks are assumed and will not be interpreted to include losses resulting from the drafting party's negligence unless expressly included.

You find three litigated provisions, two of which were held unenforceable and the other of which was enforced:

Provision 1 (held unenforceable)

It is further agreed that reasonable precautions will be taken by Camp to assure the safety and good health of said boy/girl but that Camp is not to be held liable in the event of injury, illness or death of said boy/girl, and the undersigned does fully release Camp, and all persons concerned therewith, for any such liability.

Provision 2 (held unenforceable)

I consent to the renting of a horse from _____ by _____, a minor, and to his/her assumption of the risks inherent in horseback riding. I agree, personally and on his/her behalf, to waive any claims or causes of action which he/she or I may now or hereafter have against _____ arising out of any injuries he/she may sustain as a result of that horseback riding, and I will hold _____ harmless against any and all claims resulting from such injuries.

Provision 3 (enforced)

ACCIDENTS

It is further expressly agreed that all exercises and treatments and use of all facilities shall be undertaken by Member at Member's sole risk and that Spa shall not be liable for any claims, demands, injuries, damages, actions or causes of action whatsoever to Member or property arising out of or connected with the use of any of the services and facilities of Spa or the premises where they are located, and Member does hereby expressly forever release Spa from all such claims, demands, injuries, damages, actions or causes of action, and from all acts of active or passive negligence on the part of Spa, its corporate owner, or servants, agents, or employees of Spa or its corporate owner.

_____

You also find a row boat rental contract in use at a nearby lake. It includes the following paragraph, which has not been litigated.

READ THE FOLLOWING AND ALL ADULTS MUST SIGN.

I am aware that outdoor recreational activities can be hazardous and I assume all risks of injury, loss of life, and damage to person and property during such activity, fully realizing that _____, or its agents are not responsible for any such injury, loss of life, or damage to person or property, and I agree to pay for, defend, indemnify, and hold _____, or its agents, employees, successors and assigns harmless from all liabilities, claims, demands, costs, losses, expenses or compensation of whatever nature, for loss, damage or injuries to persons and property sustained by me, my heirs, personal representatives, successors and assigns, and all other persons resulting from or in any way connected with transporting or use of equipment furnished by _____, or its agents directly or indirectly caused or contributed to the cause of said injury, loss of life or damage to persons or property by their negligent acts, gross negligence or recklessness. I understand that the use of equipment furnished by _____ constitutes an acceptance of said equipment on a lease basis "AS IS." I, as a parent or guardian or supervisor of a minor child, make this agreement individually and on behalf of this minor child to induce _____ to allow this child to participate in this activity.

_____

Drafting Assignment 4.B—Release

Often parties agree after rather than before injury that in consideration of payment of a sum of money to an injured party, that party releases from liability the one who pays the money.

Your client is Auto Mutual Insurance Company. William and Carol Jackson, husband and wife, were insured by Auto Mutual when they both suffered physical injuries in an automobile accident on March 20 of last year, on Kingston Pike outside of Charlesville in your state. The driver of the car that hit the Jacksons was George Miller of 8400 Middlebrook Pike in Charlesville. Miller was uninsured, and the Jacksons' policy included uninsured motorist coverage. Now William Jackson agrees to release the Company in consideration of payment of $72,000. Carol Jackson is seriously incapacitated; she is not willing to settle her claims.

Someone else in your office has drafted the release below for William Jackson to sign.

> RECEIVED OF AUTO MUTUAL INSURANCE COMPANY, HEREINAFTER CALLED THE COMPANY, THE SUM OF Seventy-Two Thousand Dollars ($72,000) in full settlement and final discharge of all claims under Policy # 4829309 for injuries to William Jackson arising out of the ownership or operation of an uninsured automobile by George Miller which occurred on or about the 20th day of March, 19—, in Charlesville, ————.

————

A release after injury is strictly construed against the released party just as a prospective exculpatory clause is strictly construed against the party to benefit from it. There are generally two tests of validity:

- The release must be "knowing."
- The release must be "voluntary."

In view of the first test, think about what recitals might help substantiate the released party's later claim that the releasing party signed the release knowingly.

In view of the second test, weigh the two following approaches: (1) providing a "window" period during which the releasing party can escape after signing, with the payment not made until the window closes; or (2) treating the release as a receipt for paid consideration.

The "tighter" the release, the better chance it has of precluding or surviving challenge over lack of knowledge or involuntariness. However, the more legal terms of art or legalese in the release, the greater chance there is that the releasing party will become wary and decline to sign it.

Assume you find in your files the releases below, all drafted by others. After you read them, redraft the release for William Jackson to sign.

RELEASE AND SETTLEMENT OF CLAIM

1   **For the sole consideration of** _____ Dollars, to me/us in
2 hand paid, the receipt of which is hereby acknowledged, I/we
3 _____, Releasor(s), being over 21 years of age, do hereby release,
4 and forever discharge _____,
5 Releasee(s) and all other persons, firms or corporations from any
6 and all claims, demands, rights, actions or causes of action on
7 account of or in any way growing out of any and all personal
8 injuries (and consequences thereof, including death, and specifically
9 including, also, any injuries which may exist, but which at this time
10 are unknown and unanticipated and which may develop at some
11 time in the future, and all unforeseen developments arising from
12 known injuries) and any and all property damage resulting or to
13 result from an accident that occurred on or about the _____ day
14 of _____ 19__, and do hereby for myself/ourselves, my/our heirs,
15 executors, administrators, successors, assigns and next of kin cove-
16 nant to indemnify and save harmless the said above-named
17 Releasee(s) and said persons, firms or corporations above-referred to,
18 from all claims, demands, costs, loss of services, expenses, and
19 compensation on account of or in any way growing out of said
20 accident or its results both to person and property.

21   **It is expressly understood and agreed that** the acceptance of
22 the said above amount is in full accord and satisfaction of a disputed
23 claim, and that the payment of the said above amount is not an
24 admission of liability.

25   **In Witness Whereof,** I/we have hereunto set my/our hand and
26 seal this _____ day of _____ 19__.

27   SIGNATURE: _____(L.S.)

28   _____(L.S.)

29   CERTIFICATE OF WITNESSES

30   **We certify that this release** was signed in our presence by the
31 above who acknowledged that he/they understood it fully.

32 Witness _____   Witness _____

33 Address _____   Address _____

RELEASE OF ALL CLAIMS

1   FOR AND IN CONSIDERATION OF the payment to me/us of
2 the sum of Dollars ($_____), and other good and valuable consider-
3 ation, I/we, being of lawful age, have released and discharged, and
4 by these presents do for myself/ourselves, my/our heirs, executors,
5 administrators and assigns, release, acquit and forever discharge
6 _____ and any and all other persons, firms and corporations of

7 and from any and all actions, causes of action, claims or demands
8 for damages, costs, loss of use, loss of services, expenses, compensa-
9 tion, consequential damage or any other thing whatsoever on ac-
10 count of, or in any way growing out of, any and all known and
11 unknown personal injuries and death and property damage result-
12 ing or to result from an occurrence or accident that happened on or
13 about the _____ day of _____, 19__, at or near _____.

14   I/we hereby acknowledge and assume all risk, chance or hazard
15 that the said injuries or damage may be or become permanent,
16 progressive, greater, or more extensive than is now known, antici-
17 pated or expected. No promise or inducement which is not herein
18 expressed has been made to me/us, and in executing this release I/
19 we do not rely upon any statement or representation made by any
20 person, firm or corporation, hereby released, or any agent, physi-
21 cian, doctor or any other person representing them or any of them,
22 concerning the nature, extent or duration of said damages or losses
23 or the legal liability therefor.

24   I/we understand that this settlement is the compromise of a
25 doubtful and disputed claim, and that the payment is not to be
26 construed as an admission of liability on the part of the persons,
27 firms and corporations hereby released by whom liability is express-
28 ly denied.

29   This release contains the ENTIRE AGREEMENT between the
30 parties hereto, and the terms of this release are contractual and not
31 a mere recital.

32   I/we further state that I/we have carefully read the foregoing
33 release and know the contents thereof, and I/we sign the same as
34 my/our own free act.

35   WITNESS _____ hand and seal this _____ day of _____,
36 19__.

37 **WITNESSES**

38   **CAUTION! READ BEFORE SIGNING**

_____
ADDRESS _____ } _____
_____   _____
ADDRESS _____

1   **SETTLEMENT AGREEMENT AND RELEASE ***

2   THIS SETTLEMENT AGREEMENT AND RELEASE ("Settle-
3 ment Agreement") is made and entered into this _____ day of

4 ————, 19—, by and among ———— ("Plaintiff") and ————, a
5 ———— corporation, ("Insurer").

6 RECITALS

7 (A) On or about ————, 19—, the Plaintiffs filed a complaint
8   ("Complaint") against ———— et al. ("Defendants") in the
9   ———— Court in the State of ————, ———— County,
10   (Court Action No. ————) which Complaint arose out of
11   certain alleged negligent acts or omissions by the Defen-
12   dants.

13 (B) The Insurer is the liability insurer of the Defendants and as
14   such would be obligated to pay any judgment obtained
15   against the Defendants which is covered by its policy.

16 (C) The parties desire to enter into this Settlement Agreement
17   in order to provide for certain payments in full settlement
18   and discharge of all claims which are the subject of the
19   Complaint, upon the terms and conditions set forth herein.

20 AGREEMENT

21 The parties hereto hereby agree as follows:

22 (1) *Release and Discharge*

23   In consideration of the payments called for herein, the
24   Plaintiffs and each of them hereby completely release and
25   forever discharge the Defendants and each of them, the
26   Insurer, and said parties' past, present and future officers,
27   directors, stockholders, attorneys, agents, servants, represent-
28   atives, employees, subsidiaries, affiliates, partners, predeces-
29   sors and successors in interest, and assigns and all other
30   persons, firms, or corporations with whom any of the former
31   have been, are now or may hereafter be affiliated, of and from
32   any and all past, present or future claims, demands, obliga-
33   tions, actions, causes of action, wrongful death claims, rights,
34   damages, costs, losses of services, expenses and compensation
35   of any nature whatsoever, whether based on a tort, contract or
36   other theory of recovery, and whether for compensatory or
37   punitive damages, which the Plaintiffs or any of them now
38   have, or which may hereafter accrue or otherwise be acquired,
39   on account of, or any way growing out of, or which are the
40   subject of, the Complaint (and all related pleadings) including,
41   without limitation, any and all known or unknown claims for
42   bodily and personal injuries to Plaintiffs and the consequences
43   thereof, which have resulted or may result from the alleged
44   negligent acts or omissions of the Defendants or any of them.
45   This release, on the part of the Plaintiffs, shall be a fully
46   binding and complete settlement between the Plaintiffs, the
47   Defendants and the Insurer and all parties represented by or
48   claiming through the Plaintiffs, save only the executory

49 provisions of this Settlement Agreement. The Plaintiffs agree
50 to defend, indemnify and hold the Defendants and the Insurer
51 harmless from and against all such claims, demands, obliga-
52 tions, actions, causes of action, damages, costs and expenses.

53 (2) *Payments*

54 In consideration of the release set forth above, the Insurer
55 on behalf of the Defendants hereby agrees to pay the
56 following sums as set forth in Exhibit A.

57 (3) *Plaintiff's Rights to Payments*

58 The defendant and/or the Insurer shall not segregate or set
59 aside any of its assets to fund the payments to Plaintiff
60 required herein, it being understood that Plaintiff is and
61 shall be a general creditor to the Defendant and/or the
62 Insurer and/or the Insurer's assignee. Said payments can-
63 not be accelerated, deferred, increased or decreased by the
64 Plaintiff and no part of the payments called for herein or
65 any assets of the Defendant and/or the Insurer and/or the
66 Insurer's assignee is to be subject to execution or any legal
67 process for any obligation in any manner, nor shall the
68 Plaintiff have the power to sell or mortgage or encumber
69 same, or any part thereof, nor anticipate the same, or any
70 part thereof, by assignment or otherwise.

71 (4) *Attorney's Fees*

72 Each party hereto shall bear all attorney's fees and costs
73 arising from the actions of its own counsel in connection
74 with the Complaint, this Settlement Agreement and the
75 matters and documents referred to herein, the filing of a
76 dismissal of the Complaint, and all related matters.

77 (5) *Designation of contingent Beneficiary and Revocation of Des-*
78   *ignation*

79 Any payments to be made after the death of the Plaintiff
80 pursuant to Section 2 hereof shall be made to such persons
81 or entity as shall be designated in writing by said Plaintiff
82 to the Insurer. If no person or entity is so designated by
83 said Plaintiff, such payments shall be made to the estate of
84 the Plaintiff. No such designation nor any revocation
85 thereof shall be effective unless it is in writing and deliv-
86 ered to the Insurer.

87 (6) *Assignment and Assumption*

88 The parties hereto acknowledge that the Insurer may as-
89 sign to, and arrange for the assumption by one or more
90 assignees (the "Assignee"), the obligation with respect to
91 periodic and deferred lump sum payments set forth in

92   Exhibit A. Any such assignment and assumption shall
93   completely release and discharge the Defendants and the
94   Insurer from such obligations. The Plaintiffs recognize
95   that, in the event of such an assignment, the Assignee(s)
96   shall be Plaintiffs' sole obligor with respect to the obliga-
97   tions assigned.

98   (7) *Right to Purchase an Annuity*

99   For his own convenience, the Insurer, or the sole obligor to
100   whom the Insurer assigns obligation, should such assign-
101   ment be opted for, reserves the right to fund its obliga-
102   tion(s) under Exhibit A above through the purchase of any
103   annuity policy from the _____ Life Insurance Company.
104   The Insurer, or sole obligor in the event that the insurer
105   assigns obligation, shall be the owner of the annuity policy,
106   and shall have all rights of ownership. For its own conve-
107   nience, the Insurer, or in the alternative, the sole obligor,
108   shall have the annuity carrier mail payments directly to
109   the Plaintiff. The Plaintiff shall be responsible for main-
110   taining proper mailing address and mortality information
111   to the life insurance annuity Company.

112   (8) *Discharge of Obligation*

113   The Obligations of the Insurer to make each monthly
114   installment of the annual payments and the deferred lump
115   sum payments shall be discharged upon the mailing of a
116   valid check in the amount of such payment to the address
117   designated by the party to whom the payment is required to
118   be made under this Settlement Agreement.

119   (9) *General Releases*

120   The Plaintiffs hereby acknowledge and agree that the re-
121   lease set forth in Section 1 hereof is a general release and
122   they further expressly waive and assume the risk of any
123   and all claims for damages which exist as of this date but
124   which the Plaintiffs do not know of or suspect to exist,
125   whether through ignorance, oversight, error, negligence, or
126   otherwise, and which, if known, would materially affect
127   their decision to enter into this Settlement Agreement.
128   The Plaintiffs further agree that they have accepted pay-
129   ment of the sums specified herein as a complete compro-
130   mise of matters involving disputed issues of law and fact
131   and they fully assume the risk that the facts or law may be
132   otherwise than they believe.

133   (10) *Delivery of Dismissal With Prejudice*

134   Concurrently with the execution of this Settlement Agree-
135   ment, counsel for the Plaintiffs has delivered to counsel for

136 the Insurer an executed Dismissal with Prejudice for the
137 Civil action described in Recital A above. The Plaintiffs
138 have authorized their attorneys to execute this Dismissal
139 on their behalf and hereby authorize counsel for the Insur-
140 er to file said Dismissal in the proper court.

141 (11) *Warranty of Capacity to Execute Agreement*

142 The Plaintiffs represent and warrant that no other person
143 or entity has or has had any interest in the claims, de-
144 mands, obligations, or causes of action referred to in this
145 Settlement Agreement; that they have the sole right and
146 exclusive authority to execute this Settlement Agreement
147 and receive the sums specified in it; and that they have not
148 sold, assigned, transferred, conveyed, or otherwise disposed
149 of any of the claims, demands, obligations, or causes of
150 action referred to in this Settlement Agreement.

151 (12) *Disclaimer of Liability*

152 The Plaintiffs agree and acknowledge that they accept
153 payment of the sums specified in this Settlement Agree-
154 ment as a full and complete compromise of matters involv-
155 ing disputed issues; that neither payment of the sums by
156 the Insurer nor the negotiations for this settlement (includ-
157 ing all statements, admissions, or communications) by the
158 Insurer, the Defendants, or their attorneys or representa-
159 tives shall be considered admissions by any of said parties;
160 and that no past or present wrongdoing on the part of the
161 Defendants shall be implied by such payment or negotia-
162 tions.

163 (13) *Entire Agreement and Successors in Interest*

164 This Settlement contains the entire agreement between the
165 Plaintiffs, the Defendants and the Insurer with regard to
166 the matters set forth in it and shall be binding upon and
167 incur to the benefit of the executors, administrators, per-
168 sonal representatives, heirs, successors and assigns of each.

169 (14) *Construction Law*

170 This Settlement Agreement is entered into in the State of
171 _____ and shall be construed and interpreted in accor-
172 dance with its law.

173 (15) *Representation of Comprehension of Document*

174 In entering into the Settlement Agreement the Plaintiffs
175 represent that they have relied upon the legal advice of
176 their attorneys, who are the attorneys of their own choice
177 and that the terms of the Settlement Agreement have been
178 completely read and explained to them by their attorneys,

179   and that those terms are fully understood and voluntarily
180   accepted by them.

181   (16) *Additional Documents*

182   All parties agree to cooperate fully and execute any and all
183   supplementary documents and to take all additional actions
184   which may be necessary or appropriate to give full force
185   and effect to the basic terms and intent of this Settlement
186   Agreement.

187   (17) *Effectiveness*

188   This Settlement Agreement shall become effective immedi-
189   ately following execution by all of the parties.

190 Executed at _____ this _____ day of _____, 19__

191 By _____
192   Plaintiff

193 _____
194   Plaintiff

195 _____
196   Defendant

197 _____
198   Defendant

199 _____
200   Company, Insurer

201 By: _____

202 Its: _____
203   Title

_____

1 READ CAREFULLY—By signing this you give up EVERY right you
2 have.

3   I, _____ Age _____
                (write your own name and age)

4 Address _____ in exchange for _____
                (Street number, city or town, and state)

5 dollars ($_____) which I have received, do hereby _____
                                                         (Write the word

6 _____ and forever discharge __
   "release" to show that you know what you are doing)

7 _____ and their heirs, executors,
       (Here insert full name of all those to be released)

8 administrators, personal representatives, successors and assigns
9 from each and every right and claim which I now have, or may

10 hereafter have on account of injuries and illnesses suffered by me as
11 follows:

12 _____

13 and, in addition to that, I _____
(Write the word "release" to show that you know what

14 _____ them from each and every right and claim which I now
you are doing)

15 have or may hereafter have because of any matter or thing which
16 happened before the signing of this paper, it being my intention by
17 the signing of this paper to wipe the slate clean as between myself
18 and the parties released, even as respects injuries, illnesses, rights
19 and claims not mentioned herein or not known to me.

20 READ THE FOLLOWING SIX NUMBERED STATEMENTS CARE-
21 FULLY:

22   (1) I know that this paper is much more than a receipt. IT IS A
23 RELEASE. I AM GIVING UP EVERY RIGHT I HAVE.

24   (2) I know that in signing this release I am, among other things,
25 now settling in full for all injuries, illnesses and disabilities which I
26 have had already, which I have now, and which I may have in the
27 future, either because of the particular occurrence mentioned above
28 or because of any other occurrence in the past, or because of both,
29 even though I do not know that I have had already, have now or
30 may have in the future such injuries, illnesses and disabilities, and
31 even though they are not mentioned particularly in this release;
32 and I do all this regardless of what anyone may have told me about
33 my injuries, illnesses and disabilities or about anything else.

34   (3) I know that doctors and other persons make mistakes, and I
35 am taking the risk that what they may have told me is wrong. If
36 that should be the case, it is my loss, and I cannot back out of the
37 settlement.

38   (4) I realize that the payment of the money mentioned above is
39 not an admission that anyone is liable to me for anything.

40   (5) I am signing this release because I am getting the money. I
41 have not been promised anything else.

42   (6) I am satisfied.

43   THE FOLLOWING IS TO BE FILLED IN BY THE
44   CLAIMANT HIMSELF IN HIS OWN HANDWRITING.

45   A.   Have you read this paper from beginning to end?   A.___
46   B.   Do you know what this paper is that you are
47   signing?   A.___
48   C.   What is this paper which you are signing?   A.___

49 _____
(Write here "release of everything")

50   D.   Do you make the six numbered statements printed
51   above and do you intend that the parties whom you
52   are releasing shall rely on the statements as the
53   truth?   A.___
54   E.   Do you know that signing this paper settles and
55   ends EVERY right or claim you have for DAM-
56   AGES as well as for past and future maintenance,
57   cure, and wages?   A.___
58   F.   In order to show that you know what you are doing
59   please copy in your own handwriting, in the space
60   immediately following, the third numbered state-
61   ment above.

62   _____

63   _____

64   _____

65   Therefore, I am signing my name upon the words THIS IS A
66 RELEASE and alongside the seal, which is printed below and which
67 is adopted by me as my own, to show that I mean everything that is
68 said on this paper.

69   Dated _____, 19__

70 SIGN HERE

71   THIS IS A RELEASE

72 _____   [Seal]

73   Claimant, if he wishes to sign and seal this paper, should write
74 his name upon the words "THIS IS A RELEASE" immediately
75 above and alongside the printed seal.

Drafting Assignment 4.C—Release

If the parties to a pending legal action enter a release agreement, the release should be drafted expressly with regard to that action.

• The release should refer to the action precisely.

• It should make clear that the released party makes no admissions.

• It should make clear that the releasing party is not to be regarded as prevailing for any purpose such as awarding attorney's fees.

• The consideration for the released party's payment of an agreed sum should include the releasing party's dismissal with prejudice of the pending action.

Often release and settlement agreements are drafted as court papers, complete with caption, and filed. Consider that represented parties do not normally sign court papers; their attorneys do. Represented parties can nonetheless sign affidavits. Also, an agreement can become an exhibit attached to a motion to dismiss.

Retrieve the pleadings you drafted in conjunction with Part One of this book. On behalf of one of the defendants, draft an agreement to be signed by the defendant as the released party and the plaintiff as the releasing party. Determine what you think is a reasonable sum as the settlement amount. Present the release in the form that you think is most beneficial to your client. Give special attention to how vague or precise and how general or particular the language should be.

Drafting Assignment 4.D—Lease

Your clients are Gordon and Rhonda West. They have recently moved to your city and begun a rental business as the new owners of seven different parcels of property: one garage apartment, two duplexes, and four single family homes. One of the single family homes has a detached garage that is rented as a workshop storage area. The Wests refurbish the property themselves, prepare it for rental, and handle all business and other matters associated with renting.

The Wests bring you the form lease they have used in the past in their business elsewhere. It is the lease that appears at pp. 135–37 and is the subject of Exercises 4.6 and 4.7. The Wests are not satisfied with it, and they ask you to do the following:

1. Redraft the lease to make it easy for tenants to understand.

2. Make the lease comply completely with your state's law.

3. Revise the lease to reflect the information below about their rental operations and to help prevent problems they have been encountering or might encounter in the future.

Facts for West Lease

Every lease will be for 12 months or longer. The Wests will permit a tenant to renew the lease as provided in the form they have been using. However, they have in mind one tenant who was delinquent in paying rent and continuously played his radio so loudly that it disturbed the neighbors. When he asked to renew, the Wests refused. They want the lease to make it clear that they may refuse to renew under these circumstances. Also, they want notice from a tenant one month ahead of termination if the tenant wants to renew.

Rent is due on the first day of each month. The rental amount varies from one parcel of property to another. One of their biggest problems has been getting rent on time. Instead of a flat amount for a late charge, they want to charge 1% of the rent each day the rent is late.

The tenants are to pay for all utilities. The Wests once had an argument with a tenant over whether a monthly mosquito control charge was a utility. The city imposed it after the tenant moved in. The Wests ended up paying that charge and don't want it to happen again.

According to the Wests, the biggest help in avoiding problems has been requiring the first and last months' rent plus a security deposit in advance. They prefer having rent mailed to them rather than collecting it in person.

Sometimes a tenant gives them a bad check. Then they have to pay the bank a $20 service charge. They would like not to have to bear that expense.

Tenants can have pets but only on specific written approval. Depending on the pet, there may be a deposit. In the past, the Wests have not charged a deposit for gold fish and a caged canary because they did not expect these pets to cause damage. They expect to charge a deposit for all dogs and cats. The amount will vary depending on the Wests' estimate of both the animal and the tenant.

Tenants are responsible for maintaining the yard. The Wests have had a problem with tenants littering with paper, cans, and bottles, especially on weekends. They have also had a problem with tenants breaking window panes and knocking out screens without replacing them. One tenant persistently left the Wests' garbage can out by the road where it could blow away or get stolen easily.

The Wests have found that it is to their advantage for them to make repairs rather than to require tenants to do so. However, they want tenants to replace air conditioning and furnace filters and provide for extermination of roaches. The tenants are also responsible for keeping the property clean and in good order.

The Wests will hold all security deposits in a non-interest bearing account at Reliable Bank and Trust, 3600 Main Street. The Wests want to incorporate in the lease any notices a landlord is required to give to a tenant about the security deposit. The security deposit will be the same amount as one month's rent.

The Wests want to prohibit waterbeds. The garage apartment has already suffered serious damage when a tenant's waterbed sprang a leak while the tenant was out of town one weekend.

Sometimes tenants do not park in their designated parking areas. One tenant frequently parked so as to block the adjacent tenant's parking space. Another tenant charged money for cars to park on the lawn during a nearby high school football game.

The Wests want to make sure that anyone who rents the detached garage does not use it for any business purpose. The zoning laws prohibit business use of any of the Wests' properties.

They have had the following additional problems: A tenant moved out and took a ceiling fan with him. Another tenant painted the living room walls orange and blue without permission. Another tenant decorated the refrigerator and the front of the kitchen cabinets with adhesive paper. Another tenant took the doors off the kitchen cabinets and did not put them back on at the end of the lease term. The Wests found some of the cabinet doors stacked in a closet. They never found the rest of them.

Finally, the Wests noticed that several tenants had frequent overnight guests, and they do not want to allow this. One tenant asked permission to have a roommate temporarily, but the roommate became a permanent fixture.

The Wests say that you can regard as applicable to their rental property any information in the existing form lease that is consistent with the information above.

Introduction to Drafting a Residential Lease

A real estate lease is both a conveyance of land and a contract. Because it conveys an interest in land, its contents have traditionally been somewhat formal and expressed in technical language. Relatively little content in a real estate lease is legally required to be there. The only essential parts are:

(1) the names of the parties,

(2) a description of the leased property,

(3) language showing the landlord intends to divest himself or herself of possession and the proposed tenant intends to come into possession,

(4) the duration of the lease, and

(5) the rental amount.

The law of landlord and tenant supplies for the parties the rights and obligations they do not expressly cover in the lease. For example, implied covenants or obligations arise by operation of law, such as the landlord's covenant of quiet enjoyment and the tenant's obligation to treat the leased property in such a way that no injury is done to it. Because the lease is a contract, the parties may add other terms and alter the basic principles of landlord and tenant law so long as the new terms are not illegal and do not contravene public policy.

Many states have enacted residential landlord-tenant statutes as remedial legislation to spell out the rights and duties of landlords and tenants, and partly to protect tenants against unconscionable rental agreements. These statutes codify many aspects of the residential landlord-tenant relationship. At the same time they substitute modern contractual principles for archaic conveyancing concepts.

Residential leases are traditionally drafted by the landlord, the party with the business interest in the transaction. Unlike other forms of consumer contract, there have been few form leases devised by landlord groups. As a result, relatively few form leases prepared by trade associations or legal printers are in use in any given area. Because the provisions of a residential lease are almost never negotiated between contracting parties, and instead the tenant must either "take it or leave it," landlords have a broad range of substantive and stylistic choices. A lawyer drafting for the landlord should consider the following questions:

1. In addition to the essential parts of the lease, what should be included?

  a. Should anything from the statutes be included? For example, should consumer protections afforded by law be included?

  b. Should rules for the tenants' behavior be included to protect the landlord?

2. What is the appropriate style?

3. What should be emphasized and how? [14]

Drafting Assignment 4.E—Construction Contract

Your client is Martha Isley, a local contractor doing business as Waccamaw Construction Company, a sole proprietorship. Waccamaw's address is 215 South East Boulevard. Isley was in the construction business for three years in South Carolina before moving to your city. She used a construction contract inherited along with the company from her grandfather. She has the contract language on a computer disk, and she changes the particulars for each new job. The original contract follows.

The Original Waccamaw Contract

1   A CONSTRUCTION AGREEMENT

2   This agreement, made and entered into This 26th Day of
3   February, 1968, by and between Anthony C. Carnaggio and Eulee C.
4   Carnaggio hereinafter called the Owners, and Waccamaw Construc-
5   tion Company by Gylet Lewis hereinafter called the Contractor.

6   Witnesseth:

7   Whereas, the said Anthony C. Carnaggio and Eulee C. Carnag-
8   gio are the Owners of property located in Horry County described as
9   the, Lot Four (4), Block Eighty-two (82) of Tilghman Estates, Ocean
10 Drive Beach, South Carolina.

14. For a comparative analysis of two methods of revising a lease into plain language, see A. Siegel and D. Glascoff, Jr., Case History: Simplifying an Apartment Lease, ch. 4, Drafting Documents in Plain Language 169 (1981) (course handbook of the Practicing Law Institute).

11 and

12   Whereas it is the desire of the parties to this agreement to enter
13 into an arrangement under which the Contractor will build for the
14 Owners a Residence on said property in accordance with certain
15 plans and specifications attached to this agreement, and incorporat-
16 ed herein by reference, said Residence to be paid for by the Owners
17 in accordance with the terms of this agreement. Both the agree-
18 ment and plans must be read together and not as separate agree-
19 ments.

20   The purpose of this paragraph is merely to set forth the intent
21 of both parties and purpose of the contract; the following numbered
22 paragraphs are the mutual promises between the parties. The
23 courts look to the intent as well as the specific terms agreed upon
24 therefore, if an important part of the agreement is omitted in the
25 numbered paragraphs but mentioned above in the paragraph enti-
26 tled "whereas" it would be sufficient to bind the parties to the
27 agreement.

28   Now, therefore, in consideration of the mutual promises of the
29 parties as set forth hereinbelow and in consideration of the agree-
30 ment of the Contractor to build a Residence aforesaid together with
31 the promise of the Owners to pay for same in accordance with the
32 terms of this agreement, it is mutually agreed as follows:

33   1. Contractor agrees to build a residence as described in the
34 plans and specifications attached hereto and made a part hereof on
35 the property belonging to the Owners hereinabove described in
36 accordance with the said plans and specifications, and further, the
37 contractor agrees to provide all of the labor and materials and to
38 perform, or to cause to be performed, all work necessary for the
39 proper construction and completion of the said residence in conform-
40 ity with the said plans and specifications, including all conditions
41 thereof and also in conformity with the building and zoning laws
42 and regulations of the Town of Ocean Drive Beach, State of South
43 Carolina. It is mutually agreed that all subcontractors work and
44 materials, except as otherwise hereafter agreed in writing between
45 these parties, shall be purchased and handled through the office of
46 the contractor and shall be performed under the direction and
47 supervision of the contractor, subject to the approval of the Building
48 Inspector of the Town of Ocean Drive Beach, S.C. The contractor
49 shall furnish all tools and equipment necessary for the purpose of
50 the performance of the work at his own expense. It is agreed that
51 the selection of any subcontractor shall not create an agency rela-
52 tionship between the Owners and said subcontractors, but that the
53 Owners shall have no control over the selection of said subcontrac-
54 tors.

55   2. It is further agreed that all work in connection with the
56 erection of the residence shall be carried on with all possible speed
57 consistent with reasonable cost, good workmanship and safety of

58 construction, and it is further agreed that the erection of the said
59 building shall progress continuously except for strikes, lockouts,
60 delay in delivery of materials, acts of God or other delays beyond
61 control of the contractor. The contractor agrees to commence the
62 Performance of the work immediately, and to be completed by
63 approximately July 15, 1968.

64   3. In consideration of the performance by the said contractor
65 of all of the covenants and conditions contained in this agreement
66 and contained in the plans and specifications the owners agree to
67 pay the contractor an amount equal to the amount of the material
68 furnished by the contractor and the labor furnished by the contrac-
69 tor together with payroll taxes and Insurance, also together with
70 the sum total of the net amount due the subcontractors performing
71 work or furnishing work for said construction. The Owners also
72 agree to pay to the contractor, in addition to the amount specified
73 hereinabove, a fee equal to 10% of the actual cost of the said
74 residence, said fee to be paid after completion of said residence and
75 acceptance thereof by the Owners. It is specifically agreed by and
76 between the parties that notwithstanding the agreement herein-
77 above by the owners shall not be required, under the terms of this
78 agreement, to pay to the contractor any amount in excess of the
79 sum of Thirty–Four Thousand, Five Hundred Dollars ($34,500.00)
80 which is the estimated cost of construction, plus the fee provided for
81 herein.

82   4. It is further agreed by and between the parties that the
83 payment constituting the satisfaction of the Owners obligation un-
84 der the terms of this agreement shall be made in the following
85 manner:

86   a. That the owner shall pay to the contractor at the time of
87 the signing of this agreement the sum of $3,000.00.

88   b. That from time to time, and not more frequently than once
89 each month, except in case of an emergency, the contractor shall
90 submit to the owners proper invoices or delivery tickets covering
91 labor, material or subcontract work performed in the construction of
92 the improvements on the property.

93   c. That upon receipt of the invoices or bills hereabove referred
94 to, the owners will cause same to be paid into the hands of the
95 persons furnishing labor, materials or subcontracting services; that
96 the owners shall not pay any invoice or bill for labor, materials or
97 subcontracting services without the approval of the contractor.

98   5. It is further mutually agreed by and between the parties
99 that neither party will make any change or deviation from the plans
100 and specifications set forth as Exhibit "A" attached hereto; it is
101 further agreed that should both parties agree to a change in the
102 plans and specifications, then there shall be executed an agreement
103 supplemental to this agreement setting forth the change to be made
104 and the amount of addition to or subtraction from the contract

105 price; it is further mutually agreed that should some change agreed
106 upon orally and be incorporated into the work called for under the
107 terms of this agreement, that such oral agreement shall not consti-
108 tute a waiver of the provisions of this paragraph by either or both
109 parties and notwithstanding such oral agreement, no additional cost
110 resulting from the performance of the work shall be added to the
111 contract price nor shall any savings resulting from the performance
112 of said change be deducted from the contract price.

113   6. It is further agreed that the contractor will carry adequate
114 Workmen's Compensation and Unemployment Compensation Insur-
115 ance for all the employees to be employed upon the job and the
116 contractor shall also carry public liability and property damage
117 Insurance. The contractor shall also carry Builder's Risk Insurance
118 in an amount at least equal to the estimated price as set forth in
119 paragraph 3 hereinabove. In case of loss, it is agreed that the
120 proceeds of all such risk insurance shall be used to restore and
121 replace any property damaged or destroyed, and it is especially
122 agreed that the contractor shall not be held responsible for or liable
123 for any loss, damage or delay caused by fire, cyclone, strikes,
124 lockouts, civil commotion, nor shall any loss or damage be charged
125 as a part of the work called for under the terms of this agreement.

126   This Agreement shall be binding on the parties hereto, their
127 assigns, successors, representatives or administrators.

128   Three (3) Exhibits.

129   WACCAMAW CONST. CO.

130   GYLET LEWIS

131   Contractor

132 JOHN JENRETTE, JR.

133   Witness

134   ANTHONY C. CARNAGGIO

135   Owner

136   EULEE C. CARNAGGIO

137   Owner

138 JOHN JENRETTE, JR.

139   Witness

Isley has asked you to redraft the contract to accomplish the following:

1. Avoid any ambiguity respecting the contract price.

2. Give her as much protection as possible against liability for damages due to construction delays.

3. Try to prevent interference by property owners in the construction process, either through late payments to subcontractors or unauthorized changes.

4. Adapt the contract to her next construction job, according to the following facts.

――――――

Facts for Isley's New Contract

The property owners are Patricia McMillan and I.J. Reilly, two dentists who want Isley to build an office for them. Isley and the dentists reached their agreement last Friday. They have an appointment to sign the contract next Friday. They will bring to the appointment a copy of the legal description of the property. The street address is 450 Sutter Lane in your city. The estimated date of completion is three months to the day from next Friday. The estimated cost of construction is $134,500. The owners are to pay a down-payment of $13,000 at the time they sign the contract. Isley says you can regard as applicable to the new contract any information in the original Waccamaw contract that is consistent with the information in this paragraph.

――――――

Isley's Problems on the Mulliner Project

Isley used the old Waccamaw contract without significant problems until a year ago, when she undertook to build an office for Dr. Carl Mulliner. In the past, all of her construction projects had been houses.

The cost of constructing the office was $240,800. According to her understanding of the agreement, Isley claimed that Mulliner owed her a total of $248,580. In an action in which she attempted to establish and enforce a lien for the balance due on the agreement, the trial court construed it as entitling her to only $234,500. The court found that $134,500 was a reasonable estimated price and that additional costs incurred in making changes in the project were part of the "actual cost" of construction. Moreover, the court awarded Mulliner damages of $13,950 for construction delays. Isley completed construction March 15 of last year, nearly nine months later than estimated. Isley has fired her trial lawyer and hired you to represent her on appeal (not part of this assignment). She also wants you to redraft her contract so as to avoid similar results in the future.

What happened with Mulliner was essentially as follows:

Their agreed estimated date of completion was the previous July 1. However, Isley encountered an initial two-month delay in obtaining a building permit. Then early in the construction, rain storms prevented the work from going forward on schedule.

On October 1 Mulliner ordered her to accelerate construction. However, he subsequently began asking her to make various alterations, invariably after the work had been completed. He was constantly turning up at the site with suggestions and complaints.

A central feature of the office was the "lab." The contract specifications called for a system of built-in cabinets. After these had been installed, Mulliner called them "shoddy" and announced that he wanted them ripped out and replaced with a certain substantially more expensive brand. After waiting several weeks for the replacement cabinets to come in, Isley finally called the manufacturer and learned that the line of cabinets she had ordered had been discontinued. When she called Mulliner to discuss the problem, he was on vacation and unavailable for three weeks. Under orders to accelerate, she decided to consult the interior designer who had been advising Mulliner. The designer recommended that she order similar cabinets manufactured by another company. They cost more, but Isley ordered and installed them.

Mulliner refused to pay the additional cost and berated her for making the decision without consulting him. Although the new cabinets were similar in appearance to the ones he had selected, there were only three drawers in each cabinet instead of four. According to Mulliner, efficient operation of the lab depended upon having four. In the end, Isley had to tear the cabinets out, absorb the additional cost, and order a new set. The replacement cabinets plus the additional labor cost an additional $3,000. Isley and Mulliner executed a supplemental agreement covering the cost of labor and materials for the replacement cabinets.

Mulliner also demanded that Isley replace "hollow-core" doors with "solid-core," increasing the cost by $900. There was no written agreement covering the doors; in fact, Mulliner made all arrangements with one of the subcontractors and Isley did not learn of the change until the work was completed.

After the consulting rooms and reception area were substantially complete, Mulliner decided that the intercom system was not adequate and required Isley to replace it with a more expensive system. The parties executed a supplemental agreement covering the cost of installation, $1,000. They neglected to mention the $1,000 increase in the cost of materials.

While one of the subcontracting firms was in the process of painting the interior, Isley discovered that one of her employees had inadvertently ordered the wrong brand and color of paint. Additional labor and materials to correct the mistake cost Isley $400. She absorbed the cost of correcting her employee's mistake.

Isley was also plagued by labor problems and vandalism. She became involved in disputes with the subcontracting firms she had engaged to install the plumbing and lay the asphalt for the parking lots. These disputes substantially delayed the project. The night after the sinks were installed, vandals broke in and tore them out. They also smashed several windows. Isley's insurance paid for the damage.

Long before construction was complete, Mulliner was threatening to sue Isley for breach of contract. In the end, he refused to pay her more than what he claimed was the contract price of $134,500. However, when she sued him for the balance, he counterclaimed for damages due to delay. Because he could not get into the new building, he had to continue paying $1000 a month for his downtown office and an additional $50 a month for parking. He also had to pay an additional receptionist he had hired in anticipation of an expanded practice and $500 a month to store new furniture and equipment he had ordered for his new office.

————

A Note on the Special Problem of Delay in Construction Contracts

Delay is a common problem in the performance of construction contracts. Owners want to claim damages when the contractor does not finish on time. Likewise contractors suffer a loss when the owners' interference or lack of cooperation causes delay. How either party's delay claim fares in court depends heavily on what if anything their contract says about who bears the loss in case of delay.

The lawyer who drafts for the contractor needs to think about both of these matters in respect to the possibility of delay:

(1) protecting the contractor against the owner's claim for damages if, for reasons beyond the contractor's control, the contractor finishes late, and

(2) protecting the contractor against loss if the owner causes delay.

If the contract is silent about what events will excuse nonperformance or late performance, courts may look to the common law of impossibility or to the Uniform Commercial Code on impracticability. But it is often to the parties' advantage—or to the advantage of the contractor as drafting party—to address in the contract the possibility of delay.

Here are some drafting devices for limiting liability for delay:

1. "Best Efforts" Provisions

The contractor may promise only to use "best efforts" or "reasonable efforts" to complete on or before a certain date instead of promising to complete on or before that date. In particular, a contractor may want to avoid such language as: "Contractor warrants that construction will be completed by January 15, 1992." Such language may be held to mean that the warrantor assumes the entire risk of failure to perform on time, with no excuses. In other words, the warrantor becomes indemnifier as well and forgoes excuse.

2. Liquidated Damages Provisions

The contract may include a liquidated damage provision to limit the owner's remedy if the contractor does not complete on time. The owner might, of course, insist that such a provision also limit the contractor's remedy for any delay caused by the owner.

Beware of the potential for contradiction if the contract includes both a liquidated damages provision and a "no damages for delay" provision. A party cannot be entitled to liquidated damages and no damages under the same circumstances. It is possible to have no damages under certain circumstances and liquidated damages under other circumstances, but the contract needs to clarify when each of the distinct provisions applies.

3. *Force Majeure* Provisions

Force majeure provisions list the extraordinary circumstances, such as "acts of God" for which they are named, that provide excuses for delay. Events that sometimes provide excuse are natural catastrophes ("acts of God") such as fire or flood, government actions, labor problems, or transportation problems. A war abroad or domestic economic problems may affect prices or delivery dates.

The doctrine supporting these provisions is expressed in § 261 of the Restatement (Second) of Contracts:

> **Discharge by Supervening Impracticability.** Where, after a contract is made, a party's performance is made impracticable without his fault by the occurrence of an event the non-occurrence of which was a basic assumption on which the contract was made, his duty to render that performance is discharged, unless the language or the circumstances indicate the contrary.

Force majeure provisions are commonly called "no damage for delay" provisions. Courts often uphold them so long as they are reasonable. Such a provision is most usually validated if it is:

(1) specific enough to relate to the particular kind of project that is the subject of the contract,

(2) comprehensive enough to cover various causes of delay and various forms of damage,

(3) unambiguous, and

(4) clear.[15]

It is to the contractor's advantage that the provision can be broad in its coverage and still not considered ambiguous.[16] In fact, too much particular detail without sufficient broadening language to accompany it is dangerous. The drafter is wise, however, to anticipate and be explicit about any particular kind of delay that may be peculiar to the project. A contract that mentioned late delivery of steel was held not to cover delay because of defective steel.[17] With this case in mind, think about other possibilities.

If the building department in your county is slow in granting permits, that is worth mentioning. If there is a known archeological interest in the

15. See Ace Stone, Inc. v. Wayne Tp., 47 N.J. 431, 221 A.2d 515 (1966).

16. See Western Engineers, Inc. v. Utah, 20 Utah 2d 294, 437 P.2d 216–218 (1968).

17. Southeastern Builders, Inc. of Alabama v. Joe Brashears Steel, Inc., 336 So. 2d 1228, 1228–29 (Fla.App.1976).

site or other subsurface condition that might result in delays, that is worth mentioning.[18] If your provision refers specifically and exclusively to contractual liability, it might be held not to cover tort liability.[19]

4. References to Remedies

Beware also of unintentionally limiting the contractor's possibilities for collecting damages from the owner. A contractor who claimed over $40,000 in delay damages caused by the architect's errors and interference, was unable to recover delay damages from an owner after agreeing to the provision below because it provided for extension of time as the exclusive remedy:

> The Contractor shall not be entitled to any claim for damages on account of hindrances or delays from any cause whatsoever, but if occasioned by any act of God, or by any act or omission on the part of the Owner, such act, hindrance, or delay may entitle the Contractor to an extension of time in which to complete the work which shall be determined by the Architect, provided that the Contractor will give notice in writing of the cause of such act, hindrance, or delay within ten days (10 days) after its occurrence.[20]

Surely the owner took an atypically active role in drafting that contract. The lesson of the case for the contractor is that while extension of time is one remedy worth mentioning, it should not be referred to as the exclusive one.

Just as it is dangerous to be too narrow in reference to the remedies available to the contractor, it is important to be specific enough in reference to the kinds of damages that the owner cannot claim from the contractor, such as loss of profits, loss of use, overhead expenses for home office and rental of equipment.[21]

Finally, remember that the aim of a well drafted delay clause is not merely to provide a defense when the owner sues the contractor for delay damages but, better yet, to deter the owner (1) from asserting a delay claim in the first place, and also (2) from causing delay.[22]

Drafting Assignment 4.F—Service Contract

Your client is Juan Aguilar, the President of Security Services, Inc., which does business as Security on the Spot ("SOS"). The company sells and services burglar and fire alarm systems throughout your county. The corporate office is at 9999 High Street in your city. In the

18. Lesser, The "No Damage for Delay" Clause: Avoiding Delay Claims in Construction, Oct. 12, 1987 Ohio State Bar Assn. Report 1578, 1584.

19. Id. at 1586.

20. Ericksen v. Edmonds School District No. 15, 13 Wash.2d 398, 405, 125 P.2d 275, 278 (1942).

21. Lesser, above note 18, at 1586.

22. For discussion of *force majeure* clauses in contracts generally, see Burnham, *Force Majeure*, ch. 9, above note 3, at 93. For background on other construction contract provisions as well as delay provisions, see generally S. Siegfried, Introduction to Construction Law (1987).

same building is the central monitoring station for alarm systems serviced by SOS.

When SOS went into business, it sold and serviced alarm systems exclusively for commercial properties. Recently, however, in response to wide consumer demand, SOS expanded to serve residential properties as well.

Aguilar brings you a contract that a friend of his uses in the same kind of business. Aguilar would like you to adapt it for him to use in his business. However, he is not entirely satisfied with his friend's contract. He would like you to redraft it to attend to the following matters:

1. The contract deals only with commercial properties. Redraft to make it useable with both commercial and residential properties.

2. Aguilar has found that residential clients often don't understand contracts, and that leads to disputes. Redraft to make the contract unambiguous and easy to understand.

3. There is an ordinance in your county on alarm systems. (It appears at p. 185.) Redraft the contract as needed to bring it into compliance with the ordinance and also to put SOS in as favorable a position as possible with clients who are under the jurisdiction of the ordinance.

4. SOS has had some problems in the past. Redraft Aguilar's friend's contract to reflect the information below and to help prevent problems in the future.

Facts for the SOS Contract

Aguilar tells you he has had a lot of trouble with late payments of monthly service fees. He would like to institute a late charge, but is not sure how to make it both easy to administer and successful as a deterrent. He would like you to add provisions to accomplish his intention.

Aguilar reports that a number of clients appear surprised and angry at being expected to pay for anything after they give notice that they don't want to renew the contract. He wants you to clarify the renewal terms and the consequences of notice of cancellation.

Aguilar wants to be sure there is no confusion about the right to cancel. SOS should be free to cancel on account of any damage to the system that makes it impracticable to continue service, no matter what causes the damage.

Aguilar wants to make sure SOS is as fully protected as possible against liability for interruptions in service and especially for a client's losses due to burglary.

Aguilar has had trouble from several clients who were furious with SOS when the Sheriff's Department charged them a fee for false alarms. Those clients had not called SOS to inspect their systems for malfunction after previously having a false alarm. Aguilar would like you to figure out a way to use the contract to put clients on notice of the alarm ordinance if they are under its jurisdiction, and to treat as a breach of the contract any failure to have SOS inspect and repair the system after a false alarm.

Aguilar tells you that the alarm ordinance has meant nothing but trouble for him. On occasion, he has called the Sheriff's Department to let them know that he was going to be testing a client's system and that they should disregard a signal in the next 15 minutes, but they have still sent deputies out and then charged the client for a false alarm.

On occasion lightening has set off an alarm. Sometimes the radio waves from two-way car radios set off alarms. When those things happen, no malfunction in the system causes the alarm. The client cannot help it, and SOS cannot help it. Yet under the ordinance the client has had a false alarm. Aguilar hopes you will be able to use his contract to put the client on notice of such realistic possibilities and thus direct the client's anger away from SOS.

Aguilar's Friend's Contract

CENTRALLY MONITORED SERVICE AGREEMENT

1 This agreement made and entered into as of the _____ day of
2 _____ 19__ by and between Modern Services Corporation (herein-
3 after referred to as N.S.I.), an Indiana Corporation, and _____
4 referred to as Client.

5 N.S.I. wants to provide monitored alarm services to Client and
6 Client needs said services to protect its building known as _____
7 located at _____

8 Now, therefore, it is mutually agreed by and between the parties as
9 follows:

10 TERM
11 The initial term of this agreement shall be for one year, beginning
12 _____ and ending on _____.

13 PAYMENTS
14 Client agrees to pay N.S.I. a monthly service fee of $_____
15 payable in advance on the first day of each month.

16 Client shall send all payments provided for herein to the following
17 address: National Security & Investigation, 131 Clark Street, Indi-
18 anapolis, IN 46204.

RENEWAL

After the initial term, this agreement shall automatically renew itself from year to year unless either party shall give written notice of cancellation at least thirty (30) days prior to the date of termination of an annual period. Such termination shall be without penalty provided the Client shall pay any unpaid balance of the agreed advance service or installation charge and any other charge accrued hereunder but unpaid for service rendered prior to such termination. Any payment made for service to be supplied subsequent to the date of such termination shall be refunded to the Client.

SECURITY SYSTEM

N.S.I. agrees to maintain or cause to be maintained, during the term of this agreement, in the premises of the Client, equipment, and devices to provide a centrally monitored system necessary to transmit signals from the premises of the Client to the Central Monitoring Station, and will, subject to the terms and conditions hereof, until termination of the agreement, maintain such equipment, and devices and other materials connected therewith, will remain the personal property of N.S.I.

DESCRIPTION OF EQUIPMENT

_____

_____

_____

ACCESS TO PREMISES

If the alarm is monitored at the Central Monitoring Station N.S.I. agrees upon receipt of a signal indicating the unauthorized entry of Client's premises to transmit notice of signal to the municiple police department. Client agrees to furnish N.S.I. a list of the names and individual signatures of all persons who shall have the right to enter the premises of the Client between the regularly scheduled times for opening and closing the premises and who may be called upon for a key to enter the premises of the Client during such periods.

MAINTAINING, TESTING AND INSPECTION

The Client hereby authorizes and empowers N.S.I., its agents or assigns, to maintain the aforesaid system in said premises and to inspect, test and repair the system, and further, to make any changes in or alterations to the system made at the request of the Client or made necessary by any changes in the Client's premises, property, or equipment after the original installation has been completed, at the cost of the Client upon receiving the written consent of the Client. The Client agrees to furnish any necessary electric current through the Client's meter and at the Client's own

62 expense. It is mutually agreed that the work of N.S.I.'s periodic
63 inspections and tests of the system shall be performed between the
64 hours of 8:00 o'clock A.M. and 5:00 o'clock P.M., exclusive of
65 Saturdays, Sundays, and holidays.

66 OWNERSHIP OF MONITORING EQUIPMENT UPON TERMINA-
67   TION OF AGREEMENT

68 It is understood and agreed that N.S.I. may remove or upon written
69 notice to the Client, abandon in whole or part, all devices, instru-
70 ments, appliances, cabinets, and other materials associated with the
71 system, upon termination of this agreement, without obligation to
72 repair or redecorate any portion of the Client's premises upon such
73 removal, and that the removal or abandonment of such materials
74 shall not be held to constitute a waiver of the right of N.S.I. to
75 collect any charges which may have been accrued or may be accrued
76 hereunder.

77 CANCELLATION OF AGREEMENT BY N.S.I.

78 This agreement may be cancelled, without previous notice, at the
79 option of N.S.I., in case the Central Station, connecting wires or
80 equipment within the Client's premises are destroyed by fire or
81 other catastrophe, or so substantially damaged that it is impractica-
82 ble to continue service, and may likewise be cancelled at the option
83 of the Client, in the event that the Client's plant is so destroyed or
84 damaged. Any advance payments made for service to be supplied
85 subsequent to the date of such termination shall be refunded to the
86 Client.

87 This agreement may be terminated at the option of N.S.I. at any
88 time in the event that N.S.I. is unable to secure or retain the
89 connections or privileges necessary for the transmission of signals
90 by means of conductors between the Client's premises and the
91 Central Station or between the Central Station and the municiple
92 police department and N.S.I. shall not be liable for any damages or
93 subject to any penalty as a result of such termination. Any advance
94 payments made for service to be supplied subsequent to the date of
95 such termination shall be refunded to the Client.

96 MAINTENANCE AND REPAIR OF CLIENT'S PROPERTY

97 It is understood and agreed that N.S.I.'s obligation relates to the
98 maintenance solely of the specified protective signaling system, and
99 that N.S.I. is in no way obligated to maintain, repair, service,
100 replace, operate or assure that operation of the property, system or
101 any device or devices of the Client or of others to which N.S.I.'s said
102 systems are attached unless N.S.I., its agents or employees have
103 damaged property, system or device of Client or others necessitating
104 repair or replacement.

105 DELAYS OR INTERRUPTIONS IN SERVICE

106 N.S.I. assumes no liability for interruptions of service due to strikes,
107 riots, floods, fires, or acts of God and will not be required to supply
108 service to the Client while interruption of service due to any such
109 cause shall continue; however, if an interruption in service not
110 caused by Client continues for more than thirty (30) days regardless
111 of the cause of such interruption, Client, at its option may cancel
112 this agreement without previous notice.

113 Client will be given a pro rata reduction in the monthly service fee
114 for any interruptions in service not caused by Client which last for
115 more than twenty-four (24) hours.

116 N.S.I. agrees to notify Client of any interruption in service and to
117 furnish Client at Client's request and expense with a security guard
118 for the time period during which the interruption lasts.

119 LIABILITY

120 IT IS AGREED BY AND BETWEEN THE PARTIES HERETO
121 THAT N.S.I. IS NOT AN INSURER. Insurance shall be obtained
122 by the Client. Amounts payable to N.S.I. hereunder are based on
123 the value of the services and the scope of liability as herein set
124 forth; that from the nature of the services rendered, it is impracti-
125 cal, if not impossible to fix the actual damages, if any, which may
126 proximately result from a failure on the part of N.S.I. to perform
127 any of its obligations hereunder; that if N.S.I. should be found liable
128 for loss or damage due to a failure of its services in any respect, its
129 liability shall be limited to a sum equal to ten percent of the annual
130 service charge for the above described premises or $250.00 whichev-
131 er is greater. This liability shall be exclusive. If Client desires
132 N.S.I. to assume a greater liability or responsibility than that set
133 forth herein to either Client or Client's insurance carrier by way of
134 subrogation, Client will make such requests in writing and N.S.I.
135 will quote an additional price.

136 ASSIGNMENT

137 This agreement is not assignable by either party except upon the
138 written consent of the other party first being obtained.

139 WARRANTIES AND AMENDMENTS

140 It is mutually understood and agreed that any representation,
141 promise, condition, inducement or warranty, express or implied, not
142 included in writing in this agreement shall not be binding upon any
143 party and that this agreement may not be altered, modified, or
144 otherwise changed at any time except with the written consent of

145 each of the parties hereto, and in the form of an addendum to this
146 agreement.

147 COMPANY NAME _____

148 SIGNED _____

149 TITLE _____

150 REPRESENTED BY: MODERN SERVICES
151   CORPORATION

152   d/b/a NATIONAL SECURITY
153   & INVESTIGATION

154 SIGNED _____

155 TITLE _____ 23

23. Reprinted from Materials on Legal   1981 with permission of West Publishing
Drafting by Reed Dickerson, copyright ©   Company.

Chapter 5

LEGISLATION

Table of Sections

I. PUBLIC AND PRIVATE LEGISLATION

A. VARIETIES AND SIMILARITIES

"Legislation" is most commonly thought to mean public legislation: constitutions, statutes, ordinances, and regulations. One textbook on government processes illustrates how varied are the sources of public pronouncements that "make law." In an exercise, the authors ask students to try to name the originating institutions of several unidentified quotations. The documents are subsequently identified as an NLRB opinion, a Presidential executive order, a state highway department directive, a disciplinary rule from the ABA Code of Professional Responsibility, a letter from a U.S. President to a member of the

Federal Trade Commission, a resolution of a state legislature, an act of a state legislature, and a state supreme court rule.[1]

Legislation, however, may be private as well, such as corporate by-laws or covenants and restrictions for a condominium or a subdivision. In a sense, contracts, wills, and trusts also legislate. From the perspective of drafting, an Act of Congress and a two-party residential lease are the same kind of document. "Whether a document is simple or complicated, it creates, when executed, law not only for the parties but those who are bound by or rely on it."[2] It is not surprising then that when Professor Dickerson revised his classic treatise, *Legislative Drafting*,[3] he incorporated it into *The Fundamentals of Legal Drafting*,[4] thereby emphasizing that most of legal drafting is actually legislative. Here is another writer's musing on how pervasive private legislation is:

> * * * The Congress in Washington and the legislatures in the state capitals pass laws. The administrative agencies turn out regulations. The courts hand down judicial decisions and opinions. We forget, even the lawyers themselves forget, that it is the lawyers in their offices who make the bulk of our law.
>
> I spent this morning working on a draft of an agreement for the publication of cheap paper-bound books. The signature of an author and a publisher would turn that agreement into law. This afternoon I watched a client execute a codicil to his will. After he had signed I took the pen. I took it, because it was my own. But if it had been his, he might well have given it to me as a governor might give me the quill with which he had signed a statute which I had drafted. For this codicil was none the less a part of our law. This evening I read the announcement in the afternoon paper of a new bond issue. I recognized one which three of my partners had been working on, drawing the mortgage which secured it and the agreement under which it was to be underwritten and sold. This was law for everyone who bought or sold those bonds.
>
> Where two or three, or more, are gathered together in contract, they set up a small momentary sovereignty of their own. There is nothing fanciful about this. A contract is a little code for a special occasion. A lease is a little statute for your tenancy of a house you have neither built nor bought. Partnership articles or the charter and by-laws of a corporation are quite an elaborate code of law for those who are concerned. A corporate mortgage is a piece of legislation for a large and shifting population of bondholders, affecting, it is true, only a part of their lives, but affecting that part as completely as experienced and foresighted lawyers working late into the urban night can make it.
>
> * * *

1. H. Linde, G. Bunn, F. Paff, and W. Church, Legislative and Administrative Processes 1–4 (2d ed. 1981).

2. Robinson, Drafting—Its Substance and Teaching, 25 J. Legal Educ. 514, 528 (1973).

3. (1954).

4. (2d ed. 1986).

This private legislation has something of a life of its own, irrespective of legislatures and courts. For one thing, most of it looks for its enforcement to that posse of social fears, private prides, and economic pressures which we are likely to call good faith, and which is just as powerful as the expectation of compulsion. And the more the lawyer who drafts a document anticipates enforcement by the law, the more he prevents it; and the more it takes the place of law. For the very purpose of the document is to avoid recourse to the courts. * * *

This is law which the parties make for their own small domain. As a matter of fact, much of it becomes law for others as well, by imitation. An agreement proves satisfactory. It is not copyrighted. Unlike the latest song, you can copy it for free. It may even get into a law book, and acquire the authority of print, or even of precedent. Other lawyers use it, as we all use any device that saves us time, thought, or the burden of unconventionality. Originality is a vice in this branch of literature. Any substantial change would incur responsibility as well as tempt litigation. Finally it becomes as established in our law as a folk song in our literature, and in strictly the same way. A book of legal forms is the legal cousin of an anthology of popular ballads.[5]

B. LEGISLATIVE DRAFTING DISTINGUISHED FROM OTHER LEGAL WRITING

In a sense then, all of the material in Part Two of this book is about legislative drafting, "preventive law." As such, it should be distinguished from the other forms of writing that commonly engage lawyer's expertise. In briefs, memoranda, and letters, lawyers explain their analysis of legal materials and try to persuade someone to think or behave in a certain way. In fact, the study of this kind of writing is largely a study of the strategy of persuasion, complete with attention to effective appeals to emotion.

In contrast, legislative drafting, whether public or private, is completely free from emotional content or "sales pitch." It is instead descriptive and prescriptive. The drafter has no need to convince anybody of anything. Instead the drafter describes a particular world, large or small, and either prescribes future behavior in that world or describes the consequences of anticipated behavior.

Legislative document drafting also differs from memorandum and brief writing in that memoranda and briefs usually focus on relatively few points or issues with sometimes extensive text devoted to each one. In document drafting, each sentence expresses one or more provisions, each with its own separate significance. Moreover, the exact wording of each sentence matters to an extraordinary degree. Good legislative drafting differs significantly from good writing generally. "Bill drafting must have the accuracy of engineering, for it is law engineering; it

---

5. C. Curtis, It's Your Law 42–44 (1954). Copyright 1954 by The President and Fellows of Harvard College; 1982 by Henry W. Minot, Jr. Reprinted by permission of the publisher, Harvard University Press.

must have the detail and consistency of architecture, for it is law architecture." [6]

It is in this respect that statutes, ordinances, and private rule-making documents part company with contracts. In the realm of contracts, the negotiation process sometimes makes precision more trouble than it is worth.

> No matter how much time is allowed for the negotiation, there is never time enough to think every issue through in all its possible applications, and never ingenuity enough to anticipate all that does later show up. Since the parties earnestly strive to complete an agreement, there is almost irresistible pressure to find a verbal formula which is acceptable, even though its meaning to the two sides may in fact differ. The urge to make sure of real consensus or to clarify a felt ambiguity in the language tentatively accepted is at times repressed, lest the effort result in disagreement or in subsequent enforced consent to a clearer provision which is, however, less favorable to the party with the urge. With agreement reached as to known recurring situations, questions as to application to more difficult cases may be tiredly brushed aside on the theory that those cases will never—or hardly ever—arise.[7]

Whatever earnest good faith or crossed fingers allows contracting parties to settle for ambiguity or vagueness, they themselves are the ones mainly to suffer if they are mistaken. The more widely a rule applies beyond the drafting or executing parties, the heavier burden there is to be exact.

> Every written law which goes beyond mere regulation of details is a work of art; it can no more afford to dispense with unity of design and continuity of execution than a monumental building. It should proceed from one mind, or from very few minds working in intimate association, and it should be framed, if not by one hand, at least under uniform general directions and by hands trained in one school.[8]

C. THE PROFESSION OF LEGISLATIVE DRAFTING

If legislative drafting encompassed exclusively public legislation, this chapter would not exist. Our government's legislative bodies now generally employ staffs of professional drafters. They commonly have drafting manuals to spell out for them the exact parts, formats, styles, and sometimes language prescribed by state constitutions or statutes for the bills they draft. These staff drafters are taught mainly on the job. At their service are the Uniform Statutory Construction Act, state statutory construction acts, the Drafting Rules for Writing Uniform or Model Acts promulgated by the National Conference of Commissioners on Uniform State Laws, and state legislative drafting manuals. Profes-

---

6. D. Kennedy, Drafting Bills for the Minnesota Legislature 7 (1946).

7. Shulman, Reason, Contract and Law in Labor Relations, 68 Harv.L.Rev. 999, 1004 (1955). Copyright © 1955 by the Harvard Law Review Association.

8. Sir Frederick Pollock, quoted in Read, MacDonald, Fordham and Pierce's Materials on Legislation 235 (4th ed. 1982).

sional legislative drafters also have the services of the National Conference of State Legislatures, which conducts drafting seminars to hone the drafters' skills. In short, they do not learn their work in drafting courses in law schools. And most students who study drafting in law school are not preparing to work in a state legislative drafting office.

D. LEGISLATIVE DRAFTING IN PRIVATE PRACTICE

Yet drafting private legislation is such a pervasive part of the practicing lawyer's work that every lawyer needs to know the principles that are transferable from one legislative document to another. Moreover, many a lawyer in private practice becomes involved in the process of drafting public legislation. On behalf of a client, the lawyer may respond to a call for comments on proposed federal regulations,[9] which often amounts to proposing substitute language. On behalf of another client, the lawyer may tackle a local ordinance, either as challenger or as drafter.

When a lawyer in private practice takes an active role in drafting local ordinances, the benefits to that lawyer's practice can spread widely. For example, an expert on land-use regulations comments as follows on the benefits of a zoning ordinance that is easy to use:

> Because zoning regulations are consulted so regularly by so many, there is a real payoff in making them easier to use. This is particularly true for the telephone-book-size ordinances of larger cities or counties, which are especially complex. * * *

> An ordinance designed for ease of use can help planners improve their community relations. Users of the ordinance outside local government are more likely to have a good opinion of the zoning process if the ordinance is clear and they can consult it without difficulty.

> An ordinance that is easy to use can reduce the time planning staff must spend in responding to routine questions from petitioners. It can help simplify the jobs of elected or appointed officials who must refer to the ordinance during meetings. Newly elected or newly appointed officials can become familiar with the ordinance more quickly. And amending regulations becomes more manageable.[10]

II. THEORIES AND STRATEGIES

A. A THREE–STEP PROCESS

Drafting legislation involves considerable attention to process. It is a creative process, and its fruit is public policy. Professors Eskridge and Frickey write about statutes, but it is easy enough to apply their

---

9. For practical advice on drafting effective comments, see Ridgway, Burnley, Hitchcock, and O'Neill, Influencing the Substance of Agency Action, 5 Ad.L.J. 51 (1991).

10. J. Gann, Jr., How To Write an Easy–To–Use Zoning Ordinance, PAS Memo 1, 1, July 1986; reprinted with permission from the American Planning Association.

theory of statutory drafting to other forms of legislation as well. They invite us to view the process as one with three steps.

W. ESKRIDGE, JR. AND P. FRICKEY, OUR THEORY OF STATUTORY DRAFTING, CASES AND MATERIALS ON LEGISLATION

830–33 (1988).*

* * * It is not a linear process, for you will typically have to go back and rethink each step after completing the next one. And at each step in the process, it is most critical to understand the existing statutory framework (as interpreted by courts and agencies) very carefully. Drafting statutes, like interpreting them, should be informed by Justice Frankfurter's triplex admonition: Read the statute. Read the statute. Read the statute!

The first step is to determine what you want the proposed legislation to do. This involves a determination of your ideal objective and, then, any amelioration of that objective to maximize the chance that your bill will receive the legislative attention you desire. Most of the time, the objective of the drafting project will be given to the bill drafter by someone else—by a legislator to her personal or committee staff, by an agency or executive department official to the agency or departmental lawyers, by an organized lobbying group to its counsel or staff. But, also most of the time, the objective will be set forth in a general way. The first job of a thoughtful drafter is to explore the objective more thoroughly on both a conceptual and a political level.

To the extent that the drafter is part of the process by which options are explored and narrowed, the drafter must be sensitive to what is politically possible. * * *

Even if you can envision a potential committee majority for your bill, consider that if your bill is strongly offensive to a major interest group (e.g., employers, unions, civil rights groups) it will attract a lot of adverse lobbying. You may not be able to afford this sort of opposition, because it dampens the enthusiasm of the bill's probable supporters and frightens away potential supporters. How can you avoid this problem? * * * Here is where conceptual ingenuity often comes into play. You might explore the options with the person or group desiring this legislation. Would something largely symbolic be sufficient? If not, is there a compromise solution * * *? * * * (Of course, you may want to draft a very strong bill, with the expectation that it will be diluted as part of a compromise or logrolling process.)

The second step is to determine the structure of your proposed legislation. Once you have decided on the basic idea for your proposed legislation, you need to figure out what needs to be done to implement the idea. This is more than just devising a simple format for the bill

* * *. Since most proposed legislation operates in a framework created by or molded by existing statutes, the drafter needs to decide how to fit her proposal into the * * * code of laws. * * * Is there any provision * * * that should be repealed? What sections should be amended? Should whole new sections be added, and if so where? How much should be accomplished by explicit statutory language, and how much by subsequent lawmaking by [an agency] * * * or the courts?

* * *

The third step is to draft the bill, so that the language and organization are no more complicated than necessary, serve the object of the legislation without creating unnecessary problems, and are internally coherent and consistent with usages in the existing statute. The hardest step in our process is executing the concept and the organization developed in the first two steps. (We remind you that during the process of writing the language, you may think of problems with your concept or your organization. The conceptualization and organization of a draft statute are continuous processes.) * * * [T]here are three general precepts that are particularly important.

First, is Ockham's Razor: Create the narrowest possible statute that is clear and serves your purposes. Do not clutter up the statute with unnecessary verbiage. For example, do not say: "The Commission shall undertake a determination * * *." Instead, say: "The Commission shall determine * * *." Have a compelling justification for each provision. For example, do not establish a detailed procedural set-up unless there is a good reason to do so; otherwise, leave it to the [agency] * * * to devise. Make the sections brief. If a matter requires great elaboration on the face of the statute, break up the provision into several sections, or create several subsections.

Second, be helpful to the reader. Statutes are meant to influence conduct, and that basic purpose of almost all statutes is, obviously, better served if the statute is clear, precise, and logically developed. If there is an overall purpose to your proposed statute, announce it simply. Avoid "legalese" and big words when simpler terms would convey the same meaning, for the latter will be meaningful to more people. Provide definitions when you are using common words in a narrow way. Organize the statute logically. You may want to include a table of contents in the first section of a lengthy bill. It is useful if the sections and the subsections (and further subdivisions) follow a logical pattern. Titles or captions for sections and, sometimes, for subsections are often useful.

Third, follow rules of consistency. Do not use different words to refer to the same thing. For example, do not use "affirmative action plan" in [one] * * * amendment * * * and "preferential treatment" in [another] * * * amendment * * * if you mean essentially the same thing. * * * Do not use the same word to refer to different things. For example, it would be potentially confusing to use "discrimination" in a different sense when referring to racial discrimination than when referring to sexual discrimination. * * * If your proposed legislation is to be integrated into an existing statutory scheme, be consistent with the usages adopted in the existing scheme. For example [if you are drafting an amendment to Title VII of the Civil Rights Act of 1964], do not refer to the Equal Employment Opportunity Commission as the "EEOC"; it is simply called the "Commission" in existing Title VII. The language in your bill will be codified together with the rest of Title VII—make sure that it fits in stylistically as well as substantively.

Indeed, in drafting your * * * bill, you may consider existing provisions as models, much as prior contracts are often starting points for lawyers drafting new contracts. While you do not want to adopt the vices of the existing statute * * *, its terms of art and set phrases are useful starting points in drafting a statute that will fit in with existing law.

Exercise 5.1

Following is a county ordinance on the subject of "fences and safety barriers for swimming pools." Evaluate it according to the three precepts proposed above by Professors Eskridge and Frickey as guidelines for drafting a bill.

ORDINANCE NO. 82–19

1 AN ORDINANCE PROVIDING FOR THE CONSTRUCTION
2 AND MAINTENANCE OF FENCES AND SAFETY BARRIERS
3 FOR SWIMMING POOLS, PROVIDING FOR PERMITS, PRO-
4 VIDING FOR TYPES OF SAFETY BARRIERS AND FENCES
5 PERMITTED, PROVIDING AN EFFECTIVE DATE.

6 BE IT ORDAINED BY THE BOARD OF COUNTY COMMISSION-
7 ERS OF _____ COUNTY, _____:

8   SECTION 1: Intent. It is recognized that swimming pools
9 which are not surrounded by fences or safety barriers pose a threat
10 to the safety of the citizens of _____ County, _____, especially
11 young children. The purpose of this ordinance is to provide a
12 minimum standard of protection against the hazards of unprotected
13 and easily accessible swimming pools.

14   SECTION 2: Definitions. As used in this ordinance the follow-
15 ing terms shall have the following meanings:

16 Swimming Pool—Any constructed or prefabricated pool used for
17   swimming or bathing over 24" in depth measured between the
18   floor of the pool and the maximum water level.

19 Swimming Pool (Private)—Shall be defined to include all construct-
20   ed or assembled pools which are used as a swimming pool in

21 connection with a residence whether single or multi-family and
22 are available for use only to the family of the owner or owners
23 and their private guests or invitees.

24 Swimming Pool (Public)—Shall be defined to include any construct-
25 ed or prefabricated pool other than a private pool.

26 SECTION 3: Permits. Before any work is commenced, permits
27 shall be secured for all swimming pools and for the safety barriers.
28 Plans shall contain all details necessary to show compliance with
29 the terms and conditions of this ordinance. No swimming pool
30 permit shall be issued unless simultaneously therewith a permit is
31 secured for the erection of the required safety barrier. If the
32 premises are already enclosed, as hereinafter provided, a permit for
33 the safety barrier shall not be required if, upon inspection of the
34 premises, the existing barrier and gates are proven to be satisfacto-
35 ry.

36 SECTION 4: Required for final inspection of pool. No swim-
37 ming pool final inspection and approval shall be given by the
38 Building and Zoning Codes Department, unless there has been
39 erected a safety barrier as hereinafter provided. No pool shall be
40 filled with water unless a final inspection has been made and
41 approved, except for testing purposes as may be approved by the
42 Building and Zoning Codes Department.

43 SECTION 5: Types permitted. The safety barriers shall take
44 the form of a screened-in patio, a wooden fence, a wire fence, a rock
45 wall, a concrete block wall or other materials so as to enable the
46 owner to blend the same with the style of architecture planned or in
47 existence on the property.

48 SECTION 6: Height. The minimum height of the safety barri-
49 er shall not be less than four feet.

50 SECTION 7: Location of barrier. The safety barrier shall be
51 erected either around the swimming pool or around the premises on
52 which the swimming pool is erected. In either event, it shall
53 enclose the area entirely, prohibiting unrestrained admittance to
54 the enclosed area.

55 SECTION 8: Gates. Gates shall be of the spring lock type, or
56 equivalent, so that they shall automatically be in a closed and
57 fastened position at all times.

58 SECTION 9: Wooden fences. In the wooden type fence, the
59 boards, pickets, louvers, or other such members, shall be spaced,
60 constructed, and erected so as to make the fence not easily climba-
61 ble or penetrable.

62 SECTION 10: Walls. Walls whether of the rock or block type
63 shall be erected to make them not easily climbable.

64 SECTION 11: Wire fences. Wire fences shall be the two inch
65 chain link or diamond weave nonclimbable type, or of an approved
66 equal, with top rail. They shall be of a heavy, galvanized material.

67   SECTION 12: Refusal of permit. It shall be within the discre-
68 tion of the director of the Building and Zoning Department to refuse
69 approval of any barrier which, in his opinion, does not furnish the
70 safety requirement of this section i.e., that is high enough and so
71 constructed to keep children of pre-school age from getting over or
72 through it.

73   SECTION 13: Maintenance. It shall be the responsibility of
74 the owner or occupant of the premises upon which a swimming pool
75 is hereafter erected to maintain and keep in proper and safe
76 condition the safety barrier required and erected in accordance with
77 this ordinance.

78   SECTION 14: Exemptions. The provisions of this ordinance
79 shall not apply to above ground swimming pools, access to which is
80 gained by a ladder or other portable device or movable device such
81 as a swing up ladder which can be easily removed from the pool or
82 otherwise secured to accomplish the minimum level of protection
83 afforded by this ordinance.

84   SECTION 15: Applicability. The provisions of this ordinance
85 shall apply to all new private swimming pools, the construction of
86 which commences after the effective date.

87   SECTION 16: Variances. Variances from the provisions of this
88 ordinance may be applied for and received from the _____ County
89 Zoning Board of Adjustment where it is demonstrated that unique
90 circumstances dictate that the provisions of this ordinance would
91 serve no useful purpose and further that the purposes of this
92 ordinance would not be frustrated by the granting of such variance.

93   SECTION 17: Warning. The degree of protection afforded by
94 this ordinance is considered reasonable for regulatory purposes.
95 The provisions of this ordinance shall not be construed by any
96 person to replace that degree of care which is required to properly
97 supervise and control either their own premises or their own chil-
98 dren who may wander upon the premises of another where a
99 swimming pool is located. The degree of protection afforded by this
100 ordinance is declared to be minimal and it is specifically recognized
101 that any safety barrier may be surmounted under the proper
102 circumstances.

103   SECTION 18: Severability. It is declared to be the legislative
104 intent that if any section, subsection, sentence, clause or provision
105 of this ordinance is held invalid, the remainder of the ordinance
106 shall not be affected.

107   SECTION 19: Effective date. This ordinance shall take effect
108 upon receipt of the official acknowledgement from the Office of the
109 Secretary of the State of _____ that this ordinance has been filed
110 with said office.

————

Exercise 5.2

Following is a county "false alarm ordinance." Evaluate it according to the three precepts proposed above by Professors Eskridge and Frickey as guidelines for drafting a bill.

_____ COUNTY FALSE ALARM ORDINANCE 84–10

1   WHEREAS, there are presently in use within the unincorpo-
2 rated area of _____ County certain hardware and other radio and
3 electronically controlled alarm systems which are privately owned
4 and operated; and,

5   WHEREAS, these privately owned burglary and robbery alarm
6 systems are causing substantial misuse of the manpower and re-
7 sources of the Office of the Sheriff by causing the dispatch of patrol
8 units to the scene of numerous false alarms thus removing the units
9 from patrol and causing them to be out of service when a true need
10 or emergency situation could exist; and,

11   WHEREAS, telephone alarm devices regulated or programmed
12 to make connection with the Sheriff's Office could seize and hold
13 Sheriff's office telephone lines to the exclusion of other calls; and

14   WHEREAS, the current high incidence of false alarms and the
15 misuse of telephone alarm devices is deemed to constitute a threat
16 to the people of the County and is obstructive of efficient protection;

17   NOW, THEREFORE, BE IT ORDAINED, BY THE BOARD OF
18 COUNTY COMMISSIONERS OF _____ COUNTY, _____;

19   Section 1. Definitions.

20   a) "Alarm system" shall mean any mechanical, electrical or
21 radio-controlled device which is designed to be used for the detection
22 of any unauthorized entry into a building, structure or facility, or
23 both, and which emits a sound or transmits a signal or message
24 when activated. Alarm Systems include, but are not limited to,
25 direct dial telephone devices, audible alarms and proprietor alarms.
26 Excluded from the definition of alarm systems are devices which are
27 designed or used to register alarms that are audible, visible, or
28 perceptible in or from any motor vehicle or auxiliary device in-
29 stalled by telephone companies to protect telephone systems from
30 damage or disruption of service.

31   b) "False alarm" shall mean the activation of any alarm signal
32 by an alarm system which is responded to by the Sheriff's Office,
33 and which is not caused or precipitated by an actual or attempted
34 burglary or other attempted unlawful act or activity, or other
35 emergency reasonably requiring the services of the Sheriff's Office.
36 An alarm will be deemed to be valid only when substantial physical
37 evidence exists which would clearly indicate a criminal act was the
38 sole reason for activation of the alarm. Examples include, but are
39 not limited to: freshly broken windows, doors, or locks; obvious

40 indications of forced illegal entry; missing property, etc. Alarm
41 systems which activate from simply shaking of doors or rattling of
42 windows are not properly installed or maintained and are deemed to
43 be emitting a "false alarm".

44   c) "Person" shall mean any natural person, firm, partnership,
45 association, corporation, company or organization of any kind.

46   d) "Sheriff" shall mean the Sheriff of _____ County, or his
47 designated representative.

48   e) "Automatic dialing device" shall mean an alarm system
49 which automatically sends over regular telephone lines, by direct
50 connection, or otherwise, a pre-recorded voice message or coded
51 signal indicating the existence of the emergency situation that the
52 alarm system is designated to detect, but shall not include such
53 telephone lines exclusively dedicated to an alarm system which are
54 permanently active and terminate within the communication center
55 of the Sheriff's Office.

56   f) "Residential premises" shall mean any structure or combina-
57 tion of structures which serve as dwelling units including single
58 family as well as multi-family units.

59   g) "Commercial premises" shall mean any structure or area
60 which is not defined herein as residential premises.

61   h) "Fee" shall mean an assessment of costs imposed pursuant to
62 this ordinance to defray the expense of responding to a false alarm.

63   Section 2. Notification and Registration. Every person who
64 shall own, operate, or lease any alarm system as defined herein
65 within the unincorporated area of _____ County, whether existing
66 or to be installed in the future, shall, within thirty (30) days of the
67 effective date of this ordinance for existing alarm systems or prior
68 to installation of alarm systems installed after the effective date of
69 this ordinance, notify the Sheriff, on forms to be provided by the
70 Sheriff's Office of the following information:

71   1. The type, make, model of the alarm system.

72   2. Whether installed in a residential or commercial premise,
73 and the location of the alarm system, including the street address or
74 specific directions to where the alarm system is located.

75   3. The name, address, business and/or home telephone num-
76 ber of the owner or lessee of the alarm system. In the event that
77 the owner or lessee of the alarm system is a business entity,
78 partnership, or corporation, the business shall indicate the name,
79 street address, and telephone number of the agent designated by the
80 business to be responsible for contacting.

81   4. The names, addresses and telephone numbers of not less
82 than two (2) persons to be notified to respond in the event of an
83 alarm activation. The responder persons so listed must be available
84 at all times and be authorized to enter the premises and deactivate

85 the alarm system. It shall be the responsibility of the owner,
86 operator, or lessee of the alarm system to keep the listing current.

87 5. Such other information as the Sheriff shall deem necessary
88 or appropriate.

89 Section 3. Response to False Alarm; Required Reports; Cor-
90 rective Action; Penalties and Disconnection.

91 a) For the purpose of this ordinance, responsibility for a false
92 alarm shall be borne by the owner, operator, or lessee of the alarm
93 system.

94 b) A response to a false alarm shall result when any Deputy
95 Sheriff is dispatched to or responds to the activation of any alarm
96 system.

97 c) The following shall be required by each person who owns,
98 operates or controls any premise, commercial or residential, for each
99 incident of a response to a false alarm by the Sheriff's Office.

100 1. For a response to a premise at which no other false alarm
101 has occurred from the effective date of this ordinance or within the
102 preceding six (6) month period, whichever shall be less, a written
103 report, on forms prescribed by the Sheriff's Office shall be filed with
104 the Sheriff's Office within ten (10) days after notice to do so, setting
105 forth the cause of such false alarm, the corrective action taken,
106 whether the alarm has been inspected by an authorized serviceman,
107 and such other information as the Sheriff may reasonably require to
108 determine the cause of such false alarm and corrective action
109 necessary. No fee shall be charged for the first response.

110 2. For a second or third response to false alarms to any
111 premise, commercial or residential, within six (6) months after the
112 first response, no fee shall be assessed, but a written report shall be
113 required as for a first response.

114 3. For a fourth false alarm response to any premise, commer-
115 cial or residential, within six (6) months after such third response of
116 a false alarm and for each succeeding response within six (6) months
117 of the preceding response, a fee of TWENTY–FIVE DOLLARS
118 ($25.00) shall be charged; a written report and inspection shall be
119 required/and if such fourth false alarm or any such succeeding false
120 alarm is a result of failure to take necessary corrective action, the
121 Sheriff may order the disconnection of such alarm system. For
122 failure to pay the required fee, the Sheriff may order the disconnec-
123 tion of any alarm system. It shall be a violation of this ordinance
124 not to disconnect, or to reconnect such alarm system until such
125 corrective action is taken and the fee is paid, provided that no
126 disconnection shall be ordered on any premise required by law to
127 have an alarm system in operation. Any order for disconnection
128 shall be rescinded by the Sheriff upon presentation of demonstrative
129 evidence of corrective action and inspection, as may be required by

130 the Sheriff, and a finding that adequate corrective action has been
131 taken and the required fee has been paid.

132   Section 4. <u>Requirement to Respond to Premise when Alarm is</u>
133 <u>Activated.</u> The owner, operator, or lessee or a listed responder of
134 an alarm system is required to respond by reporting to the premises
135 or facility within thirty (30) minutes from the time of the notifica-
136 tion by Sheriff of the activation of any alarm system, whether false
137 or not. Failure to respond shall be deemed a violation of this
138 ordinance by the owner, operator or lessee of the alarm system.

139   Section 5. <u>Deactivation of Audible Alarms Within Thirty Min-</u>
140 <u>utes.</u> It shall be a violation of this ordinance to maintain an alarm
141 system or audible alarm which does not deactivate within thirty (30)
142 minutes of its activation.

143   Section 6. <u>Automatic Dialing Devices.</u> It shall be a violation
144 of this ordinance for any person to install, maintain, own, possess or
145 operate any automatic dialing device alarm system regulated or
146 programmed to make connection with any telephone number in-
147 stalled in the Sheriff's Office, except to such telephone number(s)
148 which may be determined and designated by the Sheriff.

149   Section 7. <u>Requirement of Auxiliary Power Supply.</u> It shall
150 be a violation of this ordinance for any person to install, maintain,
151 own, possess or operate any alarm system which does not have an
152 auxiliary power supply which activates in the event of a power
153 failure or electrical outage.

154   Section 8. <u>Right to a Hearing.</u> Upon written request of the
155 person assessed a fee or ordered to disconnect an alarm, a hearing
156 may be held before the Sheriff or his designee to review such
157 assessment or disconnect order. Such request must be made within
158 fifteen (15) days after the date of the notice of assessment or
159 disconnect order. At the hearing, such evidence as is deemed
160 necessary may be presented.

161   Section 9. <u>General Penalty.</u> Anyone convicted of a violation
162 of, or failure to comply with, any of the provisions of this ordinance
163 shall be punished as provided by law.

164   Section 10. <u>Severability.</u> If any section, subsection, sentence,
165 clause, provision or part of this ordinance shall be held invalid for
166 any reason, the remainder of this ordinance shall not be affected
167 thereby, but shall remain in full force and effect.

168   Section 11. <u>Effective Date.</u> October 12, 1984.

B. THE DRAFTER'S ROLE IN IMPROVING LEGISLATIVE SUBSTANCE

One writer, with 24 years' experience as a state senator, regards
defective drafting not merely as a sign of poor writing skills but as

symptomatic of unclear focus on the substance of the policy expressed in the legislation.[11]

It is a commonly held but mistaken notion that the legislator, who is the policy-maker, is the one with all the ideas, and that the drafter is a mere "scrivener" with the limited role of getting those ideas into appropriate form. On the contrary, the skilled legislative drafter does far more than simplify or clarify without changing the substance of what someone else has proposed. To achieve legislation that fulfills its purpose, the more communication between proposer and drafter, the better. In fact, the more communication among proposer, potential user and drafter, the better. "The Drafter's Role in Improving the Substance of Legislation" was the title of a senior legislative drafting seminar sponsored by the National Conference of State Legislatures in 1991.[12]

To become fully engaged in achieving a legislative purpose, you need to understand the legislative process, and you need to research the present law on the subject in your jurisdiction as well as the experience of any other jurisdictions that already have a law like the one you are contemplating.

This background research will equip you to help the policy makers articulate precisely what it is they want to do. You can formulate questions and options that will help them identify:

• whether there is need for a new law;

• what purpose it will serve;

• who will benefit from the law, who will be disadvantaged;

• what the costs of administering the law will probably be;

• what the likely response to the law will be from the courts, the bureaucracy, and the public.[13]

One text provides a questionnaire as a research guide.

11. J. Davies, Legislative Law and Process in a Nutshell 182 (2d ed. 1986).

12. This seminar was held at The University of Florida College of Law, October 23–26, 1991.

13. W. Statsky, Legislative Analysis and Drafting 164 (2d ed. 1984). Copyright © 1984. Reprinted with permission of West Publishing Company.

QUESTIONNAIRE TO BE ANSWERED IN PREPARING A MEMORANDUM AS THE BASIS FOR DRAFTING A BILL, READ, MACDONALD, FORDHAM AND PIERCE'S FOURTH EDITION, MATERIALS ON LEGISLATION

233–34 (1982).*

(* * * Before answering any of the following questions read all of them, treat them as constituting a unit, and answer each in its relation to the others.)

1. What is the subject matter of the proposed new law, i.e., with exactly what phases of human affairs, economic, social, or political is the proposed law concerned?

2. What reliable data, literature, expert opinion and advice on the present problem in its economic, social, and political aspects are available? What is their accumulative effect?

3. What is the present law of this state (or country) on the subject?

4. What is the broad objective of the proposed new law?

5. What are the specific fact situations for which the present law is alleged to provide an inadequate or undesirable solution?

6. Does the alleged defect actually exist?

7. If so, is the situation unique to this state (or country), or has the same or a similar defect in the law been dealt with by the legislature of any other state or country?

8. If another state or country has dealt with such a defect, what statutory remedy did it devise?

9. What has been the experience of such other state or country in applying its statute judicially and administratively? Have any theoretical and practical difficulties been encountered? If so, what means have been taken to overcome them?

10. Have the above mentioned statutes of other states or countries been judicially or administratively construed?

11. Have the governmental officers charged with the administration of such statutes any criticism or suggestion for improving them?

12. Has the legislature of this state (or the Congress) ever considered or enacted legislation in any phase of human affairs essentially related to the subject now under consideration? If so, what has been its general policy? Would any statutes be in pari materia with the proposed new law? If so, how would they interplay? Adapt and answer questions 9 to 11 to any statutes included in question 12.

13. What specific solution do you recommend to remedy the defect you are now considering?

14. Does your solution involve legislative administration or law making in the sense of laying down rules of general application?

15. If the latter, what is the immediate and specific object or purpose of the new law that you propose?

16. What are the likely economic, social, and political results and implications of your proposed solution?

17. What are the various sanctions and other devices available for use in obtaining the objects of your proposed law?

18. With particular reference to question 17, does the subject matter of your proposed law indicate that it will be self-executory, or must administrative machinery be utilized?

19. What modifying effect, express or implied, will your new law have on presently existing law, both common and statutory?

20. Is there any question concerning the constitutionality of your proposed law: (a) under the federal constitution; (b) under the constitution of this state?

21. In the light of careful appraisal of your answers to the foregoing questions, do you recommend the enactment of a new law? If so, draft the necessary bill.

Much of the drafter's working time may be spent refining the substance of the "agreement in principle" brought to the drafter by a committee sponsoring the legislation. One commentator describes a project that involved 18 hours conference time to produce four and one-half double spaced pages. The conference time mounted because it became clear that the committee's "agreement in principle" was little more than a shared belief that there ought to be a law on the subject. Subordinate policy questions brought out their disagreements about what administrative body should enforce the statute, whether a new one should be created, what the sanctions should be for violations, and what procedural rights accused persons should have. There were major arguments over how to define terms. The account of this project [14] shows how skeptical you need to be of "agreements in principal."

Exercise 5.3

You are the county attorney. Recently a restaurant has opened just outside the city limits of the county seat. The county commission-

---

14. Jones, Some Reflections on a Draftsman's Time Sheet, 35 ABA J. 941 (1949).

ers come to tell you they have been receiving numerous complaints because the cocktail waitresses at the restaurant are nude. Moreover, a number of billboards advertising the restaurant have sprung up on the interstate highway that runs through the county. These billboards, some of which are neon lit, invite travelers to "Stop and See Us" and show pictures of nearly nude women.

The commissioners tell you they agree in principle that they want legislation to prohibit this kind of establishment from operating in the county. You have learned that there is no present county ordinance or state statute prohibiting it. What additional research would you need to undertake? What questions would you pursue with the commissioners?

Exercise 5.4

Your client is a land developer who is designing an exclusive subdivision on a lake just inside the city limits. The plans are for 50 lots, each of about 3 or 4 acres. Some will have lake frontage. Those that do not will have access to the lake through a park to be owned by all of the property owners in common as members of the property owners' association. The park will have a boat ramp, picnic tables, and grills. Your client asks you to draw up covenants and restrictions to make sure the houses that buyers build in the subdivision are up to the developer's standards. What research do you need to do? What do you need to find out from the developer?

C. DRAFTING TO GET THE LEGISLATION PASSED

Professor Davies, more concerned with immediate practical strategy than long-term speculative theory, raises different issues for a bill drafter and policy-maker to think through together.

Some provisions of a bill can be drawn (1) to offend little, but also to gain little for its sponsors, (2) to achieve 100 percent of the sponsor's objective, though to do so will spark vigorous opposition, or (3) to finesse a critical issue by leaving it up in the air. Which choice should a sponsor select? The first makes the job of passing the bill easier, for opponents are less aroused; most of the battle is left for a later day. The second choice gives a sponsor some trading stock for compromise and, if the bill is passed with the particular provision included, the victory is more significant. But the sponsor runs the risk that the tough bill will not pass. The third choice makes the bill incomplete. It will bother those who want the legislature to deliver certainty in the law. And when the issue is later decided in another arena, such as a court or agency or trade association, or by subsequent legislation, the issue that has been sidestepped may be resolved against the sponsor. On the other hand, vagueness may cause those affected to overlook some hazard in the bill or to decide they are willing to gamble on ultimately winning the finessed decision. The sponsor then faces milder opposition and a simpler legislative battle.

There is no one correct choice, but the third option, intentional vagueness, serves legislatures well and often. It may be adopted consciously, occur by oversight, or turn up as a compromise during negotiation on the bill. Legislators eagerly duck tough questions if answering them threatens the passage of a bill for which a consensus has developed.[15]

Exercise 5.5

Below are parts of the domestic violence legislation from three states, labeled State A, State B, and State C. Assume that the sponsors of the legislation in each state were special interest groups eager to get legislation passed to protect the victims of domestic violence. Assume further that they wanted the protected class to include: (1) victims who were not and never had been married to their attackers, and (2) victims who were lesbians or gay men. The sponsors were concerned that express attention to these groups might spark vigorous opposition.

Analyze the three states' legislation according to the three choices Professor Davies describes above for how to draw a bill. Which choice does it appear that each state's drafter made? Which state has the broadest protected class? Which has the narrowest? What other differences do you observe in the three states' approaches?

State A

§ 273.5   Corporal injury; infliction by spouse upon his or her spouse or by person cohabiting with person of opposite sex

1   (a) Any person who willfully inflicts upon his or her spouse, or
2 any person who willfully inflicts upon any person of the opposite sex
3 with whom he or she is cohabiting, corporal injury resulting in a
4 traumatic condition, is guilty of a felony * * *.

5   (b) Holding oneself out to be the husband or wife of the person
6 with whom one is cohabiting is not necessary to constitute cohabita-
7 tion as the term is used in this section.

8   (c) As used in this section, "traumatic condition" means a
9 condition of the body, such as a wound or external or internal
10 injury, whether of a minor or serious nature, caused by a physical
11 force.

* * *

15. Davies, above note 11, at 191–92. Reprinted from Legislative Law and Process in a Nutshell by Jack Davies, 2d ed. copyright © 1986 with permission of West Publishing Company.

§ 1000.6 [Application of chapter; Definitions]

* * *

1 (d) As used in this chapter "domestic violence" means inten-
2 tionally or recklessly causing or attempting to cause bodily injury to
3 a family or household member or placing a family or household
4 member in reasonable apprehension of imminent serious bodily
5 injury to himself or herself or another.

6 (e) As used in this chapter "family or household member"
7 means a spouse, former spouse, parent, any other person related by
8 consanguinity, or any person who regularly resides or who within
9 the previous six months regularly resided in the household. "Fami-
10 ly or household member" does not include a child.

State B

§ 2919.25 [Domestic Violence]

1 (A) No person shall knowingly cause or attempt to cause physi-
2 cal harm to a family or household member.

3 (B) No person shall recklessly cause serious physical harm to a
4 family or household member.

5 (C) Whoever violates this section is guilty of domestic violence,
6 a misdemeanor of the first degree. If the offender has previously
7 been convicted of a violation of this section, a violation of this
8 section is a felony of the fourth degree.

9 (D) As used in this section and in section 2919.26 of the Revised
10 Code, "family or household member" means a spouse, person living
11 as a spouse, parent, child, or other person related by consanguinity
12 or affinity, who is residing or has resided with the offender.

State C

§ 415.602 Definitions of terms used in §§ 415.601–415.608

1 As used in §§ 415.601–415.608, the term:

2   * * *

3 (3) "Domestic violence" means any assault, battery, or criminal
4 sexual conduct by a person against the person's spouse.

5   * * *

6 (5) "Spouse" means a person to whom another person is mar-
7 ried or a person to whom another person has been married and from
8 whom such other person is now separated or divorced.

D. DRAFTING FOR THE ADMINISTRATOR

During the mid–1970's, the American Bar Foundation undertook a series of studies on the teaching of legislative process and drafting. One of those studies involved a survey of bill-drafting offices and executive branch officials concerned with bill drafting. The responses of one state executive branch official suggest the need to draft less for the court and more for the administrative agency.

It is not often enough considered, that a large number of laws are primarily "administered" and not "adjudicated."

*   *   *

*   *   * [T]he best bill drafter is a lawyer who has worked several years in the legislative process, was not afraid to ask "dumb" questions *and* who had personal responsibility to *administer* the particular legal area for a number of years.[16]

Not only do we need to think of drafting statutes and ordinances so that agencies can easily administer them, but we also need to keep in mind how much of our law is itself in the form of administrative rules.

The legal profession has undergone a profound shift in professional challenges from a preoccupation with litigation to a broader concern that includes an enormous involvement with public and private planning.   *   *   *

Although lawyers are beginning to realize that most new law is legislative rather than judicial, few realize that statutes constitute only a small fraction of the total output of new law. How is most of it being made? Through the delegated legislation we call "administrative rulemaking." Unfortunately much, if not most, of such legal planning is being done by lawyers with inadequate training in the conceptual and architectural disciplines of planning or is being done by laymen.

*   *   *

In the nonlitigious area of legal planning, which normally culminates in definitive documents whose purpose is to inform rather than persuade, the lawyer is freest to present balanced legal truth. But this calls for an expertise of which legal education provides little and for which case law is largely irrelevant. Certainly, the law's mission is broader than the dispute resolution *   *   * represented by litigation.[17]

E. DRAFTING FOR THE AFFECTED CITIZEN

It is legitimate for the drafter to be alert to the needs of the legislating policy-makers, the administering agencies, and the courts; yet it is also important not to neglect the needs of ordinary citizens, who ought to be able to figure out whether and how a law affects them.

The first thing that any law-reader wants to know is what the law is about. Does it affect him or doesn't it? Most laws fail so utterly to answer this question that they are likely to be thrown in the waste basket before the reader even tries to decipher them.

16. B. Lammers, Legislative Process and Drafting in U.S. Law Schools 47 n. 60 (1977).

17. Dickerson, Toward a Legal Dialectic, 61 Ind.L.J. 315, 316–17 (1985–86).

A typical example is the Trading with the Enemy Act, which in time of war suddenly applies to tens of thousands of Americans. But if it came in the mail to an American who was about to send some money to a foreign creditor, he would have to parse two or three pages before he found out whether he was likely to be affected by it.

The first thing the citizen would notice is that the Act begins with section 2 (maybe section 1 got lost, he thinks). Section 2, which has no subtitle, contains a long list of definitions, starting with a half-page definition of "enemy."

Somewhere in the middle of the second page begins section 3, also with no subtitle. If the citizen is still looking, he will see—

That it shall be unlawful—

(a) For any person in the United States, except with a license of the President, granted to such person, or to the enemy, or ally of enemy, as provided in this Act, to trade, either directly or indirectly, with, to, or from, or for, on account of, or on behalf of, or for the benefit of any other person.

. . .

If he keeps on for a few lines more, and understands what he reads, he will at last find out what the law is about.

A better way to start a statute is suggested by the way OPA finally learned to open its price regulations. It learned by experience to start them this way:

"This regulation fixes ceiling prices for sales by retailers of certain commodities."

The same approach could have been used in the Trading with the Enemy Act:

"This law applies to everyone in the United States who has any dealings with foreigners."

It could then have proceeded to explain what foreigners and what dealings were specifically affected.[18]

Exercise 5.6

If you were to redraft the swimming pool barrier ordinance in Exercise 5.1 and the false alarm ordinance in Exercise 5.2 according to Professor Conard's recommendations above in order to accommodate the citizen-reader, what would be your opening sentence for each one? If you were going to follow Professor Conard's recommendation in drafting the ordinance to prohibit cocktail waitresses' being nude, what would your opening sentence be?

---

18. Conard, New Ways to Write Laws, 56 Yale L.J. 458, 470–71 (1947) (citations omitted). Reprinted by permission of The Yale Law Journal Company and Fred B. Rothman & Company from The Yale Law Journal, Vol. 56, pp. 458–481.

F.   PREPARING A LEGISLATIVE PLAN

*   *   * Legislative policy is not the same thing as the legislative plan; the former is the objective to be achieved; and the latter an outline of the method by which it is to be achieved. For example, it may be laid down as a policy that certain grants are to be paid to a class of persons under specified conditions. In order to give effect to such a policy *   *   * [the] statute must, among other things, describe the persons who are to benefit, specify the amount of the grant and the conditions under which it may be paid, and provide authority for payment out of the Consolidated Revenue Fund, for suspension for breach of the conditions and for recovery of unauthorized payments, for applications, decisions and award, for penalties for misrepresentation or other wrongful conduct. *   *   * After the legislative plan is prepared, it is discussed with the sponsors and it will undoubtedly be modified; new provisions will be added and others will be dropped or changed.[19]

III.   INTRODUCTORY FORMALITIES

A.   TITLE

Titles are generally constitutionally or statutorily required for bills, acts, and sections of legislation. The requirements generally prescribe that titles of bills express their purposes (for example, "A Bill to . . ."), and that the titles of acts and sections express their subjects. Thus the full titles of bills may be very long, giving not only their subject and their purpose with respect to that subject but also listing the statutes to be amended or repealed. The titles of acts and sections are usually much shorter. Titles implement "single subject" requirements and those designed to put people on notice of the content of legislation.

B.   ENACTING CLAUSE

The exact language of enacting clauses is prescribed: by 1 U.S.C.A. § 101 for congressional bills, by state constitutions for bills in most states, and by state statutes in a few states.[20] The congressional clauses read this way: "Be it enacted by the Senate and House of Representatives of the United States of America in Congress assembled." Failure to use exactly the prescribed language can render the legislation invalid.

19. Driedger, The Preparation of Legislation, 31 Can.B.Rev. 33, 39 (1953).

20. For the exact language prescribed for enacting clauses in each state, see R.

Martineau, Enacting Clauses, Appendix A, Drafting Legislation and Rules in Plain English 124 (1991).

C. SHORT TITLE SECTION

The first numbered section in long congressional bills and some state bills sets forth a short title by which to cite the legislation after it is enacted. These short sections are practical only if the entire act is codified in one place rather than its various sections scattered throughout a code.[21]

D. FINDINGS

Some but not all bills include a section reciting the legislating body's findings that gave rise to the legislation. In remedial legislation, these are statements of the ills that the legislation is designed to remedy. These statements may also express what policy the legislation is designed to implement. Courts may look to these statements for guidance when construing the legislation, but it is dangerous to rely on this possibility as an excuse for careless drafting.[22]

E. DEFINITIONS

Definitions are the subject of Chapter 10.

IV. ORGANIZING THE BODY OF LEGISLATION

A. THE BODY AS PART OF THE WHOLE

Assume you are preparing to draft legislation. You are not going to draft either a long or short title until everything else is finished, even though the title(s) will come at the beginning. You are not going to draft definitions until you have drafted all the provisions, even though the definitions will precede the body. You have supplied an enacting clause in whatever exact language is required. You have or have not drafted findings or purpose statements depending on whether you and the policy maker have determined them appropriate to include. You know that any housekeeping provisions, such as a savings clause, repealing clause, severability clause, effective date clause, and expiration ("sunset" or "sundown") clause will follow the body. How do you organize what comes in between?

The body of legislation generally presents the operative substance in the following sequence, although organized according to whatever scheme its codification dictates:

- The rights, privileges, statuses, and duties the legislation creates for the public as in criminal statutes or for a class of persons such as those in a particular profession, including defenses and exceptions.

---

21. Id. at 115.   **22.** Id. at 116.

• Procedures for administering the legislation, including creating or granting authority to existing officers, agencies, or departments to make rules pursuant to the legislation and to enforce it.

• Civil or criminal sanctions or penalties, remedies, and enforcement procedures.[23]

B. DIVISION, CLASSIFICATION, AND SEQUENCE OF SECTIONS

1. *Steps in the Drafting Process*

Professor Davies, the veteran legislator, gives practical advice about steps in the drafting process:

    a. Draft the easiest provisions first. These are likely to be the ones that state new rules or tasks.

    b. Wait to draft difficult provisions until you work up more confidence. These are likely to be the ones that determine the extent of applicability.

    c. Work on sequence after you have accumulated several sections.

    d. Insert additional provisions as you think of them.

    e. Rearrange the sections when logic dictates.

    f. Have at least one other person read and comment on what you have drafted and participate in redrafting.

    g. Expect new readers to discover problems and complications that may change the shape and substance.

    h. Edit the whole by going through repeatedly, checking on one kind of matter at a time, for instance, one check for accurate cross-references and sequential numbering and lettering, and another check for matters of legislative tactics.[24]

2. *Recommendations about Sections*

The National Conference of Commissioners on Uniform State Laws recommends the following about organizing sections:

    a. Do not use long sections.[25]

    b. If a section covers a number of contingencies, alternatives, requirements or conditions, break it down into subsections * * *. If a further breakdown is unavoidable, break down subsections into paragraphs * * *. Do not further break down a section or subsection.[26]

    c. Use separate sections for separate provisions.[27]

---

23. See W. Eskridge, Jr. and P. Frickey, Cases and Materials on Legislation 835 (1988); id. at 119–23.

24. Davies, above note 11, at 160–62.

25. Drafting Rules for Writing Uniform or Model Acts, Rule 11, 1970 Handbook.

26. Id. at Rule 12(a).

27. Id. at Rule 12(b).

d.   Avoid references to other sections or subdivisions. Do not refer to another section or subdivision by its number or letter without descriptive language to identify it further.[28]

e.   A lengthy act may be divided into parts, chapters or articles.[29]

3. Concepts and Subject Groupings; the "Logical Pull"

Here is one drafting manual's suggested approach:

a.   One of the most fundamental problems in drafting is that of arrangement. The main idea is to make the final product as useful as possible. Carefully select the subjects to be covered and arrange them so that they can be found, understood, and referred to with the least possible effort.

b.   In general, what subject groupings are appropriate in a particular case depends upon the needs of the persons who will use the text of the law most. Arrange provisions relating primarily to administration from the viewpoint of the persons who will administer them. Arrange provisions relating primarily to the conduct, rights, privileges, or duties of persons not administering them from the viewpoint of the persons so affected. Consider not only *who* and *how many* will use a provision but *how often* they will use it.

c.   The concepts and groupings used in the text of the law should correspond to those necessarily involved in the substantive problems faced by the persons to whom the legislation is primarily addressed. The "logical pull" of a proposed heading or grouping in the text of the law depends upon how fully it meets this test.

d.   Generally, the best arrangements require the least page-turning. Avoid any arrangement, for instance, that requires substantially more cross-references between chapters than is required by an alternative arrangement offering equal or better findability, clarity, and usability.

e.   Don't use historical groupings * * * where other groupings offer substantially greater findability, clarity, and usability. However, unless an alternative grouping offers more of these functional advantages, keep the existing arrangement. * * *

f.   Don't state the same rule of law at more than one place.

g.   Treat functionally indivisible subjects at a single place. Do not fragment them.

h.   Resist the temptation to violate paragraph *f* or *g*, even where a functionally indivisible subject falls partly within one heading and partly within another. (In some cases, the subject may fall wholly within two overlapping headings.) Although you can sometimes minimize the difficulty by narrowing or otherwise changing the scope of the respective headings, in many cases

---

28. Id. at Rule 13.   **29.** Id. at Rule 15.

conflicting pulls between overlapping or otherwise competing headings cannot be removed. In these cases, treat the subject under the heading which judgment determines to have the strongest logical pull (see paragraph *c*) and place editorial cross-references to that heading following the other sections under whose headings the materials also literally fall. * * *[30]

Exercise 5.7

Search the swimming pool barrier ordinance presented in Exercise 5.1 for all references to permits. How does the ordinance violate the suggestions in paragraph *h* above? How could you minimize the difficulty? Where does the "logical pull" described in paragraph *c* lead you to treat refusal of permits?

C. ORGANIZING MATERIAL WITHIN SECTIONS

The requirements of absolute parallelism and consistency in organizing material within sections of legislation are what make this kind of drafting more exacting than any other. It is almost impossible to write a first draft of a complex provision with sufficient attention to parallelism and consistency in its structure. It is much easier to write the provision in a solid block paragraph and then come back to perform on it the process that Professor Layman Allen calls "normalization."[31]

Normalization accomplishes the following operations:

- It organizes material to focus primarily on conditions ("if" clauses) and results ("then" clauses).

- It imposes absolute consistency on word choice so that the same word always refers to the same thing and different words always refer to different things.

- It forces parallel ideas into parallel constructions.

- It tabulates significant parallel constructions in numbered or lettered sequence.

- It draws attention to whether items in sequence are alternative or cumulative by putting "or" or "and" at the end of the item before the last one.[32]

---

30. Drafting Manual for the Army and Air Force Codes, 11 Fed.B.J. 240, 241–42 (1950). This article was originally published in the Federal Bar Journal, Vol. 11, 1950. It has been reprinted here with the permission of the Federal Bar Association.

31. For discussion of symbolic logic as a normalization mechanism, see Allen and Engholm, The Need for Clear Structure in "Plain Language" Legal Drafting, 13 J.L. Reform 455 (1980).

32. For demonstration of how these operations can be modified for use in any legal drafting through tabulated sentence structure, see Chapter 9.

Following is a demonstration of normalization by Professors Allen and Engholm.

Statutory or contractual language, although sometimes relatively free of syntactic ambiguity, is frequently unnecessarily complicated. If the purpose of carefully drafted language is to clearly communicate what conditions, when fulfilled, are sufficient to reach given results, then relating conditions and results in a simple and recognizable manner can help achieve that purpose. On the other hand, failure to do so can often render a straightforward idea virtually unintelligible. [This] * * * example is a contractual provision that details the conditions under which a life insurance policy offered by the Company will be reinstated:

> **REINSTATEMENT:** If any renewal premium be not paid within the time granted the Insured for payment, a subsequent acceptance of premium by the Company or by any agent duly authorized by the Company to accept such premium, without requiring in connection therewith an application for reinstatement, shall reinstate the policy; provided, however, that if the Company or such agent requires an application for reinstatement and issues a conditional receipt for the premium tendered, the policy will be reinstated upon approval of such application by the Company or, lacking such approval, upon the 45th day (30th day in New Mexico) following the date of such conditional receipt unless the Company has previously notified the Insured in writing of its disapproval of such application. The reinstated policy shall cover only loss resulting from such accidental injury as may be sustained after the date of reinstatement and loss due to such sickness as may begin more than 10 days after such date. In all other respects the Insured and the Company shall have the same rights thereunder as they had under the policy immediately before the due date of the defaulted premium, subject to any provisions endorsed hereon or attached hereto in connection with the reinstatement. Any premium accepted in connection with a reinstatement shall be applied to a period for which premium has not been previously paid, but not to any period more than 60 days prior to the date of reinstatement.

Consider this reinstatement provision with respect to a particular factual situation. Suppose that—

1. the insured fails to pay a premium within the required time, and

2. he later pays a premium by check which he mails to the Company, and

3. the Company normally requires an application for reinstatement in connection with such acceptance, and

4. the Company has not notified the insured in writing that the reinstatement is disapproved, and

    5.   two months have elapsed since the policyholder paid the premium.

According to the above provision, should the policy be reinstated? While it is possible to carefully read the present language and answer the question, the task would be easier if the provision were drafted in normalized form. Readers may wish to test this for themselves by answering the question on the basis of the provision as drafted above before reading the normalized version * * *.

* * *

If

1.   any renewal premium is not paid within the time granted the Insured for payment, and

2.   (A) there is a subsequent acceptance of premium by the Company or by any agent duly authorized by the Company to accept such premium, without requiring in connection therewith an application for reinstatement, or

      (B) 1.   the Company or such agent

           • requires an application for reinstatement, and

           • issues a conditional receipt for the premium tendered, and

         2.   (A) such application is approved by the Company, or

              (B) the Company has not before the 45th day (30th day in New Mexico) following the date of such conditional receipt notified the Insured in writing of its disapproval of such application,

then

3.   the policy shall be reinstated, and

4.   the reinstated policy shall cover only loss resulting from such accidental injury as may be sustained after the date of reinstatement and loss due to such sickness as may begin more than 10 days after such date, and

5.   in all other respects the Insured and the Company shall have the same rights thereunder as they had under the policy immediately before the due date of the defaulted premium, subject to any provisions endorsed hereon or attached hereto in connection with the reinstatement, and

6.   any premium accepted in connection with a reinstatement shall be applied to a period for which premium has not been previously paid, but not to any period more than 60 days prior to the date of reinstatement.[33]

33. Allen and Engholm, Normalized Legal Drafting and the Query Method, 29 J. Legal Educ. 380, 387–88, 400 (1978). Copyright © 1978 by Journal of Legal Education. Reprinted by permission of the publisher.

The benefits of normalizing are the following:

- It facilitates quick reference in legislative discussion and decision-making.

- It facilitates reading and accurately applying statutes.

- It produces statements of law that are easily manipulated by word-processing programs to generate documents.[34]

V. TERMS OF AUTHORITY: A SPECIAL CONCERN ABOUT WORD CHOICE

A. THE CONVENTIONS FOR USING TERMS OF AUTHORITY

When drafting rules, especially when drafting statutes or ordinances, it is important to observe strictly the conventions for using terms of authority. Professor Dickerson sets them out as follows:

(1) To create a right, say "is entitled to."

(2) To create discretionary authority, say "may."

(3) To create a duty, say "shall."

(4) To create a mere condition precedent, say "must" (e.g., "To be eligible to occupy the office of mayor, a person must . . .")

(5) To negate a right, say "is not entitled to."

(6) To negate discretionary authority, say "may not."

(7) To negate a duty or a mere condition precedent, say "is not required to."

(8) To create a duty not to act (i.e., a prohibition), say "shall not." [35]

B. THE IMPORTANCE OF SAVING "SHALL" FOR ORDERS

Lawyers and legislators alike make mistakes in attempting to follow these conventions. Professor Davies reports that the editorial check of bills that produces the most substantive corrections is the check for correct use of "shall," "may," "must," and "should." [36] Even he is willing to use "must" to exhort, rather than saving it strictly for conditions precedent, while he makes the major point about "shall":

> *Shall* is the most powerful word in the legislative arsenal. It must not be squandered by misuse. *Shall* must not be wasted by being used to put verbs in the future tense. The future tense is seldom needed in

34. Gray, Reducing Unintended Ambiguity in Statutes: An Introduction to Normalization of Statutory Drafting, 54 Tenn. L.Rev. 433, 434–35, 455–56 (1987).

35. R. Dickerson, The Fundamentals of Legal Drafting 214 (2d ed. 1986). Copy-

right © 1986 by F. Reed Dickerson; published by Little, Brown & Company. Reprinted by permission of the author.

36. Davies, above note 11, at 183.

statutes, for a legislative act applies to the ever-present present. The novice bill drafter finds it unnatural to write in the present tense while thinking about the future. But once the drafter learns to think in terms of the time when the statute is read, the present tense comes easily. Then those invaluable *shalls* are saved for their proper use.

    Shall is a word of command. The proper use of *shall* is to give an order.[37]

C. THE FALSE IMPERATIVE

The common error among novice drafters is known as the "false imperative." It is a false imperative to say that "it *shall* be a felony to commit murder." Such phrasing is inaccurate, assuming that the law is presently in effect; rather, it *is* a felony to commit murder. The confusion is between stating what the law is and directing people to do or not do things. To a large extent, laws and other legal statements are not directions. They are descriptions of the world as it is, or statements of policy. Thus it is appropriate to phrase them in the indicative mood.

Proper Statements of Law and Policy in the Indicative Mood

It is a felony to commit murder.

The rent is due on the first day of each month.

The landlord is entitled to reasonable access to the premises.

The imperative mood is appropriate to give commands or directions. Technically, the imperative is always used in the second person.

Proper Use of the Imperative Mood for Commands and Directions

(You) Be careful.

(You) Revise several times for good drafting.

But statutes and most other regulatory documents are written in a style too formal for the second person. In them, commands and directions about future conduct are expressed in third person, and "shall" becomes the appropriate verb form.

Proper Use of Imperative "Shall" for Commands and Directions

Dog owners shall put ID tags on their dogs.

Applicants shall file their papers by June 1.

These are proper or "true" uses of the imperative. A "false imperative" phrases something as a command about future conduct when it should be an indicative statement about the present state of the law or policy. Sometimes false imperatives produce an unintended comic effect.

37. Id. at 182. Reprinted from Legislative Law and Process in a Nutshell by Jack Davies, 2d ed. copyright © 1986 with permission of West Publishing Company.

False Imperatives

Each child shall undergo vaccination by age six. (How is a five year old supposed to comply with this order?)

Each school week shall consist of 25 hours. (In other words, "You school weeks, get busy and make sure you consist of 25 hours.")

Another common mistake is to use "must" as though it were synonymous with the imperative "shall."

"Must" Mistakenly Substituted for "Shall"

The landlord must provide clean, safe common areas.

The tenant must provide the landlord reasonable access.

Technically, "must" should be reserved for conditions precedent.

"Must" Used Properly for Condition Precedent

To be eligible, the applicant must submit a notarized form.

————

Exercise 5.8

Identify and correct all errors in the use of terms of authority in the legislation below. What other errors do you find in its internal organization?

ADVANCED WRITING AND RESEARCH REQUIREMENT

1 a.   A student must receive a certificate of completion in Advanced
2   Writing and Research to graduate from _____ School of Law.
3   Any student wishing to fulfill the advanced writing and re-
4   search requirement must register with the Associate Dean of
5   Students within six weeks after the beginning of the semester.

6   A student can earn a certificate of completion in one of the
7   following manners:

8   (1) Writing a paper to the standards specified in section d
9   below in a large class or a seminar; or in an independent
10   studies program as specified in section c below;

11   (2) Completing an article of publishable quality for the Law
12   Review that is so certified by a member or members of the
13   faculty designated by the Dean;

14   (3) Such other programs as designated by the Dean.

15 b.   Any student in a class designated as a seminar (to which a limit
16   of 18 students will be imposed) has a right to fulfill the writing
17   requirement with that professor. Any professor teaching any
18   other upper division class that has 25 or less students must
19   allow at least six students in that class to fulfill the writing
20   requirement, and any professor in an advanced course of 51 or
21   more must permit up to two students.

22   If there are more requests from students in the class, faculty
23   members will choose students to work with, based upon the
24   degree to which proposed projects fall within the professors'
25   expertise.

26   Part-time faculty may supervise papers only with the permis-
27   sion of the Associate Dean. Permission usually will not be
28   granted to supervise more than two students per semester.

29 c.   Independent Studies

30   Each professor will be required to supervise up to 3 new
31   independent study students a semester regardless of the num-
32   ber of papers being supervised in other courses. He shall not be
33   allowed to supervise more than 3 without the written permis-
34   sion of the Associate Dean.

35 d.   Qualifications

36   To fulfill the Advanced Writing and Research requirement a
37   paper must be certified as on a level of good professional work
38   for an attorney. Work which is merely passing by academic
39   standards will not necessarily complete this requirement, even
40   though the paper fulfills the requirement for the course. The
41   paper must contain original work and not merely be a rehash of
42   existing sources.

43   Faculty members supervising writing requirements under any
44   of the methods stated above are expected to work intensively
45   with the students. This includes help in shaping the topic
46   selected and/or establishing schedules which will allow the
47   student sufficient time for rewriting and editing. Professors
48   are expected to verify, with independent research, if necessary,
49   the accuracy and completeness of the student's research. The
50   supervising faculty member is expected to give ample instruc-
51   tion to aid the student in completing the project and to guaran-
52   tee that he has developed sufficient research and writing skills
53   to be able to do such work in a professional manner after
54   graduation.

55 e.   Notwithstanding the foregoing, completion of a year's work as a
56   tutor in the first year writing and research program, or the
57   academic assistance program, or a research assistantship for a
58   full-time faculty member which assistantship requires substan-
59   tial experience will satisfy this writing requirement.

VI. HOUSEKEEPING PROVISIONS

Housekeeping provisions in legislation commonly include:

• Effective date provisions, which in some states are unnecessary
because the constitution or a statute provides for an automatic

effective date unless the bill specifies an emergency, authorizing earlier effectiveness.

• "Savings" provisions, which preserve pre-existing rights and duties if the legislation is not intended to be retroactive.

• Appropriation provisions, which specify amount, source, recipient, and purpose.

• "Sundown" provisions, which provide for legislative review and prospective repeal of certain statutes establishing advisory bodies, such as commissions or boards of trustees adjunct to executive agencies.

• "Sunset" provisions, which provide for automatic repeal of certain regulatory statutes at a scheduled time unless they are reenacted.

• Severability provisions, which are generally unnecessary because courts have inherent power to sever invalid matter in order to preserve the remainder, and also power to disregard a severability provision and invalidate the whole if they find that after severing invalid matter, the remainder becomes unreasonable, absurd, or otherwise not worth preserving.

A congressional study committee mentions the following additional matters on a list of what is most frequently litigated because not clarified in legislation:

• Appropriate statute of limitation.

• Availability of a private cause of action.

• Requirement of exhaustion of administrative remedies.

• Intention to pre-empt state law.

• Effect on existing legislation on the same subject.

• Jurisdiction in state or federal court.

• Types of relief available.

• Availability of attorney's fees, including conditions.

• Potential alternative dispute resolution for enforcement.

• Degree of formality of any administrative proceedings.[38]

---

38. Report of the Federal Court Study Committee 91 (April 2, 1990), reported in Abrahamson and Hughes, Shall We Dance? Steps for Legislators and Judges in Statutory Interpretation, 75 Minn.L. Rev. 1045, 1047 n. 5 (1991).

VII. ANNOTATED SAMPLE ACT OF CONGRESS

1 **An Act to authorize the establishment of the Glorieta National**
2 **Battlefield in the State of New Mexico, and for other**
3 **purposes.**

4 *Be it enacted by the Senate and House of Representatives of the*
5 *United States of America in Congress assembled,*

6 SEC. 1. SHORT TITLE.

7 This Act may be cited as the "Pecos National Historical Park
8 Expansion Act of 1990."

9 SEC. 2. FINDINGS AND PURPOSE.

10 (a) FINDINGS.—The Congress makes the following findings:

11 (1) the Civil War battle of Glorieta Pass, New Mexico,
12 fought on March 26–28, 1862, was a decisive battle of the Civil
13 War in the Far West;

14 (2) the battle was significant because the Confederate de-
15 feat at Glorieta Pass resulted in the collapse of the Confedera-
16 cy's plan to capture the riches and support of the West, thus
17 largely ending the Civil War in the West; and

18 (3) the campsite and headquarters of the Union forces
19 during the Battle of Glorieta are currently within the boundary
20 of Pecos National Historical Park.

21 (b) PURPOSE.—The purpose of this Act is to preserve and
22 interpret the Battle of Glorieta and to enhance visitor understand-
23 ing of the Civil War and the Far West by establishing a new unit of
24 Pecos National Historical Park.

Lines 1–3   • This is the long title. It suggests considerable relaxation of the "single subject" rule, although the text of the act shows that all of the purposes do in fact relate to the same subject.

Lines 4–5   • This is the enacting clause, which is always expressed in exactly the prescribed language.

Lines 6–8   • If an act has a short title, it is expressed in the first section. Short titles are convenient for reference, although many acts, especially state acts, do not have short titles. Notice that the short title is part of the legislation, although the long title is not.

Lines 9–24   • Section 2 illustrates the current method of expressing recitals as findings and purposes rather than in clauses beginning "WHEREAS."

           • Section 2 illustrates organization of a section with lettered and headed subsections and numbered but unheaded paragraphs within a subsection. Notice that it is possible to further divide one subsection without having to divide the second subsection.

25 SEC. 3. ESTABLISHMENT OF THE GLORIETA UNIT OF THE
26   PECOS NATIONAL HISTORICAL PARK.

27   (a) ESTABLISHMENT.—In order to preserve and interpret the
28 Battle of Glorieta for the benefit and enjoyment of present and
29 future generations, there is hereby established the Glorieta Unit of
30 the Pecos National Historical Park (hereafter in this Act referred to
31 as the "Glorieta Unit"). The Glorieta Unit shall be comprised of
32 approximately 682 acres as generally depicted on the maps entitled
33 "Glorieta Unit—Pecos National Historical Park", numbered 430–
34 80,031, and dated July 1990. The boundary of Pecos National
35 Historical Park, established by title II of Public Law 101–313 (104
36 Stat. 278), is hereby modified to include the Glorieta Unit.

37   (b) ADMINISTRATION.—The Secretary shall administer the
38 Glorieta Unit to preserve and interpret the Battle of Glorieta for the
39 benefit and enjoyment of present and future generations, in accor-
40 dance with the provisions of this Act, applicable provisions of title II
41 of Public Law 101–313, and provisions of law generally applicable to
42 units of the National Park System, including the Act of August 25,
43 1916 (39 Stat. 535; 16 U.S.C. 1–4), and the Act of August 21, 1935
44 (49 U.S.C. 666; 16 U.S.C. 461–7).

45   (c) ACQUISITION.—The Secretary is authorized to acquire
46 lands, waters, and interests therein within the boundaries of the
47 Glorieta Unit by donation, purchase with donated or appropriated
48 funds, or exchange. Lands may not be acquired for purposes of the
49 Glorieta Unit without the consent of the owner thereof unless the
50 Secretary determines that, in his judgment, the property is subject
51 to, or threatened with, uses which are having, or would have, an
52 adverse impact on the Glorieta Unit or on the management of the
53 Glorieta Unit.

54   (d) TRANSFER.—Lands identified on the maps referred to in
55 subsection (a) as being within the unit number 26 in the "Historic
56 Zone" are hereby transferred from the administration of the Secre-
57 tary of Agriculture to the administration of the Secretary of the
58 Interior, to be managed in accordance with the provisions of this
59 Act.

60   (e) MANAGEMENT PLAN.—The Secretary shall incorporate
61 management direction for the Glorieta Unit into the general man-
62 agement plan for the Pecos National Historical Park, including the

---

Lines 27–36   • Subsection 3.(a) illustrates that it is possible to have multiple sentences in
              a subsection without presenting them as numbered paragraphs. Paragraphs
              should be numbered only if they are separate and equal parallels in substance
              and form, not if they develop one idea.

              • Subsection 3.(a) presents the main substance of the act.

Lines 37–67   • Although Subsection 3.(b) is entitled "ADMINISTRATION," the entire
              remainder of the act concerns administration.

63 identification of routes of travel associated with the Battle of
64 Glorieta.

65   (f) AUTHORIZATION OF APPROPRIATIONS.—There are
66 hereby authorized to be appropriated such sums as may be neces-
67 sary to carry out the purposes of this Act.

68   Approved November 8, 1990.

VIII. ANNOTATED SAMPLE STATE ACT [ABRIDGED]

1   AN ACT to protect the public health; to place responsibility on
2 the department of public health for supervising the construction
3 and the healthful and safe operation of public swimming pools; to
4 provide for the issuance of construction and operation permits; to
5 authorize rules and regulations to carry out the intent of the act;
6 and to provide penalties and remedies.

7   *The People of the State of Michigan enact:*

8 **325.601 Public swimming pools defined; exemptions from act**

9   Sec. 1. A public swimming pool is an artificial body of water
10 used collectively by a number of persons primarily for the purpose
11 of swimming, recreational bathing or wading, and includes any
12 related equipment, structures, areas and enclosures that are intend-
13 ed for the use of persons using or operating the swimming pool such
14 as equipment, dressing, locker, shower and toilet rooms. Public
15 swimming pools include but are not limited to those which are for
16 parks, schools, motels, camps, resorts, apartments, clubs, hotels,
17 trailer coach parks, subdivisions and the like. Pools and portable
18 pools located on the same premises with a 1, 2, 3 or 4 family
19 dwelling and for the benefit of the occupants and their guests,
20 natural bathing areas such as streams, lakes, rivers or man-made
21 lakes, exhibitor's swimming pools built as models at the site of the
22 seller and in which swimming by the public is not permitted, or
23 pools serving not more than 4 motel units are exempt from this act.

Lines 1–6   • These lines make up the long title. As this title demonstrates, "single subject" rules do not prevent an act from covering a number of matters so long as they are related. The long title also shows not only the purpose of the legislation but also the scope of its administration and the fact that it includes sanctions. Long titles are usually dropped before codification.

Line 7   • This is the enacting clause.

Line 8   • Like much state legislation, this act has no short title. If it did, that title would be expressed in this first section.

    • This line is a section heading. It is typical in having only its first word capitalized. This helps convey that the heading is not part of the legislation but is for convenience only. Section headings are sometimes called "catch lines." In some states they are put in brackets as a further indication that they are not part of the legislation.

Lines 8–9   • This codification shows both the code section number (325.601) and the act section number (1) for each section of the act.

Lines 9–23   • This act illustrates legislation that recites no policies, rationales, or findings but moves directly to definition.

    • This act has only one term to define for use throughout: "public swimming pools." This definition does not follow the convention that words are defined in the singular. Notice that part of the definition is expressed in terms of exemption from the act.

24 325.602 Review of design; supervision of construction and
25   operation

26   Sec. 2. The department of public health shall review the
27 design and supervise the construction and operation of public swim-
28 ming pools in order to protect the public health, prevent the spread
29 of disease and prevent accidents or premature deaths.

30 325.603 Supervisory and visitorial power

31   Sec. 3. The department of public health has supervisory and
32 visitorial power and control as limited in this act over all municipal
33 and private corporations, governmental agencies, associations, part-
34 nerships and individuals engaged in the construction and operation
35 of public swimming pools.

36 325.605 Rules and regulations

37   Sec. 5. The department of public health may promulgate rules
38 and regulations to carry out the provisions of this act. All rules and
39 regulations shall be promulgated in accordance with Act No. 88 of
40 the Public Acts of 1943, as amended, being sections 24.71 to 24.80 of
41 the Compiled Laws of 1948, and subject to Act No. 197 of the Public
42 Acts of 1952, as amended, being sections 24.101 to 24.110 of the
43 Compiled Laws of 1948.

44 325.606 Submission of plans and specifications to department;
45   fees; permit

46   Sec. 6. (1) All municipal and private corporations, governmen-
47 tal agencies, associations, partnerships or individuals intending to
48 construct a public swimming pool or intending to modify an existing
49 public swimming pool shall submit plans and specifications for the
50 proposed installation accompanied by a fee of $50.00 to the depart-
51 ment of public health for review and approval and shall secure a
52 permit for the construction of the same and any contractor, builder,
53 corporation, partnership, governmental agency, association or indi-

---

Lines 26–29   • Section 2 begins the main substance of the act. Even its purpose is
relegated to incorporation in Section 2 (lines 28–29).

Lines 26–114   • Most of the provisions in the act create duties for the department of
public health or some other entity or individual, using the appropriate verb
form, "shall."

Lines 37–43   • Section 5 illustrates the creation of discretionary authority, using the
appropriate verb form, "may."

                 • The organization of this act is somewhat uncommon in that Section 5, an
administration provision, precedes some of the major substance of the act.

Lines 46–57   • Section 6.(1) illustrates problems of over-particularity throughout the act.
The 1980 amended version illustrates the solutions. The amended version
reads: "A person intending to construct a public swimming pool or intending
to modify an existing public swimming pool shall submit plans and specifications for the proposed installation accompanied by a fee specified in section
12527a to the department for review and approval and shall secure a permit

54 vidual shall not start or engage in the construction of a public
55 swimming pool or to modify an existing public swimming pool until
56 the permit for construction of the same has been issued by the
57 department of public health.

58   (2) Nothing in this act nor any action of the department of
59 public health shall relieve the applicant or owner of a public
60 swimming pool from responsibility for securing any building per-
61 mits or complying with all applicable local codes, regulations or
62 ordinances not in conflict with this act. Compliance with an ap-
63 proved plan shall not authorize the owner constructing or operating
64 a public swimming pool to create or maintain a nuisance or a
65 hazard to health or safety.

66 **325.608 Examination of plans and specifications; issuance or**
67 **denial of permit for construction; amendments; du-**
68 **ration of permit**

69   Sec. 8. (1) The department of public health shall examine the
70 plans and specifications and determine whether the pool facilities, if
71 constructed in accordance therewith, are or would be sufficient and
72 adequate to protect the public health and safety. If the plans and
73 specifications are approved, the department of public health shall
74 issue a permit for construction. If the plans and specifications are
75 not approved, the department of public health shall notify the
76 applicant of the deficiencies. The applicant may have the plans and
77 specifications amended to remedy the deficiencies and resubmit the
78 documents, without additional fee, for further considerations.

79   (2) A construction permit shall be valid for a period not to
80 exceed 2 years from the date of issuance unless an extension of time
81 is granted in writing by the department of public health.

82 **325.610 Operation permit; display; expiration; renewal; con-**
83 **sent to transfer; fee**

84   Sec. 10. All municipal and private corporations, governmental
85 agencies, associations, partnerships or individuals engaged in the
86 operation of a public swimming pool shall obtain a permit to operate
87 the swimming pool from the department of public health and shall
88 pay an initial operation permit fee of $50.00. Operation permits
89 shall be displayed by the owner in a conspicuous place on the
90 premises. Operation permits expire December 31 of each year. A

---

for the construction. A person shall not start or engage in the construction
of a public swimming pool or modify an existing public swimming pool until
the permit for the construction is issued by the department." Section 12527a
sets out a fee schedule related to swimming pool regulation generally; since
its passage, a change in the amount of a fee requires amending only one
section rather than a search of all related sections for possible need to
amend.

Line 79   • This line illustrates a false imperative. The statute should order a
person to do or not do something. It is no use to give orders to permits.

91 swimming pool operation permit shall be renewed upon receipt of a
92 proper application, an annual renewal fee of $10.00 and evidence
93 that the swimming pool is being operated and maintained in accor-
94 dance with the provisions of this act and the rules and regulations.
95 Operation permits shall not be transferred to another person with-
96 out the express written consent of the department of public health
97 and upon payment of a $10.00 transfer fee.

98 325.612 Operation without permit prohibited

99   Sec. 12.   After the effective date of this act, no public swim-
100 ming pool may be operated without an operation permit.

101 325.614 Periodic inspections

102   Sec. 14.   The department of public health, its agents or repre-
103 sentatives, or representatives of designated city or county or district
104 health departments shall make periodic inspections of all public
105 swimming pools.

106 325.615 Revocation of permit; hearing; reissuance

107   Sec. 15.   The department of public health may revoke the
108 operation permit if it finds the pool is not being operated in
109 accordance with the provisions of this act or the rules and regula-
110 tions.   Any person aggrieved by any decision of the department of
111 public health shall be granted a hearing as otherwise provided by
112 law.   Any permit that has been revoked shall be reissued only when
113 in the opinion of the department of public health the deficiencies
114 have been corrected.

115 325.617 Order to prohibit use of pool

116   Sec. 17.   If the department of public health, its agents or
117 representatives, or representatives of designated city or county or
118 district health departments consider that conditions warrant
119 prompt closing of a swimming pool until the provisions of this act
120 and the rules and regulations are complied with for the protection
121 of the public health and safety, it may order the owner or operator
122 of the swimming pool to prohibit any person from using it until
123 corrections have been made which would adequately protect the
124 public health and safety.

125 325.619 Violation; penalties; prosecution

126   Sec. 19.   Any person violating any of the provisions of this act
127 or any rule or regulation promulgated hereunder is guilty of a

---

Lines 99–100   • The passive verb may technically save this statement from being a false
                 imperative.   There is a human being lurking in the background somewhere.
                 Nonetheless, a smart drafter would revise it.

Lines 112–14   • These lines need revising too.   Who has the duty to do what here?

Lines 126–31   • Here is the section providing sanctions.

128 misdemeanor. Each day upon which a violation occurs is a separate
129 violation for the purpose of this act. The several prosecuting
130 attorneys and the attorney general of the state shall prosecute any
131 person violating the provisions of this act.

132 **325.620 Effective date**

133   Sec. 20. This act shall take effect January 1, 1967.

Line 133   • This is a helpful effective date provision because it is explicit rather than forcing the reader to go to some other document to calculate the effective date.

     • This effective date provision, like many, is expressed in terms of a false imperative. Properly expressed, it would read: "This act takes effect January 1, 1967."

IX. ANNOTATED SAMPLE STATE RULE OF CIVIL PROCEDURE [SHOWING AMENDMENTS]

1   **(B) Service: how made.** Whenever under these rules service
2 is required or permitted to be made upon a party who is represented
3 by an attorney of record in the proceedings, the service shall be
4 made upon ~~such~~ THE attorney unless service upon the party ~~him-~~
5 ~~self~~ is ordered by the court. Service upon the attorney or ~~upon~~ a
6 party shall be made by delivering a copy to ~~him or by~~ THE PERSON
7 TO BE SERVED, TRANSMITTING IT TO THE OFFICE OF THE
8 PERSON TO BE SERVED BY FACSIMILE TRANSMISSION, mail-
9 ing it to ~~him at his~~ THE last known address OF THE PERSON TO
10 BE SERVED or, if no address is known, ~~by~~ leaving it with the clerk
11 of the court. THE SERVED COPY SHALL BE ACCOMPANIED
12 BY A COMPLETED COPY OF THE PROOF OF SERVICE RE-
13 QUIRED BY DIVISION (<u>D</u>) OF THIS RULE. ~~Delivery of~~ <u>"</u>DELIV-
14 ERING a copy<u>"</u> within this rule means: handing it to the attorney
15 or ~~the~~ party; ~~or~~ leaving it at ~~his~~ THE office OF THE PERSON TO
16 BE SERVED with ~~his~~ A clerk or other person in charge ~~thereof~~; ~~or~~,
17 if there is no one in charge, leaving it in a conspicuous place ~~therein~~
18 IN THE OFFICE; or, if the office is closed or the person to be served
19 has no office, leaving it at ~~his~~ THE dwelling house or usual place of
20 abode OF THE PERSON TO BE SERVED with some person of
21 suitable age and discretion then residing ~~therein~~ IN THE DWELL-
22 ING HOUSE OR USUAL PLACE OF ABODE. Service by mail is
23 complete upon mailing. SERVICE BY FACSIMILE TRANSMIS-
24 SION IS COMPLETE UPON TRANSMISSION.

Exercise 5.9

When you amend legislation, you have to decide whether you can achieve the changes you intend by striking out certain words and

---

Line 4   • This is the first line in this sample illustrating the process for showing amendments by striking out repealed language and putting new language in all-capital letters. An alternate method is to substitute * * * for repealed language and to underline new language. Striking out has the advantage of allowing the reader to see at once how both the old provision and new provision read. Underlining has the advantage of being more easily readable than all-capital letters.

         • This is the first line illustrating the elimination of legalese from the rule.

         • This is the first line illustrating the conversion of the rule into gender-neutral language.

Lines 7–8   • These are the first lines amending to add new substance.

Line 13   • The underline of the letter "D" in this line is to signify that "D" is to remain a capital letter; it is not capitalized as new language. The underlined quotation marks are likewise to remain.

adding others in the original text; or whether the changes you intend are so extensive that it is necessary to repeal the original wording altogether and start over again.

Amend the following provision according to the information given below it. See whether all the amendments can be accomplished by striking out or adding words.

———

1 Sec. 4. The department of public health, its agent or represen-
2 tative or a representative of a designated city or county or district
3 health department may enter upon at all reasonable times each and
4 every swimming pool premises and other property of such govern-
5 mental agencies, corporations, associations, partnerships or individ-
6 uals for the heretofore established purpose of inspecting said prem-
7 ises and carrying out the authority herein vested in him by this act.

———

The following information is the basis for amendments:

1. "Department" has been defined at the beginning of the act to mean the state department of public health.

2. It is understood that a department acts through its agents or representatives.

3. The scope of authority granted in this section is to be narrowed to the state and county departments of public health.

4. City swimming pools are being removed from the scope of the act.

5. The authorization to inspect is to be limited to times when the pool is open to the public or else during a break of no longer than one hour when the pool is not open to the public. In other words, inspections are not to take place when a pool has closed for the day or has not yet opened for the day. The rationale for this restriction is that an inspection should take place when pool personnel are on hand to answer questions.

6. Statutes being amended in this state are to be converted into plain and gender-neutral language.

———

X. ANNOTATED SAMPLE PRIVATE LEGISLATION: DECLARATION OF RESTRICTIONS AND COVENANTS FOR A SUBDIVISION

1
2

DECLARATION OF RESTRICTIONS AND PROTECTIVE COVENANTS FOR LAKEVIEW

3 Woodland Corporation, Inc. ("Declarant"), an Ohio Corporation,
4 enters into this Declaration of Restrictions and Protective Cove-
5 nants ("Declaration") as the owner of the real property located in
6 Portage County, Ohio, described as:

7 [legal description]

8 for the purpose of imposing the following restrictions and covenants
9 on the property ("development") in order to protect its value,
10 desirability, and natural beauty.

11 **ARTICLE I**

12 **DEFINITIONS**

13 "Association" means Lakeview Community Association, Inc.,
14 and its successors.

15 "Board" means the Board of Directors as established in "The
16 Articles of Incorporation of Lakeview Community Association, Inc.,"
17 and its successors.

18 "By-Laws" means the By-Laws of the Association, as they exist
19 from time to time.

Lines 1–2   • The title of a private legislative document may link it to another document. This declaration would likely be mentioned in the articles of incorporation of Woodland Corporation, Inc., and should be titled exactly as it is referred to there.

    • It is helpful to make the title as specific as possible rather than having a generic title that merely identifies the nature of the document.

Lines 3–10   • The introductory clause in private legislation operates like the introduction in a contract, identifying party and place and providing short forms for future reference.

    • The introductory clause also operates like the long title of a statute in expressing the purpose of the legislation.

Lines 11–12   • This drafter has chosen to call the major divisions "articles," to number them with Roman numerals in bold type, and to center them on the page. All of these are matters of style and are for the drafter to choose for the sake of readability and easy reference, just as in designing a contract.

Lines 13–24   • The drafter stipulates definitions here exclusively for terms that are used in more than one other section.

    • The defined terms are arranged in alphabetical order. That is not particularly significant in this short list. In a list covering more than one page, it could be very significant.

20   "Common area" means real property owned by the Association
21 for the common use and enjoyment of owners.

22   "Homesite" does not include any common area.

23   "Owner" means the record owner (other than Declarant) of a
24 fee simple title to any homesite which is a part of the development.

25   **ARTICLE II**

26   **COMMON AREAS**

27 A. PROPERTY RIGHTS

28   1. All roads in the development and lots 15–18 are common
29 areas.

30   2. An owner has a right of enjoyment in the common areas
31 limited by Article II, Section A.3. An owner may delegate this
32 right, in accordance with the By–Laws, to tenants and invitees.

33   3. The Association has the right, subject to the signed approval
34 of owners of 75% of the homesites,

35   a.   to transfer or dedicate rights, or

36   b.   to grant permits, licenses, or easements to the common
37   areas.

38   4. Declarant retains the right to enter the common areas until
39 Declarant's construction activity in Lakeview is complete.

40 B. RESTRICTIONS

41   *1. Creating a Nuisance*

42   Any offensive activity which may be a nuisance to those nearby
43 is prohibited in the common areas.

44   *2. Hunting*

45   Hunting is prohibited in the common areas.

46   *3. Altering Improvements*

47   Only the Association may alter any of the improvements in the
48 common areas.

49 C. ASSESSMENTS

50   *1. Covenant*

51   An owner, by acceptance of a deed, is deemed to covenant to pay
52 the Association assessments for each homesite owned.

Lines 25–217   • Articles II and III contain the substance of the legislation, creating
                 rights, duties, discretionary authority, and prohibitions.

Lines 49–94   • Section II.C shows that the same principle governs sequence within a
                 section as within a document: substance precedes administration and
                 sanctions.

53   *2. Purpose*

54   The Association has the right to levy, collect, and disperse:

55   a.   **annual assessments** for the purpose of

56   i.   maintaining the common areas,

57   ii.   paying the insurance and taxes on the common
58   areas, and

59   iii. managing the Association.

60   b.   **special assessments** for the purpose of building, re-
61   placing, or extensively repairing capital improvements
62   for the use and enjoyment of owners.

63   *3. Amount*

64   The Board determines the amount of **annual assessments** by
65 agreeing in a vote by a quorum, which is a majority of the Board.
66 Commencing with the recording of this Declaration, and continuing
67 until January 1 of the following year, the **annual assessment** is
68 _____ per quarter. On January 1 of that year, and each year
69 thereafter, the Board may increase the assessment by as much as
70 7%.

71   The Board may institute a **special assessment** at any time by
72 agreeing to the amount in a vote by a quorum.

73   The Board shall give owners 60 days notice of any increase in
74 the **annual assessment** and the institution of any **special assess-**
75 **ment**.

76   *4. Payment*

77   The payments for the **annual assessment** are due quarterly on
78 the last day of March, June, September, and December. An owner's
79 first quarterly payment is prorated to cover only the period of
80 ownership of the homesite, and that payment is due on the first
81 quarterly due date after the ownership begins.

82   **Special assessments** are due 60 days after the Board gives
83 notice to owners.

84   *5. Remedies*

85   If the Board determines that an owner is delinquent, the Board
86 shall give the owner notice and allow the owner 30 days after
87 receipt of the notice to pay the assessment. If an owner fails to pay
88 within the 30 days, the Association has the right to

89   a.   place a lien on the owner's homesite; and

90   b.   sue the owner for delinquent assessments, together
91   with interest, collection costs, and attorney's fees.

Lines 53–62   • Subsection II.C.2 is further subdivided than is typical. However, the
subdivisions are strictly parallel and are justifiable as means of emphasis.

92   *6. Waiver*

93   No owner may escape liability for assessments by abandoning
94 the owner's homesite or by choosing not to use the common areas.

95   **ARTICLE III**

96   **HOMESITES**

97 A. GENERAL RESTRICTIONS

98   *1. Tree Removal*

99   An owner must get approval from the Association before cut-
100 ting down any tree on a homesite which is greater than 3 inches in
101 diameter, measured at the point of greatest circumference. The
102 purpose of this restriction is to ensure, within reasonable bounds,
103 that the wooded environment in the development is preserved.

104   *2. Proposed Improvements*

105   An owner must submit plans to and receive approval from the
106 Architectural Review Board ("ARB") before improving a homesite
107 by landscaping or building any structure.

108 B. ARCHITECTURAL REVIEW BOARD

109   *1. Members*

110   The ARB consists of three members:

111   a. an architect, appointed by the Board:

112   b. an owner, appointed by the Board; and

113   c. a third person, chosen by the two appointed members.

114   The Board may dismiss, and replace the members at its discre-
115 tion.

116   *2. Responsibility*

117   The ARB's only responsibility is to ensure that proposed im-
118 provements

119   a. comply with the specific restrictions in this Declaration
120   and

121   b. are in harmony with the other improvements in the
122   development.

123   *3. Procedure*

124   If the ARB does not reject proposed improvements within 30
125 days of receiving plans from an owner, the proposed improvements
126 are considered approved.

127   *4. Liability*

128   From the time of receiving title to a homesite, an owner is
129 solely responsible for the quality and safety of any improvements
130 placed on the homesite, as well as their compliance with this
131 Declaration. The ARB, Board, and Association are not liable for

132 any claims by an owner, or owner's representatives, connected with
133 the improvements on the homesite, including claims for any negli-
134 gent act or omission on the part of the ARB, its agents, or succes-
135 sors.

136 C. SPECIFIC RESTRICTIONS ON STRUCTURES

137 *1. Type*

138 Only single-family dwellings, one per homesite, are permitted
139 on the homesites.

140 *2. Area*

141 The dwelling shall contain at least 1500 square feet of living
142 space, excluding garages, porches, and decks.

143 *3. Mobile Homes*

144 Mobile homes are prohibited on a homesite.

145 *4. Setback*

146 The setback requirement for all structures, except fences, docks,
147 and driveways is

148 a. at least 50 feet from the high water mark of the lake
149   and at least 25 feet from any street-fronting and side
150   lot lines for lakeshore homesites and

151 b. at least 25 feet from the front, back, and side lot lines
152   for landlocked homesites.

153 *5. Height*

154 The dwelling's height, if on a lakeshore homesite, shall not
155 exceed 20 feet.

156 *6. Cinder Block*

157 No cinder block is permitted on the exterior of any structure on
158 the homesite.

159 *7. Fences*

160 The only type of fence permitted on the homesite is a wooden
161 fence no taller than 5 feet.

162 *8. Docks*

163 A single dock, not exceeding 400 square feet, is allowed on each
164 lakeshore homesite.

165 D. SPECIFIC RESTRICTIONS ON USE

166 *1. Residential Use*

167 The homesite is restricted to residential use only.

168 *2. Nuisance*

169 Any offensive activity which may be a nuisance to the neighbor-
170 hood is prohibited on the homesite.

171   *3. RV's*

172   Recreational vehicles, such as travel trailers, campers and mo-
173 tor homes outside of a garage are not permitted to remain on the
174 homesite for more than 30 days within any 12-month period.

175   *4. Pets*

176   a.   The only pets permitted on the homesite are common
177   domesticated household pets.

178   b.   Dog owners shall keep their dogs on a leash or confined
179   on the homesite.

180 **E.   EASEMENTS**

181   *1. Access to Lake*

182   Declarant grants to the Association, for the common use of
183 owners, an easement for providing access to the lake. The ease-
184 ment is limited to the area which begins along the full length of the
185 lot line separating homesites 14 and 19 and extends 15 feet into lot
186 19.

187   *2. Utilities*

188   An owner grants a general utility easement over that owner's
189 homesite.

190   *3. Maintenance Access to Homesite*

191   An owner grants the Association an easement to enter that
192 owner's homesite for maintenance purposes in accord with Article
193 III.

194 **F.   MAINTENANCE**

195   *1. Owner's Covenant*

196   An owner shall maintain that owner's improved homesite by

197   a.   mowing the grass and trimming the shrubbery regular-
198   ly,

199   b.   keeping the exterior of all the structures in good re-
200   pair, and

201   c.   disposing of refuse properly.

202   *2. Notice*

203   If the Board finds that an owner has failed to maintain that
204 owner's homesite, the Board shall give the owner notice and 30 days
205 from the date of receipt of notice to maintain the homesite. The
206 Board may give the owner up to 6 months to maintain the homesite
207 or repair damage to a structure on the homesite when the structural
208 damage is caused by a circumstance beyond the owner's control,
209 such as a fire or an act of God.

₂₁₀ *3. Penalties*

₂₁₁   If the owner fails to take action in the time allowed, the
₂₁₂ Association has the right to

₂₁₃   a. enter the homesite to provide the necessary mainte-
₂₁₄   nance,

₂₁₅   b. bill the owner for the costs of the maintenance,

₂₁₆   c. place a lien against the homesite for those costs, and

₂₁₇   d. suspend the owner's right to vote as a member of the
₂₁₈   Association until the bill is paid.

₂₁₉   **ARTICLE IV**

₂₂₀   **DURATION**

₂₂₁   These restrictions and covenants run with the land for 10 years,
₂₂₂ commencing on the date this Declaration is recorded, and then
₂₂₃ become renewed automatically for successive periods of 10 years
₂₂₄ until owners of 75% of the lots vote otherwise.

₂₂₅   **ARTICLE V**

₂₂₆   **ENFORCEMENT OF DECLARATION**

₂₂₇   Declarant, the Association, and any owner has the right to
₂₂₈ enforce these restrictions and covenants against any party violating
₂₂₉ them, by proceeding in equity for an injunction. Failure of the
₂₃₀ Declarant, Association, or owners to enforce a restriction or cove-
₂₃₁ nant does not waive their right to enforce that, or any other,
₂₃₂ restriction or covenant at a later time.

₂₃₃   **ARTICLE VI**

₂₃₄   **ANNEXATION**

₂₃₅   Declarant must have the signed approval of owners of 75% of
₂₃₆ the homesites before Declarant may exercise its right to annex
₂₃₇ adjoining property to Lakeview and subject the annexed property to
₂₃₈ this Declaration.

Lines 219-55   • Articles IV through IX are housekeeping provisions for the administra-
                  tion of the declaration. Each has its own title.

Lines 221-24   • Article IV illustrates the usual expression of housekeeping provisions
                  in the present tense. They are generally constantly effective policies rather
                  than orders for someone's future conduct.

Lines 235, 241   • Articles VI and VII properly express conditions precedent by using the
                  verb form "must."

239 **ARTICLE VII**

240 **AMENDMENTS**

241 To be effective, amendments to this Declaration must be

242   a.   written,

243   b.   agreed to and signed by

244   i.   owners of 75% of the homesites, and

245   ii.   Declarant and

246   c.   recorded.

247 **ARTICLE VIII**

248 **NOTICE**

249 The Association shall give any notices to owners in writing.
250 Notice is deemed received 3 days after the Association mails it to
251 owner at owner's address listed in the Association Record Book.

252 **ARTICLE IX**

253 **SEVERABILITY**

254 Invalidation of any part of this Declaration does not affect the
255 remainder, which remains in effect.

256 Woodland Corporation, Inc.

257 By: _____

258 Rosalind Gage, President

259 _____

260 Date

261 STATE OF OHIO
262 COUNTY OF PORTAGE

263 This instrument was acknowledged before me _____, 19__ by
264 Rosalind Gage.

265 _____

——————

Lines 261–65   • Declarations are commonly notarized and become effective when recorded.

XI. CHECKLIST FOR DRAFTING LEGISLATION

Titles

1. Does the title express the nature of the legislation: constitution, bill, act, ordinance, declaration, by-laws, regulations, etc?

2. Does the title express the subject of the legislation? Is it a single subject?

3. If appropriate, does the long title list all sections that this legislation amends or repeals?

4. If appropriate, do you give a short title as well as a long one, putting the short title in the first section?

Enacting and Other Introductory Clauses

5. If you are drafting a bill, do you have an enacting clause that uses prescribed language exactly?

6. If you are drafting private legislation, do you have an introductory clause that properly repeats the nature of the document from the title, identifies parties and subject, and establishes any short forms for future reference?

Recitals

7. Do you recite background findings and purposes only to the extent that they may aid implementation of the legislation?

8. Are you careful not to rely on recitals as aids to construction in place of clear drafting?

9. Do you draft recitals in "WHEREAS" clauses only if that is the accepted mode where the legislation will be codified?

Definitions

10. Do you have a definitions section only if you need to define words that are used in more than one other section of the legislation?

11. Do you restrict yourself to stipulative definitions that broaden, narrow, or change ordinary meaning? Do you avoid lexical definitions except to restrict to one of multiple meanings in common use?

12. Do you abide by the conventions for defining and naming discussed in Chapter 10?

Substance of the Legislation

13. Do you make explicit at the beginning of the substance of the legislation to whom it applies?

14. Do provisions establishing rights, privileges, discretionary authority, duties, and prohibitions precede administrative provisions?

15. Is the substance of the legislation no broader than it needs to be to accomplish its purpose?

16. Do you properly use each of the terms of authority: "shall," "may," "must," etc.?

Administration

17. Do the administration sections attend to all matters necessary to give effect to the legislation, including authority for rule-making, designation of enforcement agent, and appropriations?

18. Do you avoid devising any more of the procedural set-up for administration and enforcement than necessary?

Sanctions

19. Do administrative provisions precede sanctions?

Housekeeping Provisions

20. Do you avoid adding an unnecessary severability provision if a construction act in the jurisdiction imposes severability automatically?

21. Do you include any needed savings clause, repealing and amending clauses, and sunset or sundown clause?

22. Do you make clear whether the legislation gives rise to a private cause of action? If it does, do you clarify what statute of limitation applies, whether exhaustion of administrative remedies is a condition precedent, what court has jurisdiction, and what relief is available?

23. In private legislation, do you provide for later modification?

24. Do you include an effective date provision that is as precise as it is possible to be?

Organization of Sections and Text

25. Does your division of provisions into sections make the legislation easy to use for reference?

26. Do you divide sections into subsections when the subsections are readily separable and of equal weight?

27. Do you further divide subsections into paragraphs only when the paragraphs are readily separable and of equal weight?

28. Do you avoid division at any level that fragments one idea rather than revealing separate and equal parts?

29. Do you give every section and subsection a heading (or "catch line")?

30. Are headings informative?

31. Are headings substantively and formally parallel?

32. Do you normalize text as much as possible within each provision?

33. Do you focus substance when possible to emphasize conditions ("if" clauses) and results ("then" clauses)?

34. Are related provisions together with no needless cross-references?

35. Are provisions that could go under more than one heading put exclusively where the "logical pull" would have them?

Across-the-Board Editing

36. If the legislation is to be codified, do you adopt word usage, style, and format that are consistent with the code as well as internally consistent?

37. After you have finished redrafting and inserting material, are your numbering and lettering sequences accurate throughout?

38. Are cross-references accurate? Are you sure that every section you have cross-referenced elsewhere in a code has not been amended or repealed?

39. Have you consistently used any short forms you established in the beginning?

40. Have you used any words for which you stipulated definitions consistently with those definitions?

XII. DRAFTING ASSIGNMENTS

Drafting Assignment 5.A—Ordinance on Swimming Pools

Redraft Ordinance No. 82–19, presented in Exercise 5.1. Assume it is for a county in Michigan, and that the state statutes on swimming pools presented in Section VIII of this chapter are in force.

Drafting Assignment 5.B—Ordinance on False Alarms

Redraft Ordinance No. 84–10, presented in Exercise 5.2. Assume that in its present form it has received considerable outcry from property owners charged for false alarms, and from alarm sales and services companies, some of whom have threatened to challenge it for vagueness, or for lack of a single subject. The county's law enforcement personnel would like to salvage as much of it as possible as a deterrent against using up too much of their time responding to false alarms.

Drafting Assignment 5.C—Ordinance on
Nudity and Alcohol

You are the county attorney mentioned in Exercise 5.3. You discover that a neighboring county has passed Ordinance No. 91–5, which follows. Analyze it and then draft the narrowest ordinance you can to address the matter your commissioners have brought to you.

————

1   ORDINANCE 91–5

2   AN ORDINANCE AMENDING THE _____ COUNTY CODE
3   BY CREATING A NEW CHAPTER 115, ALCOHOLIC BEVER-
4   AGE ESTABLISHMENTS; PROVIDING FOR DEFINITIONS;
5   PROVIDING FOR LEGISLATIVE FINDINGS; PROVIDING A
6   PROHIBITION RELATING TO NUDITY AND SEXUAL CON-
7   DUCT OR THE SIMULATION THEREOF WITHIN ALCOHOL-
8   IC BEVERAGE ESTABLISHMENT; PROVIDING FOR A PEN-
9   ALTY FOR THE VIOLATION OF SUCH CHAPTER;
10   PROVIDING FOR SEVERABILITY; PROVIDING AN EFFEC-
11   TIVE DATE.

12   WHEREAS, evidence has been propounded from other commu-
13 nities that indicates that nudity and sexual conduct and the depic-
14 tion thereof, coupled with alcohol in public places, begets undesir-
15 able behavior, and that prostitution, attempted rape, rape, and
16 assaults have occurred and have the potential for occurring in and
17 around establishments dealing in alcoholic beverages where nude
18 and sexual conduct and depiction thereof is permitted; and,

19   WHEREAS, the Board of County Commissioners wishes to
20 protect against similar conditions to the end that they not occur in
21 _____ County at or around alcoholic beverage establishments;
22 and

23   WHEREAS, _____ County possesses the authority to exercise
24 the regulatory power of the Twenty-first Amendment; and,

25   WHEREAS, the Board of County Commissioners can consider
26 other communities' experience in deciding to legislate under the
27 Twenty-first Amendment in this area.

28   NOW, THEREFORE, BE IT ORDAINED BY THE BOARD OF
29 COUNTY COMMISSIONERS OF _____ COUNTY, _____:

30   Section 1. That the _____ County Code is hereby amended
31 by adding a new Chapter 115, Alcoholic Beverage Establishments,
32 and related sections thereof which shall read as follows:

CHAPTER 115. ALCOHOLIC BEVERAGE ESTABLISH-MENTS

Sec. 115.01 Definitions.

"Alcoholic beverage" shall mean all beverages containing more than one per cent (1%) alcohol by weight.

"Establishment dealing in alcoholic beverages" shall mean any business or commercial establishment, whether open to the public at large or where entrance is limited by a cover charge or membership requirement, including those licensed by the state for sale and/or service of alcoholic beverages; a hotel; a motel; a restaurant; a night club; a country club; a cabaret; a meeting facility utilized by any religious, social, fraternal, or similar organization; or a business or commercial establishment where a product or article is sold, dispensed, served, or provided with the knowledge, actual or implied, that the same will be or is intended to be mixed, combined with or drunk in connection or combination with an alcoholic beverage served or bought on the premises; or business or commercial establishment where the consumption of alcoholic beverages is permitted, whether bought on the premises or brought onto the premises and thereafter consumed. That portion of a facility designed and equipped as a dwelling unit which is actually being used as a permanent, temporary, or transient private residence, including, but not limited to, houses, apartments, condominiums, hotel and motel rooms, dormitories, and boarding houses, is not an establishment dealing in alcoholic beverages. This definition shall not be construed or interpreted to apply to any establishment except those where alcoholic beverages, as defined herein, are sold, dispensed, consumed, or possessed on the premises, or permitted to be brought on the premises for consumption.

Sec. 115.02 Legislative Finding. It is hereby found by the Board of County Commissioners, acting in its legislative capacity for the purpose of regulating alcoholic beverage establishments, as authorized pursuant to the Twenty-first Amendment, that, considering what has happened in other communities, the acts prohibited in Sec. 115.03 below encourage or create the potential for the conduct of prostitution, attempted rape, rape, and assault in and around establishments dealing in alcoholic beverages; that actual and simulated nudity and sexual conduct and the depiction thereof, coupled with alcohol in public places begets and has the potential for begetting undesirable behavior; that sexual, lewd, lascivious, and salacious conduct among patrons and employees within establishments dealing in alcoholic beverages results in violation of law and creates dangers to the health, safety, morals, and welfare of the public and those who engage in such conduct; and, it is the intent of this ordinance to prohibit nudity, gross sexuality, and the simulation and depiction thereof, in establishments dealing in alcoholic beverages.

Sec. 115.03 Nudity, Sexual Conduct Prohibited. Within existing or newly created establishments dealing in alcoholic beverages:

a. No person shall expose to public view his or her genitals, pubic area, or buttocks, or any simulation thereof.

b. No female person shall expose to public view any portion of her breasts directly or laterally below the top of the areola, or any simulation thereof.

c. No person maintaining, owning, or operating an establishment dealing in alcoholic beverages shall suffer or permit any person to expose to public view his or her genitals, pubic area, or any portion of the buttocks or simulation thereof.

d. No person maintaining, owning, or operating an establishment dealing in alcoholic beverages shall suffer or permit any female person to expose to public view any portion of her breasts, directly or laterally, below the top of the areola or any simulation thereof.

e. No person shall engage in and no person maintaining, owning, or operating an establishment dealing in alcoholic beverages shall suffer or permit any sexual intercourse, masturbation, sodomy, bestiality, oral copulation, flagellation, any sexual act which is prohibited by law, touching, caressing, or fondling of the breasts, buttocks, anus, or genitals, or the simulation thereof.

f. No person shall cause and no person maintaining, owning, or operating an establishment dealing in alcoholic beverages shall suffer or permit the exposition of any graphic representations, including pictures or images by the projection of film or video images on a television or a monitor, which depicts human genitals, pubic area, buttocks, female breasts directly or laterally below the top of the areola, sexual intercourse, masturbation, sodomy, bestiality, oral copulation, flagellation, any sexual act prohibited by law, touching, caressing, or fondling of the breasts, buttocks, anus or genitals, or any simulation thereof. This subsection shall not be construed to prohibit the showing of movies, tapes, or video cassettes that contain a movie industry rating of "R" or "PG–13."

Sec. 115.04 Penalty. Any person violating this ordinance shall be guilty of a misdemeanor and, in addition to any other penalty provided herein, shall be subject to the penalty set forth in Section 125.69(1), _____ Statutes.

125   Section 2. Severability. If any section, subsection, sentence,
126 clause, phrase, or provision of this ordinance is held invalid or
127 unconstitutional by a court of competent jurisdiction, such invalidi-
128 ty or unconstitutionality shall not be so construed as to render
129 invalid or unconstitutional the remaining provisions of this ordi-
130 nance.

131   Section 3. Effective Date. A certified copy of this ordinance
132 shall be filed with the Department of State by the Clerk of the
133 Board of County Commissioners within ten (10) days after enact-
134 ment by the Board of County Commissioners, and shall take effect
135 upon receipt of official acknowledgment from that office that the
136 same has been filed.

137   DULY ADOPTED in regular session, this _____ day of
138 _____, A.D., 1991.

139   BOARD OF COUNTY
140   COMMISSIONERS OF _____
141   COUNTY, _____

142   By: _____
143   CHAIRMAN

144 ATTEST:

145 _____   APPROVED AS TO FORM

146 CLERK   _____

147   (SEAL)   _____ COUNTY ATTORNEY

Drafting Assignment 5.D—Declaration of Covenants and Restrictions

You represent Todd Ramsey and Elizabeth Randalla. Ramsey is the land developer mentioned in Exercise 5.4. Ramsey and Randalla are married to each other and own the property that is to become the exclusive subdivision. Your new paralegal has interviewed them and drafted the declaration that follows. Ramsey and Randalla say that its content does reflect what they told the paralegal, but they are nonetheless not satisfied with the drafting.

Test the declaration that follows against the sample declaration in Section X of this chapter. Then draft a declaration for the approval of Ramsey and Randalla, keeping the facts the paralegal gleaned from them and supplying any additional content you determine to be appropriate.

RESTRICTIVE COVENANTS

1 KNOW ALL PERSONS BY THESE PRESENTS that:

2   WHEREAS, _____ and _____, his wife, hereinafter called
3 "Owners", are desirous of placing certain restrictive covenants on
4 the use of said property, which said property is more particularly
5 described as follows:

6   NOW, THEREFORE, THESE PRESENTS WITNESSETH: That
7 the Owners, for and in consideration of the covenants herein con-
8 tained, and for other good and valuable considerations, do herein
9 and hereby covenant and agree, for their successors and assigns,
10 that the following covenants and restrictions are hereby placed
11 upon the said property above described:

12   1. All building sites shall be used solely and only for residen-
13 tial purposes and no structures, permanent or temporary, shall be
14 erected, altered, placed or permitted to remain on any lot other than
15 one detached, single-family dwelling, not to exceed two and one-half
16 (2½) stories in height.

17   2. There shall be no detached or accessory buildings except
18 cabanas which are permissible when erected adjacent to and used in
19 conjunction with a swimming pool.

20   3. No building shall be erected, placed or altered on any
21 premises until the building plans, specifications, and plot plan
22 showing the location of such building have been approved as to
23 conformity and harmony of external design with the existing struc-
24 tures in the development, and as to location of the building with
25 respect to topography and finished ground elevation, by an architec-
26 tural committee as outlined in paragraph number 17.

27   4. No building shall be located on any lot except within the
28 setback and easement lines indicated on the recorded plat, however,
29 said structures are to be at least 25 feet from the front of said
30 property line and at least 12½ feet from the side of the property line
31 and at least 20 feet from the back of the property line.

32   5. No lots shall be resubdivided into parcels smaller than that
33 recorded in Plat Book _____, Page _____, of the Public Records
34 of _____ County, _____.

35   6. No noxious or offensive trade or activity shall be carried on
36 upon any building site, nor shall anything be done thereon which
37 may be or become an annoyance or nuisance to the neighborhood.

38   7. No trailer, tent, shack, garage, barn or other out building
39 erected on a building site covered by these covenants shall at any
40 time be used for human habitation, temporarily or permanently,
41 nor shall any structure of a temporary character be used for human
42 habitation.

8. The keeping of a mobile home, either with or without wheels, on any parcel of property covered by these covenants is prohibited. Any motor boat, house boat, boat trailer or other similar water borne vehicle may be maintained, stored, or kept on any parcel of residential property covered by these covenants only if housed completely within a structure which has been architecturally approved by provisions of paragraph number 3 hereof.

9. Self propelled motor homes may be kept on the property, but only if they are placed in the back yard of the property and cannot be seen from the side boundary or the front side of the property.

10. No dwelling shall be permitted on any building site covered by these covenants, the habitable floor area of which, exclusive of basements, porches, and garages, is less than 1800 square feet.

11. Easements are hereby reserved for utility installation and maintenance as indicated on the recorded plat, and no structures of any kind shall be erected in the area of such easements. Nothing may be placed within area of the drainage easements indicated on the recorded plat to impede or alter the flow of water within such drainage easements.

12. No animals or poultry of any kind other than house pets shall be kept or maintained on any part of said property.

13. When any building site shall be for sale, only one "For Sale" sign will be permitted for each lot, and this sign shall be no larger than 6 square feet; except that a sign of up to 32 square feet may be used by a builder or real estate broker to advertise a new property for sale during the construction and sales period, the sales period to extend for no more than 3 months from the date of issuance of the building permit.

14. No fence, wall or hedge shall be permitted to extend beyond the minimum building set back lines established herein except upon approval by the architectural committee as provided in paragraph 17 hereof.

15. It is prohibited for any garage or carport to face the front of the property. All garages and carports must have side entrances with the front portion of the garage or carport being of the same type and design as the remainder of the dwelling.

16. All driveways and parking areas must be paved with either asphaltic concrete or Portland Cement concrete. Drives must be paved to the curb line and shall be continuously paved in any area meant for driving or automobile storage. There shall be garages, carports or paved area on each building site for the parking of at least four automobiles. No car shall be parked, stored or otherwise left on any unpaved area. At no time shall there be any repairing, dismantling, or other mechanical work done on any automobiles or other vehicles, except in a closed carport or garage.

89   17. An architectural control committee is hereby established.
90 This committee is composed of _____ and _____, his wife. The
91 committee may designate a representative to act for it. In the
92 event of death or resignation of any member of the committee, the
93 remaining member shall have full authority to designate a succes-
94 sor. Should the membership of such committee be changed, notice
95 of this change shall be recorded in the Office of the Clerk of the
96 Circuit Court of _____ County, _____.

97   The architectural control committee shall approve or disap-
98 prove any design within 15 days from the date of the submission of
99 these plans, and such approval or disapproval shall be in writing.
100 In the event the committee, or its designated representative, fails to
101 approve or disapprove within said 15 days, then approval is deemed
102 to have been granted and the related covenants shall be deemed to
103 have been fully complied with.

104   These covenants are to run with the land and shall be binding
105 on all parties and all persons claiming under them until January 1,
106 2005, at which time said covenants shall be automatically extended
107 for successive periods of ten (10) years, unless by vote of a majority
108 of the then owners of the lots, it is agreed to change said covenants
109 in whole or in part.

110   If the parties hereto, or any of them, or their heirs or assigns,
111 shall violate or attempt to violate any of the covenants herein, it
112 shall be lawful for any other person or persons owning any real
113 property situated in said subdivision to prosecute any proceedings at
114 law or in equity against the person or persons violating or attempt-
115 ing to violate any such covenant, and either to prevent him or them
116 from so doing, or to recover damages for such violation.

117   Invalidation of any one of these covenants, or any part thereof,
118 by judgment or court order shall in no wise affect any of the other
119 provisions, which shall remain in full force and effect.

120   IN WITNESS WHEREOF, the Owners have hereunto affixed
121 their signatures this _____ day of _____, A.D., 19__.

122 Signed in the presence of:

123 _____   _____

124 _____   _____

125 STATE OF _____ ⎫
126 COUNTY OF _____ ⎭

127   BEFORE ME personally appeared _____ and _____, his
128 wife, well known and known to me to be the individuals described in
129 and who executed the foregoing instrument as "Owners" of the
130 above named real property and severally acknowledged to and

131 before me that they executed such instrument as their own free act
132 and deed and for the reasons therein expressed.

133   WITNESS my hand and official seal this _____ day of
134 _____, A.D., 19__.

135

136   Notary Public, State at Large
137   My Commission Expires:

Assignment 5.E—By-Laws

You are counsel to the Board of your state's Wildlife Protection Institute, Inc., a not-for-profit corporation. Its by-laws were poorly drafted, by your unknown predecessor. You have received a memo from the Board Secretary reporting that the Board wants you to redraft the by-laws to make certain substantive changes. You are requested also to improve the drafting generally and to make the by-laws gender-neutral. The by-laws follow. Following them, the requested substantive changes are listed.

1   **BYLAWS OF WILDLIFE PROTECTION**
2   **INSTITUTE, INC.**

3   <u>**Article I**</u>

4   The purpose for which the Wildlife Protection Institute, Inc.
5 (hereinafter referred to as the "Institute") is organized is to foster
6 awareness of land preservation systems in the State of _____
7 devoted mainly to wildlife, to engage in education and advocacy for
8 better understanding of the management, funding, and problems of
9 these systems, and to do all things necessary through lawful means
10 to carry out this purpose, and especially through litigation to
11 prevent contamination of wildlife refuges in the State of _____ by
12 the toxic wastes of industry and agriculture.

13   <u>**Article II**</u>

14   **DEFINITION AND CLASSES OF MEMBERSHIP**

15   The Institute shall be deemed to have one class of members.
16 There are no qualifications limiting or denying membership in the
17 Institute and the right to vote. Each member of the Institute shall
18 be a person who pays dues and thereby supports the purposes of the
19 Institute. The Board of Directors shall establish such rules and
20 regulations governing admissions to membership as from time to
21 time it shall deem advisable.

22   <u>**Article III**</u>

23   The fiscal year of the WPI shall be July 1 through June 30 but
24 may be changed by resolution of the Board of Directors.

Article IV

25

26 § 1. Executive Director. The Executive Director shall be se-
27 lected by the Board of Directors.

28 § 2. Duties. The Executive Director shall carry out the poli-
29 cies set by the Board of Directors. The Executive Director shall
30 hire, terminate, and supervise the staff and shall prepare an annual
31 budget for the approval of the Board of Directors. The Executive
32 Director shall submit reports to the Board of Directors on a quarter-
33 ly basis prior to each regularly scheduled meeting of the Board of
34 Directors.

Article V

35

36 Every member of the Board of Directors, officer or employee of
37 the WPI may be indemnified by the WPI against all expenses and
38 liabilities, including counsel fees, incurred or imposed upon such
39 members of the Board, officer or employee in connection with any
40 threatened, pending, or completed action, suit or proceeding to
41 which he may become involved by reason of his being or having
42 been a member of the Board, officer, or employee of the WPI, or any
43 settlement thereof, unless adjudged therein to be liable for gross
44 negligence or willful misconduct in the performance of his duties.
45 Provided, however, that the foregoing right of indemnification shall
46 be in addition to and not exclusive of all other rights to which such
47 member of the Board, officer or employee is entitled.

Article VI

48

49 The annual membership meeting shall be held the first Tuesday
50 in February of each year in [state capital], or such other place as the
51 Board of Directors may decide. Written notice of the meeting shall
52 be mailed by the Secretary to the last recorded address of each
53 member at least 30 days before the time appointed for the meeting.
54 Where members not present have waived notice in writing, the
55 giving of notice as above required may be dispensed with.

56 Special membership meetings may be called at any time by the
57 Board of Directors within or without [state capital]. Special meet-
58 ings may also be called upon a petition to the Board of Directors by
59 50 of the voting members of the Institute. Such meeting shall be
60 held within 60 days of receipt of said petition, which shall state the
61 purpose of the special meeting. The time and place of the meeting
62 shall be set by the Executive Committee of the Board of Directors.
63 Notices of the special meeting shall be mailed to each member at his
64 last recorded address at least 10 days in advance, with a statement
65 of time, place, and purpose of said special meeting. No business
66 other than that specified in the call for the special meeting shall be
67 transacted at such special meeting.

68   At any regular meeting or special meeting a quorum shall
69 consist of at least twenty voting members present. A lesser number
70 when not constituting a quorum may adjourn the meeting from
71 time to time until a quorum be present. Each member is entitled to
72 one vote which may be cast in person or by written authority of
73 proxy. The affirmative vote of a majority of the votes entitled to be
74 cast by the members present or by written authority of proxy at a
75 meeting at which a quorum is present in person is necessary for any
76 matter voted upon.

77   **Article VII**

78   **ASSETS**

79   Upon dissolution of the WPI, all of its assets and property of
80 every nature and description remaining after the payment of all
81 liabilities and obligations of the WPI (but not including assets held
82 by the WPI upon condition requiring return, transfer, or convey-
83 ance, which condition occurs by reason of the dissolution) shall be
84 paid over and transferred to one or more organizations which
85 engage in activities substantially similar to those of the WPI and
86 which are then qualified for exemption from federal income taxes as
87 organizations described in section 501(c)(3) of the Internal Revenue
88 Code of 1954 (or corresponding provisions of any subsequent federal
89 tax laws).

90   **Article VIII**

91   **SELECTION AND OBLIGATIONS OF DIRECTORS;**
92   **ALSO RESIGNATION OR TERMINATION**

93   1. The Directors have control and management of the affairs
94 of the Institute with authority to do everything necessary and
95 desirable in the conduct of the business of the Institute and in
96 accordance with the By-Laws and purpose of the Institute.

97   2. The Directors select the members of the Litigation Screen-
98 ing Committee, and review and approve the selection of the Chair-
99 man of the Committee and the Executive Director. They shall issue
100 a financial statement and a general annual report to the member-
101 ship.

102   3. The Board of Directors shall consist of fifteen (15) members
103 initially. When Institute membership has increased to 1,000 people,
104 the Board shall expand to eighteen (18); when membership in-
105 creases to 2,000 the Board will expand to twenty-one (21) members.

106   4. Only persons who are members at the time the Nominating
107 Committee is constituted are eligible to serve on the Board of
108 Directors.

109   5. Directors shall serve three-year terms, except for the Direc-
110 tors elected in February, 1981, when eight directors elected shall

111 serve two-year terms and seven directors elected shall serve one-
112 year terms. Thereafter, all directors shall be elected for three-year
113 terms, and shall serve no more than two consecutive terms.

114   6. Directors shall be elected by a majority vote of the member-
115 ship in person or by proxy at each Annual Meeting.

116   7. At a minimum, one-half plus one of the number of Board
117 members must be residents of the [state capital] metropolitan area
118 who are committed to maintaining the activities of the Institute.

119   8. The management of the Institute shall be vested in the
120 Board of Directors, which shall consist of at least fifteen and not
121 more than twenty-one persons.

122   9. The Board of Directors shall, not less than 90 days prior to
123 the Annual Meeting, select a Committee on Nominations and set
124 the date of the Annual Meeting. The Committee on Nominations
125 shall consist of five members of WPI; two of whom shall be Board
126 members not running for office in the election year.

127   10. The committee shall nominate WPI members who shall be
128 eligible to be Directors by the date of appointment of the Nominat-
129 ing Committee. The number shall be at least one and one-third of
130 the Board positions to be filled. Members of the Committee may
131 not be included among those nominated by the committee. The
132 board shall appoint three out of fifteen directors. These three
133 appointed Directors will be phased in over a three year period, one
134 appointment per year for the next three years. Therefore, for the
135 next three years there will be a decrease by one director per year in
136 the number of Directors to be elected to the Board.

137   11. The Committee shall submit its report to the Executive
138 Director not less than 45 days prior to the Annual Meeting. The
139 Executive Director shall notify all members of WPI not later than
140 30 days before the Annual Meeting of the nominees.

141   12. In selecting Board nominees, the Committee will work for
142 diversity, including minority representatives, persons with signifi-
143 cant achievement in management fields, major contributors to the
144 Institute, and those with expertise in the Institute's primary areas
145 of emphasis. As the membership of the Institute expands, geo-
146 graphic diversity of Board members also should be sought.

147   13. One-third of the Board shall constitute a quorum for all
148 purposes, but in the event of a quorum not being present, a lesser
149 number may adjourn the meeting to some future time.

150   14. The Board shall hold at least 4 regularly scheduled meet-
151 ings a year. Special meetings may be called by the President on
152 five days notice to each Director either personally, by telephone,
153 mail or telegram.

154   15. At all meetings of the Board of Directors, each Director
155 shall have one vote which must be cast in person. The affirmative
156 vote of a majority of the votes entitled to be cast by the Directors

157 present at a meeting at which a quorum is present in person is
158 necessary for any matter voted upon.

159   16. a. The Board of Directors shall elect a President, Vice
160 President and Secretary/Treasurer who shall serve as the Executive
161 Committee at the first meeting after election of the Board of
162 Directors. The Executive Committee, whose members serve at the
163 pleasure of the Board, shall meet as needed and on an emergency
164 basis and shall exercise between Board meetings all the powers and
165 duties of the Board. The President of the Board immediately
166 previous to the present Board of Directors may serve ex officio on
167 the Executive Committee.

168   b. The Board may designate other committees which it chooses
169 to establish to conduct its business.

170   17. Although no fewer than two-thirds of the Board members
171 should be experts on environmental concerns and/or lawyers, each
172 Board must include some non-professional members.

173   18. Resignation is effective upon receipt of the written resigna-
174 tion of the Director by the Secretary of the Board or written
175 confirmation by the Board of Director's oral resignation. A Board
176 member may be removed with or without cause by a majority vote
177 of the membership. In addition, there shall be a rebuttable pre-
178 sumption of termination of any member of the Board of Directors
179 who misses two meetings of the Board during one term in office.
180 Vacancies in the Board of Directors existing by reason of resigna-
181 tion, death, or removal before the expiration of a term may be filled
182 by a majority vote of the remaining members of the Board. Direc-
183 tors so appointed hold office until their successors are elected at the
184 next annual meeting.

185   **Article IX**

186   **COMPENSATION**

187   § 1. Compensation. Officers, Directors, and members of the
188 committees of the Institute shall serve without compensation by the
189 Institute, provided, however, that expenses incurred in furtherance
190 of the business of the Institute may be reimbursed.

191   § 2. Tenure. The Board shall elect all officers of the Institute
192 for one year at the February meeting of the Board for one year
193 terms. Officers shall be eligible for reappointment.

194   § 3. Resignation and removal. Resignations of officers are
195 effective upon receipt by the Secretary of the Board of a written
196 notification. Officers may be removed with or without cause by the
197 Board.

198   **Article X**

199   These bylaws may be amended or replaced by two-thirds of the
200   members voting in person or by written authority of proxy at any
201   duly organized meeting of the WPI, provided notice of the proposed
202   change is mailed to the members as required by Article V.

Substantive Changes Requested by the Board

1.   Expand the Board to 17.   Directors to be elected by the Board.
Nominating Committee to be 5 Board members.   Board can appoint
them.   Board needs to produce a slate (same number as to be elected),
and get the names to the Board at least 15 days before the Board's
election meeting, which has to be in time for new Board members to be
seated at the annual meeting.   Make clear that the Nominating Committee cannot nominate any of themselves.   Also, the Board does not
have to elect the Committee's slate.   Any Board member can add other
names to the slate.   All that is required is to propose them in writing to
each Board member at least 5 days ahead of the election.

2.   Annual meeting is moved to October.   Special meeting requires
petition by 25% of membership, and meeting must be within 60 days of
receipt of petition.   Otherwise special meeting is just like annual
meeting—no different notice requirements and no special rules on what
petition must say.

3.   Quorum is 20.   Quorum at Directors' meeting is majority.

4.   It is acceptable for members of the Board to participate in
Board meetings by conference call.   All that matters is that everybody
at the meeting be able to hear everybody else.   In other words,
somebody attending by conference phone is there for purposes of the
quorum and can vote.

5.   Removal of a director is by $\frac{2}{3}$ of the Board.   No more 2–
meeting rule.

6.   Officers are now going to be Chair, Vice Chair, President, and
Secretary–Treasurer.   The Chair will preside over the Board, and the
President will be an employee (taking the place of the Executive
Director), who serves as Chief Operating Officer (CEO), compensation to
be determined by the Board.   The President cannot be elected to any
other office, and nobody can hold more than one office at once.   All
officers have one year terms except the President, who serves at the
pleasure of the Board.

7.   At Board meetings, votes are by majority of members present,
but amending the by-laws requires $\frac{2}{3}$ of the entire Board.   The Board
can act without meeting if all the members agree in writing to act
without a meeting and also agree to the specific action.

8. Board meetings at least twice a year, October and one other. Alternate between cities in northern and southern part of state, plus others where and when Board chooses. Special meetings to be called by President, Chair, or any 5 directors, 10 days notice if by 1st class mail, 5 days if phone, telegraph, or in person.

9. Board wants to expand to be truly representative of entire state's interests, so at least 5 Board members have to be from north of [some particular city in center of your state] and at least 5 from south of there. Also, annual meetings to rotate: one year city in northeast or northwest, next year city in southeast or southwest.

10. Directors to have 3 year terms except people starting next October. Of those, 7 have term expiring 3 years later, 5 expire 2 years later, and 5 expire 1 year later. Nobody can have more than 2 consecutive 3–year terms, but somebody can be re-elected a year after a term ends. Terms to begin and end at annual meeting.

11. Members of WPI are all people who pay dues. No other qualifications, and Board does not have to pass on admission. The Board decided it is time to nail down some dues policies. If a person has a job, that person will pay regular dues, and it is up to the Board's majority vote what that regular dues amount is. The Board will also vote (with majority ruling) on some other amount (less) that students and unemployed members pay for dues. Other members, not just students and unemployed, can make special appeals to have their dues reduced or waived altogether. All dues are due on the date a person joins and then on the anniversary date every year after that.

Chapter 6

WILLS

I. A WILL AS A CREATURE OF STATUTE

A. THE IMPORTANCE OF RESEARCH

A will is a document through which a testator (1) makes a testamentary disposition of property and (2) nominates a personal representative to administer the testator's estate. The testator may also nominate (1) a trustee, (2) a guardian for the testator's minor children, and (3) a conservator for their property. A will is in many respects governed by statutes, including statutes on everything from anatomical gifts to simultaneous death and, of course, taxes. Therefore, anyone who drafts a will needs to do up-to-date research on the statutes governing it as well as the tax implications of the estate plan. This chapter addresses drafting issues that generally arise irrespective of where the will is probated and irrespective of trusts and estate planning for tax purposes.[1]

1. For an introductory text on drafting to accompany a traditional course in wills and trusts, see L. Levin, A Student's Guide to Will Drafting (1987); for a comprehensive treatise that the editor calls a "how-to-do-it-and-why" book with abundant sample provisions, see J. Stocker, Stocker on Drawing Wills (10th ed. 1987); for a sample will drafted by an 81–member ABA Committee on Estate Planning and Drafting, containing marital deduction, generation-skipping, and trust provisions, and including copious explanatory comments and alternative texts, see A Sample Will, 27 Practical Lawyer 21 (No. 2, Mar. 1, 1981); see also A. Bove, Jr., Common Will Provi-

B. STATUTORY TERMINOLOGY

The drafter of a will is wise to use terminology consistent with that in the statutes of the state where the will is expected to be offered for probate. For example, the statutes may maintain strict distinctions among the terms "executor," "executrix," "administrator," and "administratrix"; or the statutes may collapse all of these terms into one: "personal representative."

C. THE VALUE OF FOLLOWING THE STRICTEST RULES

On the other hand, it is important to keep in mind that a will may be offered for probate in a different state from the one where it is drafted. At the very least, if the testator owns real property in more than one state, it is wise to make the will comply with the rules imposed by the strictest of those states.[2]

D. DEFAULT STATUTES

A will is ambulatory, which means that it does not "speak" until the testator dies, which may be long after the will is drafted. Thus will drafting imposes an extraordinary duty to be clear. Some of the flexibility that we purposefully build into contracts and the generality sought in much legislative drafting may produce problems in a will.

Many of the statutes that govern wills provide "default" rules that operate only when the will is silent or unclear on a matter. Depending on the testator's wishes, it may be important to draft specifically to avoid the operation of such a statute. On the other hand, if what the testator wants is what the statute provides, some drafters prefer to keep the will streamlined by leaving that matter out. This practice may be dangerous, however. The statute may change before the will is probated. Also, the will may be probated in a state with a different statute from the one the drafter is counting on to govern.[3] All things considered, completeness and precision are usually the safest values when drafting a will because of the general rule that prohibits reforming a will to correct a drafter's error.[4]

---

sions, ch. 5, The Complete Book of Wills and Estates 63 (1989).

2. Levin, above note 1, at 32.

3. For detailed analysis of fill-in-the-blank statutory will forms compared with the Uniform Statutory Will Act's incorporation by reference approach, see Beyer, Statutory Will Methodologies—Incorporated Forms vs. Fill–In Forms: Rivalry or Peaceful Coexistence? 94 Dickenson L.Rev. 231 (1990).

4. deFuria, Jr., Mistakes in Wills Resulting from Scriveners' Errors: The Argument for Reformation, 40 Catholic U.L.

Rev. 1, 2 (1990) (arguing that drafters' errors should be correctable as innocent misrepresentation by the drafter to the testator). For the shifting positions of states on whether a lawyer who negligently drafts a will is liable to a disappointed beneficiary, see Jenkins, Privity—A Texas-size Barrier to Third Parties for Negligent Will Drafting—An Assessment and Proposal, 42 Baylor L.Rev. 687 (1990); Note, Hale v. Groce: Lawyer Liability to Intended Beneficiaries of Negligently Drafted Wills—Last Stand of the Immutable Privity Doctrine, 24 Willamette L.Rev. 843 (1988) (privity doctrine removed as barrier in Ore.).

II. ANNOTATED SAMPLE WILL, SELF-PROVING AFFIDAVIT, AND CODICIL

A. SAMPLE WILL

1   WILL OF DIANE FRIEDMAN WEISS

2   I, DIANE FRIEDMAN WEISS, also known as Diane B. Weiss
3 and formerly known as Diane A. Benton before my marriage to
4 CHRISTOPHER MICHAEL WEISS, SR. ("CHRISTOPHER"), and
5 residing in _____, _____ County, _____, declare this my Will
6 and revoke all prior wills and codicils.

7   ARTICLE ONE

8   DEFINITIONS

9   "Beneficiary" means the recipient of a bequest made by this
10 Will.

11   "Bequest" means a gift made by this Will.

12   "My children" means my daughter REBECCA SUSAN WEISS
13 ("REBECCA"), born January 24, 1987; my son CHRISTOPHER
14 MICHAEL WEISS, JR. ("CHRIS"), born June 5, 1990; my stepson
15 WILLIAM PAUL WEISS, whether or not later adopted by me, and
16 any other children born to or adopted by me after I execute this
17 Will.

18   "Per stirpes" means "by stocks," referring to a method of
19 dividing shares of a bequest, according to which if a beneficiary does
20 not survive the testator, that beneficiary's children share equally
21 the bequest to that beneficiary.

22   "Testator" means a person who makes a Will.

Line 1   • It is helpful for filing purposes if the title of a will includes the full
                    name of the testator.

Lines 2–6   • The introductory clause gives all present names of the testator and any
                    former ones by which she might be known, as well as any helpful informa-
                    tion explaining a name change.

Lines 4, 14   • This will has to address the common problem of two beneficiaries with
                    the same name, here father and son. Short forms distinguish between
                    them.

Lines 7–8   • The divisions of wills are commonly called "articles." As in any other
                    document, it is a helpful reference device to give every division a heading.

Lines 9–11   • These lexical definitions of terms of art are included for the benefit of
18–22   lay readers.

Lines 12–17   • This is a common stipulative definition in a will. In many states
                    default statutes accomplish the same result regarding afterborn and adopted
                    children. This definition explicitly takes the stepchild outside of a default
                    statute that would define "child" to exclude a stepchild.

                    • Terms are commonly defined in the singular. This context makes the
                    plural definition more manageable.

23 ARTICLE TWO

24 BEQUESTS

25 A. Real Property

26 I leave to CHRISTOPHER, if he survives me, my interest in our
27 homestead located at _____, _____, and any other real property
28 interest that I have at my death, including any insurance policies on
29 this property and its contents.

30 B. Primary Bequest of Personal Property

31 "Personal property" includes all of my clothing, jewelry, house-
32 hold goods and furnishings, automobiles, and all other similar
33 property. "Personal property" does not include my paintings or my
34 books. I leave all personal property that I own at my death to
35 CHRISTOPHER, if he survives me.

36 C. Alternate Bequest of Personal Property

37 If CHRISTOPHER does not survive me, I leave all my personal
38 property that I own at my death to my children who survive me.
39 My Personal Representative shall divide the property between or
40 among them so that each receives a share of approximately the
41 same value, taking into account but not being bound by preferences
42 expressed by the children. My Personal Representative shall not

---

- Some practitioners prefer to put definitions at the end of a will, preferring to put at the beginning the bequests, which are of more interest to the testator and beneficiaries. This drafter prefers using definitions at the beginning to make the entire will more accessible to the testator and beneficiaries.

Lines 25–29   • It is customary to provide for real property separate from and ahead of personal property. In a jurisdiction where the distinction is maintained between "devises" of real property and "bequests" of personal property, Article Two might cover devises exclusively.

- Some drafters would leave out any reference to the location of the homestead in the interest of having to amend the will as little as possible over time. Here the reference to "any other property interest" is designed to eliminate that need. In general, specific references to the location of property are most helpful if the will is administered by a trust company or other professional fiduciary rather than by a family member or close friend.

Lines 30–35   • Practitioners differ in the amount of detail they give to identify personal property. Here the system is to exclude the specific property, paintings and books, that is the subject of particular bequests rather than to try to give a full definition of what "personal property" means.

- Since "personal property" appears in more than one section of Article Two, it might be included among the terms defined in Article One. Since the term does not appear outside of Article Two, this drafter chose to define it within Article Two.

Lines 36–46   • Section C illustrates the kind of attention to detail that is designed to avoid a contest later, especially a claim by one child that a gift to another child during the testator's lifetime should be considered an advancement against the latter child's share.

43 consider any gifts I make to my children during my lifetime as
44 advancements to be deducted from their shares under this Section.
45 If a child of mine does not survive me but leaves children surviving
46 me, those children shall take the deceased child's share per stirpes.

47   D.   Paintings

48   I leave all the paintings that I own at my death to CHRIS, if he
49 survives me. His share of my personal property, if any, is not to be
50 diminished by the value of the paintings. If I own no paintings at
51 my death, this bequest is of no effect.

52   E.   Books

53   I leave all the books that I own at my death to REBECCA if she
54 survives me. Her share of my personal property, if any, is not to be
55 diminished by the value of the books. If I own no books at my
56 death, this bequest is of no effect.

57   F.   General Cash Bequests

58   1.   To JOHN FRESEL

59   I leave $1,000 to my employee, JOHN FRESEL, of _____
60 Street, _____, _____ County, _____, if he survives me and if
61 he is in my employ at the time of my death, the latter condition to
62 be determined conclusively by my Personal Representative.

63   2.   To CLARE and JULIA STONEHAGER

64   I leave $1,000 to CLARE STONEHAGER, if she survives me,
65 and $1,000 to JULIA STONEHAGER, if she survives me. They are

---

Lines 47–56   • These sections are also designed to avoid contests. In particular, they should defeat a child's claim for the proceeds of the earlier sale of paintings or books or for other property of equal value in place of paintings or books no longer in the estate for any reason.

     • Depending on the facts, which the drafter should probe, it might be important to describe more particularly than the terms "paintings" and "books" do. If the testator owns line drawings and etchings as well as oil paintings, "paintings" may lead to a contest. If she owns rare comic books and a complete set of *National Geographic* magazines, "books" may lead to a contest.

Line 57   • It is important to refer to the cash bequests as "general" rather than "special" to clarify that they do not come from a particular fund.

     • In some jurisdictions where old terminology is preserved, gifts of cash would be called "legacies" rather than bequests.

Lines 58–62   • Section F.1 provides a minimal explanation for the bequest to a beneficiary outside the family. A more detailed explanation might be helpful to avoid a contest if the beneficiary is unknown to the family. Giving the Personal Representative the power conclusively to determine the condition of employment is also designed to avoid a contest.

     • The more information the testator can provide about the residence of beneficiaries outside the family, the better.

Lines 63–70   • The additional information in Section F.2 is included on the theory that these beneficiaries will be informed of the provision. If the will is not

66 both of _____ Street, _____, _____ County, _____, the
67 daughters of Thomas Stonehager and my deceased friend Marie
68 Stonehager. These bequests are in loving memory of Marie. If
69 either CLARE or JULIA does not survive me, I leave her bequest to
70 her children who survive me, per stirpes.

71   3. To CENTRAL CITY POVERTY LAW SOCIETY, INC.

72   I leave $1,000 to CENTRAL CITY POVERTY LAW SOCIETY,
73 INC., a not-for-profit corporation, of _____ Street, _____,
74 _____ County, _____. I prefer that this bequest be used for
75 impact litigation on behalf of homeless persons. However, I do not
76 restrict the bequest to that use, and I authorize CENTRAL CITY
77 POVERTY LAW SOCIETY, INC., to use the bequest as it deems
78 most appropriate in furtherance of any of its corporate purposes.

79   G. Abatement of General Cash Bequests

80   I direct my Personal Representative that the general cash
81 bequests in Article Two, Section F, shall be abated pro rata if my
82 estate is not large enough to make them in full.

83   ARTICLE THREE

84   RESIDUE

85   The "residue of my estate" means all of my assets that are not
86 effectively disposed of by this Will outside of this Article. I leave
87 the residue of my estate to CHRISTOPHER, if he survives me. If
88 CHRISTOPHER does not survive me, I leave the residue of my
89 estate in equal shares to my children who survive me. If a child of
90 mine does not survive me but leaves children surviving me, those
91 children shall take the deceased child's share per stirpes.

---

probated for many years, these beneficiaries may not then remember the
testator or her friendship with their mother. Or they may never have
heard of the testator. In other words, the testator may want to do more
here than simply give people some money.

Lines 74–75   • This is "precatory" language. It expresses a preference but does not
give mandatory directions. In lines 75–78, this will removes any question
about whether the preference is precatory.

Lines 79–82   • Section G gives directions in the event that the estate is not large
enough to accommodate all of the cash bequests. Another way to take care
of the problem would be to make those bequests in terms of percentages of
the residue rather than specific dollar amounts.

Lines 84–91   • It is important that all particular bequests precede disposing of the
residue.

92   ARTICLE FOUR

93   VESTING OF INTERESTS IN CASE OF SIMULTANEOUS
94   DEATH

95   If any beneficiary dies simultaneously with me or under condi-
96 tions causing doubt as to which one of us died first, then I direct
97 that I be deemed to have survived that beneficiary for all purposes
98 under this Will.

99   ARTICLE FIVE

100   INCAPACITATED BENEFICIARY

101   A.   Beneficiary Under Eighteen Years Old

102   Any bequest to a beneficiary who is not yet eighteen years old
103 vests in that beneficiary, with my Personal Representative retaining
104 the discretion to retain the asset until the beneficiary becomes
105 eighteen years old or dies, whichever occurs first, and retaining the
106 discretion to distribute all or part of the principal and income
107 earlier in the best interest of the beneficiary.

108   B.   Otherwise Incapacitated Beneficiary

109   Any bequest left to a beneficiary who is incapacitated by reason
110 of illness, other mental or physical disability, or other legal incapac-
111 ity, vests in that beneficiary, with my Personal Representative
112 retaining the discretion to retain the asset until the beneficiary is
113 no longer incapacitated or dies, whichever occurs first, and retain-
114 ing the discretion to distribute all or part of the principal and
115 income earlier in the best interest of the beneficiary. I direct that
116 my Personal Representative has the discretion to determine conclu-
117 sively whether a beneficiary is incapacitated.

Lines 92–98   • It is common for a state to have a default statute to address the
simultaneous or nearly simultaneous deaths of the testator and a beneficiary. Article Four in this will reflects the typical approach. Sometimes a
testator chooses instead to require all or certain beneficiaries to survive by a
given number of days to be considered survivors.

Lines 101–07   • This will makes a point of referring to incapacitated beneficiaries under
a certain age rather than "minors," on the theory that the statutory age of
majority could change over time. This testator desires the incapacity to be
removed at the age of eighteen. Another testator might prefer to refer to
minors.

Lines 108–17   • Section B is designed to avoid a contest over what constitutes incapacity. As in the distribution of personal property to the children, the testator
avoids dangerous lists of particulars and instead relies on the discretion of
the Personal Representative.

118   ARTICLE SIX

119   TAXES AND EXPENSES

120   My Personal Representative shall pay all estate and other
121 death taxes payable on account of my death as expenses of adminis-
122 tering my estate, without apportionment.

123   ARTICLE SEVEN

124   GUARDIAN

125 A. Primary Nomination

126   I nominate CHRISTOPHER as Guardian of the person and
127 property of each of my children who is not yet eighteen years old at
128 my death.

129 B. Nomination of Successor

130   If CHRISTOPHER does not survive me, fails to qualify as
131 Guardian, or ceases to act as Guardian for any reason, then I
132 nominate my sister MURIEL DAWN BENTON as Guardian of the
133 person and property of each of my children who is not yet eighteen
134 years old at my death.

135   ARTICLE EIGHT

136   PERSONAL REPRESENTATIVE

137 A. Primary Nomination

138   I nominate CHRISTOPHER as Personal Representative of my
139 estate.

140 B. Nomination of Successor

141   If CHRISTOPHER does not survive me, fails to qualify as
142 Personal Representative, or ceases to act as Personal Representative

---

Lines 118–22   • Some drafters regard the provision for payment of taxes and expenses
as a housekeeping provision and put it at the end of the will. Others regard
it as dispositive of debits and thus comparable to the disposition of assets
through bequests, therefore putting it ahead of all articles on the administration of the will.

Lines 123–34   • Article Seven refers to nomination rather than appointment because
technically the court, not the testator, has the power to appoint. Nonetheless, many drafters do refer to the testator's appointment of a Guardian.

Lines 129–34   • It is important to nominate at least one successor as Guardian, if not
more than one. Line 131 is designed to replace any dangerously specific list
of reasons why a Guardian might cease to act.

Lines 137–44   • Article Eight provides the same safeguards with respect to the Personal
Representative.

              • Nomination rather than appointment is the technically appropriate
terminology here too, although many wills refer to appointment.

143 for any reason, then I nominate my sister MURIEL DAWN BEN-
144 TON as Personal Representative of my estate.

145 ### C. Powers

146   I give my Personal Representative full powers over all of the
147 assets in my estate, including the powers granted by law and those
148 granted by this Will, with the right to do anything I could do if
149 living, including invest, sell, mortgage, lease, dispose of, and dis-
150 tribute in kind all property, real and personal, when and upon
151 whatever terms and conditions my Personal Representative deems
152 appropriate.

153   ARTICLE NINE

154   WAIVER OF BOND

155   I direct that my Personal Representative, the Guardian of my
156 Children, and any Successor of either of them serve without bond or
157 other security required of them.

158   ARTICLE TEN

159   LAPSE

160   If a beneficiary under this Will does not survive me or is
161 deemed under this Will not to have survived me, then the bequest to
162 that beneficiary lapses unless this Will specifies otherwise.

163   I am signing this instrument, which is my Will, and which is
164 typewritten on ___ sheets of paper, on _____, 19__. I am signing
165 immediately below in the presence of the three persons witnessing
166 my signature at my request.

167
168   DIANE FRIEDMAN WEISS

Lines 146–52   • Many wills go into far more detail with respect to the powers of the
Personal Representative, especially if the estate property includes intangibles and business assets.

Lines 154–57   • The waiver of bond or other security is common when the Personal
Representative is a family member.

Lines 159–62   • This lapse provision recites the approach commonly taken by default
statutes. The reference to the will specifying otherwise is to account for the
instances where the will provides for per stirpes distribution to children of a
deceased beneficiary.

Lines 163–66   • This is the testimonium. The details in it are helpful to avoid a will
contest. Some practitioners go further even than to recite the number of
pages in the will; they have the testator initial each page, usually after the
last word on the page.

169 On _____, 19__, DIANE FRIEDMAN WEISS, Testator, de-
170 clared to us that the above instrument was her Will. She requested
171 that we serve as witnesses to her signing the Will. She signed the
172 Will in our presence, and there was no one else in the room at the
173 same time. At her request, in her presence, and in each other's
174 presence, we sign below as witnesses.

175   _____
176   WITNESS
177   [address]

178   _____
179   WITNESS
180   [address]

181   _____
182   WITNESS
183   [address]

Lines 169–74   • This is the attestation. The details in it are also designed to avoid a will contest. It is especially helpful to have the attestation and the witness- es' signatures on the same page as the testator's signature.

Lines 175–83   • It is common for state statutes to require only two witnesses rather than three. It is helpful to include three in case the will might be probated in a state requiring three, or in case one witness is unavailable at the time of probate.

                    • The witnesses' addresses may turn out to be essential information.

B. SAMPLE SELF–PROVING AFFIDAVIT

1 STATE OF _____ ⎫
2 COUNTY OF _____ ⎬

3   We, DIANE FRIEDMAN WEISS, Testator, and _____, _____,
4 and _____, Witnesses, whose names are signed to the attached
5 instrument, being sworn, declare to the undersigned authority that:

6   1. the Testator declared the instrument to be her Will;

7   2. she signed it on _____, 19__, at _____, _____;

8   3. she signed it willingly;

9   4. she signed it in the presence and hearing of these Witness-
10 es;

11   5. she executed it as her voluntary act for the purposes it
12 expresses; and

13   6. the Witnesses, in the presence and hearing of the Testator
14 and of each other, and at the request of the Testator, signed the Will
15 as witnesses.

16   _____
17   DIANE SUSAN WEISS,
18   TESTATOR

19   _____
20   WITNESS

21   _____
22   WITNESS

23   _____
24   WITNESS

25 Subscribed and sworn to before me by DIANE SUSAN WEISS,
26 Testator, and _____, _____, and _____, Witnesses, on
27 _____, 19__.

28 _____
29 My Commission expires:

Lines 3–5   • This is the introductory clause to an affidavit to make the will "self-
proving." The self-proving affidavit may be the most effective single way to
avoid a will contest. The introductory clause links the body of the affidavit to
the will itself and includes appropriate recitations to link it to the notarization
at the end.

Lines 6–15   • The body of this affidavit covers the same information as that provided in
the Uniform Probate Code Form (Section 2–504) but sets it out in tabulated
form for easier reading and checking that all information is included.

Lines 16–24   • The testator and the same witnesses who signed the will sign the
affidavit, preferably before they leave the room on the same occasion when
they sign the will.

C. SAMPLE CODICIL

1   FIRST CODICIL TO THE WILL OF DIANE FRIEDMAN
2   WEISS

3   I, DIANE FRIEDMAN WEISS, residing in _____, _____
4 County, _____, declare this my first Codicil to my Will dated
5 _____, 19__.

6   A. Amendments

7   1. I revoke Article Two, Section F.1 of my Will, with the result
8 that I leave nothing to JOHN FRESEL.

9   2. I leave $500 to my employee, ROBERT SIMS, of _____
10 Street, _____, _____ County, _____, if he survives me and if
11 he is in my employ at the time of my death, the latter condition to
12 be determined conclusively by my Personal Representative.

13   3. I revoke the following portion of Article Two, Section F.2 of
14 my Will:

15   "I leave $1,000 to CLARE STONEHAGER, if she survives me,
16   and $1,000 to JULIA STONEHAGER if she survives me. They
17   are both of _____ Street, _____, _____ County, _____,
18   the daughters of Thomas Stonehager and my deceased friend
19   Marie Stonehager."

20 I substitute for the revoked portion of Article Two, Section F.2 of my
21 Will the following:

22   "I leave $1,000 to CLARE STONEHAGER, of _____ Street,
23   _____, _____ County, _____, if she survives me. I leave
24      $1,000 to JULIA STONEHAGER MARSH, of _____ Street,

Lines 1–2   • For reference purposes, it is helpful to title a codicil as informatively as possible.

Lines 3–5   • The introductory clause identifies the will by its date as well as the testator.

Lines 6, 32   • A codicil not only amends a will but also ratifies all of it that is not amended. This codicil is organized to emphasize the two functions.

            • Some drafters call the divisions of a codicil "articles." That terminology can be confusing, however, because the numbering of articles in the codicil would likely not mirror the numbering of articles in the will, assuming that not all articles in the will are being amended. Calling the divisions of this codicil "sections" could be equally confusing. Therefore "A" and "B" have no other designation than their headings: "Amendments" and "Ratification."

Lines 6–31   • The amendments appear in the same sequence as the articles being amended. Amendment 2 is essentially a substitute for Article Two, Section F. 1 of the will, which is revoked by Amendment 1. However, it is not presented as a substitution because the change involves not only a substitute beneficiary but also a different dollar amount.

Lines 13–27   • Amendment 3 is designed to make it easier to find Julia Stonehager after her name change and her moving out of her father's house. The amendment requires considerable rewriting because the original bequest dealt with both Stonehager beneficiaries in the same sentence. To avoid this problem, the drafter might always treat each beneficiary in a separate sentence.

25 ————, ———— County, ————, if she survives me. They
26 are the daughters of Thomas Stonehager and my deceased
27 friend Marie Stonehager."

28 4. In Article Two, Section F.3 of my Will, the reference to
29 CENTRAL CITY POVERTY LAW SOCIETY, INC. is amended to
30 refer to it under its new name, METROPOLITAN POVERTY LAW
31 CENTER, INC.

32 B. Ratification

33 Except for the amendments above in Section A of this Codicil, I
34 ratify my Will.

35 I am signing this instrument, which is a Codicil to my Will, and
36 which is typewritten on ———— sheets of paper, on ————, 19—.
37 I am signing immediately below in the presence of the three persons
38 witnessing my signature at my request.

39 _____

40 DIANE FRIEDMAN WEISS

41 On ————, 19—, DIANE FRIEDMAN WEISS, Testator, de-
42 clared to us that the above instrument was a Codicil to her Will.
43 She requested that we serve as witnesses to her signing the Codicil.
44 She signed the Codicil in our presence, and there was no one else in
45 the room at the same time. At her request, in her presence, and in
46 each other's presence, we sign below as witnesses.

47 _____   _____
48 WITNESS   WITNESS
49 [address]   [address]

50 _____
51 WITNESS
52 [address]

———

III. ORGANIZING THE BODY OF A WILL

A. ORGANIZING FOR VARIOUS USERS

Estate practitioners vary considerably in how they organize the
body of wills. The choices depend primarily on what users they have in

---

Lines 28–31 • Amendment 4 is also designed to make a beneficiary easier to find after a name change.

Lines 35–38 • The testimonium is phrased to mirror that of the will.

Lines 41–46 • The attestation is phrased to mirror that of the will also.

Lines 47–52 • It is as useful to have three witnesses for a codicil as it is for a will. Of course, they need not be the same three.

• Likewise, a self-proving affidavit would be as useful for the codicil as for the will.

mind. Is the will being drafted to dispose of a relatively small estate with a family member to administer it? Or is the will drafted for professional fiduciaries who will administer a complex estate plan, and for lawyers and judges who will take part in its probate?

Some estate practitioners whose practice entails many wills like to have the same provisions with the same headings in the same sequence in every will they draft. This consistency is for their own convenience, without regard to variation among clients and their property. This approach also makes it possible to produce will forms or use computer drafting programs.[5] A practitioner who relies on form language, even in a self-created form, has a special need to keep up to date on case law construing that language.

A variation on using a standard form is to have prepared provisions on every possible contingency and then to choose the ones that apply in a given will and fill in the blanks with appropriate information. Even this approach, however, is likely to produce wills that are less than precisely tailored to each individual testator's circumstances and desires. In fact, it may be that the more a lawyer's practice involves will drafting, the less that lawyer is able to produce appropriate wills from predrafted programs without considerable redrafting in each case.

B. SOME CONVENTIONS

1. Definitions

Definitions belong at the beginning if they are there for the benefit of users who need lexical definitions of terms of art. Definitions are more safely put at the end if they are exclusively stipulative ones for the benefit of professional fiduciaries, lawyers, and judges. See Chapter 10 on definitions in legal documents.

2. Family Relationships

Some drafters choose to present as part of a definition article the names of family members and their relationship to the testator.[6] The sample will in Section II of this chapter uses that method in defining "my children." The issues to be addressed, unless the testator is to rely on default statutes or case law, are whether an adopted child, a child born after the execution of the will ("afterborn child"), a stepchild, or a child born outside of marriage are to be included in the definition of "child."

Some drafters prefer not to present this information in the form of definitions but instead have an article consisting of recitals laying out family relationships, providing short forms for future reference, and including addresses. This system is more accommodating in the will of

---

5. See, for example, D. Silver, Computers and Estate Planning: How to draft wills, trusts and probate documents using Wordperfect (1988).

6. Levin, above note 1, at 30.

a testator with a large and scattered family, many of whom are beneficiaries.

3. *Dispositive Provisions*

Conventionally, dispositive provisions precede administrative ones. The testator needs to make all bequests of specific property and general cash bequests (technically "legacies") before disposing of the residue of the estate in order for the residue to be determined.[7] Also, the will should make clear whether taxes and expenses are to be paid out of the residue as expenses of administration, or whether cash bequests are to be abated pro rata if necessary to pay them. This can be an important distinction if the bequest to the spouse or other primary beneficiary is mainly through the residue. The choice may also have estate tax consequences.

Bequests often begin with real property, then dispose of personal property, and finally dispose of cash. How many articles the will devotes to the bequests depends both on how many categories of property there are and how many beneficiaries there are. Even if one beneficiary is receiving more than one form of property, it is customary to organize by types of property rather than having one article on all bequests to the spouse, then an article on those to the children, etc.

4. *Administration*

Practitioners differ considerably in their approaches to provisions on administration of the will. First, some practitioners regard the nomination and powers of the personal representative as administrative matters and thus put them near the end, ahead only of housekeeping provisions.[8] Others regard the personal representative as so critical that provisions regarding this fiduciary precede even the bequests.[9] Likewise a provision nominating a guardian for minor children may be regarded as critical and thus put near the beginning or administrative and thus put near the end. Some put the payment of taxes and expenses at the end; others put it very near the beginning. It is often tied to a marital deduction provision or a bypass trust provision in a will disposing of a large estate because of the tax implications. Some view provisions on simultaneous death, gifts to minors, and lapse as so closely related to bequests that they put these provisions in or near the article(s) on bequests. Others regard them as matters of construction and thus essentially housekeeping provisions. For some, housekeeping in the context of a will includes nothing more than a severability

7. Gaubatz, Drafting Systems, Will Drafting Techniques 237, 239 (ALI–ABA Video Law Review Study Materials) (1989).

8. See, e.g., Schlesinger, Will of Robert Q. Attorney, Will Drafting Techniques 7, 17 (ALI–ABA Video Law Review Study Materials) (1989).

9. See, e.g., Brink, Last Will and Testament, Will Drafting Techniques 37, 39 (ALI–ABA Video Law Review Study Materials) (1989).

provision or one on article headings being only for convenience; others regard these provisions as needless and do not include them anywhere.

All this variety does not justify throwing together articles in a will without regard to sequence. Rather it reinforces the point that sequence reflects thinking about what users are to be primarily accommodated. Either the will is organized according to order of importance of matters to the testator and beneficiaries or according to the order of usefulness of information to the personal representative, litigator, and judge.

IV. DRAFTING TO PREVENT CONSTRUCTION PROBLEMS

A. SOLUTIONS OUTSIDE THE WILL

The main challenge of drafting a will is always to make the testator's intentions and wishes so clear that no one will ever have occasion to go outside the will for aid in construing it. Going outside the will may mean going to a default statute. It may mean going to cases that have construed similar or identical language. Ultimately, going to those cases usually means going to some canon of construction, which runs a risk of having the will administered or adjudicated in a way very different from what the testator intended.

B. INCORPORATING STATUTES BY REFERENCE

Some drafters attempt to prevent construction problems by incorporating by reference the statutes that reflect the testator's intentions. Incorporating statutes by reference is preferable to quoting statutes at length in a will, although short quotes are probably preferable to incorporation in the interest of making the will accessible to the nonprofessional user.

C. THE ROLE OF PLAIN LANGUAGE

1. "The Plain English Will": The Real Thing or A Spoof?

Plain language is becoming more highly regarded as appropriate for will drafting, even in spite of some clients' insistence that they want the "legal language" that makes their will sound important. The idea of drafting wills in plain language has lent itself to some spoofing on the part of those who suspect that advocates of plain language ultimately intend to produce legal instruments readable by first graders. For example, here is one idea of a will in plain language:

The Plain English Will

I am John Doe. This is my will. See my signature on this will. See my witnesses' signatures.

I revoke all my other wills and codicils.

See Sam Brown. I want him to be my personal representative.
Please court, make him my personal representative. Sam is honest, I
hope, and fair, I hope.

Sam won't serve? See Bob Baker. Bob will be personal representative.

See Mary Doe, my wife. Mary likes my personal effects. I give
them to her. Also my bubble gum cards. My comic books. My
baseball glove. My bat. My dog, Spot. If Mary kills me, naughty
Mary. Do not give her my dog Spot. Nor my comic books.

See Tom. See Dick. See Harry. All Does' folks. Also, issue of
me and Mary, I hope. Tom is 2. Dick is 3. Harry is 4. Mary is
fertile.

See the residue of my estate. Give the residue to Mary. If she
dies first, give it to Does' folks. Equally and outright.

See my personal representative. He is wise. He is strong. He
has powers: to sell, to lease, with notice, without notice. Also to
invest.

I'm not crazy. I know what I'm doing.

See my signature on _____ at _____, _____.

See my witnesses' signatures. We sign, watching each other. I
say: "This is my will." They say, "Yes." Now see their signatures.[10]

2. *A Will Form in Plain Language*

A will in plain language need not be a joke. In fact, Lawrence X.
Cusack, a New York estate practitioner, has published a suggested
form.[11] He drafted it after acknowledging that wills generally are "a
warehouse of clutter," including unnecessary synonyms, recitals, and
particularity.[12] He admits that many clients expect legalese in a will
and might question the legal sufficiency of plain language. However,
he also says that six other lawyers who studied his will in plain
language agree with him that it is legally sufficient and does not suffer
from any ambiguities.[13] He is careful to point out that modifications or
additions may be necessary in particular cases, and on the form itself,
he expressly warns against non-lawyers using it without advice of
counsel.[14] He also acknowledges that certain terms of art such as *per
stirpes* are worth keeping, but with a brief explanation provided.[15] His
premise is that a will needs to speak clearly both to the client and for
the client to the probate judge.

10. Anonymous (contributed by Professor David T. Smith).

11. The Plain English Will Revisited,
July 1980 Tr. & Est. 42, 43.

12. Cusack, The Blue–Pencilled Will,
August 1979 Tr. & Est. 33, 33.

13. Id. at 33–34.

14. Cusack, above note 11, at 42–43.

15. Id. at 44.

3. *Reducing Legalese to Plain Language*

Edward S. Schlesinger, also a New York practitioner, stresses that if the client does not understand what you draft, the will does not reflect the client's intent; furthermore, he cautions against depending on the client to read the definitions to find out what the will means.[16]

Thomas S. Word, Jr., a Virginia practitioner, supports his arguments for plain language with demonstrations of how to eliminate legalese. Here is an example:

Original Will

I, John Quincy Doe, now residing in the city of Richmond, State of Virginia, being of sound mind and memory, do hereby make, publish and declare this to be my last will and testament, hereby revoking, annulling and canceling any and all wills and codicils heretofore made by me.

Revised Will

I, John Quincy Doe, of Richmond, Virginia, make this will, and revoke all earlier wills and codicils.[17]

Here is Mr. Word's commentary on the above reduction from 49 words to 17:

The distinction between "will" and "testament" left us long ago. "Publish and declare" should come at the end, in the attestation clause, if at all. Do annul and cancel add anything to revoke? * * * Would anyone think we were revoking someone else's will? ("And codicils" could be omitted, but I left it as a bow to tradition and because for some strange reason clients savor the word. In fact, the whole revocation clause is surplus—a *complete* will revokes all prior ones by operation of law.)[18]

4. *The Danger in Not Using Plain Language*

The lawyer who is tempted to rely on legalese might consider the following case. A millionaire's trust contained an in terrorem clause that became an issue when the judge had to decide whether the clause should force the deceased millionaire's friend to forfeit her share of his estate. Here is the clause:

[The beneficiaries shall not] directly or indirectly aid, counsel, commence or prosecute any demands, claims, negotiations, suits, actions or proceedings in any court of law, or other arenas, having as an object: * * * the obtaining for anyone of (i) anything of value from this Trust or my estate, (ii) any of the assets of this Trust or my estate, or (iii) any assets in which I had an interest immediately prior to my

---

16. Drafting and Document Planning; How to Draft in Plain English, Will Drafting Techniques (ALI–ABA Video Law Review, April 13, 1989).

17. Word, A Brief for Plain English Wills and Trusts, 14 U.Rich.L.Rev. 471, 472 (1980).

18. Id. (citations omitted; emphasis supplied to stress that only a complete will revokes prior ones, and then only so far as an inconsistency exists). Copyright © 1980 by University of Richmond Law Review. Reprinted by permission of the publisher.

death, grounded on, arising out of, or related to any claimed or actual agreement, representation or understanding not expressly set forth in a written and executed agreement that I would (or would not cause another to) deliver to anyone anything of value (directly or indirectly, in trust, by will, or otherwise) as a gift, or for services or any other thing of value (including by way of example but not limitation any employment or assistance) received by me or another. The word "another" includes any one or more (or combination thereof) people, partnerships, corporations, trusts, estates or other entities.[19]

The judge "wrestled with the clause for at least a year," eventually decided it was incomprehensible, and held it to be of no effect, so that the millionaire's friend took her share.[20]

5. Thoughtful Drafting and Boilerplate Clauses

Rohan Kelley, a Florida practitioner, focuses in his continuing legal education presentations on what it means to be a thoughtful drafter and how to approach boilerplate clauses:

"Thoughtful drafting" is precise drafting. If you have not already done so, put yourself on a "drafting diet". Use only words that are necessary precisely to communicate what is required for the purpose you intend. Develop your own drafting style but make that style thoughtful.

Generally beware of and avoid using "boilerplate" clauses. The reason for this admonition is that the boilerplate clause may not be adequate for the purpose you intend or it may be adequate for some other purpose instead of or in addition to the intended purpose. No language should ever be inserted into a document unless you fully understand the meaning and the implication of that language. Only use a "boiler plate" clause if: 1) the author is a more thoughtful draftsman than you are (and you are willing to admit it) and 2) you fully understand the meaning and the legal effect of every word of what he or she has written. * * *

If you are a lawyer with limited experience in drafting, then try to find a thoughtful draftsman and learn from him or her. Still, you must understand what you are drafting, even if you don't have your own style and even if you must use boilerplate. If you are an experienced draftsman and a student of the law, you have no excuse for ever using boilerplate.

Becoming a thoughtful draftsman * * * begins by analyzing each sentence in your document. For example, take your favorite will or trust form (or a recent client document) and have your secretary put several extra blank lines after each sentence. Then make a notation of the purpose of that sentence in the document; what was it intended to accomplish. Then, in the same space, write "yes" or "no" in response to the question, "Would the document have been deficient if this

19. In re Weingart, No. P663511 (L.A. Super.Ct. March 21, 1983), quoted in Benson, Plain English Comes to Court, 13 Litigation No. 1, 21, 22–23 (1986).

20. Id. at 23. In *terrorem* clauses are generally unenforceable as a matter of public policy. See Section V.C of this chapter.

sentence had been omitted?". If the answer is yes, then edit the sentence to simplify the language and add clarity and precision. If the answer is no, delete the sentence. You should be able to work at the rate of about 5 sentences per hour. When you have concluded an entire paragraph or article, have your secretary retype the edited paragraph or article. Compare the new paragraph or article with the old, in its entirety. This will show you some of the results of thoughtful drafting.

Thoughtful drafting does not come easy. It is a "practice lifestyle" which must be adopted * * *. * * * It requires you to be a student of the law and an inquisitive observer. Each time you probate an estate and run up against a problem, learn from it. Ask yourself, "Could I have drafted the document to avoid this problem?". If so, incorporate the change into your forms if it might have more than a single application. Similarly, when you read a case involving a probate problem, ask yourself whether the document draftsmen have avoided this problem. Again, if it has possible general application, redraft your forms. When you attend a seminar and you hear a good idea from the podium, make a note and go back to your office and redraft your form. After many years of such thoughtful drafting, your forms will evolve into thoughtful forms and you will attain the enviable status of a thoughtful draftsman.[21]

6. *Plain Language Approach in Law School Wills Textbooks*

Law school textbook treatment of will drafting increasingly reflects the same appreciation as the expert practitioners express for drafting wills in plain language. Professors Shaffer and Mooney, for example, refer to wills and trusts as "charters for human conduct, which must or should be used routinely by lay fiduciaries, beneficiaries and parties to contracts."[22] These professors have no compliments for drafting in legalese.

> * * * Dispositive instruments, to a greater extent than business contracts and corporate forms, retain a level of legalese that betrays a black-magic theory of interpersonal relations in the law office—an inarticulate fear that everything the relatively undereducated 19th century lawyer used had cabalistic significance; although a modern person is incapable of understanding it, it is vital to a document's success. Law, according to this theory, is witch-doctoring with a pencil, and drafting is half exposition and half ritual.[23]

Shaffer and Mooney devote two chapters of their text specifically to language, the first beginning with an indictment of legalese [24], and the

---

21. R. Kelley, Thoughts of a Thoughtful Trust Draftsman 1-2 (1990) (unpublished manuscript on file in this author's office at University of Florida College of Law). Copyright © 1990 by Rohan Kelley. Reprinted by permission of the author. See also Bove, Jr., above note 1, at 63–65 (assessing proper and improper use of boilerplate).

22. T. Shaffer and C. Mooney, The Planning and Drafting of Wills and Trusts 184 (3d ed. 1991).

23. Id. at 183.

24. Id. at 181–84.

second revealing the chapter's approach in its title, "Justified Simplicity." [25]

Exercise 6.1

Redraft "The Plain English Will" in Section IV.C.1 of this chapter into plain language that is appropriate for a legal document.

D. ATTENDING TO PARTICULARS

1. *The Value of General Language*

Schlesinger cautions against excessive specificity, warning that "the more specific you are, the more likely you are to make a mistake." [26] He makes his point in the context of a will drafted with the intention of administration by a professional fiduciary. The professional fiduciary prefers powers to be stated generally, for example. In fact, Schlesinger's ultimate point is that how you draft depends on whether the fiduciary is to be a professional or a lay person.[27]

No matter who the fiduciary is, the drafter needs to take care regarding particulars and generalities. If the will refers to "my boat," and the testator dies owning two boats, how is the fiduciary to resolve the problem? Should "my homestead at 6264 Lakeview Drive" be construed to apply to my house on West Shore Drive after I move there?

For matters like these, the drafter might well choose general language rather than specific, assuming that the testator would want as many boats as are owned and the homestead no matter where located to go to the named beneficiary. General language is especially helpful as a way of avoiding frequent need for codicils for clients who frequently change their minds.[28]

2. *The Importance of Accuracy About Specifics*

Nonetheless, when specific information is to be included, it is worth it to take the care needed to be accurate. Giving a beneficiary the option to choose "an item" of personal property can produce a problem when the beneficiary chooses the 60–piece silver service or the $11,000 stamp collection.[29] There is no excuse for neglecting to distinguish between two beneficiaries with the same name or misspelling a beneficiary's name and thus risking that the intended beneficiary not receive the bequest. Yet that may result because, unlike contracts, wills are normally not reformed on account of mistake.

---

25. Id., ch. 9, at 202.

26. See above note 16.

27. Id.

28. Id.

29. See Bove, Jr., above note 1, at 72–73.

Of course, the drafter needs to find out from the testator what should happen under various possible future circumstances.

3. *Future Circumstances to Be Anticipated*

a. *Property no Longer in the Estate*

If specified property is no longer in the estate at the time of probate, is other similar property to be substituted for it? Are the proceeds of sold property to go to the beneficiary? Is the beneficiary to receive the cash value of the property regardless of how it came to be gone from the estate?

b. *Gift to Beneficiary During Testator's Lifetime*

If a beneficiary receives a substantial gift from the testator after the execution of the will but during the testator's lifetime, does the testator wish such a gift to be regarded as an advancement and its value to be deducted from the amount of the bequest to that beneficiary?

c. *Beneficiary Who Does Not Survive Testator*

If a beneficiary does not survive the testator, does the bequest to that beneficiary lapse? Do the beneficiary's lineal descendants share the bequest? If so, do they share *per stirpes* or *per capita* with other beneficiaries of the deceased beneficiary's class? In other words, for example, do the testator's grandchildren divide among themselves their deceased parent's share (*per stirpes*), or do they share equally with other grandchildren (*per capita*)?

Exercise 6.2

Diane Weiss brings you her will, which appears in Section II.A of this chapter, and which someone else has drafted for her. How would you need to redraft it, if at all, to make clear that if she owns no books when she dies, Rebecca gets nothing instead of books and no greater share of Diane's personal property?

Exercise 6.3

How would you need to redraft Diane Weiss's will, if at all, to make clear that if after executing the will she gives any gifts to Chris, Rebecca, or William during her lifetime, those gifts do not satisfy any part of her bequests to each of them?

Exercise 6.4

Assume that the following statute is in effect in your state:

732.601   Simultaneous Death Law.—

(1) When title to property depends on priority of death and there is insufficient evidence that the persons have died otherwise than simultaneously, the property of each person shall be disposed of as if he or she had survived, except as provided otherwise in this law.

(2) This law does not apply in the case of wills in which provision has been made for distribution of property different from the provisions of this law.

————

Before executing her will, Diane Weiss decides that she wants all bequests to her husband to depend on his surviving her by at least a month. But if anyone else who is a beneficiary dies less than a month after she does, that person is to be considered to have survived her unless it is impossible to tell which of them died first.

How, if at all, do you need to redraft her will before she signs it?

————

V.   DRAFTING TO DISCOURAGE A WILL CONTEST

A.   RECITALS

1. Recital of the Testator's Sound Mind

Many of the particulars recited in wills are there to discourage a will contest, even though some of them are of doubtful value for that purpose. The testator's recital of being of sound mind does no good if someone with evidence to the contrary contests the will. On the other hand, it is useful to include recitals that *demonstrate* that the testator is of sound mind. For example, recitals are useful that identify: (a) the persons who are the natural objects of the testator's bounty and (b) the nature and extent of the testator's property.

2. Revocation of Prior Wills and Codicils

The common recital of revoking previous wills and codicils may accomplish little because the latest dated will that is offered for probate is the one that ordinarily will be accepted irrespective of that recital. However, if a will appears not to dispose of all of the testator's property, an issue may arise as to whether a previous document that is inconsistent with the will is revoked by it. In that instance, expressly reciting revocation would be important.

3. *Reasons for Bequests*

The testator may discourage a will contest by reciting reasons for bequests to beneficiaries who are not natural objects of bounty, that is, persons outside the family and especially persons who are unknown to the family.

Exercise 6.5

Before signing her will, Diane Weiss decides to leave her entire art collection to her stepson William except for two Picasso sketches, which she wants to leave to her son Chris. The Picasso sketches are in pen and ink. They are authentic originals as far as she knows. They are both nudes, one male and one female. She has had them appraised, and they are worth $5000 apiece. Chris is too young to understand art at all. She is leaving him the sketches for their monetary value.

William is seventeen years old and has decided to go to art school. He is a talented artist, working in both water colors and oils. He also does etchings. He is not fond of Picasso's work. Diane and William have gotten along well since she married his father, and she would like to foster his interest in art. Aside from the Picasso sketches, she estimates that her whole collection is probably not worth over $1000. It includes mainly prints, but many of these are Van Gogh prints, and William is especially fond of Van Gogh.

How would you redraft Article Two of Weiss's will?

B. DECLARATIONS

1. *Testimonium*

The testimonium is one of the testator's means of discouraging a will contest. Some people erroneously refer to the introductory clause as the testimonium because it declares that this is the testator's will. However, the testimonium functions at the end. At that point, the testator declares that the above document is that person's will, being signed on a certain date in the presence of persons who witness the testator's signature at the testator's request.

2. *Attestation* [30]

Another major means of discouraging a will contest is the declaration of witnesses who attest to the following:

    (a) the testator told them that the instrument was that person's will;

    (b) the testator requested that they witness its being signed;

---

30. For a proposal that states abolish the attestation requirement, see Lindgren, *Abolishing the Attestation Requirement for Wills*, 68 N.C.L.Rev. 541 (1990).

(c) they did so; and

(d) they signed it in the presence of the testator and each other.

The function of attestation, as well as the testimonium, is largely ceremonial but nonetheless crucial inasmuch as validity of the will depends on due execution. How successfully the process functions depends largely on how much the lawyer says to the testator and witnesses about what is happening. If the witnesses are ever called upon to testify to these matters, the quality of their testimony may depend on how much they remember of that event, often far in the past. How much they remember may depend more on how formal the ceremony was than on what the words on the paper say. Also, if witnesses testify that procedures required by statute were not followed, the will is invalid. The words on the paper are there in part to impress on everyone the seriousness of what is happening. It is essential that they say all the right things.

Thus, for example, the drafter may mention in the attestation that no one else is present, as a means of discouraging a later claim of undue influence by some other person present. Also, the drafter may provide for three witnesses even in a state that requires only two, to avoid a challenge later if after all the will is probated in a state requiring three,[31] or if one of the witnesses is unavailable at the time of probate.

3. "Self-Proving" Affidavit

A useful device for discouraging a will contest is the "self-proving" affidavit, which is the sworn statement of the testator and witnesses about the execution ceremony. Its purpose is to establish a presumption of due execution. Ideally, this affidavit is signed and notarized immediately after signing and witnessing the will; it is then attached to the will, where it remains, with the intention of obviating any need to bring the witnesses forth later to be deposed or testify about what they witnessed. It is crucial that the testator and witnesses execute both the will and the affidavit. Signing the affidavit is no substitute for the testator's signing the will or for the witnesses' signing their attestation of the testator's signature.

C. THE *IN TERROREM* PROVISION

Another device intended to discourage a will contest is the *in terrorem* provision, in which the testator directs that a beneficiary who contests the will automatically forfeits any bequest under the will. This device does not usually accomplish its intended result, however. Some state statutes make these provisions unenforceable. In other states, although they are technically enforceable, they are so strictly construed as to be rarely enforced.[32] Finally, they may merely goad a

---

31. See Levin, above note 1, at 32. If a will is drafted in a state requiring only two witnesses, a reciprocity statute would likely validate it in a state requiring three.

32. Id. at 60–61 and cases cited.

litigious beneficiary to fight a good fight. On the other hand, in some jurisdictions at least, an *in terrorem* provision might be fully enforced. Therefore, if the testator wishes to have one, the will should provide for what happens to the property forfeited by the contesting beneficiary.[33]

Exercise 6.6

Read and evaluate the will below. Pay particular attention to the following questions:

    1. For whose convenience is the will organized?

    2. Is it written in legalese or plain language?

    3. Are there ambiguities that require going outside the will to construe?

    4. Has the drafter inadvertently given any ammunition to anyone inclined to contest the will?

1   LAST WILL AND TESTAMENT OF
2   Andrew R. Fulton

3   I, Andrew R. Fulton of _____, County of _____ and State of
4 _____, being of sound mind, hereby revoke my former Wills and
5 Codicils and declare this to be my Last Will and Testament.

6   FIRST: I hereby direct that the expenses of my last illness and
7 funeral be paid out of my estate.

8   SECOND: I devise certain items of tangible personal property
9 not otherwise specifically disposed of by this Will, excluding money
10 and items used in my trade or business, if any, to the persons listed
11 on the last dated writing made for this purpose, signed by me and in
12 existence at the time of my death. Such writing shall have no
13 significance apart from its effect on the distribution of my property
14 by this Will. In the event no such list is discovered within thirty
15 (30) days after the appointment of my Personal Representative, then
16 and in that event, it shall be presumed I have left no such writing,
17 and all of my personal property shall pass in accordance with the
18 other provisions of this Will.

19   THIRD: That all of the property which I own at my death save
20 only those specific bequests referred to in the preceding paragraph
21 and those expenses imposed by operation of law, shall be transferred
22 to Leland Malvern of _____, _____, as trustee, to be retained,
23 managed and distributed by him under the following trust provi-
24 sions. The trust corpus is to include proceeds of any life insurance
25 policies insuring my life, which are payable to the trustee who is
26 provided for by the terms of this Will. If said trustee does not
27 accept the duties of trustee or ceases to act in such capacity for any
28 reason, I hereby request that the Circuit Judge in and for _____,

---

33. See Stocker, above note 1, at 277.

29 County, _____, or the Judge of the Court which has probate
30 jurisdiction at the time such vacancy occurs appoint a corporate
31 trustee to act in such capacity. The trustee is to hold said trust
32 corpus and earning for the benefit of my parents, John D. Fulton
33 and Mary R. Fulton.

34   FOURTH: The purpose of this trust is to provide for the
35 support and general welfare of my parents, and the survivor of
36 them.

37   (a) The trust estate, including all income therefrom and in-
38   crease thereof, is to be retained, invested or reinvested by
39   said trustee, without any statutory restriction. He may sell
40   any property, real or personal, publicly or privately, with-
41   out court order and without notice, upon such terms and
42   conditions as he believes to be satisfactory. He may man-
43   age, control, lease or encumber the assets of the trust estate
44   in any way he believes will fulfill the purpose of this trust.

45   (b) Such of the income and corpus as is needed shall be applied
46   or distributed by said trustee, in cash or in kind, for the
47   support and general welfare of each beneficiary. Said
48   distribution shall be made to those persons in such manner
49   and amounts as said trustee, in his unrestricted discretion,
50   believes will fulfill the purposes of this trust, regardless of
51   the existence of other funds available for these purposes;
52   and trustee is authorized to make said distributions directly
53   to said beneficiary, to his guardian, or to any other person
54   in behalf of said beneficiary without the trustee being liable
55   to see to the application thereof.

56   (c) If the trustee shall believe that the interest of the benefi-
57   ciaries is threatened to be diverted in any manner from the
58   purposes of this trust as stated above, the trustee shall
59   withhold the income and principal from distribution, and
60   shall apply payments in his discretion in such manner as
61   he shall believe contributes to the maintenance, comfort
62   and necessities of the beneficiaries. Whenever the trustee
63   shall be satisfied that such diversion is no longer effective
64   or threatened, he may resume the distributions of income
65   and principal authorized.

66   (d) If either beneficiary dies before the assets of the trust are
67   exhausted, the trustee shall use such of the balance as is
68   needed for payment of funeral expenses and related ex-
69   penses of said beneficiary and the remainder of said assets
70   shall be retained in trust for the benefit of the surviving
71   beneficiary.

72   (e) Upon the death of both of said beneficiaries, the trust shall
73   terminate and the balance of funds remaining in the trust
74   shall be divided between Linda Peet and Mary Fulton. If
75   either of said beneficiaries predecease the time of such

76   distribution leaving children then surviving, the share that
77   would have gone to such distributee shall pass to the child
78   or children of said distributee per stirpes.

79   FOURTH: I instruct my Personal Representative hereinafter
80 named to see to my burial wherever my parents are then located.

81   FIFTH: I hereby appoint John Levine of _____, _____, as
82 Personal Representative of this Will. I empower said Personal
83 Representative to sell, lease, or mortgage any property, real or
84 personal, publicly or privately, without an order of the court and
85 without notice to anyone, upon such terms and conditions as shall
86 seem best to said Personal Representative and without liability on
87 the part of any purchaser, tenant or mortgagee to see to the
88 application of the consideration; to permit any of the beneficiaries
89 named herein to enjoy the use in kind, during probate of this Will,
90 of any tangible, personal property without liability on the part of
91 said Personal Representative for any injury to, consumption or loss
92 of any such property so used; and to settle, compromise or pay any
93 claim, including taxes, asserted in favor of or against me or my
94 estate. The beneficiaries, or their Personal Representative shall not
95 be liable for any unintentional, non-negligent injury to, consump-
96 tion of or loss of any property used as provided herein.

97   SIXTH: Any beneficiary under this Will who contests this Will
98 or any article, provision, or clause thereof, shall forfeit any bequest
99 to said beneficiary as an automatic result thereof.

100   IN WITNESS WHEREOF, I sign, seal, publish and declare this
101 instrument to be my Last Will and Testament in the presence of the
102 persons witnessing it, this _____ day of _____, 1977.

103   _____
104   Andrew R. Fulton

105   SIGNED, SEALED, PUBLISHED AND DECLARED by the
106 above-named person as and for a Last Will and Testament, and we
107 did, in his presence hereunto subscribe our names as witnesses
108 thereto.

109 _____

110 _____

111 STATE OF _____ ⎫
112 COUNTY OF _____ ⎭

113   We, being first duly sworn, do hereby declare to the under-
114 signed officer that the testator signed the instrument voluntarily
115 and that each of the witnesses signed as a witness and that to the
116 best of the knowledge of each witness, the testator was, at the time,

117 18 or more years of age, of sound mind and under no constraint or
118 undue influence.

119   _____

120   _____

121   _____

122   SUBSCRIBED AND SWORN to before me on the _____ day
123 of _____, 1977

124   _____

125   Notary Public, State of _____

Exercise 6.7

If you have a will, evaluate it according to the same tests you
applied to Fulton's will in Exercise 6.6.

VI. CHECKLIST FOR DRAFTING WILLS AND CODICILS

Title and Introductory Clause

1. Do you identify the instrument both in its title and in its
introductory clause as either a will or a codicil?

2. Do you make clear whose will or codicil it is? If a codicil, do
you make clear whether it is first, second, etc., and the date of the will
which it amends?

3. Do you include the domicile of the testator?

Definitions and Recitals

4. Either in an article giving definitions or in early recitals, do
you make clear who the testator's family members are by name and
relationship to the testator?

5. Are all beneficiaries' names correctly spelled? Are distinctions
clear between two beneficiaries with the same or nearly the same
name?

6. Do you establish short forms for reference to persons who will
be mentioned in more than one article?

7. Do you use terminology that is generally consistent with that of
the statutes in the state where you expect the will to be probated?

8. Do you define terms of art that the testator, beneficiaries, and
perhaps even the personal representative are not likely to know?

9. Do you stipulate definitions as needed to clarify classes of beneficiaries, especially the children of the testator?

Organization of the Body

10. Do you organize the articles according to some plan that either focuses first on what is important to the testator and beneficiaries or arranges information for the convenience of professionals?

11. Do you number and head the articles for easy reference?

12. Is your numbering and lettering scheme consistent throughout?

13. In general, do you put dispositive provisions before administrative ones?

Bequests

14. Do you dispose of real estate before personal property?

15. Do you avoid ambiguity in all expressions of which beneficiary is to receive what property?

16. If there are charitable bequests, is it clear whether language about the testator's wishes for the use of the property is merely precatory or intended to be binding?

17. Are charitable beneficiaries clearly identified, preferably with addresses, especially if they are not well known?

18. Do you provide for bequests of specific property and general cash bequests before the residue?

19. Do you make clear what is to happen if willed property is no longer in the estate at the time of the testator's death?

20. Do you make clear what effect, if any, gifts during the testator's lifetime to a beneficiary will have on a bequest to that beneficiary?

21. Do you make clear whether a bequest to a beneficiary who predeceases the testator lapses?

22. Do you make clear what happens in case of "simultaneous" death of a beneficiary and the testator, or else do you rely on a default statute that provides what the testator wishes?

23. Do you make appropriate arrangements for incapacitated beneficiaries?

24. Do you recite the rationale for bequests to unexpected beneficiaries?

Administration

25. Do you make clear whether debts, taxes, and expenses are to be paid out of the residue of the estate, or otherwise?

26. Do you provide for the nomination of trustees, guardians, and personal representatives, including alternates?

27. Do you make a purposeful choice to be either general or particular in stating the powers of trustees and personal representatives?

28. If appropriate, do you provide that trustees, guardians, and personal representatives should serve without bond or other security?

29. Do you avoid including an *in terrorem* or severability provision that you have reason to believe would not be enforced?

30. If you do include an *in terrorem* provision, do you provide for alternate disposition of forfeited property?

Testimonium

31. Does the testimonium declare that the instrument is the testator's will or codicil?

32. Does the testimonium declare how many pages the instrument has?

33. Does the testimonium declare the date on which the instrument is being signed?

34. Does the testimonium declare that the testator is signing in the presence of those requested to serve as witnesses?

Attestation

35. Do you provide for three witnesses as a safeguard?

36. Do the witnesses attest to having witnessed the testator's signature on the will or codicil at the testator's request?

37. Do the witnesses attest to signing in the presence of the testator and each other?

38. Are the signature lines for witnesses on the same page as the testator's signature line?

39. Are spaces provided for the witnesses' addresses?

40. Do you include a self-proving affidavit for the testator and witnesses to make a sworn statement of the facts regarding execution?

Codicils Only

41. Do you make clear exactly what articles or parts of an article are revoked?

42. Do you make clear whether amendments are additions or substitutions?

43. Do you make clear exactly what language substitutes for exactly what language?

44. Do you use an organizing scheme for the codicil that avoids confusion between the scheme in the codicil and the scheme in the will?

45. Does the codicil expressly ratify all of the will that has not been amended by the codicil?

46. Does the codicil attend to all of the same formalities as the will regarding testimonium, attestation, and self-proving affidavit?

VII. DRAFTING ASSIGNMENTS

Drafting Assignment 6.A—Codicil

Assume that Diane Weiss executed the will in Section II.A of this chapter. Recently her sister Muriel has died. Weiss decides to have Jane Jones as successor personal representative if for any reason Weiss's husband does not serve. Jones is not a relative. She is a friend who happens to be a lawyer, although she is not Weiss's lawyer. (You are.) Jones lives next door to the Weisses.

Diane and Christopher Weiss agree that if he dies before she does, then his sister Ruth Miller should serve as guardian of their children. Ruth is a 37–year old widow. Her husband's name was Tony. He died last year.

Draft a codicil to Diane Weiss's will to take care of these substitutions.

————

Drafting Assignment 6.B—Article of a Will

Assume that the following statute is in effect in your state:

732.515 Separate writing identifying devises of tangible property.—A will may refer to a written statement or list to dispose of items of tangible personal property not otherwise specifically disposed of by the will, other than money and property used in trade or business. To be admissible under this section as evidence of the intended disposition, the writing must be signed by the testator and must describe the items and the devisees with reasonable certainty. The writing may be referred to as one in existence at the time of the testator's death. It may be prepared before or after the execution of the will. It may be altered by the testator after its preparation. It may be a writing that has no significance apart from its effect upon the dispositions made by the will.

————

In view of § 732.515, study the article numbered "SECOND" in the will of Andrew Fulton, presented in Exercise 6.6. On August 1, 1976, he wrote on a piece of his letterhead paper a statement that when he died, his nephew Brian Fulton should have his gold watch and his nephew Gordon Kosel should have the gold and diamond rings that Andrew wore all the time. Andrew signed the paper and put it in his safety deposit box at the Third World Bank. It was still there when he executed his will.

In view of this information, redraft the article numbered "SECOND" in his will.

————

Drafting Assignment 6.C—Codicil

Over the years Andrew Fulton has seen less and less of his nieces Linda Peet and Mary Fulton. He has decided that after both his parents die and the trust for their benefit terminates, he no longer wants the balance of the funds in the trust to go in equal shares to his nieces. Instead he says he wants his nieces and the American Civil Liberties Union to share the balance equally.

Draft a codicil to Fulton's will to reflect his new intent. What must you find out from Fulton before you draft?

———

Drafting Assignment 6.D—Will

Your client is Eleanor Stacey, who is 47 years old, and who has been divorced from her ex-husband Jack Joslin for 20 years. She has no children. However, she has maintained friendly relations with Jack and his second wife Cynthia and has been close to the children of Jack and Cynthia, Amy and Michael. Amy and Michael have called her "Aunt Eleanor" for years.

Eleanor's only living relatives are the children of her deceased sister, Joyce Demmary. Their names are Gretchen and Stephen Demmary. They have always lived thousands of miles away, and since Joyce died two years ago, Eleanor has not seen or heard from Gretchen or Stephen at all.

Eleanor has always worked waiting tables in one restaurant or another. She has made enough money to get by but has never had any luxuries, and she has never owned her own home. She has no life insurance or retirement fund other than her savings account.

Eleanor has always had a savings account and tried to put something into it every month, although sometimes no more than $5 or $10. When she comes to see you, the savings account has a balance of $3450.

Her other treasure consists of the jewelry that her mother left to her, which she keeps in a safety deposit box at the Third World Bank. In the box are a diamond ring, a pearl necklace and earrings, and two cameo broaches. When Eleanor's mother died five years ago and the jewelry was willed to Eleanor, all of it together was appraised at $4000. The appraisal did not itemize.

Eleanor devotes all of her spare time to her volunteer work for the local child abuse prevention program sponsored by a not-for-profit corporation called Children First, Inc.

Eleanor would like you to draft her will. She wishes to leave $100 to her nephew, $100 to her niece, and $1000 to Children First, Inc., with the understanding that if Children First, Inc., is no longer a functional organization when she dies, then that money should go to whatever local organization has taken over its work.

Eleanor would like Amy Joslin to choose one item of Eleanor's mother's jewelry. The rest should be sold, along with all the rest of her personal property. Then after payment of her funeral expenses and other expenses related to her death, the rest of her estate should be divided equally between Amy and Michael Joslin, except that $500 of Michael's share should be the forgiveness of the $500 debt he owes her. She made an interest-free loan to him last April 1. He has not repaid any of it.

Eleanor would like Vincent Docker, a vice president of Third World Bank, to serve as her personal representative. She asks you to serve as an alternate.

Draft Eleanor's will. What, if anything, do you need to discuss with her first?

Drafting Assignment 6.E—Will

Draft a will for yourself, irrespective of tax considerations. If you already have a will, redraft it to reflect what you have learned about drafting wills.

Drafting Assignment 6.F—Codicil

Draft a codicil to your will. In it, revoke at least one provision, add at least one, and make at least one substitution.

Drafting Assignment 6.G—Living Will

If your state has statutes authorizing "living wills" but not prescribing the language to be used in a living will, draft a form consistent with your statutes for use by your firm's clients. If your state has no such statutes, for the purpose of this assignment assume the following sections apply.

765.02 Right to make declaration instructing physician concerning life-prolonging procedures; policy statement. The Legislature finds that every competent adult has the fundamental right to control the decisions relating to his own medical care, including the decision to have provided, withheld, or withdrawn the medical or surgical means or procedures calculated to prolong his life. This right is subject to certain interests of society, such as the protection of human life and the preservation of ethical standards in the medical profession. The Legislature further finds that the artificial prolongation of life for a person with a terminal condition may secure for him only a precarious and burdensome existence, while providing nothing medically necessary or beneficial to the patient. In order that the rights and intentions of a person with such a condition may be respected even after he is no longer able to participate actively in decisions concerning himself, and to encourage communication among such patient, his family, and his physician, the Legislature declares that the laws of this state recognize the right of a competent adult to make an oral or written declaration instructing his physician to provide, withhold, or withdraw life-prolonging procedures, or to designate another to make the treatment decision for him, in the event that such person should be diagnosed as suffering from a terminal condition.

765.03 Definitions. As used in ss. 765.01–765.15, the term:

(1) "Attending physician" means the primary physician who has responsibility for the treatment and care of the patient.

(2) "Declaration" means:

(a) A witnessed document in writing, voluntarily executed by the declarant in accordance with the requirements of s. 765.04; or

(b) A witnessed oral statement made in accordance with the provisions of s. 765.04 by the declarant subsequent to the time he is diagnosed as suffering from a terminal condition.

(3) "Life-prolonging procedure" means any medical procedure, treatment, or intervention which:

(a) Utilizes mechanical or other artificial means to sustain, restore, or supplant a spontaneous vital function; and

(b) When applied to a patient in a terminal condition, serves only to prolong the process of dying.

The term "life-prolonging procedure" does not include the provision of sustenance or the administration of medication or performance of any medical procedure deemed necessary to provide comfort care or to alleviate pain.

(4) "Physician" means a person licensed to practice medicine in the state.

(5) "Qualified patient" means a patient who has made a declaration in accordance with ss. 765.01–765.15 and who has been diagnosed and certified in writing by the attending physician, and by one other physician who has examined the patient, to be afflicted with a terminal condition.

(6) "Terminal condition" means a condition caused by injury, disease, or illness from which, to a reasonable degree of medical certainty, there can be no recovery and which makes death imminent.

765.04 Procedure for making a declaration; notice to physician.

(1) Any competent adult may, at any time, make a written declaration directing the withholding or withdrawal of life-prolonging procedures in the event such person should have a terminal condition. A written declaration must be signed by the declarant in the presence of two subscribing witnesses, one of whom is neither a spouse nor a blood relative of the declarant. If the declarant is physically unable to sign

the written declaration, his declaration may be given orally, in which event one of the witnesses must subscribe the declarant's signature in the declarant's presence and at the declarant's direction.

(2) It is the responsibility of the declarant to provide for notification to his attending physician that the declaration has been made. In the event the declarant is comatose, incompetent, or otherwise mentally or physically incapable, any other person may notify the physician of the existence of the declaration. An attending physician who is so notified shall promptly make the declaration or a copy of the declaration, if the declaration is written, a part of the declarant's medical records. If the declaration is oral, the physician shall likewise promptly make the fact of such declaration a part of the patient's medical record.

765.06　Revocation of declaration. A declaration may be revoked at any time by the declarant:

(1) By means of a signed, dated writing;

(2) By means of the physical cancellation or destruction of the declaration by the declarant or by another in the declarant's presence and at the declarant's direction; or

(3) By means of an oral expression of intent to revoke.

Any such revocation will be effective when it is communicated to the attending physician. No civil or criminal liability shall be imposed upon any person for a failure to act upon a revocation unless that person has actual knowledge of such revocation.

————

If you use the above statutes as the applicable law, assume you have received the following memorandum from a senior partner in your firm, directing your attention to a variety of matters.

MEMORANDUM

TO:　　　Junior Partner

FROM:　Senior Partner

RE:　　　Living Will Form

When you draft a living will form for us, will you keep in mind the following:

1. Some of our clients are far more sophisticated than others—everybody from Ph.D.'s to people who never graduated from high school. They all need to understand what the declaration says; on the other hand, the form should not insult anyone's intelligence.

2. Please get into the form a place for the client to say who is to make treatment decisions if the client cannot communicate.

3. Section 765.04 restricts who can be witnesses. Our form should have language to make the restriction clear to the people getting ready to sign as witnesses. Also, I have read that some other states require that both witnesses not be related to the declarant by blood or marriage

and also that they not be entitled to any of the declarant's estate either by will or by operation of law. Some have gone even further and disallowed the attending physician, the physician's employees, employees of a health facility where the declarant is a patient, or anyone who has a claim against the declarant's estate. I can't make up my mind whether it would be a good idea to add some or all of these restrictions. Will you think about them and add any that you decide belong there. Then, after I see your draft, we can talk about this whole issue of whether we should urge our clients to restrict the witnesses more tightly than our statute does.

4. Section 765.03(5) purports to be a definition, but it actually turns out to express a rule about physicians certifying terminal conditions. Most of our clients probably won't be diagnosed and certified to be afflicted with a terminal condition at the time they sign their declarations; however, some may be. See if you can make the form flexible enough to provide for listing the name and address of any physicians who have certified that the declarant has a terminal condition.

5. I think it would be a good idea to mention in the declaration the right to revoke it and also the basic information about how to revoke. In other words, let's use the form itself as a means of making sure our clients know about their revocation rights. Some states make living wills automatically expire after a certain period of time, usually five years. Think about building in automatic expiration as an alternative to—or in addition to—reciting the revocation rights. Draft according to what you conclude would be the best way to handle the possibility of clients changing their minds.

6. I would like to protect our clients by adding a provision that a copy is going to the client's doctor with directions to make it part of the client's medical record. This way, if the client has a doctor who will not comply with the living will, the client will have a better chance of finding that out in time to decide whether to change doctors.

7. I read a horror story once about living wills being put in a hospital emergency room file because they were understood to be directions not to resuscitate declarants who suffered heart failure at the hospital resulting from injuries in car accidents and other such casualties. Please take special care to prevent our form from being misconstrued that way.

8. We seem to be stuck with the vague term "terminal condition" as defined by Section 765.03(6). See if you can figure out a way for our form to give the client more power and the doctor less to determine what "imminent" means in the statement that a terminal condition is one which makes death imminent.

9. Our clients might want to specify whether food and water are to be provided by gastric tube or intravenously or not at all. What do you think of adding language to give them the option?

P.S. Here are some forms I have come across. If you find anything useful, help yourself.

———

TO MY FAMILY, MY PHYSICIAN, MY LAWYER, MY CLERGY-
MAN—

TO ANY MEDICAL FACILITY IN WHOSE CARE I HAPPEN TO BE—

TO ANY INDIVIDUAL WHO MAY BECOME RESPONSIBLE FOR
MY HEALTH, WELFARE OR AFFAIRS

Death is as much a reality as birth, growth, maturity and old age—it is the one certainty of life. If the time comes when I, _____, can no longer take part in decisions for my own future, let this statement stand as an expression of my wishes, while I am still of sound mind.

If the situation should arise in which there is no reasonable expectation of my recovery from physical or mental disability, I request that I be allowed to die and not be kept alive by artificial means or "heroic measures". I do not fear death itself as much as the indignities of deterioration, dependence and hopeless pain. I, therefore, ask that medication be mercifully administered to me to alleviate suffering even though this may hasten the moment of death.

This request is made after careful consideration. I hope you who care for me will feel morally bound to follow its mandate. I recognize that this appears to place a heavy responsibility upon you, but it is with the intention of relieving you of such responsibility and of placing it upon myself in accordance with my strong convictions, that this statement is made.

Signed _____

Date _____

Witness _____

Witness _____

Copies of this request have been given to _____

_____

_____

_____

———

DECLARATION

Declaration made this _____ day of _____, 19__. I, _____, willfully and voluntarily make known my desire that my dying not be artificially prolonged under the circumstances set forth below, and I do hereby declare:

If at any time I should have a terminal condition and if my attending physician has determined that there can be no recovery from such condition and that my death is imminent, I direct that life-prolonging procedures be withheld or withdrawn when the application of such procedures would serve only to prolong artificially the process of dying, and that I be permitted to die naturally with only the administration of medication or the performance of any medical procedure deemed necessary to provide me with comfort care or to alleviate pain.

In the absence of my ability to give directions regarding the use of such life-prolonging procedures, it is my intention that this declaration be honored by my family and physician as the final expression of my legal right to refuse medical or surgical treatment and to accept the consequences for such refusal.

If I have been diagnosed as pregnant and that diagnosis is known to my physician, this declaration shall have no force or effect during the course of my pregnancy.

I understand the full import of this declaration, and I am emotionally and mentally competent to make this declaration.

(Signed) _____

The declarant is known to me, and I believe him or her to be of sound mind.

Witness _____

Witness _____

_____

DECLARATION

I have the primary right to make my own decisions concerning treatment that might unduly prolong the dying process. By this declaration I express to my physician, family and friends my intent. If I should have a terminal condition it is my desire that my dying not be prolonged by administration of death-prolonging procedures. If my condition is terminal and I am unable to participate in decisions regarding my medical treatment, I direct my attending physician to withhold or withdraw medical procedures that merely prolong the dying process and are not necessary to my comfort or to alleviate pain. It is not my intent to authorize affirmative or deliberate acts or omissions to shorten my life rather only to permit the natural process of dying.

Signed this _____ day of _____

Signature _____

City, County and State of residence _____

_____

DIRECTIVE TO PHYSICIANS

Directive made this _____ day of _____ (month, year).

I _____, being of sound mind, willfully and voluntarily make known my desire that my life shall not be artificially prolonged under the circumstances set forth below, and do hereby declare:

1. If at any time I should have an incurable injury, disease, or illness certified to be a terminal condition by two physicians, and where the application of life-sustaining procedures would serve only to artificially prolong the moment of my death and where my physician determines that my death is imminent whether or not life-sustaining procedures are utilized, I direct that such procedures be withheld or withdrawn, and that I be permitted to die naturally.

2. In the absence of my ability to give directions regarding the use of such life-sustaining procedures, it is my intention that this directive shall be honored by my family and physician(s) as the final expression of my legal right to refuse medical or surgical treatment and accept the consequences from such refusal.

3. If I have been diagnosed as pregnant and that diagnosis is known to my physician, this directive shall have no force or effect during the course of my pregnancy.

4. I have been diagnosed and notified at least 14 days ago as having a terminal condition by _____, M.D., whose address is _____, and whose telephone number is _____. I understand that if I have not filled in the physician's name and address, it shall be presumed that I did not have a terminal condition when I made out this directive.

5. This directive shall have no force or effect five years from the date filled in above.

6. I understand the full import of this directive and I am emotionally and mentally competent to make this directive.

Signed _____

City, County and State of Residence _____

The declarant has been personally known to me and I believe him or her to be of sound mind.

Witness _____

Witness _____

*

Part Three

A PROCESS MANUAL: INTRODUCTION TO THE PROCESSES

I. USING CLIENTS AND DOCUMENTS AS RESOURCES

Part Three addresses principles of drafting that are intended to serve you no matter what document you are drafting. Part Three is for your reference *while, not after,* you are drafting the documents covered in Parts One and Two.

This entire book operates on the principle that clients and existing documents are valuable drafting resources. Chapter 7 focuses in particular on how to make the most of these resources before you begin drafting a document. First, it discusses the process of gathering information from the client, including making checklists of questions and also giving attention to what kinds of questions are and are not appropriate to ask the client. The discussion addresses the roles of drafting lawyer and client with respect to policy-making.

Chapter 7 also discusses processes for explicating a document, whether it is the client's document in current use that is to be redrafted, or whether it is another's document that you are contemplating using as a model. Explication is presented as a tool for critical analysis of an existing document, with the ultimate purpose of improving both the substance and the form of the document to be drafted or redrafted.

II. CHOOSING FLEXIBLE LANGUAGE

Choosing language is a constant process while you are drafting. Legal documents benefit from flexibility to the extent that they are plans for an uncertain future. Vague language often serves better than precise language, and general better than particular. Chapter 8 distinguishes these qualities of language from each other and offers suggestions about how to make appropriate choices in various contexts. The chapter also shows why excessive precision and particularity cause more problems than vagueness and generality.

III. ACHIEVING CLARITY AND AVOIDING AMBIGUITY

Making documents clear and unambiguous is usually more a product of editing and redrafting than choosing language in a first draft. Ambiguity is usually inadvertent rather than purposeful. Finding and removing it is easier than preventing it. Chapter 9 discusses the forms of ambiguity: semantic, syntactic, and contextual. It also demonstrates techniques for avoiding ambiguity, with special attention to tabulated sentence structure.

IV. DEFINING TERMS AND NAMING CONCEPTS

Even though definitions generally belong near the beginning of a document, it makes sense to wait until you have finished a complete draft of a document to go through the process of deciding what terms need definition and where to put the definitions. Chapter 10 discusses lexical and stipulative definitions, full and partial definitions, methods of defining, and conventions about the form of definitions. The chapter also addresses a variation on defining: the process of creating terms to name concepts or label collections of particulars.

V. MAKING STYLISTIC CHOICES

Style in legal drafting is the composite of choices the drafter makes about how to handle numerous matters of word choice, sentence structure, form, and even graphics. Trying to attend to all of these matters while composing a first draft would seriously interfere with expressing the substance. Therefore, attention to style is better left for the editing and redrafting stage when you can impose a system of stylistic controls on whatever inconsistencies you find in your first draft. Chapter 11 discusses the issues that require stylistic control. It also gives suggestions about what values might guide the choices, such as a preference for plain and gender-neutral language.

Chapter 7

USING CLIENTS AND DOCUMENTS AS RESOURCES

Table of Sections

I. DRAFTING AS A PROCESS

Drafting is a process, but it is misleading to spell out its steps in any particular order, for that might suggest that the steps are, or should be, the same for everybody every time. That is not the case, and yet it is possible to make some suggestions based on the experience of successful practitioners. Also, it is important to recognize that drafting is itself part of a larger planning process that lawyers undertake for their clients. The steps do not occur separately, one at a time, but are inextricably linked.[1]

1. See Macneil, A Primer of Contract Planning, 48 S.Cal.L.Rev. 627, 643 (1975). Sections II and III of this chapter reflect Macneil's discussion at 643–51. Although Macneil focuses expressly on contracts, the process also applies to other planning documents. See also R. Dick, Legal Drafting 29–40 (2d ed. 1985); R. Dickerson, The Fundamentals of Legal Drafting 51–69 (2d ed. 1986); Haynsworth, How To Draft Clear and Concise Legal Documents, 31 Practical Lawyer 41 (1985), adapted from The Professional Skills of the Small Business Lawyer (1984).

II. SOME CONTINUING CONCERNS

A. LEGAL CONTEXT

The external legal context in which the document is to function should figure into all parts of the planning. It should go without saying that you need to research all applicable law thoroughly.

B. CIRCUMSTANTIAL CONTEXT

You should become as fully informed as is feasible about the circumstantial context in which the document is to operate, such as the customs of any businesses involved. In this regard, it may be necessary to consult experts on technical matters outside the realm of your expertise.

C. NEGOTIATING CONTEXT

Keep in mind that negotiation is usually not finished before the drafting starts. Moreover, one of the effects of the continuing nature of negotiation is that all plans are to some extent subject to change.

III. GETTING INFORMATION FROM THE CLIENT

A. GENERATING QUESTIONS TO ASK THE CLIENT

The lawyer engaged in planning needs to gather facts about the parties' goals and also about the means by which they expect to attain those goals. This is not merely a matter of gathering information. As you begin to ask questions, that process can give new shape to the facts. Pursuing details about means, for instance, can produce new perceptions about goals. At this stage, you might uncover potential conflicts of interest among multiple parties. You also might discover that the client has not planned carefully enough. Advising the client about such matters requires tact because the client may think you are too cautious about remote possibilities and what appear to the client as minor risks.

When preparing to draft a document for an individual client, you should regard that client as one of your most valuable resources. "Researching the client" should not be left to casual conversation. It is a good idea to have questions written down to make sure nothing is left out. Many lawyers develop checklists for frequently drafted documents such as wills, corporate by-laws, or marital separation agreements. The more work you do in a given field, the more refined the checklist or intake questionnaire becomes.[2]

---

2. To get an idea of what good checklists encompass in a variety of legal con- texts, see B. Becker, B. Savin, D. Becker, and D. Gibberman, Legal Checklists (1975

Questions can be generated from a number of sources:

- Research into the law on the subject.
- Conversations with experts on technical matters involved.
- Study of the client's document that is to be redrafted.
- Study of similar documents or forms used by others.
- Study of checklists or questionnaires used by others.

To demonstrate how comprehensive a good checklist can be, following is a sample checklist for drafting a partnership agreement.

R. DICK, LEGAL DRAFTING
40–46 (2d ed. 1985) *

CHECK-LIST FOR PARTNERSHIP AGREEMENT

1. *Name*

(1) What is the proposed name of the partnership?

(2) Is this name likely to be confused with any other well-known names in this type of business?

2. *Partners*

(1) What are the names and addresses of all partners?

(2) Are all partners over the age of majority?

3. *Business Aspects*

(1) What type of business is proposed?

(2) Will the partnership require leased premises or ownership of buildings and what will be needed for inventory, furniture, fixtures and equipment?

(3) Do one or more of the partners already have a suitable lease or own a suitable building? If not, how much cash outlay is required for periodic payments under a lease or for a purchase? If a purchase is in the offing, will there be mortgage financing? Will the building be acquired as partnership property? Can the partnership realistically meet mortgage payments, utility costs, salaries and other expenses?

(4) Have the proposed partners discussed appropriate banking arrangements and fixed on a suitable line of credit for this type of business?

(5) If expansion of business is contemplated, where will the capital come from for expansion?

(6) What are the financial backgrounds and resources of the partners?

and cumulative supplements in Callaghan
looseleaf service).

(7) Is the partnership to take over an existing business? If so, are properties of that business to be transferred into the partnership? Are any insurance policies, manufacturing licenses or royalty agreements to be assigned to the partnership? Will the new partnership assume all debts and liabilities of an existing business? Will the fiscal year and auditors for the existing business be the same for the new partnership? Will the existing business be formally dissolved?

(8) Will the partnership business be one with a high element of risk? If so, would a corporation be preferable?

4. *Principal place of business*

(1) Where will the partnership locate?

(2) Will there be branch offices in the same province or in other provinces?

5. *Life of partnership*

(1) When will the partnership begin?

(2) How long is the partnership expected to last? If indefinitely, then what are the contingencies for dissolution?

6. *Capital contributions, percentage division of profits and percentage interests*

(1) What is each partner expected to contribute in money or property? Is there a time limit when contributions are to be made? If contributions are periodic what is the interest rate to be charged, if any, on the unpaid balance?

(2) Is any property being loaned by a partner (such as a library, vehicles or tools)?

(3) What is the value of any property contributions made by a partner?

(4) Is part of the profits to be left in the partnership business as extra capital?

(5) What is the percentage division of the initial money and property contributions?

(6) If the partnership is an existing one, what percentage interest has each partner in the new partnership after adding new partners? In other words, what percentage of capital, goodwill, work in progress, receivables and furniture and fixtures will each partner own in the new partnership?

(7) Does goodwill have any value at all in this type of partnership? If so, should a formula be inserted in the agreement for calculation of goodwill on the admission of new partners?

(8) Does the percentage division of profits correspond to the percentage ownership interest in the partnership? Will this division of profits change periodically depending on the performance of each partner? How will the performance of each partner be measured? If the per-

centage division of profits changes, will there be a corresponding adjustment in the percentage ownership interest?

(9) Will new or young partners be permitted to acquire a percentage ownership interest or will they be confined to a percentage division of profits?

(10) Will there be ownership and non-ownership units or common, profit-sharing units and preferred-ownership units for the partnership? For any common profit-sharing units will goodwill be fixed or frozen?

(11) If there is to be a periodic change of the percentage division of profits, will this be done by secret ballot under the control of an auditor with each partner evaluating only the performance of the other partners according to an agreed method?

(12) Are profits divisible quarterly? Will monthly statements be prepared by the auditors to watch closely the performance of the business?

(13) Will the partners have entertainment or promotional expense accounts or will these be personal?

7. *Management*

(1) Are the partners to have equal authority in management?

(2) Will there be two groups of partners—ownership and non-ownership partners, senior and junior partners, active and silent partners or partners owning common units and others owning common and preferred units?

8. *Attention to partnership matters*

(1) Are all partners to attend to partnership matters full time?

(2) Are there any activities that are prohibited?

(3) What will happen if one partner is asked to serve on a government board, committee or commission for a temporary period?

9. *Accounting matters*

(1) Will the partnership accounting be on an accrual basis?

(2) May any partner inspect the books at any time?

(3) Will there be a reserve for bad debts?

(4) Will the partners have drawing accounts?

(5) Are the partners to share any loss according to their percentage-ownership interests?

10. *Expulsion, mental incompetency, withdrawal, death, disability or bankruptcy of a partner*

(1) What are the grounds and method for expulsion of a partner?

(2) How long must a partner be disabled to fall within the disability provisions?

(3) What notice of withdrawal is required and how is it to be given?

(4) Should there be a restraint-against-trade clause if a partner withdraws, such as not engaging in medical practice for five years within five miles of a medical clinic?

(5) Is there to be a clause enabling the continuation of the business by the remaining partners after expulsion, mental incompetency, withdrawal, death, disability or bankruptcy?

(6) How is the value of the interest of the withdrawing partner to be determined? What is the time period for payment? Will an expelled partner have any right to be compensated for goodwill?

(7) Will there be a separate buy-sell agreement to compel the estate of a deceased partner to sell his interest and the surviving partners to buy that interest?

(8) Will the buy-sell agreement be funded by life insurance? If so, will term insurance, convertible term or whole life insurance be used?

(9) What proportion of each policy on the life of any one partner will the other partners own?

(10) Is any partner uninsurable or rated as a high risk because of a lung condition, etc.?

(11) Will there be a trustee under the buy-sell agreement?

(12) Should the surviving partners be entitled to an assignment to them of any policy or policies held by the deceased on their lives upon payment of the cash surrender values to the estate of the deceased?

(13) If a partner is found by court order to be mentally incompetent or incapable of managing business affairs, is that partner considered to have withdrawn from the partnership and offered that partner's interest for sale at a valuation to be determined under the partnership agreement?

(14) Will there be a compulsory retirement clause at 65 or will the partner at 65 be bought out over a period of 5 years until age 70 and still be active in the business?

(15) Will the partners collectively wish to direct the investment of cash reserves built up under the insurance policies that fund the buy-sell agreement where interest rates are higher than insurance lending rates?

11. *Dissolution*

(1) Under what conditions is the partnership dissolved?

(2) Do only senior partners act as liquidators? How are "senior partners" defined for this purpose?

B. QUESTIONNAIRES USING COMPUTER PROGRAMS

Computer software is now available to improve client questionnaires that serve as the basis for complex documents. The process works this way. The law firm first creates a master form on the computer that contains all of the various provisions that have appeared in all of the individual documents of some particular type drafted in the past by senior members of the firm. From the master form a questionnaire is produced. The questions appear on the screen. When the answers are typed on the keyboard, the answers trigger which follow-up questions to ask and which irrelevant questions to skip. The computer program also checks for consistency among answers; it adjusts tenses, plurals, and other grammatical matters. It allows for editing in response to both law and fact changes. The ultimate effect of such a program is that every lawyer in the firm can draft even complex documents that benefit from the best thinking of all the members of the firm.[3]

C. AREAS OF FOCUS FOR A CHECKLIST

1. Questions About Client's Purposes

a. What is the client's present situation in relation to the document?

b. Does the client expect the document to change the situation or to solidify it? What does the client expect the document to accomplish?

c. How does the client expect to use the document? Is it to cover one situation with one other party, or is it to be used as a form over time and thus to apply to many parties and many variations in situation?

d. Has the client negotiated with anyone regarding this document? Are negotiations still in progress? Have negotiations resulted in any oral agreements or anything else that needs to be incorporated into the document?

e. Has the client had previous transactions similar to the one to which this document will relate? What were those previous transactions like?

f. Does the client know other parties to be involved? What does the client know about them? How does the client feel about them?

2. Trouble–Shooting Questions

a. What potential problems should the document resolve so as to keep the law from stepping in to resolve them?

b. What are any potential threats to a smooth-sailing transaction?

c. Does the client want a "tight" document that covers everything and leaves nothing to risk or a "loose" document that assumes some risks in the interest of doing good business? It is important to consider

---

3. See Dziewit, Graziano, and Daley, The Quest for the Paperless Office—Electronic Contracting: State of the Art Possibility But Legal Impossibility? 5 Santa Clara Computer & High Tech.L.J. 75 (1989).

the client's style and understand that sometimes legal decisions are made in a context that also contains business decisions.

3. *Questions to Assess the Client*

a. How much does the client understand about the transaction and its legal ramifications? Is the client sophisticated or naive?

b. Is the client perceptive? Can the client's statements be trusted as accurate, honest, and consistent?

c. Is the client so totally focused on one aspect of the transaction that others are being neglected? Does the client need help to think about neglected matters?

D. THE LAWYER AS TROUBLE SHOOTER AND THE CLIENT AS POLICY MAKER

It is important to remember that the lawyer is the trouble shooter, and the client is the policy maker. Finding out what the client wants to accomplish is often a matter of finding out about underlying policies that may or may not be expressed directly in the document. Nonetheless, short of drafting an unconscionable or otherwise illegal document, the lawyer must never lose sight of the goal: achieving what the client—not the lawyer—wants.

Exercise 7.1

Develop a list of questions to ask your client for each type of planning document you draft. To the extent possible, follow these guidelines:

1. Try to group your questions under subject headings that at least roughly correspond to possible section headings in the document.

2. Ask the client only questions that the client can answer. Do not ask legal questions or questions about drafting that require you to exercise your own judgment.

3. Do not ask broad, open-ended questions that seek lengthy answers. Make sure you seek specific information rather than merely identifying a subject for inquiry. For example, avoid questions like these: "What about covenant not to compete?" or "Policy on termination?"

4. Feel free to include items of advice if you think you ought to handle something differently from the way you understand the client wants it handled. In other words, plan to use your questions as a springboard for conferring with the client, not merely as a means of learning facts.

IV. WORKING FROM A "MODEL" DOCUMENT

Only rarely must a drafter operate in a vacuum with no models at all, but commonly the available models are poorly drafted or not entirely relevant. Using a model fosters a temptation to accept something that looks all right under cursory inspection even though careful analysis would reveal serious flaws in it. Sometimes the "model" is the client's or another party's existing document, and the drafting job involves redrafting all or part of it.

————

V. EXPLICATION: THE TESTING PROCESS

If a document or a section of a document is so densely packed that it is not easily penetrable, it should be regarded as suspect. The density may result from exceptionally complex substance, or it may result from poor drafting and thus signal that the provision is potentially fraught with ambiguities. Dense material warrants the sort of explication that a scholar might perform on a literary text.[4] The process entails close reading, line by line, for both semantic and syntactic analysis. In other words, it is important to attend both to what individual words mean and to how the words and phrases relate to each other. A technical knowledge of linguistics is not necessary to perform a careful explication.

Through explication, you can discover far more than simply what a provision purports to say. If you criticize while you are analyzing, you can discover how best to redraft the provision to make it better meet its users' needs. The analysis usually involves questioning not only the meaning of individual sentences but also the purposes of the whole document. The questions may be ones to ask the client, who is the policy maker. They may lead to other forms of research. In any event, the important thing is to write them down as they occur to you. They will be useful later, and it is often a mistake to rely on memory to dredge them up on cue.

VI. EXPLICATION TECHNIQUES

A. THE ROADMAP [5]

Initially it may be helpful to analyze a suspect provision in a loose, informal way by making a rough chart of it with circles and arrows and

---

4. But see Rabinowitz, Our Evaluation of Literature Has Been Distorted by Academe's Bias Toward Close Reading of Texts, 34 Chronicle of Higher Educ. A40 (April 6, 1988) (criticizing close reading as preferred approach to literary texts).

5. See Benson, Up a Statute with Gun and Camera: Isolating Linguistic and Logical Structures in the Analysis of Legislative Language, 8 Seton Hall Legis.J. 279, 287–91 (1984).

notes in the margin. This is akin to book-briefing an opinion in a casebook. You can grasp major concepts and find major gaps or contextual ambiguities. If the hieroglyphics are easily decoded, this may be the only explication device needed.

A variation of this technique is to make a roadmap of the logical structure by going through the material and circling the words "if," "then," "and," "or," and "but." "However" and "except" can be regarded as variants of "but." "Also" and "in addition" can be regarded as variants of "and." Other variants may appear as well. It is also a good idea to circle "not" and its variants.

B. THE SENTENCE DIAGRAM [6]

If the structure of an individual sentence is garbled or particularly dense, it is helpful to draw a rough sentence diagram. You do not need to be an expert at diagraming formalities. The only grammatical skills needed are the ability to distinguish subjects, verbs, and objects, and the ability to attach modifiers to what they modify. Diagraming is especially useful for weeding out syntactic ambiguities, particularly squinting modifiers.

C. COMPLETE TABULATION

1. Tabulation as an Explication Device Distinguished From Presenting Material in Tabulated Sentence Structure

If the troublesome material is too long and complicated to yield to charting by the roadmap or the diagram, then you can test it by setting it out on paper with its compounds and items in series grouped and set apart by tabulation. This process is essentially the same as using tabulated sentence structure to present material, with one major difference. Tabulated sentence structure as a presentation device [7] indents compounds and series only when the tabulation resolves potential ambiguity or achieves special emphasis.

When you use tabulation as a testing device, however, it involves indenting virtually if not literally every set of compounds and every series in the material under scrutiny. The process reveals syntactic ambiguities and other problems in sentence structure. Sometimes the process can both reveal an ambiguity and provide the mechanism for resolving it.

---

6. See id. at 292–96.

7. See Chapter 9, Sections IV–VII for discussion of how to use tabulated sentence structure, comparison with list structure, and a checklist.

2. *An Example of Complete Tabulation Used to Test Dense Material*

   a. *The Dense Material* [8]

CANCELLATION BY SOS

1   This agreement may be canceled, without previous notice, by
2 SOS if the Central Station, connecting wires or equipment within
3 Client's premises are destroyed by fire or other catastrophe, or so
4 substantially damaged that it is impracticable to continue service.
5 It may likewise be canceled by Client if Client's plant is so destroyed
6 or damaged. Advance payments made for service to be supplied
7 after the date of termination will be refunded to Client. This
8 contract may be terminated by SOS at any time if it is unable to
9 secure or retain the connections or privileges necessary to send
10 signals between Client's premises and the Central Station or be-
11 tween the Central Station and the _____ Police Department.
12 SOS is not liable for any damages or penalty as a result of such a
13 termination. Advance payments made for service to be supplied
14 after the date of termination will be refunded to Client.

   b. *The Dense Material Completely Tabulated*

A. This agreement may be canceled, without previous notice, by SOS
    if
    1. the Central Station,
    2. connecting wires or
    3. equipment within Client's premises
    are
    1. destroyed by
        a. fire or
        b. other catastrophe, or
    2. so substantially damaged that it is impracticable to continue
        service.

B. It may likewise be canceled by Client if Client's plant is so
    1. destroyed or
    2. damaged.
    Advance payments made for service to be supplied after the date of
    termination will be refunded to Client.

C. This contract may be terminated by SOS at any time if it is unable
    to
    1. secure or

8. Adapted from a contract that ap-   from R. Dickerson, Materials on Legal
pears in full at p. 170, where it is quoted   Drafting 106–10 (1981).

2. retain

the

1. connections or

2. privileges

necessary to send signals

1. between Client's premises and the Central Station or

2. between the Central Station and the _____ Police Department.

SOS is not liable for any

1. damages or

2. penalty

as a result of such a termination.

Advance payments made for service to be supplied after the date of termination will be refunded to Client.

c. Questions Raised About the Dense Material

The process of setting the material out in this structure generates a number of questions. Some are simple questions of fact, but others are major conceptual questions that warrant discussion with SOS, the drafter's client. Consider the following questions, and decide whether they are easily answerable. Which ones would warrant discussion with SOS before redrafting? What further questions does the explication raise?

1. Why does "A" say the agreement may be "canceled" and "C" say "terminated"? What is the difference?

2. Should "A" refer to "connecting wires within Client's premises" as well as "equipment within Client's premises"?

3. In "B," what does "likewise" mean? Does it mean without previous notice? If not, why should Client have to give notice under these circumstances but SOS not have to?

4. Why is "A" about premises and "B" about plant? Are they the same place?

5. In "B," what does "so" mean? Is this a reference to fire or other catastrophe?

6. Why does Client get no refund under "A" but only under "B" and "C"?

7. May SOS be liable for damages or penalty under "A"? Under "B"?

8. Why is a provision for cancellation by Client buried in the middle of a section headed "Cancellation by SOS"?

———

Exercise 7.2

Test your understanding of explication techniques on one or more of the following provisions. Explicate by the method you find best suited for the provision. Remember that for the purposes of explication, you need to work with language and syntax exactly as they are.

Provision 1 (Statutory Definition of "Consumer Transaction")

1 "Consumer transaction" means a sale, lease, assignment, award
2 by chance, or other disposition of an item of goods, a consumer
3 service, or an intangible to an individual for purposes that are
4 primarily personal, family, or household or that relate to a business
5 opportunity that requires both his expenditure of money or property
6 and his personal services on a continuing basis and in which he has
7 not been previously engaged, or a solicitation by a supplier with
8 respect to any of these dispositions.

Provision 2 (Election Statute)

1 If no candidate has been elected to a nonpartisan office pursu-
2 ant to Section 6611 or if the number of candidates elected at the
3 primary election is less than the total number to be elected to that
4 office, then candidates for that office at the ensuing election shall be
5 those candidates not elected at the primary who received the next
6 highest number of votes cast for nomination to that office, equal in
7 number to twice the number remaining to be elected to that office,
8 or less, if the total number of candidates not elected is less.

Provision 3 (Statutory Exemption From Liability for Unauthorized Commercial Publication)

1 No relief may be obtained under Section 540.08 or Section
2 540.09, against any broadcaster, publisher or distributor broadcast-
3 ing, publishing or distributing paid advertising matter by radio or
4 television or in a newspaper, magazine or similar periodical without
5 knowledge or notice that any consent required by Section 540.08 or
6 Section 540.09, in connection with such advertising matter has not
7 been obtained, except an injunction against the presentation of such
8 newspaper, magazine or similar periodical.

Provision 4 (Official Leaflet on Unemployment Benefits)

1 *What is a seasonal worker's rate of unemployment benefit in his*
2 *season?*

3 For the ordinary benefit claimant, full rate benefit requires 50
4 contributions to have been paid or credited in the preceding contri-
5 bution year. Of these 39 must be in Class 1. Benefit, even at a
6 reduced rate, is not payable unless 26 Class 1 contributions have
7 been paid or credited in the contribution year. But if a seasonal
8 worker has not less than 13 Class 1 contributions paid or credited in
9 a contribution year, he may count as Class 1 contributions any other

10 contributions paid or credited in that year for the purpose of
11 determining his rate of benefit if he is unemployed during his
12 season. Thus if he should become unemployed in that part of the
13 year when he is normally working for an employer, he should be
14 entitled to full rate benefit so long as he has contributed according
15 to his class of insurance throughout the preceding contribution year.

Provision 5　(Exemption Provision in Equal Opportunity Legislation)

1 　　　Nothing in division H of this section * shall bar any religious or
2 denominational institution or organization, or any charitable or
3 educational organization that is operated, supervised, or controlled
4 by or in connection with a religious organization, or any bona fide
5 private or fraternal organization, from giving preference to persons
6 of the same religion or denomination, or to members of such private
7 or fraternal organization, or from making such selection as is
8 calculated by such organization to promote the religious principles
9 or the aims, purposes, or fraternal principles for which it is estab-
10 lished or maintained.

Provision 6　(Rule of Civil Procedure on Defenses and Objections)

1 　　　A party waives all defenses and objections which he does not
2 present either by motion as hereinbefore provided or if he has made
3 no motion, by responsive pleading or an amendment thereof made
4 as a matter of course under Rule 15(A), except (1) the defense of
5 failure to state a claim upon which relief can be granted, the
6 defense of failure to join an indispensable party, the defense of lack
7 of jurisdiction of the subject matter, and the objection of failure to
8 state a legal defense to a claim, may be made by a later pleading, if
9 one is permitted, by motion for judgment on the pleadings or at the
10 trial on the merits; and except (2) whenever it appears by sugges-
11 tion of the parties or otherwise that the court lacks jurisdiction of
12 the subject matter, the court shall dismiss the action.

Provision 7　(Mortgage Provision on Protecting Secured Interest)

1 　　　The Mortgagors have agreed and do hereby agree to pay
2 promptly, as the same become due and payable, to the proper
3 officers chargeable with the collection, all taxes, assessments and
4 other public charges levied or assessed against or payable in respect
5 to the above described premises or any part thereof including all
6 taxes which may be levied or assessed under any law, now or
7 hereafter existing, against the interest in said premises created by
8 this mortgage; and to keep the buildings and improvements now or
9 hereafter erected on said premises insured against loss or damage

---

* [This passage is an excerpt from a state's equal opportunity legislation. Division H bars certain forms of discrimination in the sale, transfer, assignment, rental, lease, sublease, and financing of housing accommodations and burial lots.]

10 by war damage, fire, lightning, tornado, windstorm or cyclone, in
11 such amounts and with such companies as may be satisfactory to
12 the holder of this mortgage, by a policy or policies to be left in such
13 holder's possession with loss, if any, payable to such holder as such
14 holder's interest may appear by a standard mortgage clause at-
15 tached thereto, and at least five (5) days before the expiration of any
16 such policy to deposit with such holder an approved renewal policy
17 of like amount; or at the option of the Mortgagee, to deposit with
18 the Mortgagee on each monthly payment day of the note herein
19 referred to a sum equal to one-twelfth ($^1/_{12}$th) of the amount of
20 annual premiums on said insurance required by the Mortgagee, plus
21 one-twelfth ($^1/_{12}$th) of the amount of the annual taxes and assess-
22 ments levied, or to be levied on the premises herein conveyed as
23 estimated by the Mortgagee, which payments shall be held by the
24 Mortgagee in trust, without interest, and used by it to pay such
25 insurance premiums, taxes and assessments before the same become
26 delinquent.

Provision 8   (Section from Condominium By–Laws)

1   Except for the construction of the condominium by the Declar-
2 ant or its agents and any improvement to any condominium unit or
3 to the common elements accomplished concurrently with said origi-
4 nal construction, and except for purposes of proper maintenance
5 and repair or as otherwise provided in the Condominium Act or in
6 these By–Laws, it shall be prohibited for any unit owner to install,
7 erect, attach, apply, paste, hinge, screw, nail, build, alter, remove or
8 construct any lighting, shades, screens, awnings, patio covers, deco-
9 rations, fences, walls, aerials, antennas, radio or television broad-
10 casting or receiving devices, slabs, sidewalks, curbs, gutters, patios,
11 balconies, porches, driveways, walls or to make any change to or
12 otherwise alter (including any alteration in color) in any manner
13 whatsoever the exterior of any condominium unit or upon any of the
14 common elements within the project or to combine or otherwise join
15 two or more condominium units, or to partition the same after
16 combination, or to remove or alter any window or exterior doors of
17 any condominium unit, or to make any change or alteration within
18 any condominium unit which will alter the structural integrity of
19 any building or otherwise affect the property interest or welfare of
20 any other unit owner, materially increase the cost of operating or
21 insuring the condominium or impair any easement, until the com-
22 plete plans and specifications, showing the location, nature, shape,
23 change (including, without limitation, any other information speci-
24 fied by the Board of Directors or its designated committee) shall
25 have been submitted to and approved in writing as to safety, the
26 effect of any such alterations on the costs of maintaining and
27 insuring the condominium and harmony of design, color, and loca-
28 tion in relation to surrounding structures and topography, by the
29 Board of Directors of the Council of Unit Owners, or by an Architec-

30 tural and Environmental Control Committee designated by the
31 Board of Directors.

————

VII. CONTINUING EXPLICATION IN LATER STAGES OF DRAFTING

The process of explication continues throughout the redrafting stages. After discovering what an initial explication yields, you can decide how to organize a redraft to meet the client's needs. Deciding about organization leads to deciding about related conceptual problems in the original document. Issues about structure lead to issues about substance. Structure and substance are inextricably related; explication refines that relationship.

Professor David Mellinkoff's central approach to improving bad legal writing is explication.

* * * Whether it's your legal writing or someone else's, THE QUESTION is always in order: *"Does it have to be like this?"*

If you are writing, The Question will keep you from becoming another piece of office equipment, unconcerned with consequences or the possibilities of improvement.

If you are reading, vary the emphasis. First, softly: "Does it *have* to be like this?" Then louder: "Does it have to be like *this* ?" Annoy the writer into explaining. Occasionally, the explanation will be convincing. More often, it won't satisfy you—or the writer. And you may end up with something closer to human understanding.[9]

9. Legal Writing: Sense and Nonsense xiii (West Publishing Co., 1982). By Permission.

Chapter 8

CHOOSING FLEXIBLE LANGUAGE: VAGUENESS AND GENERALITY VS. PRECISION AND PARTICULARITY

Table of Sections

I. FLEXIBILITY THROUGH VAGUENESS AND GENERALITY

A. PRECISION AS AN UNDESIRABLE GOAL

It is a widely held but mistaken notion that the goal of legal writing, particularly legal drafting, is absolute precision. Not only is such a goal impossible to reach; in legal drafting, it is undesirable. Instead the goal is, or should be, "a precisely appropriate degree of imprecision." [1]

This is not double-talk. This goal recognizes that legal documents are plans for a future full of circumstances that neither the drafter nor the client can presently know about. Thus documents need to be flexible. The most useful language to accomplish flexibility is often vague rather than precise, general rather than particular.[2] When the drafter uses language to make a document flexible, the user receives the delegated authority to interpret later when the circumstantial context can be brought to bear on the interpretation.[3]

---

1. C. Curtis, It's Your Law 76 (1954).

2. See Kirk, Legal Drafting: Some Elements of Technique, 4 Tex.Tech L.Rev. 297, 300 (1973).

3. Curtis, A Better Theory of Legal Interpretation, 3 Vand.L.Rev. 407, 419–25 (1950).

B. VAGUENESS DISTINGUISHED FROM AMBIGUITY

Professor Dickerson has defined vagueness as "the degree to which, independent of equivocation, language is uncertain in its respective application to a number of particulars." [4] This definition's reference to equivocation distinguishes between vagueness and ambiguity. It is a useful distinction because vagueness is often both purposeful and valuable while ambiguity is usually inadvertent and dangerous.[5]

Some commentators use the terms "ambiguity" and "vagueness" as though they were synonymous. However, when they treat "purposive" ambiguity as a deliberate device to delegate the authority to interpret, the commentators appear to be talking about vagueness but calling it ambiguity.[6] For example, here is historian Henry Steele Commager writing about the framers of the United States Constitution:

> * * * Quite deliberately, they fell back on ambiguous words and phrases: "Republican form of government," "unreasonable searches and seizures," "cruel and unusual punishment," "provide for the general welfare" and many others, confident that future generations would have the good sense to define this language in terms "adequate to the exigencies" of politics and government.[7]

The distinction between ambiguity and vagueness is worth preserving. Ambiguity equivocates; if a word is ambiguous, there are usually only two or three possibilities as to what it means. If a word is vague, there are many more possibilities. Vagueness is a matter of degree.

The only words that are totally precise (the opposite of vague) are words that refer to only one thing or one person such as "the Mona Lisa," "William Shakespeare," or "the current Queen of England." Note that the reference to the current Queen is more precise than a reference to Queen Elizabeth would be. "England's Queen Elizabeth" could refer to Elizabeth I as well as Elizabeth II. That term is ambiguous. A reference to "Queen Elizabeth" is also vague. There may be unknown numbers of local festival queens and the like named Elizabeth as well as somebody's dog or cat. But there is only one "current Queen of England."

It is true, however, that context can eliminate vagueness just as it can ambiguity. A reference to Queen Elizabeth's meeting on a particular date with England's Prime Minister John Major would be neither vague nor ambiguous.

4. R. Dickerson, The Fundamentals of Legal Drafting 39 (2d ed. 1986); see Farnsworth, Some Considerations in the Drafting of Agreements: Problems in Interpretation and Gap Filling, 23 Record of N.Y. C.B.A. 105, 106 (1968) (vagueness as result of words that do not refer to "a neatly bounded class but a distribution about a central norm").

5. But see for discussion of purposeful ambiguity, Triggs, The Antarctic Treaty Regime: A Workable Compromise or a "Purgatory of Ambiguity"? 17 Case W.Res.J.Int'l L. 195 (1985).

6. See Dickerson, above note 4, at 35, note 5; see, for example, Miller, Statutory Language and the Purposive Use of Ambiguity, 42 Va.L.Rev. 23, 23–24, notes 29, 30 and accompanying text (1956).

7. Meese Ignores History in Debate with Court, N.Y. Times, Nov. 20, 1985, at A31, col. 3.

As this example illustrates, nearly all terms are vague to some degree. Even though precise reference is the exception rather than the rule, some words are more vague than others. Perhaps the most vague are references to colors, smells, sounds, and other things that we know by the senses. What does "red" mean? Or "loud" or "bitter" or "cold"? What does "high" mean? Or "near"? Even though we might have a difficult time explaining such concepts to make sure someone else perceives them in exactly the same way we do, we do not avoid using the terms at all. We largely rely on context to make meaning precise. For example, people do not have difficulty distinguishing between a "bitter divorce" and a "bitter lemon pie."

C. VAGUENESS ASSOCIATED WITH GENERALITY

Just as the distinction between vagueness and ambiguity is worth preserving, the association between vagueness and generality is worth acknowledging. "Vagueness is normally used in the philosophy of language in connection with general terms * * *."[8]

Strictly speaking, vagueness and generality are distinguishable. General terms refer to several, perhaps many, particulars, but the exact particulars referred to are capable of being identified. In other words, the intended scope of general terms is clear, while the intended scope of vague terms is not. A reference to "this state's statutes" is general but not vague, assuming the context provides the name of the state. A reference to "my heirs at law" is general but not vague, assuming the context indicates whose heirs, when they are to be determined, and according to what state's law.

Although it is possible to distinguish between vague and general terms, it is of dubious value to devote very much time and energy to doing so. It is not the label that matters. What matters is that the drafter be alert to the need for flexibility, or elasticity, in documents that describe future events and prescribe or proscribe future behavior. Here is Henry Steele Commager again on the delegates to the 1787 Constitutional Convention:

> * * * Because the delegates were free from the arrogance of supposing they could anticipate the future, that is just what they did. They laid down broad general principles for grants of power, and restraints on power, assigning to the national Government powers of a general nature and leaving to the states those of a local nature—and this in language flexible enough to anticipate an ever-changing society, economy and political crises. That is how Abraham Lincoln interpreted the Constitution during the greatest crisis of our history: The Constitution was flexible enough to enable him to do whatever was necessary to save the union.[9]

If the distinction between vagueness and generality is to be preserved at all, it may help to remember the difference between type facts

---

8. Christie, Vagueness and Legal Language, 48 Minn.L.Rev. 885, 886 (1964).

9. Above note 7, at A31, col. 2–3.

and unique facts. Unique facts get expressed in more particular terms. They report the past and are the language of pleadings and other litigation documents. Thus a complaint alleges that "the landlord failed to repair the front steps." In contrast, a lease, looking to the future, expresses type facts in general terms. It refers to "the landlord's duty to maintain the common areas." It may move still farther from precision and refer to "remedies for breach of duty."

It often does not matter at what point the language is no longer merely general but becomes vague as well.[10] "Language, at any rate in legal documents, does not fix meaning. It circumscribes meaning."[11]

D. TIGHTENING AND LOOSENING LANGUAGE

What matters is whether the term you choose will stretch to cover the particular circumstance to which somebody later wants to apply it—or the circumstance somebody wants it not to reach. For example, Charles C. Curtis describes the process of drafting an agreement for an unsecured loan. The vice-president of a bank, the client, wants a provision about the borrower's duty to keep a certain amount of "working capital." But "working capital" might be too vague. The drafter chooses to say, "the excess of the total current assets over current liabilities, determined in strict accordance with sound accounting practice by * * * independent certified accountants * * *." The drafter chooses the modifiers with special care. "Independent certified" keeps "accountants" from stretching far enough to cover the borrower's own accountants or uncertified accountants. On the other hand, "sound" allows "accounting practice" to stretch far enough to cover current practices that are subject to customary discretion within the profession of accountancy.[12] This kind of elasticity should not be denigrated as an abdication of the power to legislate precisely. Instead the elasticity acknowledges that the fabric of business dealings and the fabric of the social structure require individuals to be able to decide what is reasonable under the current circumstances.

This same recognition of the value of imprecision is reflected in the concepts that serve as constitutional principles.

> The constitution unavoidably deals in general language. It did not suit the purposes of the people, in framing this great charter of our liberties, to provide for minute specifications of its powers, or to declare the means by which those powers should be carried into execution. It was foreseen that this would be a perilous and difficult, if not an impracticable, task.[13]

Thus our legal literature is full of references to "due process," "equal protection," and a wealth of other such imprecise terms. They were intended to be so. Now and then someone urges something like the

---

10. For discussion of the theory that lawyers deal in the general and the particular rather than the abstract and the concrete, see Curtis, above note 1, at 59–60.

11. Id. at 67.

12. Id. at 67–68.

13. Martin v. Hunter's Lessee, 14 U.S. (1 Wheat.) 304, 326 (1816).

argument that "interstate commerce" does not include interstate telegraph companies because telegraph did not exist when the framers chose that term, but such an argument does not usually get very far.[14] One of the clearest instances of choosing vague terms on purpose to allow for future variations in circumstance was in the U.S. Supreme Court's direction to integrate the schools "with all deliberate speed." [15] Legislators assume the same kind of general control over the future without committing anyone to specifics when they direct:

> The tenant shall not unreasonably withhold consent to the landlord to enter the dwelling unit from time to time.

Likewise, contracting parties engage in the same sort of flexible social control when they agree in a lease:

> In case the premises should be damaged by fire, wind, rain, or other cause beyond the control of both landlord and tenant, then the premises will be repaired within a reasonable time at the expense of landlord.

II. THE DANGERS OF VAGUENESS AND GENERALITY

Vagueness and generality do sometimes cause trouble. Occasionally a statute is held void for vagueness. In the realm of both public and private documents, there is always the possibility of the reader in bad faith who insists that now means next year or here means three states to the west.

For instance, the story is told of the man who posted a sign on his barn saying, "Please do not ask permission to hunt." When he found hunters in his woods and asked them whether they had read his sign, they told him they had and assumed from it that he meant he wanted hunters to go ahead without bothering him. What this amounts to, of course, is "purposely pretending not to hear." [16]

But the danger of someone's saying "this" means "that" exists with respect to almost any term. For example, parties to a contract have argued about the word "chicken." Did it mean only a young chicken suitable for broiling or frying or any chicken meeting the contract's specification on weight and quality? [17] In another sales contract, one party argued that "minimum 50% protein" in horsemeat scraps could stretch to mean 49.5%.[18] An insured once argued that a fire insurance policy covering lumber stored in "sheds" covered lumber in the basement of a two-story warehouse.[19]

14. For example, see Pensacola Tel. Co. v. Western Union Tel. Co., 96 U.S. (96 Otto) 1 (1877).

15. Brown v. Board of Educ. of Topeka, Kansas, 349 U.S. 294, 301, 75 S.Ct. 753, 757 (1955).

16. AP dispatch, reported in Christie, above note 8, at 887, note 3.

17. Frigaliment Importing Co. v. B.N.S. Intern. Sales Corp., 190 F.Supp. 116, 117 (S.D.N.Y.1960).

18. Hurst v. W.J. Lake & Co., 141 Or. 306, 309, 16 P.2d 627, 628 (1932).

19. Easton v. Washington County Ins. Co., 391 Pa. 28, 32–33, 137 A.2d 332, 335 (1957).

It probably would be impossible to anticipate and thus prevent such interpretations. Even if it were possible, it would require such wordy detailing of particulars that documents would become nearly impossible to wade through.

      * * * [T]he generality, the vagueness, the flexibility, of the "language of the law" puts the lawyer on the horns of a dilemma. By assumption, the parties to the document are agreeing to specific solutions to specific problems that may possibly arise in the course of their transaction; but the "language of the law" that the lawyer has available inevitably depends upon the circumstances. Charles P. Curtis once suggested that drafting be done in these general, vague, flexible terms.[15] The parties could wait until the difficulty had arisen—and the facts were known—and could then, in a retrospective decision true to common law method, determine what the term meant under the circumstances. But this means that the parties to the document have abandoned, to the generality of the language of the law, and to the retrospective method of the common law, the opportunity to agree in advance upon the rules that are to be used to settle the difficulties that arise in their transaction.

      The maxims or principles of legal interpretation—for wills, for statutes, for contracts, and the like—are the means by which courts retrospectively give particular substance to the general, vague, flexible "language of the law." [16] These maxims and principles will always be necessary because it is impossible to predict all of the difficulties that can arise in a transaction or all of the circumstances under which these difficulties can occur. Nevertheless, in the transaction that is based on the consent of two parties, the assumption is that the parties have the opportunity to fix the rules that will be used to solve difficulties that occur during their transaction and that they have in fact done so.[17] * * *[20]

---

15. Curtis says the author of a word or phrase delegates to the user of the document the power to interpret it when necessary—and when the circumstances surrounding the need for interpretation are known. The most important criterion for interpretation is consistency with the rest of the law. Curtis, A Better Theory of Legal Interpretation, 3 Vand.L.Rev. 407, 419–25 (1950).

16. This is the basis for the concept that language that is clear on its face not only need not be interpreted but cannot be interpreted by a court. As to statutes, see 2 J.G. Sutherland, Statutes and Statutory Construction § 4502 (3d ed. F. Horack

1943). As to contracts, see 3 A. Corbin, Contracts § 542 (1960); 4 S. Williston, Contracts § 609 (3d ed. W.H.E. Jaeger 1961).

17. The parol evidence rule is a codification of these assumptions; and the broadened recognition of "partial" integration extends the concept to all contractual transactions. Restatement (Second) of Contracts §§ 235(3), 236(2), 237(1) (Tent. Draft No. 5, 1970).

20. Kirk, Legal Drafting: Some Elements of Technique, 4 Tex.Tech L.Rev. 297, 300 (1973). Copyright © 1973 by Texas Tech University Law Review. Reprinted by permission of the publisher.

III. THE DANGERS OF PRECISION AND PARTICULARITY

A. LISTING PARTICULARS

Listing particulars or even several fairly general terms is a common device to try to give a clear idea of the meaning of vague terms. This has been likened to drawing several overlapping circles to bring attention to the overlapping area. It is a way of using vagueness to aid precise understanding.[21]

Thus the lease provision about damage to the premises does not refer merely to "cause beyond the control of both landlord and tenant" but also mentions "fire, wind, and rain" to give more of an idea of the kind of damage contemplated. Snow damage would probably be included. A baseball through a window thrown by the tenant's visiting grandchild might not be.

B. *EXPRESSIO UNIUS EST EXCLUSIO ALTERIUS*

However, this device for clarifying vague terms can produce a great deal of trouble through the operation of the canon *expressio unius est exclusio alterius,* which means that to express one thing is to exclude similar alternatives not mentioned. The lesson the canon teaches is to avoid lists of particulars because they usually cannot be exhaustive. The danger is that some particular that is left out will be regarded as purposefully omitted.[22]

Omitting a particular can cause trouble; so can applying the canon to determine it a purposeful omission. Consider the case of the physician who withdrew from his partnership in a clinic. The partnership agreement limited his right to practice for two years within a given area, and the remaining partners in the clinic sued to enforce the agreement. The trial court found for the clinic. The appellate court reversed the judgment, holding that the partnership agreement was void under a statute respecting contracts in restraint of trade. Here is the pertinent part of the statute.

> (1) Every contract by which anyone is restrained from exercising a lawful profession, trade or business of any kind, otherwise than is provided by subsections (2) and (3) hereof, is to that extent void.
>
> (2) One who sells the good will of a business, or any shareholder of a corporation selling or otherwise disposing of all of his shares in said corporation, may agree with the buyer, and one who is employed as an agent or employee may agree with his employer, to refrain from carrying on or engaging in a similar business and from soliciting old

---

21. Christie, above note 8, at 895–96.

22. For analysis of how this canon has been called into service to help reverse a well established interpretation of federal immigration law, see INS v. Phinpathya, 464 U.S. 183, 104 S.Ct. 584 (1984); Pelta, INS v. Phinpathya: Literalist Statutory Interpretation in the Supreme Court, 23 San Diego L.Rev. 401 (1986).

customers of such employer within a reasonably limited time and area, so long as the buyer or any person deriving title to the good will from him, and so long as such employer continues to carry on a like business therein. Said agreements may, in the discretion of a court of competent jurisdiction be enforced by injunction.

(3) Partners may, upon or in anticipation of a dissolution of the partnership, agree that all or some of them will not carry on a similar business within a reasonably limited time and area.

The court figured out that since subsection (1) refers to "profession, trade or business," and subsection (2) refers only to "business," then subsection (2) must omit professions and trades on purpose. Accordingly, the court decided that the exception described in subsection (2) did not apply to the professional partnership. The applicable provision of the clinic's agreement was unacceptably in restraint of trade.[23]

The state supreme court quashed the decision, taking the position that the statute had been adopted from another state and thus should be construed as it had been in the courts of the other state, where the exception applied to professions and trades as well as businesses.[24] The supreme court relied heavily on the dissent to the appellate opinion, which has no kind words for the majority's use of the canon.

In the search for meaning there are no shortcuts, and Latin is no substitute for thought. Of course expressio unius est exclusio alterius if the alterius is excluded from the unius by context or common sense. But in the statute we here interpret, "business " is first used following the words "profession, trade or " and followed by "of any kind." Thus where "business" recurs in subsections (2) and (3) it is used in its generic sense which includes within ejusdem generis "profession" and "trade." At least the Attorney General, mirabile dictu, so thought in 1964 when he opined that physicians could indeed enter into such an agreement as is here involved. Op.Atty.Gen. 064–121. But neither expressio nor ejusdem determines the correct interpretation of a statute. These Latin labels are affixed after interpretation by us judges. When they are taken seriously, as expressio unius is here, as factors in the process of decision, the result often distorts legislative intent.

The first step in statutory construction is a reading of the entire statute:

* * *

I cannot read into that statute any intention on the part of our Legislature to enact a blanket prohibition against contracts not to compete and then to permit them between those engaged in business but not between those engaged in professions or trades.

* * *

In truth the time is overdue to rescue the law of statutory interpretation from Latin as the Second Vatican Council rescued the Mass. Max Radin wrote: "In all this what room is there for the standard 'canons of interpretations,' for ejusdem generis, expressio

23. Akey v. Murphy, 229 So.2d 276, 279 (Fla.App.1969).

24. Akey v. Murphy, 238 So.2d 94, 95–96 (Fla.1970).

unius, and the entire coterie or band of phrases and tags and shibboleths which are so wearisomely familiar? I should be tempted to deny that they have ever resolved an honest doubt, if a general negative were provable. Certainly it is hard to find an instance in which they did more than invest with the appropriate symbolic uniform a conclusion that should have been quite as respectable in the ordinary civilian clothes of sober common sense." A Short Way With Statutes, 56 Harv. L.Rev. 388 (1942).[25]

Even though the canons do not fare well in this dissent, it is also true that adopting another state's construction of an adopted statute is itself only another construction device, not inherently more, or less, sensible for its lack of a Latin name.

C. *EJUSDEM GENERIS*

Ejusdem generis is another Latin-named canon that poses a threat to the drafter of lists. *Ejusdem generis* means "of the same kind." The canon provides a method for limiting the meaning of a general term at the end of a list of more particular ones. For example, if a statute allows a tax deduction for losses from "fire, storm, shipwreck, or other casualty," a deduction is probably not allowed for loss of a diamond ring by negligently dropping it into a lake. When figuring out how restrictive the general term is, the interpreter should keep in mind that the purpose of adding the general term was presumably to account for reasonable possibilities left out of the list of particulars because the drafter did not think of them.[26]

The canon poses a threat to the drafter because an interpreter may excessively narrow the meaning of a term in light of the preceding terms associated with it. For instance, the Williams Act prohibits "any fraudulent, deceptive, or manipulative acts or practices, in connection with any tender offer." [27] In 1985, the U.S. Supreme Court held that a withdrawal of one tender offer and substitution of another was not manipulative because "manipulative" meant deceptive or fraudulent.[28]

The dangerous error of over-particularity is especially common in wills [29] and trusts.[30] Consider, for example, the following all too typical directions to an executor. The particularity works as a constant invitation to think about what other particulars are not mentioned and why not.

25. Akey v. Murphy, 229 So.2d at 279–80 (Mann, J., dissenting).

26. See W. Statsky, Legislative Analysis and Drafting 90–91 (2d ed. 1984).

27. 15 U.S.C. § 78n(e) (1982).

28. Schreiber v. Burlington Northern, Inc., 472 U.S. 1, 8, 105 S.Ct. 2458, 2462 (1985).

29. See E. Schlesinger, English as a Second Language for Lawyers, 12 Inst. on Est. Plan. para. 708 (1978).

30. See J. Johnson, A Draftsman's Handbook for Wills and Trust Agreements 10–13 (1961).

<u>Section 1.</u> I direct my Executor, as promptly as practicable after my death, to pay from and out of my residuary estate all my just debts, if any there be, my burial expenses, including the cost of a marker and the engraving of the marker at my grave, all costs and expenses of administering and settling my estate and all lawful taxes assessed by reason of my death against my taxable estate or any part thereof, including estate, inheritance, succession, transfer and any other taxes, by whatever name called, whether levied by the Federal Government or by any State Government or political subdivision of any State, and such taxes shall not be charged against or collected from any legatee or devisee of any share or part of my estate, other than my residuary estate, or from the beneficiary or beneficiaries of any insurance policy or policies on my life and the proceeds of which are included as a part of my taxable estate, or from any person who receives or acquires at my death, in any manner whatsoever, any property or any interest in any property which is considered or treated as a part of my estate for the purpose of computing any one or more of the aforesaid taxes.[31]

For comparison, consider the following recitation of the powers of a personal representative. Without the redundancies of the above provision, it is easier to assess the value of the particulars included here.

I appoint my wife, _____, as PERSONAL REPRESENTATIVE of my estate and direct that she serve without bond. In addition to the powers conferred upon personal representatives by law, she shall have full power, in her discretion and without any court order or proceeding to lease, or to sell pursuant to option or otherwise at public or private sale and upon such terms as she shall deem best, any real or personal property belonging to my estate, without regard to the necessity of such sale for the purpose of paying debts, taxes or devises; or to retain any or all of such property not so required, without liability for any depreciation thereof; to make distribution in kind; to assign or transfer certificates of stock, bonds or other securities; to adjust, compromise and settle all matters of business and claims in favor of or against my estate; to continue any unincorporated business for the period of administration, or to incorporate any business in which I may be engaged at the time of my death and to continue that incorporated business throughout the period of administration; and to do any and all things necessary or proper to complete the administration of my estate, all as fully as I could do myself.

Instead of trying to predict every possible particular, the drafter should reduce general terms to the lowest common denominator. The drafter walks a tightrope between language so vague that it invites misunderstanding and language so particular that an interpreter in bad faith is able to slip out from under some provision by claiming not to be covered by its exact terms. Learning to be sure-footed on the tightrope between precision and imprecision becomes increasingly important as the scope of malpractice continues to widen. Lawyers who draft wills

---

31. Quoted in Word, A Brief for Plain English Wills and Trusts, 14 U.Rich.L.Rev. 471, 473 (1980).

and contracts must be especially on guard against being found negligent for drafting errors,[32] especially errors arising out of some form of ambiguity.

Exercise 8.1

You are legal advisor to your county commissioners. One of them has brought you the text of a proposed ordinance and asked you to evaluate its choice of language. Section 1 of the ordinance is below. Evaluate it, especially with respect to degree of generality and particularity and of vagueness and precision.

```
 1    SECTION 1.  It shall be unlawful for any person, firm or
 2  corporation to convey or transport garbage, offal or other rubbish
 3  upon any public highway, road or street in that part of _____
 4  County outside the incorporated cities located therein, unless such
 5  garbage, offal or other rubbish is conveyed or transported in a
 6  vehicle with a water-tight metal body provided with a tight metal
 7  cover or covers and so constructed as to prevent any of the contents
 8  from leaking, spilling, falling or blowing out of such vehicle, and
 9  such vehicle shall at all times, except when being loaded or unload-
10  ed, be completely and securely covered so as to prevent offensive
11  odors escaping therefrom and so that no part of the contents thereof
12  shall be at any time exposed.
```

Exercise 8.2

You represent a local moving company engaged exclusively in local moves of household goods. Your client has been using a bill of lading form that is common, with minor variations, among national moving companies. Your client operates in a heavily competitive market and does not want unnecessarily to scare off business. You have been asked to evaluate the form.

Below are the first three paragraphs, which recite the terms of the carrier's liability. Evaluate their choice of language, and also evaluate conceptualization and organization.

TERMS AND CONDITIONS

```
1    1.  PERILS ASSUMED—The carrier assumes obligation against all
2  risks of direct physical damage or loss to the property to be moved,
3  packed, stored, shipped, forwarded, or otherwise handled from any
4  external cause except as hereinafter excluded.
```

32. For discussion of cases in which vagueness or ambiguity has led to liability to clients and sometimes to third parties, see Comment, Attorney Malpractice in California: The Liability of a Lawyer Who Drafts an Imprecise Contract or Will, 24 U.C.L.A.L.Rev. 422 (1976). See also Note, Lawyer Liability to Intended Beneficiaries of Negligently Drafted Wills—Last Stand of the Immutable Privity Doctrine, 24 Willamette L.Rev. 843 (1988).

2. The carrier shall be liable only for its failure to use ordinary care and then only on the basis of customer's declared valuation of the goods. The burden of proving negligence or failure to use the care required by law shall be upon the customer.

3. No liability shall be provided for loss or damage caused by or resulting from: An act, omission, or order of shipper, including damage or breakage resulting from improper packing by shipper; insects, moths, vermin, ordinary wear and tear, or gradual deterioration; defect or inherent vice of the article, including susceptibility to damage because of atmospheric conditions such as temperature and humidity or change therein; hostile or war-like action in time of peace or war including action in hindering, combating, or defending against an actual, impending or expected attack; any weapon of war employing atomic fission or radioactive force whether in time of peace or war; or insurrection, rebellion, revolution, civil war, usurped power, or action taken by governmental authority in hindering, combating, or defending against such occurrence, seizure, or destruction under quarantine or customs regulations, confiscation by order of any government or public authority, or risks of contraband, or illegal transportation or trade; any strike, lockout, labor disturbance, riot, civil commotion, or any act of any person or persons taking part in any such occurrence or disturbance; and acts of God.

Chapter 9

ACHIEVING CLARITY AND AVOIDING AMBIGUITY

Table of Sections

I. THE NATURE OF AMBIGUITY

Written material is ambiguous if on its face it has two or more distinct and mutually exclusive meanings. Usually an ambiguity is an equivocation, that is, an uncertainty between two meanings. The writing literally says two things equally.

Example A

Only persons who are doctors and lawyers qualify.

Must one be both a doctor and a lawyer to qualify, or is it enough to be one or the other? Also, what about a Ph.D.? Does one with a doctorate in literature qualify?

Example B

Persons who reside in New York and New Jersey have 90 days in which to file claims.

Does the 90–day rule apply to everyone who resides in New York and also to everyone who resides in New Jersey? Probably. Possibly, however, the rule applies only to a much smaller group—those who have at least two residences, one in New York and one in New Jersey. Thus the statement of the rule is equivocal.

Usually the word "equivocate" has derogatory connotations. A person who equivocates is thought to be evasive, Janus-faced or "two-faced," one who "speaks out of both sides of the mouth." On the other hand, in some contexts—poetry, in particular—ambiguity deserves praise. The language of metaphor is the language of ambiguity. Likewise in some legal writing, ambiguity is a valuable tool. The defense counsel, composing answers to interrogatories or a letter to plaintiff's counsel, may benefit from ambiguity as a means of keeping from making dangerous admissions while still being technically responsive to questions asked.

Professor Arthur Leff's definition of "ambiguity" in his unfinished law dictionary discusses both its virtues and vices.

> **ambiguity.** A state of language in which the meaning to be conveyed is subject to uncertainty, in which the writing can plausibly mean one thing, or another, or still another or more. In legal writing, of course, it is always said that ambiguity is to be avoided, since people's rights and duties so often arise out of language and depend upon its meanings. But every natural language is to some extent ambiguous. Unlike languages of mathematical logic, which are designed for almost no purpose but to avoid ambiguity, ordinary languages have other jobs to do—to express nuance, to be pleasant to the mind and ear, subtly to reverberate word to word and context to context so as to express things not just accurately, but richly and fully. Thus, almost anything written in a real language *can* be seen to convey more than one precise meaning, and indeed the creation and use of ambiguity is one of the prime techniques of literature. In fact, intentional ambiguity is sometimes desired in law too, as when parties to a contract would rather not face a potential issue, preferring instead to deal with the issue ambiguously and leave the solution of the problem, should it arise, to determination by subsequent litigation.

> Hence, while unambiguous writing is important to law, even when desired it is an aim never fully realizable. One does the best one can. While there are famous instances of apparently perfect clarity being insufficient (as when "one thousand" turned out to mean "1200" in the rabbit trade, and "white selvage" was shown to refer to "dark selvage"), it is usually possible to write most things with enough exactness to serve the legal purpose at hand, *i.e.,* to express only one plausible meaning in the particular context. Legal problems do arise, however, because one wants neither to bind people to things they did not mean, nor to allow every previous agreement and meaning to be opened up to the uncertainty of subsequent litigation. A contract should not *ordinarily* be at risk of a subsequent claim by a party that by "black" he meant "white." But what if he did—and the other party knew it?

> The central problem is this: Once something is found "ambiguous" *at law,* it is up for grabs. There is, for instance, an "ambiguity

exception" to the **parol evidence rule.** Testimony about unwritten understandings is allowed to clarify "ambiguities" in contract interpretation. There are even rules of thumb, *e.g.,* that ambiguous language should be interpreted "*contra proferentem,*" or "*contra stipulatorem,*" *i.e.,* against the profferer or writer thereof, or even "*contra venditorem,*" *i.e.,* against the seller in an ambiguous sales contract. And there is the practically important rule that all ambiguities in any insurance contract will be interpreted against the insurance company. The difficulty, then, is to take a language necessarily always somewhat ambiguous, and decide when it is ambiguous enough that one should allow subsequent argument about what it really was meant to mean in the face of a pretty clear "objective" meaning.[1]

Ambiguity in legal drafting is almost never appropriate. When it happens, it is usually inadvertent, not purposeful. The owner and contractor who sign the building contract do not want to go to court after the house is built to have a judge or jury determine the price. When the contract is discovered to be ambiguous, it is so in spite of the intentions of the parties. Each of them knows precisely what the contract says. It is not at all vague. The trouble is that it says one definite thing to one person and another definite thing to the other.

Figure 1[2] is a classic demonstration of the way ambiguity works. If you show this picture to a group of people, you can count on some of them to see an old woman and some to see a young one. Some people do readily see both. But for those who do not, it can take a long time and a great deal of pointing to noses and mouths and hair before both faces appear. The problem is that once one image is set in the mind's eye, it is difficult to see a contrary one.

Thus it is not surprising that when confronted with an ambiguous writing, readers often do not acknowledge the ambiguity and explain how they resolve it. Rather they insist the writing is not ambiguous and it says the one thing they read it to say. They may, of course, know perfectly well that it is ambiguous and simply not be willing to say so. But it is entirely possible that, like the person who only sees one woman in Figure 1, they honestly report seeing only one meaning in the ambiguous writing.

Therefore, an important task of the lawyer as drafter is to be aware of the potential for ambiguity in documents and to edit carefully to remove inadvertent ambiguity. If an ambiguity is patent, in other words, obvious on the face of the document, courts commonly construe it against the drafter. If the ambiguity is latent and not discovered until trouble develops, the drafter will still suffer the results of confusion where there might have been clarity. Occasionally a contract that

1. The Leff Dictionary of Law: A Fragment, 94 Yale L.J. 1855, 2007 (1985). Reprinted by permission of The Yale Law Journal Company and Fred B. Rothman & Company from The Yale Law Journal, Vol. 94, pp. 1855, 2007.

2. R. Dickerson, Teacher's Manual for Materials on Legal Drafting 54a (1981). Reprinted with permission from West Publishing Company.

contains neither patent nor latent ambiguity is treated as ambiguous if applying its terms literally would produce an absurd result.[3] Ambiguity comes in three forms: semantic, syntactic, and contextual.[4]

Figure 1

3. See, e.g., Tumlinson v. Norfolk & Western Railway Co., 775 S.W.2d 251 (Mo. Ct.App.1989); see also Note, Absurdity as an Indication of Ambiguity in Missouri Contract Law, 55 Mo.L.Rev. 617 (1990) (discussing Tumlinson and citing other cases in several states).

4. For detailed discussion of the forms of ambiguity, with examples of the many possibilities, see R. Dick, Legal Drafting 61–73 (2d ed. 1985).

II. THE FORMS OF AMBIGUITY

A. SEMANTIC AMBIGUITY

1. Double- and Multi-meaning Words

Semantic ambiguities occur because words often have more than one meaning. Most double-meaning words cause no confusion because the context of surrounding words clarifies the meaning. This is true of homonyms, which are words spelled and pronounced identically but different in meaning. For example: After a game of pool, they jumped in the pool. Another example: She serves on boards that are concerned about the price of shingles and boards. Notice that there are no homonyms in this sentence: He is bored with serving on the board. Here the difference in spelling clarifies meaning without any need to look to context.

In the sentence above about doctors and lawyers, the uncertainty whether "doctor" includes Ph.D. is a problem of semantic ambiguity. In fact, in that sentence, "doctor" has more than two possible meanings. What about veterinarians, dentists, osteopaths, and chiropractors? Do they qualify? Here the context is no help.

When one discovers potential semantic ambiguity in one's own drafting, it is wise to look first to the context. Can the ambiguity be prevented by choosing surrounding words carefully? If context is no help, then it is wise to add words, perhaps a synonym, to clarify which meaning is intended. For instance, "residence" may mean legal domicile; it may also mean usual place of abode. In a contest between economy and clarity, clarity should always win.

2. Saying the Same Thing the Same Way and Different Things Differently

Many people learn in English composition classes that repetition is a weakness and that variety in word choice is a strength. Certain misguided fiction writers take this advice to heart and try to tag every line of dialogue differently. The first speaker may be allowed merely to have "said" something, but the next one "replied," and then the first "answered," and after that somebody "whispered," "sighed," "breathed," or even "smiled" words in response. Sports reporters are particularly prone to this habit of using a different verb in every sentence. If one team "beat" another, the next team "defeated," "trounced," or "tromped" its opponent.

This constant variation, sometimes derogatorily called "elegant variation," can be irritating and distracting in any context. In legal drafting, it is totally unacceptable because the shifts make a reader wonder whether there is some hidden difference in meaning or reference. If you are writing about condominiums and at one point refer to "units," you dare not later refer to "dwellings" unless you intend a different referent. If you are writing about "rules," they should not later become "regulations."

Just as it is important to use the same term consistently to refer to the same thing, it is also important not to give the same term more than one meaning or referent in the same document. For example, in a provision about "the United States" as a country, or as a geographical place, it would be inappropriate to say something like this: "The United States grants its citizens specified immunities." Such a statement refers to the United States government, not to the country itself.

3. *Some Special Problems*

a. Dates [5]

Careless references to dates can produce inadvertent ambiguity.

"From _____ to _____"

The option extends *from* May 5 *to* May 8.

Is the option available on May 5? On May 8? As "from" and "to" are usually, but not always, construed, the option would not be available on May 5 but would be on May 8. In other words, usually the beginning date is excluded and the ending date included.

"Until _____"

The option extends *until* May 8.

Is it available on May 8? Probably. Again, the ending date is usually, but not always, included.

"Between _____ and _____"

The option is open *between* May 5 *and* May 8.

Is it open on May 5? On May 8? Probably not on either date.

"By _____"

The option must be exercised *by* May 8.

May it be exercised *on* May 8? Probably.

"Prior to _____"

The option must be exercised *prior to* May 8.

May it be exercised on May 8? Probably not. But a case went to the U.S. Supreme Court on the issue of whether claims to federal land could be filed on December 31, in accord with a statute that said "prior to December 31." The majority required filing on or before December 30, but a dissenting opinion would have allowed filing before the end of the year.[6]

---

5. For many examples of litigated ambiguous date and time references, see J. Aitken, ed. Expressions Relating to Time, ch. 11, Piesse's The Elements of Drafting 107 (7th ed. 1987) (citing Australian, Canadian, and English cases).

6. United States v. Locke, 471 U.S. 84, 105 S.Ct. 1785 (1985).

Clearer Substitutes

The option is available *after* May 4 and *before* May 8.

The option must be exercised *before* May 8.

b. *Other Periods of Time*

"Month"

Today is August 28. You have one *month* in which to exercise the option.

May you exercise it on September 30? It is almost impossible to say. If today were August 15, it might be easier to speculate that you could exercise the option on September 14 or 15, and that "month" means 28 (or 30?) days from today. But the nearer you get to the beginning or ending of a calendar month, the more "month" seems to mean calendar month.

"Week"

Today is Thursday. You have one *week* in which to exercise the option.

May you exercise it next Friday? It is almost impossible to say. Complicating the concept of "week" is the concept of the five-day business week.

"Midnight"

The option expires Thursday at *midnight.*

Is it open at 12:01 a.m. on Thursday? Probably. It probably will still be open at 11:59 p.m. on Thursday, but it may be open only through 11:59 p.m. on Wednesday.

Clearer Substitutes

You may exercise the option on or before September 29.

You may exercise the option on or before next Wednesday.

The option expires at 11:59 p.m. on Wednesday.

c. *Ages*

Careless phrasing of references to age can also produce inadvertent ambiguity.

Ambiguous

This option is open to anyone between the ages of 21 and 30.

Clearer Substitute

This option is open to anyone 21 years old or older and under 31.

Ambiguous

This option is open to anyone who is more than 21 years old.

Clearer Substitutes, Depending on Intended Meaning

This option is open to anyone who has passed his or her 21st birthday.

This option is open to anyone who is 22 years old or older.

d. Number

Using the singular rather than the plural often prevents ambiguity.

Ambiguous Plurals

Persons with hardships shall file affidavits in support of applications for exemption.

Must one person have more than one hardship to be entitled to exemption? How many affidavits per person? Per hardship? Using the singular makes the muddle disappear.

Clearer Substitute Using Singular

A person with a hardship shall support an application for exemption by affidavit.

Another solution is to take people out of the sentence altogether and make it generic.

Clearer Generic Substitute

The way to prove hardship is by affidavit.

e. Provisos

The phrase "provided that" produces so much ambiguity that it is wise to avoid it as much as possible. For example:

These by-laws may be amended at any regular meeting at which a quorum is present, by a majority vote of the members present, *provided* that notice of the vote was given as *provided* in the by-laws, and further *provided* that amendments that affect requirements of these by-laws for votes other than majority votes must pass with votes of not less than the amount called for in the requirements to be affected by the proposed amendment.

The proviso about notice is a condition precedent. The sentence should say: "*if* notice was given."

The phrase "notice of the vote was given as provided in the by-laws" produces no ambiguity. This sentence uses "provided" to refer to a provision in a document. It is not a proviso.

The final use of "provided that" does not set forth another condition precedent for conducting the vote. This proviso introduces a new rule altogether. It would better be stated in a separate sentence with a transitional signal such as "however."

B. SYNTACTIC AMBIGUITY

Syntactic ambiguity is uncertainty of meaning resulting from the arrangement of words in a sentence rather than from multiple meanings of an individual word. Context is often no help at all in clarifying the meaning. In fact, it is the arrangement of words together in the immediate context that produces the ambiguity. Professor Layman Allen argues that lawyers tend to be experts in their manipulation of semantic uncertainty; however, he offers no such compliments regarding lawyers' skills at manipulating syntax.

> The members of the legal profession, which holds itself out to the public as expert in the art of communicating, perform at about the level of rank amateurs in the expression of structure. We are innocently and inadvertently introducing structural uncertainties into our writings to a degree that is a professional disgrace—enough so, that it often ought to be sufficient grounds for a successful malpractice action.[7]

1. Conjunctions and Other Verbal Glue

In the sentence, "Only persons who are doctors and lawyers qualify," it is syntactic ambiguity that makes it impossible to know whether one person must have two professions to qualify. The troublesome word is "and," a coordinating conjunction. Conjunctions and prepositions are often responsible for syntactic ambiguity because they are the glue in a sentence, the words that signify how the content words—the nouns and verbs—relate to each other.

It is possible, of course, to say that common sense resolves the ambiguity if context does not. Relatively few people are both medical doctors and lawyers. The number practicing both professions simultaneously is minuscule. Thus common sense dictates that the sentence means that those who qualify are both doctors and other people who are lawyers. Besides, if the sentence appeared in the context of some paragraph, that wider context would probably resolve the ambiguity.

However, "common sense" does not always solve such problems. It is particularly dangerous to rely upon in a world of legal interests and potential readers in bad faith.

a. The Ambiguous "Or"

For instance, consider the effects of the emphasized "or" in this U.S. Department of State form.

> I certify that I have read the names of the above listed organizations, and that I am not now, nor have I ever been, a member of, in association with, or affiliated with, *or* that I have not contributed to any of such organizations, except as indicated and explained below [emphasis added].

---

7. Towards a Normalized Language to Clarify the Structure of Legal Discourse, Vol. II, Deontic Logic, Computational Linguistics and Legal Information Systems 349, 349 (1981).

Professor Allen has used this sentence to show the value of tabulated form as a tool for revealing syntactic ambiguities:

I certify

1. that I have read the names of the above listed organizations, and

2. A) that I am not now, nor have I ever been, a member of, in association with, or affiliated with, or

   B) that I have not contributed to any such organizations,

3. except as indicated and explained below.

Is it possible that the draftsman really meant "or" between 2A and 2B; so that merely having failed to contribute to any such organization allows one to sign the oath with impunity?

Now consider the emphasized "or" in this statute.

> Any male person who, knowing a female person is a prostitute, lives or derives support or maintenance in whole or in part from the earnings or proceeds of her prostitution, or from money loaned or advanced to or charged against her by any keeper or manager or inmate of a house or other place where prostitution is practiced or allowed, or who solicits *or* receives compensation for soliciting for her, is guilty of pimping, a felony * * * [emphasis added].[8]

A man charged under this statute argued that the final clause should be read to mean "who solicits compensation or receives compensation." Since there was no evidence that he either solicited compensation or received compensation, he argued he was innocent. The State of California, wanting to convict him for pimping, argued that the clause should be read to mean "who solicits for her or receives compensation for soliciting for her." In this case, the trial judge construed the ambiguous "or" in favor of the defendant.[9]

b. The Ambiguous "And"

Now consider the final "and" in this statute.

> No person shall engage in or institute a local telephone call, conversation or conference of an anonymous nature and therein use obscene, profane, vulgar, lewd, lascivious or indecent language, suggestions or proposals of an obscene nature *and* threats of any kind whatsoever [emphasis added].

A man charged under this statute argued that there was nothing in the State's bill of particulars to substantiate that he had made any threats. The statute, he argued, outlawed obscene language *and* threats in an anonymous phone call. One without the other was not enough to violate the statute. His position was not only arguable; he prevailed, that is, until the Louisiana Supreme Court deduced that

8. Logic and Law, Law and Electronics 203 (1962).

9. People v. Smith, 44 Cal.2d 77, 79–80, 279 P.2d 33, 34–35 (1955).

"and threats" was properly interpreted as "or threats." [10]   Here is an analysis of the statute.

ALLEN AND ENGHOLM, NORMALIZED LEGAL DRAFTING AND THE QUERY METHOD
29 J. Legal Educ. 380, 384–87, 399 (1978).*

Hill was charged with unlawfully making an anonymous telephone call to a woman during which he used obscene, profane, vulgar, lewd, lascivious and indecent language and threats. In response to a motion for a bill of particulars, the state conceded that Hill made no specific threats other than those inherent in words to the effect that he desired sexual intercourse with the woman he called. Subsequently, the district court dismissed the prosecution, basing the dismissal on an interpretation of the statute that required both obscene language and threats as distinct elements of the crime.

The state appealed to the Louisiana Supreme Court, contending that the district court's dismissal was based upon an erroneous interpretation of the statute. As originally enacted, the statute read:

> No person shall engage in or institute a local telephone call, conversation or conference of an anonymous nature and therein use obscene, profane, vulgar, lewd, lascivious or indecent language, suggestions or proposals.

and the phrase "of an obscene nature and threats of any kind whatsoever" was added later. The prosecution argued that the "and" in the added phrase should be read disjunctively in order to fulfill the intent of the legislature in enlarging the scope of the statute. The intended effect would have been achieved by drafting the statute to read "No person shall X or Y". Therefore, it argued, the court should construe the "and" as an "or".

This same position can be expressed differently—and more persuasively—to achieve the same result. Instead of the straining argument to interpret the "and" as "or" to achieve the legislative intent, the more persuasive argument is to merely interpret "and" as a full-sentence connecting "and" rather than a sentence-part connecting "and".

Thus, where the statute formerly said, "No person shall X", it was amended to say, "No person shall X and Y". The intent of this language, it could have been argued, was to provide that "No person shall X, *and* no person shall Y", rather than as "No person shall (X *and* Y)". Represented diagramatically (using the actual language of the statute), the state's position, in effect, was (and could have actually been so argued):

10. State v. Hill, 245 La. 119, 125–26, 157 So.2d 462, 464 (1963).

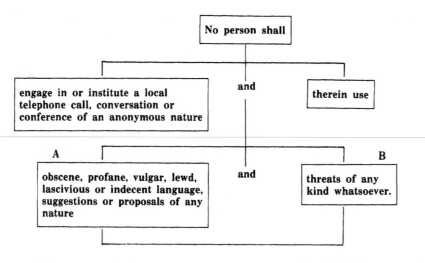

1. No person shall engage in or institute a local telephone call
    * * * and therein use **A,** and

2. No person shall engage in or institute a local telephone call
    * * * and therein use **B.**

Hill argued the opposite. He claimed that the legislature used the
word "and" in order to restrict the scope of the statute. Where there
was formerly a single element to the crime, now it was necessary to
show that the defendant made threats in a telephone call in addition to
using obscene, profane, etc., language. Since he had failed to make
threats in the telephone call upon which his prosecution was based, the
district court had properly dismissed the charge. Hill's position can
also be represented by a diagram:

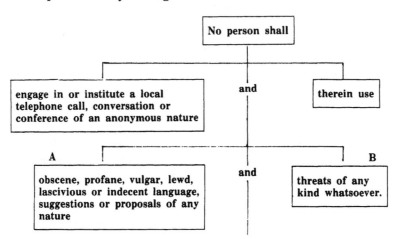

No person shall engage in or institute a local telephone call * * *
and therein use **A** and **B.**

Ultimately, the Louisiana Supreme Court resolved the case by
interpreting the disputed "and" as an "or".

* * *

It is notable that in reaching the conclusion it did, the court ignored the common law maxim that criminal statutes are to be construed strictly. It is fair to ask whether the ambiguity was deliberate. Does deliberately incorporating this syntactic ambiguity (if it was done deliberately) in this Louisiana criminal statute serve a useful policy goal? Or is it simply another example of inadvertent ambiguity that is easily overlooked when drafting statutory language?

* * *

The results of this normalizing process are two ways of normalizing the Louisiana statute that regulates anonymous telephone conversations (1) by converting its ambiguous within-sentence syntax into unambiguous between-sentence syntax, and (2) by merely disambiguating the relevant aspects of its within-sentence syntax. From the viewpoint of facilitating the more extensive use of computers in helping to process and analyze legal prose, the first alternative is preferable. It could be written as follows:

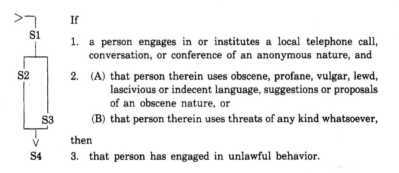

If

1. a person engages in or institutes a local telephone call, conversation, or conference of an anonymous nature, and

2. (A) that person therein uses obscene, profane, vulgar, lewd, lascivious or indecent language, suggestions or proposals of an obscene nature, or

   (B) that person therein uses threats of any kind whatsoever,

then

3. that person has engaged in unlawful behavior.

The second alternative could be written:

No person shall engage in or institute a local telephone call, conversation or conference of an anonymous nature and therein use any of the following:

1. obscene, profane, vulgar, lewd, lascivious or indecent language, suggestions or proposals of an obscene nature, or

2. threats of any kind whatsoever.

Neither of these alternatives deals with the other ambiguities (other than the one that arose in the Hill case) in this statute. They are probably inadvertent ones, also, that should be resolved.[11]

---

c. *The Ambiguous Hybrid, "And/Or"*

The hybrid conjunction and disjunction, "and/or" has caused legal trouble for years. Critics have railed against it, and judges have construed it against lawyers who were foolish enough to persist in using

---

11. See also Dickerson, Obscene Telephone Calls: An Introduction to the Reading of Statutes, 22 Harv.J. on Legis. 173 (1985).

it.[12] In case after case, the comments about "and/or" reflect an extraordinary degree of anger from the bench. Here is a typical condemnation.

> It is manifest that we are confronted with the task of first construing "and/or", that befuddling, nameless thing, that Janus-faced verbal monstrosity, neither word nor phrase, the child of a brain of someone too lazy or too dull to express his precise meaning, or too dull to know what he did mean, now commonly used by lawyers in drafting legal documents, through carelessness or ignorance or as a cunning device to conceal rather than express meaning with view to furthering the interests of their clients.[13]

Among contemporary scholars of legal drafting, Professor Mellinkoff is especially helpful in going beyond invective to show how "and/or" sometimes results in contradiction and other times in redundancy. He explains both what the trouble is and what to do about it.

> The high failure rate of legal papers that depend on *and/or* for anything of importance should have long since eliminated it from the legal vocabulary. Yet it persists, and is widely used in legal and ordinary writings. For the writer in a hurry, for the writer content to let others solve the problems created by the writer, *and/or* is such a short, quick, and easy way out. It has a special currency in academia, where the lure of the scientific (*interface, parameter*) gulls some into confusing the compact form of *and/or* with the precision of a lopsided fraction.

> One book on usage says its popularity even in "respectable places" means that it "is therefore acceptable current English." Most of the English usage people condemn it as ugly, unnecessary, and confusing. They usually end up blaming it on the law, saying (in charitable ignorance), "Maybe it's all right for them, but let them keep it."

> This reverse smugness should give lawyers pause. Instances of non-legal *and/or* do not encourage imitation. They demonstrate its mindlessness ("Rape: The Hidden Crime.' [sic] Also shown is how other women can prevent *and/or* survive rape."), and its complicated silliness. (We look forward to seeing *and/or* hearing from you.)

> Despite the relative simplicity of *A or B or both* (when such specification is necessary), legal writings continue to spew contradictions joined by an habitual *and/or*.

☐ For example:

  * * * the order was not made *and/or* was kept in abeyance.

  [Make it *or*.]

  * * * might be discharged *and/or* paroled at any time.

  [Make it *or*.]

---

12. See numerous citations in McCarty, That Hybrid "and/or," 39 Mich.St.B.J. 9 (No. 5, May 1960).

13. Employers' Mutual Liability Ins. Co. v. Tollefsen, 219 Wis. 434, 437, 263 N.W. 376, 377 (1935).

* * * it was uniformly specified *and/or* implied.

[Make it *or*.]

Like a tic, *and/or* intrudes without effort, even when the writer has already covered all the possibilities.

☐ For example:

* * * the application of one or more of doctrines of A, B, C, *and/or* D.

[Make it *and*.]

If the lawyers did invent *and/or*, they owe it to the common language to atone, by now eliminating *and/or* from the legal vocabulary, and hope that the common language will follow. It is still confusing readers and costing litigants money. Anything *and/or* can do, ordinary English can do better.[14]

2. *Modifiers*

a. *Squinting Modifiers*

The expression "squinting modifier" is a somewhat awkward but nonetheless standard metaphor used to refer to a modifier that may modify what precedes it or what follows it.

Example 1

One section needing revision surely is not to be quoted.

Does the section surely need revision, or is it surely not to be quoted?

Example 2

The client with the foot broken recently filed an action.

Was the foot broken recently, or did the client file recently?

b. *Modifiers Preceding or Following Compounds*

Modifiers preceding or following compounds may modify all compounded items or only the closest item.

Example

The report is required of educational institutions and corporations making charitable donations.

Is the report required of a corporation that is not educational?

Is it required of an educational institution that makes no charitable donations?

Example

The secretary of state may revoke a license issued under this act if the secretary determines that the licensee has been convicted of a felony or misdemeanor involving dishonesty or fraud.

14. David Mellinkoff, Legal Writing: Sense and Nonsense 55–56 (West Publishing Co., 1982). By permission.

May the secretary revoke a license if the licensee has been convicted of a felony not involving dishonesty or fraud?

Some grammarians insist that the doctrine of the "last antecedent" resolves these questions by dictating that the modifier modifies only the noun nearest to it. But many people do not understand the doctrine, and many who do understand it nonetheless do not uniformly apply it. Relying on it to resolve a doubtful construction would be foolish indeed.[15]

3. Pronoun Reference

The most common pronominal ambiguity occurs in a sentence with a plural pronoun and more than one plural noun as possible referent.

Example A

The parties have reviewed the contractual terms, brought in their witnesses, and have several disagreements about them.

Do the parties disagree about the witnesses, about both the witnesses and the terms, or possibly about only the terms?

Some ambiguous pronominal references have nothing to do with plurals, however.

Example B

The lawyer told her client that she was right.

Who was right? The lawyer? Or the client?

Example C

The accountant tried to keep the client from losing the tax advantages, which was not easy.

What was not easy? Losing the tax advantages? Or trying to keep the client from losing them?

4. Punctuation

a. Comma

Sometimes careless placement of a comma produces ambiguity.

Example

Have you used another name in employment, or in making applications within the last five years?

The comma suggests that if you used another name in employment ten years ago, you should answer the question yes. In other words, the five-year limitation seems to refer only to making applications even though the "common sense" analysis suggests that probably the questioner cares only about uses of another name in the past five years either in employment or in applications.

15. For more examples and suggestions about rephrasing to eliminate the ambiguities, see Aitken, above note 5, at 21–25.

Irregular punctuation in a provision of the Florida Constitution produced a syntactic ambiguity that sent a case to the Florida Supreme Court. Article V, Section 4(b)(1) reads:

> District courts of appeal shall have jurisdiction to hear appeals, *that may be taken as a matter of right*, from final judgments or orders of trial courts * * * not directly appealable to the supreme court or a circuit court * * * [emphasis added].

The State wanted to appeal an order granting a motion for judgment of acquittal in a criminal case; it relied on the commas setting off "that may be taken as a matter of right," arguing that the provision authorized appeal as a matter of right from every order. Here is the outcome of the State's argument.

STATE v. CREIGHTON

469 So.2d 735, 739 (Fla.1985) (footnotes omitted).

Principles of English usage indicate that the present language was not intended to provide that all final orders and judgments are appealable as a matter of constitutional right. The word "that" is the restrictive, or defining pronoun. It introduces matter that defines, restricts, modifies, or qualifies the matter to which it refers. On the other hand, the word "which" is the nonrestrictive or nondefining pronoun and is used to introduce a separate, independent, or additional fact about the matter referred to. W. Strunk and E.B. White, *The Elements of Style* 53 (1972). So, the clause, "that may be taken as a matter of right," restricts the term "appeals" so as to apply the grant of jurisdiction only with regard to appeals that may be taken as a matter of right. Nothing is said about the circumstances under which a litigant has the right to take an appeal. The reader is in effect told to look elsewhere to determine whether there is such a right. In order to plainly say that all final judgments may indeed be appealed as a matter of right, the constitution would have to use the clause "*which* may be taken as a matter of right." In such a context, "which" does not define or restrict such appeals but independently describes them, adding information in a way that would have independent substantive effect. *See* M. Kammer and C. Mulligan, *Writing Handbook* 117–18, 138, 151–52 (1953). If the word "which" had been used instead of "that," one could logically interpret the language to confer upon a litigant the right to appeal a final judgment or order. *See also* H.W. Fowler, *Modern English Usage* 713 (1937). But we must look at the language actually used, and that language indicates that the question of when an aggrieved litigant is entitled to an appeal is a matter to be determined by sources of authority other than the constitution.

————

The combination of questionable punctuation—or lack of it—and an ambiguously placed modifier can produce no end of trouble. Consider the case of the trucking company ordered by the Interstate Commerce Commission (ICC) to stop shipping in certain parts of Connecticut, Pennsylvania and New Jersey. The ICC Certificate of Public Convenience and Necessity that caused the trouble authorized the company to ship:

> Between points in Connecticut, Pennsylvania, New Jersey, and New York *within 100 miles of Columbus Circle, New York, N.Y.,* on the one hand, and, on the other, points and places in Connecticut, Delaware, Maryland, Massachusetts, Pennsylvania, New Jersey, New York, and Rhode Island [emphasis added].

The company argued that "within 100 miles of Columbus Circle, New York, N.Y." modified only "New York," leaving the company free to ship anywhere in Connecticut, Pennsylvania, and New Jersey. The ICC argued that the 100–mile limitation applied to all 4 states. Here is how the federal district court in New Jersey resolved the problem.

T.I. McCORMACK TRUCKING CO. v. UNITED STATES

298 F.Supp. 39, 41–42 (D.N.J.1969).

* * *

Initially, it must be noted that, as a matter of grammatical construction, there can be no question but that the 100–mile provision in the Sub 70 Certificate applies only to New York. Whether the grammatical rule be designated as the "Doctrine of the Last Antecedent," or as a matter of simple common sense, the absence of a comma after the Certificate's first reference to "New York" indicates most clearly that this is the case. As a result, all that remains for consideration is the Commission's contention that the effect to be given to its own special expertise in construction of technical terms of art compels that this court defer to it in a case of simple grammatical construction such as is presented here.[2]

That contention was dealt with thoroughly in the first *McCormack* opinion, 251 F.Supp. at 534–536, where strong distinction was made between Commission construction of "commodity descriptions" and Commission construction of territorial descriptions. In the case of the former, it was pointed out, there is involved "an area wherein the Commission's great familiarity with customary trade usage and with industry-wide understanding of prior Commission interpretations is critical." As a result, it was concluded, wide latitude should be given to Commission interpretation of commodity descriptions. However, in the case of Commission construction of territorial descriptions, such as are involved in the McCormack matter, it was pointed out, with citation to the Commission's own statements in its original Order of March 26, 1962:

2. In framing the issue in such a manner, the court, of course, does not find it necessary to consider the merits of the Commission's attempted invocation of its "expertise." On this question, see the dissenting opinion of Commissioner Webb, 102 M.C.C. at 583.

"The disputed language in McCormack's certificate is non-technical in nature. *There is no apparent reason for example, why a similar territorial description in a statute or contract should be given any different meaning,* * * * no policy or presumption favoring a liberal or strict construction for the purpose of granting a larger or smaller quantum of operating authority. (Emphasis supplied). 89 M.C.C. at 10."

251 F.Supp. at 536. This court continues to believe that the conclusion reached in the original *McCormack* decision was a cogent one; as a result, no great deference will be paid to the Commission's rather unusual reading of the Sub 70 Certificate. The court holds that, as a matter of law, the Certificate permits plaintiff to deal in Connecticut, Pennsylvania, and New Jersey, without reference to the 100 mile limitation contained therein, which applies only to operations in New York State.

The Order of the Interstate Commerce Commission dated August 5, 1966 will be set aside and enjoined.

*   *   *

The majority opinion gives the impression that the disputed provision is actually quite simple and not worthy of such controversy. However, that is the way it is with ambiguities. One person reads something one way; someone else reads it another. Each one has a theory about punctuation, grammar, "plain meaning," or legislative history as the only proper foundation on which to base a reading. Often neither acknowledges that the provision is ambiguous, in spite of the fact that if it were not, they probably would not be arguing about it in the first place.

In the trucking company's case, the majority consisted of only two people, members of a three-judge panel. The dissenting third judge wrote more than twice as much about the case and the presence or absence of a "dangerous comma." Here is part of the dissenting opinion.

T.I. McCORMACK TRUCKING CO. v. UNITED STATES

298 F.Supp. 39, 45–47 (D.N.J.1969) (McLaughlin, J., dissenting).

What we have before us is a 1948 certificate of public convenience and necessity issued by the Interstate Commerce Commission. The unquestioned intent of the Commission was to apply the hundred mile limitation to all points and places in the four states named in the document. Because of the involved irregular routes allowed, the certificate was obviously not easy to draft; to a layman that task could well have been nigh impossible. Even so, as we have seen, the Commission never contended that each of the words in the "within 100 hundred miles of Columbus Circle, N.Y. * * *" phrase were technical words of art but does say and has established that "Collectively the words have a definite and distinctive meaning in the context here considered." As such and having in mind that in this connection the uncontradicted intent of the Commission as to the content of the certificate was to include all four states of the certificate within the hundred mile limitation of Columbus Circle, it was not only "common sense" but high level specialized judgment to use the Commission rightly recognized expertise to make sure that the language chosen supported the Commission's purpose. That was only the beginning of the firm, unalterable designation of the routes allowed by the granting Authority. McCormack Company which had applied for and had received the said certificate knew exactly what the Commission had allowed in its territorial designation. McCormack formally verified that in writing and under those precise conditions accepted the certificate as drafted and without reservation. Not long after that, definitely at least by the time its new ownership took over, plaintiff was deliberately transporting interstate freight over routes beyond the scope of its certificate. Plaintiff has persisted in that course down to and including this moment. It never brought a proceeding before the Commission in an effort to vindicate its action. The only reason it appears here as plaintiff is because it is again in effect appealing from a Commission decision upholding the certificate as granted.

We have seen how McCormack in the beginning contended that the Commission by some mysterious informal wave of the hand allowed plaintiff the additional routings. In passing, that of itself is the strongest possible admission that the original, sharply limited certificate meant what the Commission had always maintained it did. Having made no progress with its enlargement allegation, McCormack came into this Court in its 1966 appeal with a new proposition. It produced a person described in the prior court opinion as a "linguist". He, from the absence of a comma after the first "New York" in the phrase involved, concluded that McCormack was given unrestricted rights in all four states. The "New Standard Dictionary of the English Language" (1944) states the prime meaning of linguist to be "an adept in languages; one who is acquainted with several languages". The second meaning of the word is given as "a student of the history or science of language; a philologist". This particular linguist has no Interstate Commerce Commission experience whatsoever. There is no suggestion that he has any understanding of irregular routings. The linguist's pronouncement is seconded by four attorneys also produced on behalf of the plaintiff. At oral argument the main reliance for the plaintiff for the comma disposition was stated as the truly scholarly H.W. Fowler in his book "Modern English Usage" (1965 Ed.) p. 588. However, there is no mention of Fowler in plaintiff's briefs. What Fowler deals with on p. 588 and also on pp. 587 and 589 is the murky comma world. The most Mr. Fowler and his revisionist suggest is the recasting of sentences instead of using the crude device of the intrusive comma. On p. 588, it is said "In ambiguous appositions. Insertion or removal of commas is seldom a sufficient remedy, and indeed it is usually impossible. The thing is to remember that arrangements in which apposition commas and enumeration commas are mixed up are dangerous and should be avoided."

Amazingly there is no mention either oral or written by plaintiff of the great American authority in this field, Wilson Follett. The latter's definitive book "Modern American Usage" (1966) is of much the same view as Fowler. Follett lays the comma to an uneasy rest at p. 401, saying "The comma can cause trouble equally by its absence, by its presence, and by wrong placement." Neither Fowler nor Follett ever intimate that a comma quibble in circumstances as those before us should ever be given serious attention.

The certificate, intended to be granted by the Commission and so granted in 1948, down to and through the current litigation has never been attacked as unreasonable. And there is no claim that the Commission has ever varied from its 1948 view of its grant. Plaintiff, having agreed to and accepted the original territory, later desiring more, simply took it. Its unfounded statement that the Commission merely closed its eyes, went beyond its statutory grant, beyond its authority and extended the area allowance, just fell apart and is not here referred to by plaintiff. Instead came the incredible argument that despite the Commission's intention, the plaintiff's acquiescence and the fact that the Commission had always upheld its 1948 position completely, nevertheless, because of the absence of at best a most questionable comma, the certificate, which contained what the Commission intended to grant and did grant and what plaintiff intended to receive and did accept, is to be construed twenty years after it was allowed in a manner significantly different from what the Commission gave and what the plaintiff knowledgeably was given.

There has been nothing arbitrary, capricious or clearly erroneous in the Commission's actions throughout the twenty years of this certificate. There is no excuse in this case to allow the desperate use of a "dangerous comma" to reverse a decision of the Commission which was soundly within its discretion.

I would affirm the decision of the Commission.

Exercise 9.1

Explain what produces the ambiguity in each of the following provisions. Then redraft each provision to make it unambiguous.

a. My executor shall divide the remainder of my property equally between all of my nieces and my nephew.

If there are 11 nieces, does the nephew get ½ or ¹⁄₁₂?

   b. I hereby deed the property to Michael Howard, a single man, and Robert Mern and Anne, his wife.

Does Howard get ½ or ⅓ interest?

   c. Officers shall be elected on a vote of the members representing not less than ¾ of the capital stock of the membership.

Must a candidate receive ¾ of the vote to be elected, or do ¾ of the members constitute a quorum for voting purposes?

   d. No person shall have sexual intercourse with a child of the age of 14 years, or under.

If a person has sexual intercourse with a child whose fourteenth birthday was three months ago, is the act in violation of the statute?

Exercise 9.2

Identify the semantic and syntactic ambiguities in the following price provision from a construction contract. (This provision is excerpted from the contract presented in full at p. 160).

1   3. In consideration of the performance by the said contractor
2 of all of the covenants and conditions contained in this agreement
3 and contained in the plans and specifications the owners agree to
4 pay to the contractor an amount equal to the amount of all material
5 furnished by the contractor and the labor furnished by the contrac-
6 tor together with payroll taxes and Insurance, also together with
7 the sum total of the net amount due the subcontractors performing
8 work or furnishing work for said construction. The Owners also
9 agree to pay to the contractor, in addition to the amount specified
10 hereinabove, a fee equal to 10% of the actual cost of the said
11 residence, said fee to be paid after completion of said residence and
12 acceptance thereof by the Owners. It is specifically agreed by and
13 between the parties that notwithstanding the agreement herein-
14 above by the owners shall not be required, under the terms of this
15 agreement, to pay to the contractor any amount in excess of the
16 sum of Thirty–Four Thousand, Five Hundred Dollars ($34,500.00)
17 which is the estimated cost of construction, plus the fee provided for
18 herein.

------

b. Semi-colon

Although most ambiguous punctuation problems are comma problems, the semi-colon is also sometimes the culprit. Does it separate phrases or clauses that stand independently on their own, or is it merely a comma in disguise?

Consider the case of an Indiana couple who appealed their conviction for illegal sale of fireworks. Here is the statute they relied upon for their defense.

> Nothing in this act shall be construed to prohibit any resident whole-saler, dealer, or jobber to sell at wholesale such fireworks as are not herein prohibited; *or the sale of any kind of fireworks provided the same are to be shipped directly out of state;* or the use of fireworks by railroads or other transportation agencies for signal purposes or illumi-nation, or the sale or use of blank cartridges for a show or theater, or for signal or ceremonial purposes in athletics or sports, or for use by military organizations [emphasis added].

The defendants had sold at retail some fireworks that were permitted by statute only to be sold wholesale. They argued that this was legally acceptable because they ascertained that the purchaser was from Illi-nois and he signed a statement that he was "going to immediately ship all Indiana illegal fireworks directly out of the state of Indiana * * *."

The court of appeals accepted the defendants' view of the matter and reversed the conviction. Here is what the Indiana Supreme Court had to say about it.

HILL v. STATE
488 N.E.2d 709, 710–11 (Ind.1986).

* * *

Counsel points out that this section is structured as a series, each ending with a semicolon, followed by the word "or" as an introduction to the next exception on the list. The common understanding of such a series of phrases is that each stands on its own as a separate exception. Under this reading, he argues, the Hills engaged in a "sale of any kind of fireworks provided the same are to be shipped directly out of state" and thus did not violate the law.

The State's position has been that Ind.Code § 22–11–14–4 was intended to exempt wholesale transactions for shipping out of state. Responding to this argument, defense counsel interrupted the prosecu-tor five times during final argument in the trial court to insist that the sale to Oakley was a retail sale. The prosecutor provided the trial judge with copies of minutes from the town planning commission indicating that the operator of New–Line Fireworks, which was on land zoned for wholesale operations, represented that fireworks were not stored on the premises and were delivered to customers "through the mail or by a truck." When a party cannot keep his own story straight, it requires additional concentration to treat his arguments seriously.

While it is true that the common meaning given the punctuation used in Ind.Code § 22–11–14–4 would suggest that an exemption exists for fireworks sold wholesale or retail for shipment out of state, we are not obligated to engage in a debate on the significance of semicolons and disjunctives when doing so renders the statute absurd or produces a result repugnant to the apparent intent of the legislature. *Spaulding v. Harvey* (1856), 7 Ind. 429.

The framework provided by the General Assembly seems plain enough. It manifests a desire to reduce the number of children and adults burned or injured by fireworks. The legislature has determined that certain fireworks are safe for retailing to the general public and that others are not. Dealers are allowed to sell all fireworks at wholesale and all fireworks may be shipped out of state. Appellants see in this scheme the proverbial loophole: the customer walks in the store, signs a statement that he intends to ship all illegal fireworks out of state, buys individual items, and drives away. Although Oakley was asked to show his drivers license to show that he was not an Indiana resident, if we accept the Hills' argument that they are exempted because the fireworks were to be "shipped directly out of state", the residence of the purchaser would be of little moment.

We conclude that reading the phrase "shipped directly out of state" as an exception to the rule that only certain listed fireworks can be sold at retail required that the term "shipped" be read to mean a method of delivery which does not result in the product being placed in general distribution within the state. It means that jobbers may sell crates of fireworks and ship them to Illinois; it does not mean that fireworks salesmen can have their customers sign a form and then hand them a paper bag of cherry bombs.

This loophole is closed. The judgment of the trial court is affirmed.

C. CONTEXTUAL AMBIGUITY

Contextual ambiguity results when two different parts of the same document say contradictory things. Contextual ambiguity may result from contradiction between two sentences in sequence. Occasionally contextual ambiguity occurs within one sentence. For example:

> State regulations are not preempted only when they conflict with federal law.

Common sense suggests that the drafter intends to say that the regulations are preempted only when they conflict or that the regulations are not preempted except when they conflict. However, the sentence combines two ways to make its point and so says the opposite of what the drafter presumably intends.

More often contextual ambiguity results from contradiction between two sentences rather than within one. For example, consider what it would be like to try to conduct a college inventory of equipment according to the following instructions:

> Items valued at more than $100 are included in the inventory. The standard items consist of desks, chairs, credenzas, tables, lamps, typewriters, personal computers, filing cabinets, dictating equipment, calculators, and other electrical equipment. Items omitted from the lists include: library chairs, wastebaskets, staplers and other desk accessories.

When the contradictory phrases are close together, the contradiction is at least easy to spot. Contextual ambiguity is often the most difficult type to discover, however, because the contradictory clauses or sentences may be far removed from each other. It is not until one party relies on one of them and another party relies on the other that the ambiguity is discovered.

The case below illustrates the typical process a court goes through to attempt to reconcile contradictory clauses. Here the customers of a truck rental company thought they had a lease with an option to purchase, giving them the right to return the trucks when the contract was terminated. The rental company read the "Truck Lease Service Agreement" to say that at termination, there was to be an absolute sale of the trucks to the customers. When the customers returned the trucks, the rental company sold them at a loss and sued for breach of contract to collect the difference. The court resolved the controversy by looking to a section of the contract that both the rental company and the customers overlooked.

TRANSPORT RENTAL SYSTEMS, INC. v. HERTZ CORP.

129 So.2d 454, 455–56 (Fla.App.1961).

* * *

The contract in question is very complete and in great detail. It contains 29 provisions, all of which apply only to the leasing of trucking equipment, with the exception of the two sections hereinafter quoted.

The breach of the contract for which damages were claimed was alleged to have occurred under Section (18) and subsections (a) and (b) thereof which read as follows:

> "(18) Either party shall have the right to cancel this agreement on any Anniversary of the date on which the last vehicle delivered to Customer hereunder shall have entered Customer's service under this agreement, by giving to the other party, at least thirty (30) days prior to such termination date, notice in writing of its intention so to terminate this agreement.

> (a) In the event either party shall elect to cancel this agreement, then Customer agrees to purchase the vehicles then covered by this agreement and Lessor agrees to sell said vehicles to Customer, upon the basis set out in sub-section (b) hereof.

> (b) In the event of cancellation of this agreement, the purchase by Customer of the vehicles covered hereby shall be for cash or upon terms suitable to Lessor and at the original value thereof, as specified in Schedule A and/or other Schedule A's attached hereto, less depreciation, computed upon the bases of the time which has elapsed from the date the vehicles shall have entered the service of Customer until the date Customer shall have exercised this option to purchase, and at the depreciation rate set forth in Schedule A and/or other Schedule A's attached hereto, provided, however, that the purchase price of such

vehicles under this option shall not in any event be less than fifteen (15) per cent of the original value, as set out in Schedule A and/or other Schedule A's attached hereto."

the plaintiff claiming that same provided for an absolute sale of the vehicles to the defendants.

The vehicles were returned by the defendants to the plaintiff upon termination of the contract. The plaintiff then sold the vehicles at private sale. The damages for the breach were claimed to be a sum of money equal to the difference between the amount realized from the sale of the vehicles and the amount the plaintiff would have been entitled to receive for the vehicles under the terms of the contract. This amount was established to be the sum of $18,000. It is apparent that the jury allowed only one-half of this amount as plaintiff's damages for the breach, but this is not material in resolving the issue.

The main contention of the defendants was that the above-quoted provision of the contract was only an option to purchase, giving the defendants, lessees under the contract, the right to return the goods upon termination of the contract.

Defendants' motion to dismiss the complaint for its failure to state a cause of action was denied. Likewise, defendants' motion for a directed verdict upon the issue involved because of the plaintiff's failure to show a breach by the defendants of the contract was denied.

The arguments of counsel were centered primarily around an interpretation of the above referred to provision of the contract. Also, the briefs of the parties are confined almost entirely to a construction of this provision. Apparently, Section (16) of the contract, which reads as follows:

"(16) Customer agrees that upon the expiration of the period for which any vehicles delivered under this agreement respectively shall have been leased or upon the cancellation or termination of this agreement, all of the vehicles delivered under this agreement to Customer will be returned to Lessor at the garage at which such delivery shall have been made (or such other garage in the same city as may have been designated by Lessor), in as good mechanical condition and running order as they were when received by Customer, ordinary wear and tear excepted."

was either disregarded or entirely overlooked. This provision can only be construed as implying a right to return the vehicle upon termination of the contract and sets forth the conditions upon which the return is to be made. This is a reasonable inference and no other inference or intention can possibly be applied to its terms. When this provision is considered along with Section (18) and its subsections and the other provisions of the contract, the contract must be considered as a lease agreement with an option, upon termination of the contract, in the lessees to either return the vehicles or buy the same upon the terms set forth in Section (18) and its subsections.

Section (16) would not have been inserted had it not been intended to serve some purpose in expressing the intention of the parties. An implication of law arising from one clause of a contract indicating that another is unnecessary does not justify that such other clause is superfluous. 7 Am.Jur., Contracts, 95. It is a cardinal rule in the construction of contracts that the intention of the parties thereto will be ascertained from a consideration of the whole agreement. 7 Fla. Jur., Contracts, Sec. 77. If a contract contains clauses which are apparently repugnant to each other, they must be given such an interpretation as will reconcile them if possible. 7 Fla.Jur., Contracts, Sec. 91. The real intention, as disclosed by a fair consideration of all parts of a contract, should control the meaning given to mere words or particular provisions when they have reference to the main purpose. 7 Fla.Jur., Contracts, Sec. 88, p. 155; 12 Am.Jur., Contracts, Sec. 252; 7 Fla.Jur., Contracts, Sec. 87. These general principles of construction are well-settled statements of the law in this state.

Upon applying these general principles of construction to the contract in question, it can only be concluded that the contract in question was a lease agreement with an option to the lessees, upon termination of the lease agreement, to either return the property or buy the same. The lessees chose to return the same to the lessor's assignee, the appellee herein. There was, therefore, no breach of the contract and the defendants, the appellants herein, were entitled to judgment as a matter of law upon this particular element of alleged damages.

* * *

Exercise 9.3

Do an across-the-board check of the construction contract presented at p. 160, looking at all provisions related to price. What contextual ambiguities do you find?

Do another across-the-board check of the same contract, looking at all provisions related to insurance. What contextual ambiguities do you find?

Are additional contextual ambiguities revealed by additional across-the-board checks of the same contract?

Exercise 9.4

Your client AM brings you a handwritten page and tells you, "My friend MG and I own a big piece of land together, which we have subdivided into 10 lots. Now we're ready to sell the land. Here is the contract we drew up. We trust each other, but we want a good legal contract. Get this into proper form for us, okay?"

After reading the handwritten contract, what would you need to ask AM before redrafting? Try to anticipate as fully as possible any problems you would have redrafting the contract so that you could do the job after only one conversation with AM. Here is what the handwritten page says over the signatures of the two friends.

1) 50%/50% of quick bulk sale that both parties agree to.

2) $\frac{2}{3}$ (MG) $\frac{1}{3}$ on profits up to $91,000. 50%—50% on anything over $91,000.

3) 150 K or better offer on bulk sale we will both agree to sell.

4) Money will be divided: According to above formulas.

III. CANONS OF CONSTRUCTION

If the drafter does not take charge of making meaning clear, courts sometimes rely upon the canons, or rules, of construction to govern how to choose one of two or more contradictory meanings. However, these are not actually rules with the force of law. They are customs, and a given canon may or may not be followed in a given situation.[16]

Restrictive canons of construction were originally an English device to preserve the common law from legislative meddling, and that sense of them became an American idea as well in the maxim: "Statutes passed in derogation of the common law * * * should be construed strictly * * *."[17] However, the twentieth century has given us some changing views of the relationship between the common law and the canons of statutory construction. The New Deal era brought constrictions on the common law and more liberally construed remedial legislation.[18] The era of expansion of civil rights legislation brought new deference to administrative interpretations of legislation through regulations.[19] The 1980's brought back deference to the common law accompanied by a reluctance to interfere with contract and property rights and an inclination to construe regulatory statutes narrowly.[20] One study notes that nineteenth century restrictive canons were used more in the 1980's than during the New Deal era and that expansive

16. For a detailed discussion of how the canons function, see the examples in a specific context—the interpretation of collective bargaining agreements by labor-management arbitrators—in Elkouri and Elkouri, How Arbitration Works 342–65 (4th ed. 1985).

17. Ross v. Jones, 89 U.S. (22 Wall.) 576, 591 (1874).

18. See, for example, SEC v. C.M. Joiner Leasing Corp., 320 U.S. 344, 350–51, 64 S.Ct. 120, 124–25 (1943).

19. See, for example, Griggs v. Duke Power Co., 401 U.S. 424, 433–34, 91 S.Ct. 849, 854–55 (1971).

20. See, for example, Schreiber v. Burlington Northern, Inc., 472 U.S. 1, 8, 105 S.Ct. 2458, 2462 (1985).

canons were used far less in the 1980's.[21] In such an era, the plain meaning doctrine reigns.[22] Broad remedial purposes get short shrift.

Some states codify some of the canons in their constitution or in an opening code title to govern the entire code. Even more common are statutes directing a given construction of a particular chapter or even a particular section. The Commissioners on Uniform State Laws have drafted rules of construction for uniform statutes. It may be interesting to speculate whether codification of a canon gives it any greater weight than those that remain grounded only on case law, but ultimately it matters more what courts do than what they say about why they do it.[23] The most important thing to recognize about the canons is how slippery they are and how dangerous it is to rely on any of them.[24] Professor Llewellyn gives ample evidence of why this is so.[25]

LLEWELLYN, REMARKS ON THE THEORY OF APPELLATE DECISION AND THE RULES OR CANONS ABOUT HOW STATUTES ARE TO BE CONSTRUED

3 Vand.L.Rev. 395, 401–06 (1950) (footnotes omitted).*

CANONS OF CONSTRUCTION

Statutory interpretation still speaks a diplomatic tongue. Here is some of the technical framework for maneuver.

THRUST	BUT PARRY
1. A statute cannot go beyond its text.	1. To effect its purpose a statute may be implemented beyond its text.
2. Statutes in derogation of the common law will not be extended by construction.	2. Such acts will be liberally construed if their nature is remedial.

---

21. Harris, The Politics of Statutory Construction, 1985 Brigham Young U.L. Rev. 745, 787.

22. See, for example, Aultman Hosp. Ass'n v. Community Mut. Ins. Co., 46 Ohio St.3d 51, 544 N.E.2d 920 (1989).

23. Memorandum from Professor Mary Ellen Caldwell to Barbara Child (Fall 1986) (on file at U. of Fla. College of Law Legal Drafting Dept.).

24. There is no absolute certainty even in such trusted maxims as the rule that penal statutes are to be strictly construed. "The rule is still invoked, but so variously and unpredictably, and it is so often conflated with inconsistencies, that it is hard to discern widespread adherence to any general policy of statutory construction."

Jeffries, Legality, Vagueness, and the Construction of Penal Statutes, 71 Va.L.Rev. 189, 219 (1985).

25. See also Farber and Frickey, Legislative Intent and Public Choice, 74 Va.L. Rev. 423 (1988); Posner, Legal Formalism, Legal Realism, and the Interpretation of Statutes and the Constitution, 37 Case W.Res.L.Rev. 179 (1986). For discussion of how the canons operate in the context of employment contracts, see N. Brand, Interpreting and Applying Contract Language, ch. 2, Labor Arbitration: The Strategy of Persuasion 33 (1987).

* Copyright © 1950 by Vanderbilt Law Review. Reprinted by permission of the publisher.

THRUST	BUT	PARRY

3. Statutes are to be read in the light of the common law and a statute affirming a common law rule is to be construed in accordance with the common law.

3. The common law gives way to a statute which is inconsistent with it and when a statute is designed as a revision of a whole body of law applicable to a given subject it supersedes the common law.

4. Where a foreign statute which has received construction has been adopted, previous construction is adopted too.

4. It may be rejected where there is conflict with the obvious meaning of the statute or where the foreign decisions are unsatisfactory in reasoning or where the foreign interpretation is not in harmony with the spirit or policy of the laws of the adopting state.

5. Where various states have already adopted the statute, the parent state is followed.

5. Where interpretations of other states are inharmonious, there is no such restraint.

6. Statutes *in pari materia* must be construed together.

6. A statute is not *in pari materia* if its scope and aim are distinct or where a legislative design to depart from the general purpose or policy of previous enactments may be apparent.

7. A statute imposing a new penalty or forfeiture, or a new liability or disability, or creating a new right of action will not be construed as having a retroactive effect.

7. Remedial statutes are to be liberally construed and if a retroactive interpretation will promote the ends of justice, they should receive such construction.

8. Where design has been distinctly stated no place is left for construction.

8. Courts have the power to inquire into real—as distinct from ostensible—purpose.

9. Definitions and rules of construction contained in an interpretation clause are part of the law and binding.

9. Definitions and rules of construction in a statute will not be extended beyond their necessary import nor allowed to defeat intention otherwise manifested.

10. A statutory provision requiring liberal construction does not mean disregard of unequivocal requirements of the statute.

10. Where a rule of construction is provided within the statute itself the rule should be applied.

11. Titles do not control meaning; preambles do not expand scope; section headings do not change language.

11. The title may be consulted as a guide when there is doubt or obscurity in the body; preambles may be consulted to determine rationale, and thus the true construction of terms; section headings may be

THRUST   BUT   PARRY

THRUST	PARRY
	looked upon as part of the statute itself.
12. If language is plain and unambiguous it must be given effect.	12. Not when literal interpretation would lead to absurd or mischievous consequences or thwart manifest purpose.
13. Words and phrases which have received judicial construction before enactment are to be understood according to that construction.	13. Not if the statute clearly requires them to have a different meaning.
14. After enactment, judicial decision upon interpretation of particular terms and phrases controls.	14. Practical construction by executive officers is strong evidence of true meaning.
15. Words are to be taken in their ordinary meaning unless they are technical terms or words of art.	15. Popular words may bear a technical meaning and technical words may have a popular signification and they should be so construed as to agree with evident intention or to make the statute operative.
16. Every word and clause must be given effect.	16. If inadvertently inserted or if repugnant to the rest of the statute, they may be rejected as surplusage.
17. The same language used repeatedly in the same connection is presumed to bear the same meaning throughout the statute.	17. This presumption will be disregarded where it is necessary to assign different meanings to make the statute consistent.
18. Words are to be interpreted according to the proper grammatical effect of their arrangement within the statute.	18. Rules of grammar will be disregarded where strict adherence would defeat purpose.
19. Exceptions not made cannot be read.	19. The letter is only the "bark." Whatever is within the reason of the law is within the law itself.
20. Expression of one thing excludes another.	20. The language may fairly comprehend many different cases where some only are expressly mentioned by way of example.
21. General terms are to receive a general construction.	21. They may be limited by specific terms with which they are associated or by the scope and purpose of the statute.
22. It is a general rule of construction that where general words follow an enumeration they are to be held as applying only to persons and things of the same general kind or	22. General words must operate on something. Further, *ejusdem generis* is only an aid in getting the meaning and does not warrant confining the operations of a statute

Thrust	But	Parry
class specifically mentioned (*ejusdem generis*).		within narrower limits than were intended.
23. Qualifying or limiting words or clauses are to be referred to the next preceding antecedent.		23. Not when evidence sense and meaning require a different construction.
24. Punctuation will govern when a statute is open to two constructions.		24. Punctuation marks will not control the plain and evident meaning of language.
25. It must be assumed that language has been chosen with due regard to grammatical propriety and is not interchangeable on mere conjecture.		25. "And" and "or" may be read interchangeably whenever the change is necessary to give the statute sense and effect.
26. There is a distinction between words of permission and mandatory words.		26. Words imparting permission may be read as mandatory and words imparting command may be read as permissive when such construction is made necessary by evident intention or by the rights of the public.
27. A proviso qualifies the provision immediately preceding.		27. It may clearly be intended to have a wider scope.
28. When the enacting clause is general, a proviso is construed strictly.		28. Not when it is necessary to extend the proviso to persons or cases which come within its equity.

IV. TABULATED SENTENCE STRUCTURE

A. A DEVICE FOR RESOLVING AMBIGUITY

Instead of counting on some canon of construction to clarify meaning, it is worth taking care to avoid ambiguity. The single most useful device for avoiding syntactic ambiguity is tabulated sentence structure, which sets material out on the page in a form that makes clear how its parts relate to each other.[26]

Here is a conversion of a sentence into two alternate tabulated structures, each one resolving syntactic ambiguity a different way.

Untabulated Provision

Psychiatric service is covered only if it is furnished by a group practice organization, by a hospital, or by a community mental health center which furnishes comprehensive mental health services.

---

26. For discussion of tabulation as an explication device, see Chapter 7, Section VI.C.

Notice first how the provision is ambiguous. Does it require only community mental health centers to furnish comprehensive mental health services in order to have psychiatric service covered? Or does the requirement also apply to group practice organizations and hospitals? The provision can be tabulated one of two ways to clarify which meaning is intended.

Tabulated Version with Meaning 1

Psychiatric service is covered only if it is furnished by

    (a) a group practice organization,

    (b) a hospital, or

    (c) a community mental health center which furnishes comprehensive mental health services.

Set out this way, the provision expressly requires that a community mental health center furnish comprehensive mental health services. It also expressly does not impose that requirement on group practice organizations and hospitals.

Tabulated Version with Meaning 2

Psychiatric service is covered only if it is furnished by

    (a) a group practice organization,

    (b) a hospital, or

    (c) a community mental health center

which furnishes comprehensive mental health services.

Set out this way, the provision expressly imposes the requirement on all three furnishers of service.

B. A DEVICE FOR EMPHASIZING ALTERNATIVE AND CUMULATIVE ITEMS

Another advantage of tabulated sentence structure is that it provides visible emphasis of whether the tabulated items are alternative or cumulative.

Emphasis of Alternative Items

If the company defaults in paying

    (a) taxes,

    (b) rents, or

    (c) other like charges,

the security under this mortgage becomes enforceable.

Emphasis of Cumulative Items

Any person guaranteeing a signature warrants that

    (a) the signature was genuine;

    (b) the signer was an appropriate person to endorse; and

    (c) the signer had legal capacity to sign.

For additional emphasis, some drafters prefer to put "and" or "or" after every item in the series except the last one. In a short series, especially one appearing in full on the same page, the repeated conjunction serves little purpose. In a long series covering several pages, there may be more justification for repeating. However, for that long a series, the better aid to the reader is to indicate in the introductory words ahead of the series whether it is alternative or cumulative.

C. TESTING TABULATED MATERIAL FOR COHERENCE

If you read a tabulated sentence out loud, it should sound to a listener like a coherent sentence. In addition, each tabulated item should follow smoothly from any introductory words that precede the tabulated material. Likewise, any concluding words should follow smoothly from each tabulated item. Thus, if any introductory words and any concluding words are read with any one of the tabulated items alone, a coherent statement should result.

For example, we can extract from the second version of the sentence about psychiatric service a coherent statement exclusively about service furnished by a hospital. If we read the introductory words and the concluding words together with our chosen item (b) from the tabulated series, the result is the following statement:

Psychiatric service is covered if it is furnished by a hospital which furnishes comprehensive mental health services.

The sentence is coherent. Thus the tabulated structure passes the test.

Tabulated sentence structure can go wrong if you do not carefully integrate both the introductory and the concluding words with each tabulated item individually.

Tabulated Sentence for Testing

If the estate exceeds $30,000

  (a) each child is entitled to a distributive share in the balance over $30,000; and

  (b) if the estate is $30,000 or less, no child is entitled to any distributive share.

Reading the introductory words with part (b) makes clear what has gone wrong. The result makes no sense.

Introductory Words with Part (b) Failing the Test

If the estate exceeds $30,000, if the estate is $30,000 or less, no child is entitled to any distributive share.

Here is how the material should have been presented.

Corrected Tabulation

  (a) If the estate exceeds $30,000, each child is entitled to a distributive share in the balance over $30,000; and

(b) if the estate is $30,000 or less, no child is entitled to any distributive share.

Exercise 9.5

Explain what is wrong with the structure in the following sentences.

Sentence a

(1) The application shall contain:

    (a) The applicant's name and address.

    (b) Birthday.

    (c) Shall be filed with the Department of State.

Sentence b

(a) The landlord shall make reasonable provisions for:

    1. The extermination of rats, mice, roaches, ants, wood-destroying organisms, and bedbugs. When vacation of the premises is required for such extermination, the landlord shall abate the rent.

    2. Locks and keys.

    3. The clean and safe condition of common areas.

Sentence c

(a) General Rule. If

    (1) any improvements located on the premises at the time of the execution of this binder are damaged by fire or other casualty prior to closing; and

    (2) those improvements can be restored to substantially the same condition within a period of 30 days after such destruction occurs; and

    (3) the Seller restores the improvements, then the closing date shall be extended accordingly, and

    (4) the Buyer shall have no option to terminate this contract.

    (5) All risk of loss prior to closing shall be borne by the Seller.

D. TABULATED SENTENCE STRUCTURE DISTINGUISHED FROM OUTLINE

A sentence set out with its parallel parts tabulated looks somewhat like an outline in that outlines also have parallel parts indented and numbered or lettered. However, it is important to distinguish tabulated sentence structure from outlines. A sentence of text presented in tabulated structure is still a *complete sentence*. An outline, in contrast, is an *abbreviated version* or a skeleton of a whole rather than the whole itself broken into parts.

V. LISTS DISTINGUISHED FROM TABULATED SENTENCE STRUCTURE

Sometimes it is convenient to indent and number or letter items merely because they form a list. If the list is preceded by introductory words, the result may look like tabulated sentence structure. However, lists differ from tabulated sentence structure essentially in that the point of the sentence with a list in it is clear before the list begins, and the items in the list function almost as various possible ways to fill a blank.

List Structure

This chapter applies to the purchase by any of the following agencies of all services for which payment is authorized:

    (a) The Department of the Army.

    (b) The Department of the Navy.

    (c) The Department of the Air Force.

Same Sentence Using Blank

This chapter applies to the purchase by _____ of all services for which payment is authorized.

Any one of the listed agencies may be written into the blank, and later if someone with the power to do so decides that the chapter also applies to the Coast Guard, it may also be written into the blank, whereupon it becomes item (d).

Depending on the formality of the document, indicators other than letters or numbers, such as bullets, could mark the items. Notice that each item is presented as an independent unit beginning with a capital letter and ending with a period rather than a comma or semi-colon.

Also notice that neither "and" nor "or" joins the last item in the list to those preceding it. The items are neither cumulative nor alternative. Rather, the same thing (the introductory words) is being stated independently about each item. Conceivably, it could be stated about other items as well, either now or later; therefore, what happens to be the last item on the list now should not be thought of as finally the last item, or even as the end of the sentence. For all practical purposes, the "end of the sentence" is the end of the introductory words preceding the list, and each item on the list is an equally available substitute for the language "any of the following agencies," which is essentially nothing more than a blank to be filled in.

VI. VERSATILITY OF THE TABULATION PROCESS

Presenting material in tabulated sentence structure involves essentially the same process as tabulating it to explicate it. The difference is that explication requires tabulating all or nearly all the parallel items rather than just those deserving special attention. Here is a demonstration showing the same provision tabulated fully for explication, then presented in tabulated sentence structure, and finally restructured using a list.

Untabulated Provision

You are exempt from this requirement if you are 18 or older and a full-time student, and this requirement also does not apply in the event that you are legally responsible for the support of one child under school age or two or more children, or medically exempt.

Same Provision Tabulated for Explication

You are exempt from this requirement if you are

     1.   a.   18 or

              b.   older and

     2.   a full-time student, and

this requirement also does not apply in the event that you are

     1.   legally responsible for the support of

              a.   one child under school age or

              b.   two or more children or

     2.   medically exempt.

Same Provision Presented in Tabulated Sentence Structure

You are exempt from this requirement if

     1.   you are 18 or older and a full-time student;

     2.   you are legally responsible for the support of one child under school age or two or more children; or

     3.   you are medically exempt.

Same Provision Presented in List Structure

You are exempt from this requirement if you meet any of the following requirements:

     1.   You are 18 or older and a full-time student.

     2.   You are legally responsible for the support of one child under school age or two or more children.

     3.   You are medically exempt.

The list structure is probably the preferable one for this provision because a reader would likely look to see if any one listed item applied, not all three.

VII. CHOOSING TABULATED SENTENCE STRUCTURE OR LIST STRUCTURE

Tabulated sentence structure and list structure lend themselves to different kinds of material, so that you should make a conscious choice to use one or the other.

A. TABULATED SENTENCE STRUCTURE

Tabulated sentence structure is appropriate only when dividing up an existing complete sentence to show the relationships among its parts. This structure is especially useful to set out cumulative requirements, as in: "You must do this, this, *and* this to comply with the law," or alternative prohibitions, as in: "If you do this, this, *or* this, you will incur a penalty."

B. LIST STRUCTURE

List structure is appropriate for giving examples. The words "for example" or "for instance" or "the following" often signal list structure. List structure is also appropriate for material in which a reader might be expected to look up just one item on the list rather than having an equal interest in all the listed items.

VIII. CHECKLIST FOR USING TABULATION

1. Use either structure judiciously. Do not over-tabulate uncomplicated, unambiguous material. Do not automatically indent and number or letter every sentence in a section of a document.

2. Make sure that tabulated items are parallel in both substance and form.

3. Decide whether the material lends itself to tabulated sentence structure or list structure, and then observe the formalities for the chosen structure.

4. In tabulated sentence structure, make sure to indicate whether the items are alternative or cumulative.

5. Make sure that a tabulated sentence makes sense when you read the introductory words followed by each item alone. If there are concluding words after the tabulated material, make sure the sentence

makes sense when you read each tabulated item alone followed by the concluding words.[27]

Exercise 9.6

Below are three provisions that have figured in court disputes. Decide how you would construe them and why. Then redraft them to remove any possible ambiguity and ensure that even a reader in bad faith could not plausibly support an interpretation other than yours. Remember that the goal of careful drafting is not merely to prevail in litigation; it is to prevent litigation. Moreover, one cannot be sure that a court's construction of an ambiguous provision will be sensible, assuming "sensible" means according to the drafter's intention.

Case 1

The judge dismissed an indictment against the defendant for Class B theft. The State appealed, arguing that the governing statute authorizes dismissals only involving Class D and Class E crimes. Here is the statute.

1   When a person has been admitted to bail or is committed by a
2 judge, or is indicted, or held upon a complaint and warrant for an
3 assault or other Class D or E crime as defined by Title 17–A, section
4 4–A, for which the party injured has a remedy by civil action, except
5 aggravated assaults, assaults upon or resistance of a law enforce-
6 ment officer as defined by Title 17–A in the execution of his duty,
7 and assaults of such officers, if the injured party appears before the
8 judge or court, and in writing acknowledges satisfaction for the
9 injury, the court, on payment of all costs, may stay further proceed-
10 ings and discharge the defendant. The judge may exonerate the
11 bail and release the obligors, supersede the commitment by his
12 written order and exonerate the bail of the witnesses.

Should the Class B theft dismissal stand?

Case 2

The defendant was found guilty of violating a zoning ordinance prohibiting lodging houses in a Class 1A District. She rented rooms on the second and third floors of her house in a Class 1A District to six roomers. She did not serve meals to anyone. Her roomers paid rent either weekly or monthly. There was no dispute that her house was occupied as a lodging house, but the defendant claimed that the ordinance permitted her to rent rooms to five or more roomers as long as she did not furnish table board to more than four. Here is the relevant part of the ordinance.

---

27. For comparison of different styles of tabulating for different purposes and levels, see Aitken, Drafting in Paragraphs, ch. 4, above note 5, at 26.

1   Subject to the off street parking regulations set forth in Sec-
2 tions 800 to 814, an accessory use customarily incident respectively
3 to a Class 1A or Class 1B District use shall be permitted in such
4 respective district when such accessory use, building or structure is
5 located upon the same lot with the main use or building to which it
6 is accessory provided that:

7   *   *   *

8   (4) Rooms only in the main building may be rented, and table
9 board furnished for pay to not more than four persons, for definite
10 periods of not less than one week, provided no window display sign,
11 sign board or other visual or sound device is used to advertise such
12 use and no culinary facilities in addition to those provided for one
13 family are used.

Should the defendant be able to keep her roomers as long as they take their meals elsewhere?

Case 3

Four town council members were defendants in a civil action to oust them from office for paying themselves a salary. In a separate civil action, a court had adjudged the salary void. They repaid the money, and there was no criminal prosecution. When the State sought to oust them from office, they argued there could be no ouster without prior criminal conviction. The State argued that ouster was a separate penalty authorized by statute and not dependent on conviction. Here is the statute.

1   No alderman or councilman of any town, organized hereunder,
2 shall, during the term for which he shall have been or shall be
3 elected, accept, take or receive to his own use, from the town of
4 which he shall be an alderman or councilman, any sum of money or
5 other thing of value, other than that which is, by this chapter
6 provided to be paid to such alderman or councilman, for his services
7 as such alderman or councilman; and every person who shall
8 violate the provisions of this section, shall be deemed guilty of a
9 misdemeanor and upon conviction thereof, in any court of compe-
10 tent jurisdiction, shall be fined not less than one hundred dollars,
11 nor more than three hundred dollars, such fine to go to the school
12 fund of the county in which such town shall be located; and he shall
13 also cease to be an alderman or councilman, as the case may be, of
14 such town.

Should the council members be allowed to stay in office?

Chapter 10

DEFINING TERMS AND NAMING CONCEPTS

Table of Sections

I. DRAFTING DEFINITIONS: A LATE STAGE IN THE DRAFTING PROCESS

It is wise to wait until you have finished a first draft of a document to attend to definitions. Only then do you know what terms, if any, warrant definition as you have used them; and only then can you tell what is the most appropriate place to put definitions. If you are using defined terms in more than one section, then it is appropriate to gather definitions together in a section at the beginning of the document. A term used in only one section is more appropriately defined at the beginning of that section. Above all, if a definition is to aid a user of the document, it needs to appear before rather than after the user encounters the defined term.

Whenever you are inclined to define a term, the threshold question is whether the reader might be better served if you did not. If you use a term as it is commonly used, there is no need to provide a definition. If you are drafting legislation, it may become part of a larger body of legislation that already provides definitions. Then your task is either to draft according to those definitions, citing them if necessary, or to stipulate different definitions if necessary.

Even if you are convinced that every definition you provide is necessary, or at least helpful, beware if you have a long list. You do not serve the document user well if you provide such a complicated system of definitions with cross-references among them that the user must constantly recheck them to have a clear sense of the substance to which they relate. Some drafters get carried away with the power to define and end up defining term after term.

In the realm of definitions, it is usually wise to try to be a minimalist, in other words, to try to convey everything you have to say clearly without using definitions at all. Then, if you discover that you do have some terms for which definitions will benefit the reader, try to put them in the sections where the terms are used. Then, finally, if you still end up with a definition section, it should have in it as few definitions as possible.

Drafting the definitions last can prevent two embarrassing problems:

- A term given one meaning in the definitions section and used with a different meaning later in the document.

- A term defined in the definitions section and never mentioned again.

Definitions do in fact serve the user very well if they have an appropriate purpose and if they are of the type appropriate to the purpose.

II. PURPOSES AND TYPES OF DEFINITIONS

A. LEXICAL DEFINITION

1. *Lexical Definition as Full Definition, Using "Means"*

Dictionary definitions are lexical. They describe accepted current usage; they do not prescribe rules for correct usage. Lexical definitions are full, not partial. If they are written out in sentence form, they say that the defined term *means* whatever the given definition says.

2. *Appropriate Lexical Definitions in Legal Documents*

In a legal document it is sometimes helpful to give a lexical definition of a technical term. In a consumer document, it is helpful to define a legal term of art.

3. *Inappropriate Lexical Definitions in Legal Documents*

Otherwise, there is generally no need to give lexical definitions in legal documents. If a reader is unfamiliar with the common meaning of a term, then that reader can consult a dictionary. Nonetheless needless lexical definitions do often appear in legal documents. For example, here is part of the definitions section of a zoning ordinance regulating commercial advertising:

> (4) *Sign* means any display of characters, letters, illustrations, or any ornamentation designed or used as an advertisement, announcement or to indicate direction.

*   *   *

> (6) *Temporary* sign means sign to be erected on a temporary basis, such as sign advertising the sale or rental of the premises on which located; sign advertising a subdivision of property; sign advertising construction actually being done on premises on which the sign is located; sign advertising future construction to be done on the premises on which located, and special event such as public meeting, sporting event, political campaign or event of a similar nature.

B. STIPULATIVE DEFINITION

1. Stipulative Definition as Full Definition, Using "Means"

a. Stipulating One of Several Lexical Definitions

A stipulative definition does not merely describe; it prescribes the meaning of a defined term as used within the scope of a specified document, part of a document, or set of documents. The power to stipulate meaning is significant among your powers as a drafter. When you stipulate, you demand that a document user accept the meaning you provide. Many words in common use have more than one lexical definition. The simplest form of stipulation is to restrict the range of lexical definition or single out one of multiple lexical definitions of a term.

Definitions Restricting the Lexical Range

"Writing" *means* writing in longhand.

"Conveyance" *means* a conveyance made before May 4, 1970.

"Department" *means* the Department of Natural Resources.

In each of these stipulations, the common (lexical) meaning does not change, and the definition only restricts the number of particulars to which it applies. In the three examples above, notice that the stipulation may restrict a little or a lot, even as far as having the term apply to only one particular as "Department" does here.

The restricting definition is most useful as a form of shorthand. If the only department mentioned in the document is the Department of Natural Resources, it is convenient to be able to refer to it throughout by the single word "Department." The restricting definition eliminates constant and lengthy repetition.

In some respects, the restricting definition is a variation on the process of providing short forms for references to parties in the introductory clauses of pleadings and contracts. Put another way, those introductory clauses stipulate definitions for the short forms they provide, the parties' full names being the definitions.

b. Naming Concepts: Creating the Defined Term Instead of the Definition

The process of defining terms is closely related to the process of conceptualizing. The client brings you a welter of particulars and either no concept at all or poorly conceived concepts. You may increase your store of essential but chaotically disorganized facts by looking at the client's business records, assessing business risks, and trying to attend to all of the client's particular requests. As you try to bring order to the chaos, you are trying to reach an appropriate level of generalization. Put another way, you are looking for the lowest common denominator among the particulars. To find the concept best adapted to reach the desired result, you search for what Professor Irvin Rutter calls a "type fact," a generalization about the behavior of a kind of thing, as opposed to a "unique fact," which is a statement about a particular thing that happened.[1] The statements that lawyers produce as planners rely heavily on type facts, just as the statements we produce as litigators rely heavily on unique facts. In short, for the planner, type facts turn into concepts.[2]

To be manageable, concepts need names. When you name a concept, you create a defined term instead of a definition. This term is another helpful form of shorthand.

> * * * Take a statute which regulates physicians, hospitals and nursing homes which provide health care and are reimbursed by the government with respect to needy patients. Obviously, the statute will be referring repeatedly to these regulated persons and entities. How convenient to create a defined term like "Service Provider—any physician, hospital or nursing home which provides health care to needy patients and is reimbursed for the cost of such care under a program of the U.S. Government." * * * [T]his definition * * * illustrat[es] the economy to be achieved by thereafter providing merely that, "A Service Provider shall . . ." and "A Service Provider shall not . . ." and "This section shall not apply to a Service Provider who . . ." throughout the body of the statute.[3]

Creating a term to name a concept, or choosing an existing term for that purpose, takes some care. Practitioner Hollis T. Hurd uses the shorthand referent "employee" in the National Labor Relations Act to

1. Designing and Teaching the First-Degree Law Curriculum, 37 U.Cin.L.Rev. 9, 85 (1968).

2. See Dickerson, Toward a Legal Dialectic, 61 Ind.L.J. 315, 326–27 (1986).

3. H. Hurd, Writing for Lawyers 114 (1982). Copyright © 1982 by Hollis T. Hurd; published by Journal Broadcasting & Communications, P.O. Box 3084, Pittsburgh, Pa. 15230. Reprinted by permission of the author.

show what can go wrong if the term chosen has a load of baggage that we would rather not bring along.

   * * * The Act protects various types of activity by employees, among them strikes. Clearly there is a recurring necessity to refer to these protected individuals, and the Act naturally refers to them as "employees," who are defined as including individuals whose work has ceased as a consequence of a current labor dispute. Now take a striker: the company is operating the plant and the striker refuses to come to work. Shouldn't that be regarded as a quit, just the same as when an employee voluntarily chooses to stay home for any other reason? Or, at the very least, shouldn't such absence justify the employer in discharging him and thus terminating the employer-employee relationship? You would think so, but the drafters of the NLRA have seduced all its readers by the choice of the defined term "employee".

   As for a striker, the NLRA provides that he is entitled in some circumstances to receive his job back when the strike ends and in other circumstances merely to stand at the top of the list of applicants for future openings. That is the basic protection which the Act affords to a striker. However, this protected individual is always called an "employee" in the Act, and this has led to the startling conclusion, which is now widely held, that a company cannot discharge a striker, nor has a striker quit. We know this because strikers are "employees."

   We wouldn't have this problem if the Act called these people "Protected Individuals." That title would make clear that such individuals have only the protection afforded by the Act and, while preferential re-hire may be one of them, continuous employment status is not. Or the defined term could be anything else, like "Martians" or "Yellow Vegetables." The whole point of defined terms is that, like symbols in algebra, they stand for something else; they have no intrinsic meaning. The NLRA intends only to say that people who can be described as members of this particular class with these characteristics (i.e., they used to be employees but went on strike) have certain rights. Any name would do, since it would serve only to incorporate the definition by reference.

   But noooo! They had to choose the word "employee", and now most everyone thinks that strikers are still employees, as required by the Act. Strikers are "Protected Individuals"; they are not necessarily employees. Tempest in a teapot? Well, how about all the employee benefit plans of the company which, by their terms, cover "employees". Do strikers get continued free medical care, free life insurance, service credit toward pensions, and even vacations? And if they do, what incentive will there be to settle the strike? A poor choice of words can be very expensive indeed.

   So, as a reader, always treat defined terms as merely incorporating their definitions by reference. In your mind, expand the document by adding back in all the redundancy which the defined terms removed.

That is the only way to assure that you will not be seduced by the terms.

And as a writer, consider very carefully whether the obvious and natural choice for a defined term really fits in with your thesis in the document. If not, choose one that does. * * *[4]

Practitioner Hurd suggests, not entirely facetiously, that it would be smart to create nonsense words as concept names to avoid other meanings creeping in.[5]

———

Exercise 10.1

Evaluate "Extortion by Theft" as the name chosen for the concept that is the subject of the statute below.

SECTION 4. Extortion by Theft of Agricultural Products

It shall be unlawful for any person to obstruct, retard, prevent, delay or otherwise interfere with the production, transportation, shipment, delivery, purchase, sale, barter or marketing of any perishable agricultural or dairy product, or to cause the transportation, shipment, delivery, purchase, sale, barter or marketing of any perishable agricultural or dairy product to be obstructed, retarded, prevented, delayed or otherwise interfered with, by coercing, threatening, intimidating, or attempting to coerce, threaten or intimidate any person who owns, grows, produces, buys, sells, barters or markets any such product, or who is engaged in the transportation, delivery, shipment or marketing of any such product, for the purpose of inducing, extorting or compelling such person to join any organization, or to contribute money, services or any other thing of value to such organization or to any person or persons whomsoever, or to contribute money or other thing of value to any person or persons on the condition, express or implied, that the production, transportation, shipment, delivery, marketing, purchase, sale or barter of such product will not be obstructed, retarded, prevented, delayed or otherwise interfered with. Any person who shall violate any of the provisions of this act shall be deemed guilty of a felony and upon conviction thereof shall be fined in any sum not exceeding one thousand dollars ($1,000) and imprisoned for a period of not less than one (1) nor more than five (5) years.

———

Gaining insight into "type facts" can lead to changing the general terms that name concepts. Changing existing conceptual names can have far reaching legal consequences, however. Consider what happened at the University of California at Berkeley when the University announced a plan to reclassify all its various graduate student teaching positions under the single general title: "graduate student instructor."

---

4. Id. at 115–17. Reprinted by permission of the author.

5. Presentation for Southeastern Paralegal Institute (June 5, 1991).

Before the reclassification in July 1985, there had been three classifications: "teaching assistant," "teaching associate" and "acting instructor." The acting instructors had received higher pay than those in the other classifications. Their status had also enabled them to teach beyond the four years to which other graduate students were limited. The additional teaching years were critical to a student working on a Ph.D. These benefits disappeared with the reclassification. However, it appeared to the graduate students that the main purpose for the reclassification was to defeat their attempt to unionize. The University wanted to regard them as teacher trainees rather than employees and thus ineligible to bargain.[6]

In short, concepts—and the terms that name them—can be used as tools to achieve a particular legal result; they can also spark a legal battle.

2. *Partial Definitions*

a. *Enlarging Definitions*

In an enlarging definition, the common meaning changes to add to the number of particulars to which the term applies. Enlarging definitions use the verb "includes." They also serve as a form of shorthand.

Appropriate Enlarging Definitions

"Mortgage" *includes* deed of trust.

"House" *includes* the lot on which it stands.

If an enlarging definition goes too far, it strains the reader's willingness to accept the stipulation. You have the power to order a reader to accept your definition, but if you contradict ordinary use too much, the reader may have trouble following your orders. "Few principles of legal drafting call for more scrupulous adherence than the principle that a term should not be defined in a sense that significantly conflicts with the way it would normally be understood in that context by the legislative audience to whom the law is primarily addressed."[7]

The principle is rooted in human psychology. No matter how explicitly you stipulate, a reader cannot easily substitute a new set of connotations for very different ones that automatically come to mind. Professor Dickerson illustrates by asking us to contemplate what would happen if a mathematics professor suddenly asked the class to assume that "two" meant "four" and "four" meant "eight." The student asked

6. For an account of the Berkeley students' charges of unfair labor practices filed with the California Public Employment Relations Board, see Berkeley Graduate Students Protest Job Reclassification, Chron. of Higher Educ., Oct. 2, 1985, at 27, 30. For a report of the Administrative Law Judge's ruling in the graduate students' favor, see Cal. Graduate Students Eligible for Bargaining, Chron. of Higher Educ., Mar. 4, 1987, at 2; but see Graduate Students Strike Over Union at Berkeley, Chron. of Higher Educ., May 10, 1989, at A2 (reporting that the Public Employment Relations Board ruled the graduate students ineligible to bargain).

7. R. Dickerson, Legislative Drafting 90–91 (1954). Copyright © 1954 by Reed Dickerson; published by Little, Brown & Co. Reprinted by permission of the author.

to recite multiplication tables would encounter terrible psychic contortions.[8] There is no good reason to impose such difficulty on the users of documents.

Strained Enlarging Definitions

"Automobile" includes all motor vehicles with four or more wheels.

"Bicycle" includes every vehicle propelled solely by human power.

In other words, a tractor-trailer rig is an automobile, and a unicycle is a bicycle.

These definitions appear in the definitions section of the Traffic and Parking Rules and Regulations for a university campus. The definitions also illustrate another common error in the use of "includes." They do not just enlarge the lexical definition. They present lexical definition plus enlarged definition. In other words, they are full definitions, and as such, they should use the verb "means," not "includes." For example, a passenger car is commonly understood to be an automobile. That is a lexical definition. There is no need in a legal document to give such a definition. Yet, as a motor vehicle with four wheels, the passenger car is made part of the Traffic and Parking definition.

If you wanted to enlarge the definition of "automobile" to include eight-passenger vans, or even tractor-trailers, the definition should state that "automobile" includes vans and tractor-trailers; it should not use language conveying the lexical definition as well. Adding the lexical definition defeats the purpose of using the enlarging definition as a form of shorthand.

On the other hand, drafters misuse "includes" so often, giving lexical definition along with the enlargement, that some argue that to leave lexical definition out is to leave the door open to a reader in bad faith who insists that an unmentioned part of a definition is an excluded part.

Exercise 10.2

Below are definitions from legislation for the protection of coastal zones. Evaluate them as enlarging definitions. Do they appropriately use "includes"? To what extent, if any, do they strain ordinary understanding and connotations? How well does "nonhabitable major structure" work as a created defined term?

>   (a) "Major structure" includes houses, mobile homes, apartment buildings, condominiums, motels, hotels, restaurants, towers, other types of residential, commercial, or public buildings, and other construction having the potential for substantial impact on coastal zones.

* * *

---

8. Id. at 90.

(c) "Nonhabitable major structure" means swimming pools; parking garages; pipelines; piers; canals, lakes, ditches, drainage structures, and other water retention structures; water and sewage treatment plants; electrical power plants and all related structures or facilities, transmission lines, distribution lines, transformer pads, vaults, and substations; roads, bridges, streets, and highways; and underground storage tanks.

If a drafter tries to force a strained definition on a consumer in a standardized form contract, there is increasing danger that the courts will not honor it. This is in part the result of a theory of contract, expressly adopted in several jurisdictions and implicitly accepted in others,[9] to the effect that "contract" means the parties' reasonable expectations regardless of what the document says that purports to manifest mutual assent. This theory is largely a response to the growing use of standardized forms. It assumes that the consumer does not read the document before becoming bound, which is probably true in many instances and certainly true in regard to insurance policies sent to the insured after they purchase insurance.[10]

If the meaning of the contract exists in spite of what the document says, then does it not matter what you write down? Yes, it does matter. The reasonable expectation theory probably applies less strictly to contracts that are not standardized forms and to contracts between businesses rather than adhesion contracts. In any event, to the extent that the reasonable expectation theory applies at all, you should be particularly careful not to attempt to impose strained definitions. Here is a case in point.

An insurance company issued a policy entitled, "BROAD FORM STOREKEEPERS POLICY" and "MERCANTILE BURGLARY AND ROBBERY POLICY." The policy defined "burglary" as meaning a felonious entry leaving "visible marks" on "the exterior of the premises at the place of such entry." Based on this definition the insurance company denied a claim for a burglary during which the burglar left visible marks of forcible entry on interior doors but not on exterior ones.[11] The Iowa Supreme Court refused to apply the policy's definition, finding that it contradicted common understanding of burglary and thus contradicted the reasonable expectation of the insured. The policy had not been delivered until after the purchase, but the definition in it was nonetheless treated as unconscionable.[12]

9. See Slawson, The New Meaning of Contract: The Transformation of Contracts Law by Standard Forms, 46 U.Pa.L.Rev. 21, 30–31 (1984).

10. Id. at 26.

11. C & J Fertilizer, Inc. v. Allied Mutual Insurance Co., 227 N.W.2d 169, 171 (Iowa 1975).

12. Id. at 177, 178–79, 182. For a case in which judgment was for the insurance company on the same theory, see Farm Bureau Mutual Insurance Co. v. Sandbulte, 302 N.W.2d 104, 110–14 (Iowa 1981) (implied warranties, insured's reasonable expectations, and standard policy provisions found to be the same).

b. Confining Definitions

A confining definition deletes some of the particulars that are part of the common meaning. Confining definitions use the verb "does not include."

Appropriate Confining Definitions

"Faculty" *does not include* part-time faculty.

"Writing" *does not include* typewriting.

In some respects a confining definition may be regarded as a different way to accomplish the same result as a restricting definition.

Confining Definition

"Faculty" does not include part-time faculty.

Same Result Through Restricting Definition

"Faculty" means full-time faculty.

Confining Definition

"Writing" does not include typewriting.

Same Result Through Restricting Definition

"Writing" means handwriting.

The choice usually depends on which form produces the more concise statement and the preferred emphasis—on the positive or the negative, or on the expected or the unexpected.

3. Choosing Between Full and Partial Definition

Remember that partial definitions, both those stipulating that X *includes* Y and those stipulating that X *does not include* Y, can be valuable tools of shorthand. They eliminate the obligation to set forth in exhaustive terms every particular that comprises the full definition. In contrast, a full definition, stipulating that X *means* Y, carries a heavy obligation to be complete. If X means nothing else but Y, it also means every bit of Y. Furthermore, by implication, Y means nothing but X, and it also means every bit of X.

Inexperienced drafters are often drawn to the power of stipulating full definition. They pour out detail after detail, increasing the danger of leaving something out. They would do well to concentrate instead on the lighter burden of partial definition.

4. Combining Full and Partial Definition

a. Acceptable Practice: "Means" Definition Followed by "Includes" or "Does Not Include" Definition

Sometimes it is helpful after giving a full definition, using "means," to tack on a partial definition, using "includes" or "does not include," to emphasize something and to remove any doubt about the scope of the full definition. The combination is acceptable as long as the two parts of the definition do not contradict each other.

Acceptable Combination of Full and Partial Definitions

"Expressway" means the Cross–Town Expressway including related approaches, viaducts, bridges, interchange facilities, and service roads.

"Doctor" means any person who has been granted a doctoral degree but does not include a J.D.

b. Unacceptable Practice: "Means and Includes"

If a definition purports to say that a term both "means and includes" a definition, without giving the full definition before signaling the partial one, then it is a self-contradictory hybrid of restricting and enlarging.

Unacceptable Combination of Full and Partial Definitions

"Expressway" means and includes the Cross–Town Expressway, related approaches, viaducts, bridges, interchange facilities, and service roads.

Exercise 10.3

Evaluate the following combined full and partial definition. Do the two sentences contradict each other in any respect? Does the first sentence give an appropriate full definition? Does the second sentence give an appropriate partial definition?

"Tangible personal property" means personal property which may be seen, weighed, measured, felt, touched, or which is in any other manner perceptible to the senses. It also includes services and intangibles, including communications, laundry and related services, furnishing of accommodations and sales of electricity, the sale or use of which is subject to tax under this chapter and does not include stocks, notes, bonds, mortgages, or other evidences of debt.

III. METHODS OF DEFINING [13]

A. MORE PARTICULAR OR FAMILIAR TERMS

Define by equating the term with a more particular or more familiar term. For example:

---

13. For a comprehensive discussion of the various methods of defining along with particular uses and misuses of stipulative definitions, see R. Dick, Legal Drafting 73–82 (2d ed. 1985). For an abbreviated version of the same discussion and additional examples of all methods, see Younger, The Definitive Word on Definitions, 72 ABA J. 98 (1986).

"Reserved Area" means the kitchen, club room, and sitting room in the clubhouse building.

"Rate card values" means rate card values published by Standard Rate and Data Service, Inc.

"Good faith" means honesty in the transaction concerned.

B. DIVISIONS

Define by analyzing the term's divisions or sub-divisions. For example:

"Rental agreement" means any written agreement, or oral agreement if for less duration than one year, providing for use and occupancy of premises.

"Condominium" means that form of ownership of condominium property under which units of improvements are subject to ownership by one or more owners, and there is appurtenant to each unit, as part thereof, an undivided share in the common elements.

C. LARGER CATEGORIES

Define by establishing the term's referent as part of some larger thing or category. For example:

"Common elements" means the portion of the condominium property not included in the units.

"Assessment" means a share of the funds required for the payment of common expenses which, from time to time, are assessed against the unit owner.

D. LIST OF REFERENTS

Define by listing the term's referents. For example:

"Institutional First Mortgagee" means a bank, savings and loan association, insurance company, mortgage company, real estate investment trust or other construction lender, or individual mortgage lender authorized to do business in the State of _____.

"Deposit money" means any money held by the landlord on behalf of the tenant, including, but not limited to, damage deposit, security deposit, advance rent deposit, pet deposit, or any contractual deposit agreed to between landlord and tenant either in writing or orally.

————

IV. CONVENTIONS REGARDING THE FORM OF DEFINITIONS

A. INTRODUCING DEFINITIONS

If you have a definitions section and you wish to begin the section with an introductory clause, say in the present tense that the definitions "apply" or the terms "mean" whatever you say they do. Avoid the falsely imperative statement that terms "shall mean."

B. ORDER

If you have a single definition to put in a section of substantive text where it applies, put the definition at the beginning. If you have a definitions section, put that at the beginning of the document. Put a list of definitions in alphabetical order, not in the order in which the terms come up in the document or in any other order.

C. FORM FOR DEFINED TERM

It is important to make a defined term stand out as such in the sentence giving its definition. The most common convention for doing this is to put a defined term in quotation marks. Some drafters prefer italics, underlining, bold type, or all-capital letters. A related device is to present all defined terms in the same emphasized form whenever they occur throughout the document to signal the document user that definitions of these terms appear in the definitions section. This device is a variation on the practice of putting parties' names in all-capital letters throughout pleadings. If you use this device, you need to restrict your use of whatever form you choose to this one purpose. For example, it will not work if you use italics throughout the text to signal defined terms but also use italics for emphasis or for foreign words.

It is conventional to define words in the singular, not in the plural.

V. RULES BURIED IN DEFINITIONS

A. RESULTING PROBLEMS

Drafters who get carried away with drafting definitions often allow substantive rules to creep into the definitions. Two problems result. One is that the rules are of no use in defining the terms. The other is that the rules themselves become difficult to locate because they are out of their normal place. Rules buried in a definitions section may be seldom invoked—or followed. Here are purported definitions illustrating how a definition can go astray. Note that it is a sign of trouble when a new sentence begins in the midst of a definition.

B. EXAMPLES

1. Definition of "Wine"

(1) "Wine" means all beverages made from fresh fruits, berries, or grapes, either by natural fermentation or by natural fermentation with brandy added, in the manner required by the laws and regulations of the United States, and includes all sparkling wines, champagnes, combination of the aforesaid beverages, vermouths, and like products. Sugar, flavors, and coloring materials may be added to wine to make it conform to the consumer's taste, except that the ultimate flavor or the color of the product may not be altered to imitate a beverage other than wine or to change the character of the wine.

(2) "Fortified wine" means all wines containing more than 14 percent of alcohol by weight.

2. Definition of "Retail Sale"

(3)(a) "Retail sale" or a "sale at retail" means a sale to a consumer or to any person for any purpose other than for resale in the form of tangible personal property and includes all such transactions that may be made in lieu of retail sales or sales at retail. A resale must be in strict compliance with the rules and regulations, and any dealer making a sale for resale which is not in strict compliance with the rules and regulations shall himself be liable for and pay the tax. A dealer may, through the informal protest provided for in s. 213.21 and the rules of the Department of Revenue, provide the department with evidence of the exempt status of a sale. The department shall adopt rules to implement this act which shall provide that valid resale certificates and consumer certificates of exemption executed by those dealers or exempt entities which were registered with the department at the time of sales shall be accepted by the department when submitted during the protest period but shall not be accepted in any proceeding under chapter 120 or any circuit court action instituted under chapter 72.

Exercise 10.4

The following definition sections come from a variety of documents. Evaluate them according to the principles discussed in this chapter.

Document 1. Declaration of Condominium

1 DEFINITIONS: As used in this Declaration of Condominium
2 and By–Laws and Exhibits attached hereto, and all Amendments
3 thereof, unless the context otherwise requires, the following defini-
4 tions shall prevail:

5   A. Declaration, or Declaration of Condominium, or Enabling
6 Declaration, means this instrument as it may be from time to time
7 amended.

8   B.   Association, means the _____ non-profit corporation
9   whose name appears at the end of this Declaration as "Association",
10 said Association being the entity responsible for the operation of
11 said Condominium.

12   C.   By–Laws, means the By–Laws of the Association specified
13 above, as they exist from time to time.

14   D.   Common Elements, means the portion of the Condominium
15 property not included in the Units.

16   E.   Limited Common Elements, means and includes those com-
17 mon elements which are reserved for the use of a certain unit or
18 units, to the exclusion of all other units.

19   F.   Condominium, means that form of ownership of condomini-
20 um property under which units of improvements are subject to
21 ownership by one or more owners, and there is appurtenant to each
22 unit, as part thereof, an undivided share in the common elements.

23   G.   Condominium Act, means and refers to the Condominium
24 Act of the State of _____.

25   H.   Common Expenses, mean the expenses for which the unit
26 owners are liable to the Association.

27   I.   Common Surplus, means the excess of all receipts of the
28 Association from this condominium, including, but not limited to,
29 assessments, rents, profits, and revenues on account of the common
30 elements, over and above the amount of common expenses of this
31 condominium.

32   J.   Condominium property, means and includes the land in a
33 condominium, whether or not contiguous, and all improvements
34 thereon, and all easements and rights appurtenant thereto, intend-
35 ed for use in connection with the condominium.

36   K.   Assessment, means a share of the funds required for the
37 payment of common expenses which, from time to time, are assessed
38 against the unit owner.

39   L.   Condominium Parcel or Parcel means a unit, together with
40 the undivided share in the common elements which are appurte-
41 nant to the unit.

42   M.   Condominium Unit, or Unit, is a unit as defined in the
43 Condominium Act, referring herein to each of the separate and
44 identified units delineated in the survey attached to the Declaration
45 as Exhibit "1", and when the context permits, the condominium
46 parcel includes such unit, including its share of the common ele-
47 ments appurtenant thereto. The physical boundaries of each unit
48 are as delineated in the survey aforedescribed, and are as more
49 particularly described in Article III and Article XIX.B. of this
50 Declaration.

51   N. Unit Owner, or Group of Unit Owners, or Owner of a Unit,
52 or Parcel Owner, means the owner or group of owners of a single
53 condominium parcel.

54   O. Developer, means the _____ corporation whose name
55 appears at the end of this Declaration as "Developer", its successors
56 and assigns.

57   P. Institutional First Mortgagee, means a bank, savings and
58 loan association, insurance company, mortgage company, a real
59 estate investment trust or other construction lender, or individual
60 mortgage lender authorized to do business in the State of _____.

61   Q. Occupant, means the person or persons, other than the unit
62 owner, in possession of a unit.

63   R. Condominium Documents, means this Declaration, the By-
64 Laws and all Exhibits annexed hereto, as the same may be amended
65 from time to time.

66   S. Unless the context otherwise requires, all other terms used
67 in this declaration shall be assumed to have the meaning attributed
68 to said term by Section 3 of the Condominium Act as of the date of
69 this Declaration.

Document 2. By-Laws of Condominium (Same Condominium as Document 1)

1   ARTICLE I

2   GENERAL

3   Section 3. <u>Definition</u>: As used herein, the term "corporation"
4 shall be the equivalent of "association" as defined in the Condomini-
5 um Declaration, and the words "property", "Unit owner", and
6 "condominium" are defined as set forth in the Condominium Decla-
7 ration, etc., of the corporation, to which these By-Laws are at-
8 tached.

*　*　*

9   ARTICLE IV

10   MEMBERSHIP

11   Section 1. <u>Definition</u>: Each parcel (apartment) owner shall be
12 a member of the corporation, and membership in the corporation
13 shall be limited to owners of condominium parcels.

*　*　*

14   ARTICLE VI

15   NOTICES

16   Section 1. <u>Definition</u>: Whenever under the provisions of the
17 statutes or of the Certificate of Incorporation or of these By-Laws,
18 notice is required to be given to any director or member, it shall not

19 be construed to mean personal notice; but such notice may be given
20 in writing by mail, by depositing the same in a post office or letter
21 box in a postpaid, sealed envelope, addressed as appears on the
22 books of the corporation.

Document 3. Rules and Regulations of Condominium Association

1 15. PARKING AND TRAFFIC CONTROL

2   a) Parking and traffic control shall at all times be subject to
3 such rules and regulations as the Board of Governors may establish.

4   b) Definitions: For the purpose of these rules and regulations, a
5 private passenger automobile is an operable, self-propelled vehicle
6 which is designed primarily for the transportation of people, togeth-
7 er with ancillary provision for their baggage and parcels. A private
8 passenger automobile includes the vehicle known generally as the
9 station wagon. The definition excludes trucks, commercial vehicles,
10 vehicles carrying visible watercraft, or vehicles containing facilities
11 for sleeping, cooking or waste disposal.

* * *

12 16. RECREATIONAL FACILITIES

13   a) Definitions:

14   i) "Recreational Facilities" as used herein means the
15   entire area lying between the northwesterly side of the
16   tennis court (projected) and the two creeks (_____
17   and _____), including structures and improvements
18   thereon.

19   ii) "Swimming Pool" includes the aprons and contiguous
20   paved areas, and the Shuffleboard Court and the Play-
21   ground.

22   iii) "Clubhouse" means the building housing the club facil-
23   ities and porches, balconies, patios and paved areas
24   adjacent thereto (excluding the Swimming Pool).

25   iv) "Reserved Area" means the kitchen, Club Room and
26   the Sitting Room in the Clubhouse building. The Pool
27   Room and the entire Health Club area are specifically
28   excluded from the "Reserved Area".

29   v) The arts and crafts facilities in Condominium Building
30   No. II are not included in Recreational Facilities for
31   the purpose of this Rule No. 16 only.

32   vi) A "house guest" is an invitee to a condominium unit
33   whose stay is temporary but includes staying over-
34   night. A "party guest" is an invitee to a social or
35   entertainment event in the Reserved Area. A "guest"

36   is an invitee of a condominium unit resident who is not
37   a party guest or a house guest.

38   vii) For the purpose of these rules an "outside organiza-
39   tion" or "outside organized group" is an aggregation of
40   persons, a majority of whom are not residents of
41   _____ Condominium, who associate together on spe-
42   cific occasions under a common name such as, but not
43   limited to, "club", "association", "society", "fellow-
44   ship", "auxiliary", "fraternity", "sorority" or word of
45   similar import.

Document 4. Law School Faculty Handbook

1 4.2 Appointments, Faculty

2 Definitions

3   For the purpose of participating in the governance of the
4 College of Law by attending and voting at faculty meetings,
5 "faculty" means those persons whose primary function is teaching
6 and research and who hold the rank of professor, associate professor
7 or assistant professor and includes the dean, associate dean, assis-
8 tant dean and persons holding similar administrative positions if
9 they also hold professorial rank but does not include the assistant to
10 the dean, persons holding the rank of instructor or any interim rank
11 or a member of the library staff, whether engaged in teaching or
12 not, except that the law librarian by action of the faculty may be a
13 member of the faculty. Persons serving in the College of Law with
14 professorial rank as visitors, or holding an interim instructional
15 rank, or otherwise directly engaged in the instructional program,
16 are invited and encouraged to attend faculty meetings but are not
17 eligible to vote.

Document 5. Automobile Rental Agreement

1   PAGE ONE (REVERSE SIDE)

2   _____ RENTAL AGREEMENT

3 1. DEFINITIONS

4 This is an **Agreement** between you and the Company to rent to you
5 a motor **Vehicle** ("car") (including tires, tools, accessories and
6 equipment).

7   The **Vehicle** is described on Page 2 (front side).

8   The rentor (lessor) is called the **Company** and is identified in
9 the upper lefthand corner on Page 2.

10   The renter (lessee) is you (sometimes called the **Customer**) and
11 you also are identified on Page 2. You must sign this Agreement.

12 An Authorized Driver is you (the Customer) and/or an addition-
13 al Authorized Driver who has been approved in writing by the
14 Company and has signed his or her name at the time of rental in
15 Area 87 on page 2 of this agreement. The only other Authorized
16 Driver is a person who has your permission to use the Vehicle, but
17 that person must have a valid drivers license and be at least 18
18 years old. Some locations require that he or she must be 21 or 25
19 years old (check this with the location where you rent the car). In
20 addition, such person must be a member of your immediate family
21 who permanently resides in your household or must be your busi-
22 ness associate (for example, partner, employer, employee or fellow
23 employee) and be driving the Vehicle for customary business pur-
24 poses. Customer agrees not to permit use of Vehicle by any other
25 person without obtaining the prior written consent of Company.

Document 6. Residential Lease

1 G. Our office hours are from 10:00 A.M.–12:00 noon and 1:00–5:00
2   P.M. Monday thru Friday; after hours we will respond only to
3   emergencies.

4   The definition of an emergency is basically as follows:

5   "An emergency is one that if not followed thru promptly will
6   result in severe damage to your unit." We will also consider as
7   emergency calls those items which will make it prohibitive for
8   you to occupy your unit such as a heater breakdown in 35
9   degree weather, water leaks, power failure as a result of compo-
10   nents in your units, or any acts of God such as storm, fire, etc.

Exercise 10.5

Evaluate the definitions section of Ordinance No. 82–19, the swimming pool barrier ordinance that is presented at p. 182.

Exercise 10.6

Evaluate the definitions section of Ordinance 84–10, the false
alarm ordinance that is presented at p. 185.

VI. CHECKLIST FOR DRAFTING DEFINITIONS

1. Do you try to have as few definitions as possible rather than as
many as possible?

2. Do you have a definitions section only to define terms used in
more than one other section of a document?

3. Do you keep all rules and other substance out of definitions, so that definitions do absolutely nothing but define terms?

4. Do you introduce a definitions section by reciting that the given definitions "apply" or words "mean," avoiding the false imperative statement that definitions "shall apply" or words "shall mean"?

5. In a definitions section do you put defined words in alphabetical order?

6. Do you put each definition ahead of the first use of the defined term, whether you collect definitions in a definitions section or put them within individual sections where defined terms are used?

7. Do you use some device such as quotation marks or all-capital letters to set off defined terms from the rest of the text? Do you then avoid using that same device for other purposes as well?

8. Do you provide lexical definitions only of technical terms, terms of art that users of the document might not know, or terms with multiple common meanings from which you choose one?

9. When you provide a definition using "means," is it full, not partial?

10. When you provide a definition using "includes," is it partial, not full?

11. When you create a term to name a concept or serve as a shorthand referent for a number of particulars, do you choose a term that does not have other inconsistent meanings firmly attached to it?

12. Do you avoid definitions that strain common meanings?

13. Do you avoid "means and includes"?

14. Do you use each defined term consistently with your definition throughout?

15. Do you use every term you have defined?

Chapter 11

MAKING STYLISTIC CHOICES

Table of Sections

I. THE CHALLENGE TO REMAIN INCOGNITO

In E.B. White's famous essay on style in the little book that is generally referred to as "Strunk and White," he writes of style "in the sense of what is distinguished and distinguishing. * * * When we speak of Fitzgerald's style," White writes, "we don't mean his command of the relative pronoun, we mean the sound his words make on paper. Every writer, by the way he uses the language, reveals something of his spirit, his habits, his capacities, his bias. * * * No writer long remains incognito." [1]

Like White's comments, most comments about style are subjective. Someone has a bold style; someone else has a turgid style. Style is flashy or tangled or refreshing. It is long-winded and pompous, or it is breezy or matter-of-fact. To characterize a novel in such terms is one thing. It is quite another thing to determine standards for appropriate style in drafting a contract or a will. If White is right about writers not being able to remain incognito, his words issue a challenge to legal

---

1. W. Strunk, Jr. and E. White, The
Elements of Style 66–67 (3d ed. 1979).

drafters, whose personality and beliefs have no business in legal documents.

II. CONSISTENCY

A. THE CUMULATIVE EFFECT OF MANY PARTICULARS

Consistency is the stylistic principle most highly valued in drafting legal documents. To some extent it does not matter what conventions you adopt as long as you observe them consistently. If there is anything that characterizes the style of a well drafted legal document, it is that the drafter always says the same thing the same way and different things differently. Improving style, therefore, amounts to attending consistently to a whole collection of particulars that merit attention throughout any legal document.[2]

> * * * It is only the cumulative effect of a large number of minor changes which can bring about a major improvement. In this respect, the analogy to streamlining is close. In the process of streamlining a locomotive, probably the removal of no single protuberance or angle would produce a perceptible difference in the operation of the train. The removal of fifty does.[3]

B. PARALLEL STRUCTURE

1. Parallel Sentence Structure

Parallel ideas belong in parallel structures whenever possible. The consistency in structure helps a reader recognize the relationship in the substance. For example, compare the following two sentences:

Sentence With Parallel Objects

Seller will pay for inspection, repairs, and painting.

Same Substance Without Parallel Objects

Seller will pay for repairs, the bill for painting, and getting an exterminator to inspect for termites.

Here are two more sentences for comparison:

Sentence With Parallel Verb Phrases

The applicant shall obtain an application form from Room 250, fill it out, have his or her signature notarized, and file the completed form with the clerk in Room 254.

---

2. For further discussion of style in specific contexts, see I. Alterman, Plain and Accurate Style in Court Papers (1987); C. Felsenfeld and A. Siegel, Writing Contracts in Plain English (1981); W. Statsky, Legislative Analysis and Drafting, (2d ed. 1984). On legal style generally, see B. Garner, The Elements of Legal Style (1991).

3. Cavers, The Simplification of Government Regulations, 8 Fed.B.J. 339, 345 (1947).

Same Substance Without Parallel Verb Phrases

The applicant shall obtain an application form from Room 250 and fill it out, remembering that the signature must be notarized, and all completed applications must be filed with the clerk in Room 254.

The recommended parallel structures reinforce substance. In the first example, the series of objects ("inspection," "repairs," and "painting") makes it easy to see at a glance that the seller will pay for three things. In the second example, the series of verbs ("obtain," "fill out," "have notarized," and "file") makes it easy to see that the application process has four steps.

2. *Normalized Form*

When there are several items in a parallel series, especially if they are parallel conditions and parallel results, it is helpful to number or letter the items and thus to use consistency of form even more bluntly to reinforce substance. The next step is to indent the numbered or lettered items. If the process is rigorous enough, the material becomes normalized. The manner of presentation may aid the reader even further by capitalizing "IF," "AND," "THEN," etc., a convention among many users of normalization.[4] For example, compare the following four versions of a statute.

A. Pure paragraph form

If a certificate of need for commitment to care and treatment as a patient or resident is authorized or required to be made by a physician, psychologist, or other professional under this title, and it is made by such a professional who is the spouse, parent, grandparent, brother, sister, child, aunt, uncle, nephew, or niece of the individual who is the subject of the petition, application or certificate, or it is made by a professional who has an ownership interest in a private facility in which the individual is to be detained, then it shall not be considered under this title.

B. Paragraph form with item labeling and without item indentation

If (1) a certificate of need for commitment to care and treatment as a patient or resident is authorized or required to be made by a physician, psychologist, or other professional under this title, and (2)(A) it is made by such a professional who is the spouse, parent, grandparent, brother, sister, child, aunt, uncle, nephew, or niece of the individual who is the subject of the petition, application or certificate, or (B) it is made by a professional who has an

---

4. Letter from Grayfred B. Gray to this author (Aug. 26, 1991).

ownership interest in a private facility in which the individual is to be detained, then it shall not be considered under this title.

C. Normalized form without full item indentation

IF

(1) A certificate of need for commitment to care and treatment as a patient or resident is authorized or required to be made by a physician, psychologist, or other professional under this title, AND

(2)(A) It is made by such a professional who is the spouse, parent, grandparent, brother, sister, child, aunt, uncle, nephew, or niece of the individual who is the subject of the petition, application or certificate, OR

(B) It is made by a professional who has an ownership interest in a private facility in which the individual is to be detained,
THEN

(3) It shall not be considered under this title.

D. Normalized form with full item indentation

IF

(1) A certificate of need for commitment to care and treatment as a patient or resident is authorized or required to be made by a physician, psychologist, or other professional under this title, AND

(2)(A) It is made by such a professional who is the spouse, parent, grandparent, brother, sister, child, aunt, uncle, nephew, or niece of the individual who is the subject of the petition, application or certificate, OR

(B) It is made by a professional who has an ownership interest in a private facility in which the individual is to be detained,

THEN

(3) It shall not be considered under this title.[5]

---

3. The Decision Tree

A decision tree[6] first reduces conditions and results into a consistently phrased series of "yes" or "no" questions and answers. The

5. Gray, Reducing Unintended Ambiguity in Statutes: An Introduction to Normalization of Statutory Drafting, 54 Tenn. L.Rev. 433, 452–53 (1987) (footnote omitted). The full text of this article appears at 54 Tennessee Law Review 433 (1987) and is reprinted by permission of the Tennessee Law Review Association, Inc.

6. See Benson, Up a Statute with Gun and Camera: Isolating Linguistic and Logical Structures in the Analysis of Legislative Language, 8 Seton Hall Legis.J. 279, 296–300 (1984).

decision tree can be a useful tool for presenting complex rules in some contexts. An accurate and complete decision tree makes a provision easy for a reader to follow, but it is not always easy to produce. It involves three stages:

(a) Divide the material into as many discrete propositions as you can.

(b) Divide each proposition into an assertion and its negation, in order to make the list exhaustive and the propositions mutually exclusive.

(c) Put the propositions into a logical sequence.[7] They should move from general to specific subject matter so that the first question produces an immediate result in as many cases as possible, and each successive question moves to a lower common denominator, producing a result for fewer cases.[8]

To illustrate, here is a provision in a homeowner's insurance policy and the same provision presented in a decision tree (Figure 1).[9]

This policy insures against direct loss to the property covered by the following perils:

1. Fire or Lightning, excluding loss resulting from electrical injury or disturbance to electrical appliances, devices, fixtures or wiring caused by electrical currents artificially generated, unless fire ensues, and then only for the loss caused by such ensuing fire.

The decision tree is also useful as a device for assessing the over-all conceptual scheme of a provision. If the provision is irrational or arbitrary or if there is a gap in its coverage, the decision tree is likely to reveal the problem.[10] The decision tree can also be adapted to produce and fill out standard forms through computer programs.[11]

---

7. Wason, The Drafting of Rules, 118 (Part 1) New L.J. 548, 549 (1968).

8. Benson, above note 6, at 298.

9. Id. at 297, 298. Reprinted with permission from Seton Hall Legislative Journal Vol. 8 (1984), pp. 297, 298. Copyright © 1984 by Seton Hall Legislative Journal. All rights reserved.

10. Fitzgerald and Spratt, Rule Drafting—I, 119 (Part 2) New L.J. 991, 992 (1969).

11. For an example of the transformation of a tax statute into a computer program for computing individuals' tax liability, see Fitzgerald and Spratt, Rule Drafting—III, 119 (Part 2) New L.J. 1052, 1052–54 (1969).

Figure 1

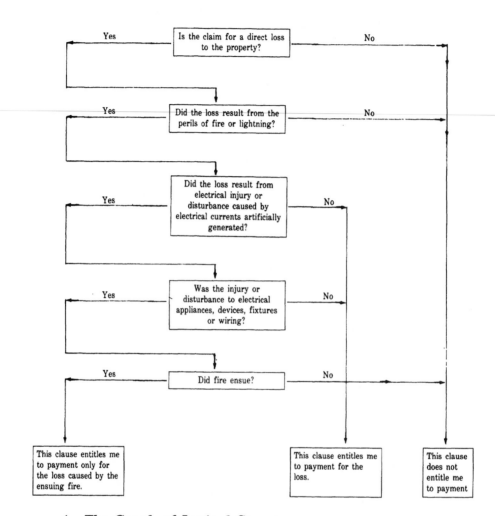

4. The Graph of Logical Structure

The graph of logical structure [12] is a variation on a decision tree. Instead of focusing on "yes" and "no" questions, the graph focuses on the logical relationships expressed by "if" (conditions), "then" (results), "and" (cumulatives), "or" (alternatives), and "but" (exceptions). To illustrate, here is a provision about retirement pensions, a representation of it through a decision tree (Figure 2), and a graph of its logical structure (Figure 3).[13]

The earliest age at which a woman can draw a retirement pension is 60. On her own insurance she can get a pension when she reaches that age, if she has then retired from regular employment. Otherwise she has to wait until she retires or reaches age

12. See Benson, above note 6, at 301–05.   13. Wason, above note 7, at 548. Copyright © 1968 by New Law Journal. Reprinted by permission of the publisher.

65. At age 65 pensions can be paid irrespective of retirement. On her husband's insurance, however, she cannot get a pension, even though she is over 60, until he has reached age 65 and retired from regular employment, or until he is 70 if he does not retire before reaching that age.

Figure 2

MARRIED WOMAN'S (FLAT RATE) RETIREMENT PENSION			
1. I am under 60	Yes	..	.. NO PENSION
	No	..	.. read Q.2
2. I am claiming	(a) on own insurance		.. read Q.3
	(b) on husband's insurance		.. read Q.5
3. I am under 65	Yes	..	.. read Q.4
	No	..	.. PENSION
4. I am working	Yes	..	.. NO PENSION
	No	..	.. PENSION
5. my husband's age is	(a) less than 65		.. NO PENSION
	(b) between 65 and 69		.. read Q.6
	(c) 70 or more		.. PENSION
6. my husband has retired	Yes	..	.. PENSION
	No	..	.. NO PENSION

Decision trees and graphs may be too schematic to serve as the sole method of presenting contractual and legislative provisions. It would be difficult, for instance, to quote part of a graph, and legal documents need to be easily quoted with precise reference given. On the other hand, in informal settings, users may benefit from the presentation of rules and regulations in tree or graph form.

One study compared a group of people who read a complex set of regulations in its original textual form and another group who read the regulations in the form of a decision tree. The group who used the decision tree solved problems according to the regulations in hypothetical cases faster and more accurately than the other group. They also made more favorable comments about the regulations.[14]

Decision trees and graphs are especially helpful for document users who want to find the answer to a particular problem. They can quickly rule out the details and alternatives that do not apply, and they need not try to keep in mind all the answers to earlier questions as they move down the tree or graph.[15]

14. Id. at 549.

15. Fitzgerald and Spratt, above note 10, at 991.

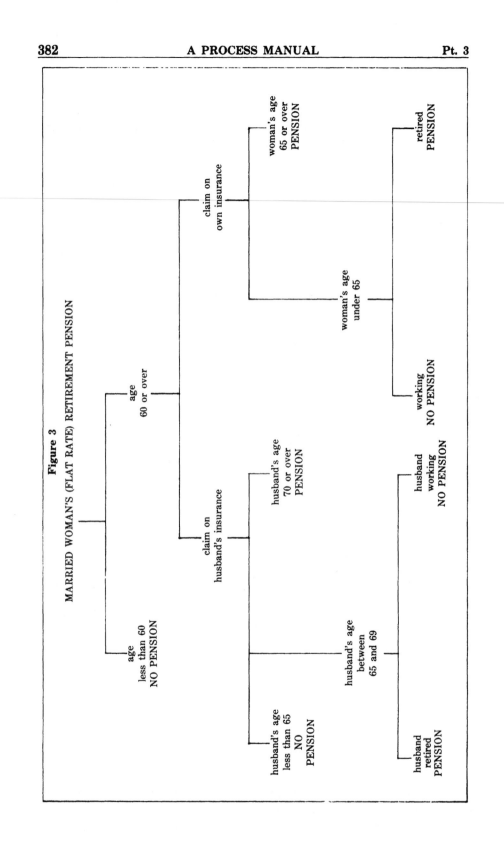

Figure 3

MARRIED WOMAN'S (FLAT RATE) RETIREMENT PENSION

C. TENSE

1. *Present Tense*

It is advisable to draft policy statements, conditions, and recitals as well as descriptions in a consistent present tense sequence. This is because of the convention that documents "speak constantly." In other words, they "speak" when they are used rather than when they are drafted.

Policy Statements in the Present Tense

Unless one party gives the other party written notice of intent to terminate this agreement 30 days before the end of the term, this agreement renews itself from month to month.

If any provision in this agreement is held invalid, the remaining provisions continue in effect.

Many drafters violate the present tense convention, drafting policy statements in the future tense by mistake.

Mistaken Use of Future Tense for Policy Statements

Unless one party shall give notice, this agreement shall renew itself.

If any provision shall be held invalid, the remaining provisions shall continue in effect.

Sometimes, in a mistaken zeal for precision, drafters make things even worse by using the future perfect tense.

Mistaken Use of Future Perfect Tense

Unless one party shall have been given notice. . . . If any provision shall have been held invalid. . . .

2. *Past and Present Perfect Tenses*

Occasionally it is acceptable when stating conditions to use the past tense or the present perfect tense.

Condition Stated in the Past Tense

If a person other than the landlord repaired the damage, the landlord is not responsible for the quality of the work.

Condition Stated in the Present Perfect Tense

If the premises have been condemned, this agreement terminates.

However, since documents "speak constantly," these conditions could just as well be expressed in the present tense.

3. *Future Tense*

The future tense is appropriate to express duties with respect to future conduct that are either imposed by some form of legislation or accepted by agreement. "Shall" expresses orders. "May" expresses discretionary authority. "Will" expresses agreement.

Order in Statute

The landlord *shall* provide locks and keys.

Assertion of Discretionary Authority in Contract

The landlord *may* enter and repossess the premises upon termination of this contract.

Agreement in Contract

The tenant *will* keep the premises in good repair.

Many consumer contracts, drafted by the more powerful party, read more like statutes than contracts. They recite what the seller, lender, or landlord *will* do, but they order what the buyer, borrower, or tenant *shall* do. As consumer law imposes more plain language requirements on contracts, there is more pressure to produce contracts that read like agreements instead of rule books.

D. SINGULAR AND PLURAL

It is conventional to use the singular consistently, even when the sense is plural. For example, it is conventionally understood that the singular reference to "tenant" throughout a lease applies to all the tenants if more than one are parties to the lease.

Singular Reference for Possibly Plural Referents

The tenant is responsible for any minor repair.

Using a consistent singular is helpful to avoid some ambiguities that the plural can produce.

Ambiguous Plural

Applicants shall file their forms before January 1.

Does one applicant have more than one form to file? If the number of forms per applicant is not at issue, it may be preferable to make a generic statement about forms without reference to applicants at all.

Generic Solutions

Forms are due before January 1.

December 31 is the deadline for filing forms.

On the other hand, using the plural in reference to people is one convenient way to avoid the problems involved in using gender-specific pronouns.

E. NUMBERS

A drafter needs a consistent approach to presenting numbers: words, figures, or a combination of words and figures, as in "forty-seven dollars ($47)." Some drafters regard the combination as a useful safeguard against being harmed by a typographical error in figures, since such errors are easy to overlook in proofreading. If there is a conflict between the words and the figures, it is usually understood that the words prevail.[16]

The most common approach to numbers is to use words for numbers one through nine and figures for 10 and higher numbers. However, when 2 or more numbers appear in the same sentence, 1 of which is 10 or higher, figures are commonly used for all of the numbers. This approach, of course, does not address the problem of potential typographical errors. It is conventional in any approach to use words for any number that begins a sentence.

It is also conventional to use figures for the following: dates ("January 4"), time ("4 p.m."), measurements ("6 miles"), amounts of money ("$17"), and percentages ("3 percent" or "3%").

III. BREVITY

A. NEEDLESS ELABORATION

"Wordiness is a natural enemy of clarity * * *."[17] This is not to say that the shorter sentence is always the clearer one. If it takes more words to make a complicated concept clear, then clarity justifies the added words. However, lawyers are more often inclined to be too wordy than too brief.

One of the most common forms of wordiness peculiar to legal documents is elaboration of details with no particular legal significance. Here is a discussion of how various consumer forms were streamlined by eliminating needless detail.

C. FELSENFELD AND A. SIEGEL, WRITING CONTRACTS IN PLAIN ENGLISH
118–19, 121–23 (1981).*

The unsimplified model forms contain many examples of unnecessary elaboration. For instance, the old loan note refers to amounts that are unpaid "for a period in excess of 10 days." The new note uses the shorter but equally informative "more than 10 days."

Consider also the old note's description of debts that are covered by the collateral security. The security first applies to the loan that is covered by the note. The note calls this "the indebtedness of the undersigned hereunder." In the new note, it is called "this * * * debt."

---

16. For a tongue-in-cheek view of one who believes that such careful people are actually taking the whole business (or themselves) too seriously, see Vanneman, Jr., Blame It All On O.P.E.C.? 65 ABA J. 1266 (1979).

17. Siegel, To Lift the Curse of Legalese—Simplify, Simplify, 14 Across the Board 64, 70 (No. 6, June 1977).

The same security also covers the borrower's other debts to the bank. The old note calls them

> all other indebtedness or liabilities of the undersigned to the bank, whether joint, several, absolute, contingent, secured, unsecured, matured or unmatured, under any present or future note or contract or agreement with the bank.

The new note just refers to "any other debt."

> The old note starts listing default events with these words:

> In the event of default in the payment of this or any other Obligation or the performance or observance of any term or covenant contained herein or in any note or other contract or agreement * * *

A less verbose substitute (the concept not being carried into the new note) might be this: "If I break any promise to you * * *."

Both the old and new notes list various remedies that the bank will have if the borrower defaults. In general, these exist as a matter of law. There is therefore no requirement that they be catalogued in an agreement. While special consequences of a default, or special remedies—particularly "specific performance" of an obligation [73]—can be important in special cases, this consumer loan note involves none of them. The old note is being verbose when it describes the bank's legal rights upon the borrower's default by saying:

> * * * the Bank shall have the right to exercise all the rights and remedies available to a secured party upon default under the Uniform Commercial Code (the "Code") in effect in New York at the time, and such other rights and remedies as may otherwise be provided by law.

The bank enjoys those enforcement rights whether or not they are mentioned in the note.[74] So the only apparent reason for this language is to inform the borrower. But what does the consumer borrower know of rights and remedies under the Code and other laws? The words are meaningless to the very audience to whom they are addressed. The new note eliminates this unjustifiable elaboration by saying:

> You will also have other legal rights, for instance, the right to repossess, sell and apply security to the payments under this note and any other debts I may then owe you.

In the old note, the bank has the right upon default "to declare all or any part of the Obligations to be immediately due and payable, whereupon such Obligations shall become and be immediately due and payable." That language vibrates with importance. But it lacks legal significance. If the bank can declare the debts due, of course they *become* due; otherwise the declaration should not be there in the first place. The new note cuts through the pomposity and says: "You can then demand immediate payment of the balance * * *".

---

73. See *Williston on Contracts,* Third Ed., Sec. 1423 B. fn. 4.

74. The ability to resort to collateral under the Code and also sue on the debt are permitted by Section 9–504 of the Code. Section 9–501 makes it clear that a secured party enjoys those rights even if they are not enumerated in the contract.

Here is another passage from the bank loan note where familiar, concrete words were used to supplant windy jargon:

Old	New
Acceptance by the Bank of payments in arrears shall not constitute a waiver of or otherwise affect any acceleration of payment hereunder or other right or remedy exercisable hereunder.	You can accept late payments or partial payments, even though marked "payment in full", without losing any of your rights under this note.

Obviously, the traditional legal skills must be used to ensure that meaningful protection is not lost in the cause of simplification. Much elaboration may be meaningless. On the other hand, some words with the appearance of dross may be significant. Research must often precede the correct choice. The cooperative apartment sale contract is designed to bind both the seller and the buyer, one to sell and the other to buy. To accomplish this, the earlier text explicitly covered both sides of the transaction: "Seller agrees to sell and transfer and Purchaser agrees to buy the * * *". Is this cumbersome construction essential to the desired result? If it merely reads "Seller agrees to sell the * * *", is the buyer contractually bound to buy? * * *

* * *

* * * A reformation of the sentence can explicitly bind seller and buyer. Some creativity in writing achieves both clarity of language and legal specificity. While one continues to question the specific inclusion of both seller and buyer as a legal necessity, the solution eliminates any doubt that might result from a "Seller will sell the * * *" approach.

The old cooperative apartment sale contract, derived as it is from musty real estate forms, buries simple thoughts beneath needless elaboration. Paragraph 6, for example, begins:

> This sale is subject to the approval of the directors or shareholders of the Corporation as provided in the Lease or the corporate bylaws.

This sentence serves a much smaller purpose than the number of words would indicate. Who is to approve the sale—the directors or the shareholders? Is the underlying requirement in the lease or the bylaws? The buyer cannot tell. More important, even if these questions were answered they would not help the buyer understand or complete the transaction. If the granting of approval is a routine formality, it requires less elaboration than this; if it's more than routine, it requires more detail. Strictly speaking, this is a matter of choosing content, not just language. But it shows how a drafter who sought to be thorough has only been elaborate. In contrast, the new version says that: " * * * the Corporation must also give its approval."

Paragraph 16 of the old cooperative sale agreement illustrates another kind of elaboration:

All representations, understandings and agreements had between the parties with respect to the subject matter of this agreement are merged in this agreement which alone fully and completely expresses their agreement.

Compare this with the new version, which cuts through the elaboration. In the paragraph titled "Complete Agreement," it says: "Both parties agree that this contract sets forth all of their understandings." We discuss "word strings" below, but it is worth noting here that a traditional word string, "representations, understandings and agreements," has been replaced by a single word—"understandings"—which carries the intended meaning.

Here are more illustrations of needlessly elaborate language, and their plain English counterparts, from the old and new insurance policies.

BEFORE

This Policy shall not apply with respect to coverage

* * *

(e) to personal injury or property damage with respect to which an Insured under this Policy is also an Insured under a nuclear energy liability policy issued by Nuclear Energy Liability Insurance Association, Mutual Atomic Energy Liability Underwriters or Nuclear Insurance Association of Canada, or would be an Insured under any such Policy but for its termination upon exhaustion of its limit of liability.

AFTER

3. We won't cover any liability connected with a nuclear energy incident that's covered by one of the specialized nuclear energy insurance groups. Or would've been covered if the insurance liability limit hadn't been used up.

BEFORE

In the event that any provision of this policy is unenforceable by the Insured under the laws of any State or other jurisdiction wherein it is claimed that the Insured is liable for any injury covered hereby, because of non-compliance with any statute thereof, then this policy shall be enforceable by the Insured with the same effect as if it complied with such statute.

AFTER

If any of the terms of this policy should conflict with state or local law, you can enforce them as if they'd been changed to conform.

As these examples show, attempts to make a sentence all-inclusive only make it harder to understand. This form of verbosity creates another problem as well, by destroying the connective links between sentences. The result appears to be a list of separate, independent sentences, rather than a natural discourse in which each sentence builds on the one before and flows into the one that follows. Where the sentences in a text are not strongly linked, the whole text becomes difficult to follow:

BEFORE

Cancellation

This Policy may be cancelled by the Named Insured by surrender thereof to the Company or any of its authorized agents, or by mailing to the Company written notice stating when thereafter such cancellation shall be effective. This Policy may be cancelled by the Company by mailing to the Named Insured at the address shown in this Policy written notice stating when, not less than thirty (30) days thereafter, such cancellation shall be effective. The mailing of notice as aforesaid shall be sufficient notice and the effective date of cancellation stated in the notice shall become the end of the policy period. Delivery of such written notice either by the Named Insured or by the Company shall be equivalent to mailing. If the Named Insured cancels, earned premium shall be computed in accordance with the customary short rate table and procedure. If the Company cancels, earned premium shall be computed pro rata. Premium adjustment may be made at the time cancellation is effected or as soon as practicable thereafter. The check of the Company or its representative, mailed or delivered, shall be sufficient tender of any refund due the Named Insured. If this contract insures more than one Named Insured, cancellation may be effected by the first of such Named Insured for the account of all the Named Insureds: notice of cancellation by the Company to such first Named Insured shall be deemed notice to all Insureds and payment of any unearned premium to such first Named Insured shall be for the account of all interests therein.

AFTER

Can This Policy Be Cancelled?

Yes it can. Both by you and by us.

If you want to cancel the policy, hand or send your cancellation notice to us or our authorized agent. Or mail us a written notice with the date when you want the policy cancelled. We'll send you a check for the unearned premium, figured by the short rate table—that is, pro rata minus a service charge.

If we decide to cancel the policy, we'll mail or deliver to you a cancellation notice effective after at least 30 days. As soon as we can, we'll send you a check for the unearned premium, figured pro rata.

B. NEEDLESS SYNONYMS

The other most common form of wordiness in legal documents is the needless synonym, as in "authorize and empower" or "rest, residue, and remainder." The old habit of using synonyms may have had sensible beginnings when legal documents in English had to be understood by people who spoke Anglo–Saxon and others who spoke French or Latin. Also, when scriveners were paid by the word, some of them may have added words on their own initiative. However, the synonym habit has hung on long after any rationale has disappeared. Today it is usually enough to pick one term, probably the most familiar or legally significant, and then use it consistently. Here are Felsenfeld and Siegel on the subject of strings of synonyms in the Citibank forms:

C. FELSENFELD AND A. SIEGEL, WRITING CONTRACTS IN PLAIN ENGLISH
124–26 (1981).*

Consider some of the word strings in the old bank promissory note and their treatment in the new version. Note that writing in a simpler manner often involves a new approach to the subject matter and not merely the elimination of words or the substitution of more familiar words. Sentences can be restructured entirely to read better. Generalizations can be made specific. Ideas scattered about the agreement can be brought together. Unnecessary substantive provisions can be dropped altogether.

For example, the old note, in providing for a late charge on installments in default, uses the essentially unnecessary string to describe them:

due and remaining unpaid.

The revised version refers to the:

overdue instalment.

As another example, the old note holds the defaulting borrower obligated to pay the lender's:

costs and expenses.

The newer note reflects a combined legal, business, and language decision. Instead of generalizing and creating an open-ended world of "costs and expenses" to be paid for by the consumer, the new note establishes realistic events in advance. It refers specifically to:

attorney's fees * * * and court costs.

Many other word strings appear in the old bank promissory note. The new one handles them in a variety of ways. For some, the unnecessary verbosity was eliminated:

Old	New
• indebtedness or liabilities (of the undersigned to the bank)	• debt (to you)
• shall have made and is hereby granted (a security interest)	• give (you what is known as a security interest)
• in and to	• in
• then and in any such event (describing the consequences of a default)	• you can then

- due and payable
- rights and remedies

- immediate payment of the balance
- legal rights

For other word strings in the old note, the substantive content was eliminated, or the provisions were rewritten in an entirely new way. The old word strings in this category include:

- any and all
- performance or observance
- term or covenant
- contract or agreement

- evidencing or relating to
- nature or description
- fact or notice

Here are some additional word strings and their alternatives as they appear in the old and new versions of the cooperative apartment sale agreement:

Old	New
• sell and transfer (Par. 1)	• this sale
• represents, warrants and covenants (Par. 4)	• assures
• right and power (Par. 4(a))	• has the right
• full force and effect (Par. 4(e))	• in effect
• representations, understandings and agreements (Par. 16)	• understandings
• changed, discharged or terminated (Par. 17)	• to change this contract, or to cancel it completely
• cease and terminate (Par. 18)	• be considered cancelled

Other strings in the old agreement that were not specifically replaced in the new are:

- right, title and interest (Par. 2)
- in and to (Par. 2)
- terms, covenants and conditions (Par. 7)
- rules and regulations (Par. 7)
- cancel and terminate (Par. 13)
- fair and reasonable (Par. 15)
- obligation and liability (Par. 18)

The words in each string obviously do not have the same meaning. In many cases, such as *evidencing or relating to* and *in and to,* the differences are substantial. The drafter's job is to decide whether the several meanings are needed, in context, to accomplish the purpose of the contract.

C. LEGALESE

Wordy legal documents are often stuffed with words like "aforesaid," "hereinbefore," "witnesseth," and "to wit." The drafters of these documents are usually especially enamored of "said" as in: "I bequeath to my said wife all my said personal effects." In his Persuasive Writing column in the ABA Journal, Professor Irving Younger had this to say about legalese: "These are show-off words. Anyone who uses them wants the world to see that it's a lawyer talking, for only lawyers use these words. There's no need to remind the world that you're a lawyer * * *." [18]

The beginnings of documents are especially vulnerable to legalese. Opening boilerplate full of legalese hangs on out of tradition rather than legal necessity.[19] Perhaps this is so because getting started is often the hardest part of drafting a document and drafters borrow legalese from old forms just to get underway.

IV. NOUNS AND VERBS

A. NOMINALIZATIONS

Professor Joseph M. Williams devotes considerable attention in his book on style to what he calls "nominalizations": nouns that have been derived from verbs or adjectives,[20] such as "rejection" and "violation" or "adjustment" and "alignment." Using nominalizations is not in itself a stylistic blunder. However, many sentences full of nominalizations produce a heavy, turgid style. Professor Williams uses the following sentences to illustrate the problem:

Sentence Relying on Nominalizations

The claimant's *testimony* was that there was no medical *treatment* from July 27 until his *consultation* with a doctor on December 12.

Same Substance Presented Through Verbs

The claimant *testified* that he was not medically *treated* from July 27 until he *consulted* a doctor on December 12.

The first sentence is heavy with nouns that focus on abstractions rather than human beings. No human being is doing anything in that sentence. In the second sentence, the claimant comes to life. He acts and is acted upon.

Sentence Relying on Nominalizations

Your *compliance* with this provision is mandatory and *failure* to provide S with *proof* that such *insurance* is in effect constitutes *violation* of the Contract.

Same Substance Presented Through Verbs

You *must comply* with this provision. If you *do not prove* to S that you *are insured,* you *will violate* the Contract.

18. Symptoms of Bad Writing, 72 ABA J. 113 (May 1, 1986).

19. For demonstration of how to convert to simpler beginnings with valid effect, see Kirk, Legal Drafting: How Should a Document Begin? 3 Tex.Tech L.Rev. 233, 233–38, 247–63 (1972).

20. Style: Ten Lessons in Clarity and Grace 11–20 (2d ed. 1985).

Sentences describing human beings in action make documents easier to follow, just as they make any writing more interesting to read.[21]

B. ACTIVE AND PASSIVE VERBS

Many books about writing exhort writers to use active verbs instead of passive ones. Generally that is good advice.

Sentence with Generally Preferred Active Verb

The insured shall give notice to the insurer within 90 days.

Sentence with Passive Verb

The insured shall be given notice within 90 days.

In the second sentence, the actor is not mentioned at all. In some sentences using passive verbs, the actor is relegated to the lesser status of an object.

Sentence with Passive Verb and Actor as Object

The insurer shall be given notice by the insured.

When you want to impose an affirmative duty on a person or class of persons, then the passive does not serve you well.

Sentences with Passive Verbs That Fail to Impose a Duty

All work shall be carried on with all possible speed.

All work shall be handled through the contractor's office.

These are the kinds of sentence that give passive verbs a bad name.

Another reason to prefer active verbs is that they take fewer words than passive verbs; therefore, writing with active verbs produces more energetic, fast-paced prose.

Sometimes, however, passive verbs are useful. For example, if there is some reason not to spell out who is responsible for something, then the passive verb serves well.

Sentence Using Passive Verb on Purpose To Focus on Concept

The notice shall be filed within 30 days.

Policy statements may purposely focus on abstract concepts rather than people doing things. It is possible to argue that the passive verb produces a false imperative even though the sentence is grammatically acceptable. Most people would agree, however, that the sentence does not direct the notice to do anything.[22] There is no particular reason to recast the sentence so that the person filing the notice manages to get into it as its subject. In short, passive verbs are not automatically inferior to active verbs.

---

21. J. Williams, The Dispositive Edge: Inventing Responsibility (July 19, 1986) (presentation at Conference of The Legal Writing Institute).

22. But see Kirk, Legal Drafting: Some Elements of Technique, 4 Tex.Tech L.Rev. 297, 311–12 (1973).

Exercise 11.1

Figure 4 [23] is a survey on language preferences that was sent to lawyers and judges in several states. Determine what your preferences are and why.

V. GENDER–NEUTRAL LANGUAGE

A. PROBLEMS CAUSED BY GENDER–SPECIFIC LANGUAGE

Gender-neutrality has received detailed coverage in much of the recent writing by experts on legal drafting.[24] They recognize the difficulties of avoiding gender-specific pronouns altogether, but they also take seriously the attempt to remove sexual bias and its appearance from legal documents. Most understand that even though it may be technically "correct" to use the word "man" to refer to both sexes, it is also true that when someone uses "man" as a generic term, the reader or listener is likely to visualize or think of a man.[25]

Moreover, legal classifications that use gender-specific words such as "he" and "man" always refer to men but may or may not refer to women.

Sentence with Ambiguous Masculine Pronoun

A person is eligible if he is married and over the age of 18.

Such ambiguous classifications, especially in statutes, have produced enough legal problems to warrant finding a more effective solution than boilerplate gender-construction provisions [26] to the effect that masculine pronouns include the feminine.[27]

23. Child, Language Preferences of Judges and Lawyers: A Florida Survey, Feb. 1990 Fla.B.J. 32, 33 (quoting Harrington and Kimble, Survey: Plain English Wins Every Which Way, 66 Mich.B.J. 1024, 1024 (1987)). Copyright 1990 by the Florida Bar. Reprinted by permission of the publisher.

24. See R. Dickerson, The Fundamentals of Legal Drafting 221–39 (2d ed. 1986); Felsenfeld and Siegel, above note 2, at 139–41; D. Mellinkoff, Legal Writing: Sense and Nonsense 47–51 (1982); Bagin, Are All Men Equal: The "Generic" Dilemma, Simply Stated 1 (No. 62, Jan. 1986) (Document Design Center newsletter); Romm, Avoiding Sexist Language, Quaint and Otherwise, 71 ABA J. 126 (May 1985).

25. For a detailed study of the ramifications of this process, see C. Miller and K. Swift, Words and Women (1976). For discussion in a legal context, see Collins, Language, History, and the Legal Process: A Profile of the "Reasonable Man," 8 Rut.–Cam.L.J. 311 (1977). For a study of how assumptions about the sexes affect thinking as well as writing, see Hofstadter, Metamagical Themas, 247 Scientific American 18 (Nov. 1982). For a full-length study of linguistic sexism in scholarly and professional writing as well as suggestions about nondiscriminatory usage, see F. Frank and P. Treichler, Language, Gender, and Professional Writing: Theoretical Approaches and Guidelines for Nonsexist Usage (1989).

26. See Comment, Sexism in the Statutes: Identifying and Solving the Problem of Ambiguous Gender Bias in Legal Writing, 32 Buffalo L.Rev. 559, citations throughout (1983).

27. See, e.g., 1 U.S.C. § 1.

Figure 4
Legal Language Survey

Below are paragraphs taken from legal documents. Please mark your preference for paragraph A or B in the space provided.

1. ___ A) Now comes the above named John Smith, plaintiff herein, by and through Darrow & Holmes, his attorneys of record, and shows unto this Honorable Court as follows:

   ___ B For his complaint, the plaintiff says:

2. ___ A) I received a completed copy of this note and disclosure statement before I signed the note.

   _____ Date _____

   ___ B) Maker(s) hereby acknowledge receipt of a completely filled in copy of this note and disclosure statement prior to execution hereof this ____ day of _____, 19__

3. ___ A) Petitioner's argument that exclusion of the press from the trial and subsequent suppression of the trial transcripts is, in effect, a prior restraint is contrary to the facts.

   ___ B) Petitioner argued that it is a prior restraint to exclude the press from the trial and later suppress the trial transcripts. This argument is contrary to the facts.

4. ___ A) One test that is helpful in determining whether or not a person was negligent is to ask and answer whether or not, if a person of ordinary prudence had been in the same situation and possessed of the same knowledge, he would have foreseen or anticipated that someone might have been injured by or as result of his action or inaction. If such a result from certain conduct would be foreseeable by a person of ordinary prudence with like knowledge and in like situation, and if the conduct reasonably could be avoidable, then not to avoid it would be negligence.

   ___ B) To decide whether the defendant was negligent, there is a test you can use. Consider how a reasonable careful person would have acted in the same situation. To find the defendant negligent, you would have to answer "yes" to the following two questions:

   (1) Would a reasonably careful person have realized in advance that someone might be injured by the defendant's conduct?

   (2) Could a reasonably careful person have avoided behaving as the defendant did?

   If your answer to both of these questions is "yes," then the defendant was negligent. You can use the same test in deciding whether the plaintiff was negligent.

5. ___ A) The company will pay benefits only if the insured notifies the company of the loss.

   ___ B) Payment of benefits will not be made by the company if the insured fails to provide notification of the loss.

6. ___ A) If attorneys want to comment on the proposed change in court procedures, they may send comments in writing to the Clerk, 233 Main St., Gotham City, before Feb. 21, 1987.

   ___ B) Interested attorneys may, on or before February 20, 1987, submit to the Clerk, 233 Main St., Gotham City, written comments regarding the proposed change in court procedures.

B. AVOIDING SEXIST LANGUAGE GRACEFULLY

It is essential to find gender-neutral language that does not succumb to incorrect grammar, awkwardness, or simple nonsense. Professor Richard Wydick's practical advice is particularly attentive to these concerns.

The very first section of the United States Code says that: "words importing the masculine gender include the feminine as well." Women are tired of that, and legal writers can no longer get away with it.

Whatever your personal beliefs about the role of women in society, you should avoid sexist language for the same reason that you avoid other language quirks—if you use sexist language, you will distract a part of your audience. And you will distract another part of your audience if you resort to clumsy or artificial constructions when trying to avoid sexist language.

Avoiding sexism gracefully is no easy task. Here are four suggestions that may help:

1. *Expressions Implying Value Judgments*

First, don't use expressions that imply value judgments based on sex. (For example, *a manly effort,* or *a member of the gentle sex.*)

2. *Sex-neutral Terms*

Second, use sex-neutral terms where you can do so without artificiality. (For example, use *workers* instead of *workmen* and *reasonable person* instead of *reasonable man.* But don't concoct artificial terms like *waitpersons* to refer to servers in a restaurant.

3. *Parallel Construction*

Third, use parallel construction when you are referring to both sexes. (For example, *husbands and wives,* not *men and their wives,* or *President and Mrs. Kennedy,* not *President Kennedy and Jackie.*)

4. *Sex-based Pronouns*

Fourth, don't use sex-based pronouns when the referent may be of the opposite sex. For instance, don't use *he* every time you refer to judges. And don't use *she* either. The latter is just as distracting as the former. You can resort to the clumsy phrase *he or she* in moderation, but you can often avoid the need by using one of the following devices:

> Omit the pronoun: For example, instead of *"the average citizen enjoys his time on the jury,"* you can say *"the average citizen enjoys jury duty."*

> Use the second person instead of the third person: For example, instead of *"each juror must think for herself,"* you can say *"as a juror, you must think for yourself."*

> Use the plural instead of the singular: For example, instead of *"each juror believes that he has done something worthwhile,"* you can say *"all jurors believe that they have done something worthwhile."*

> Repeat the noun instead of using a pronoun: For example, instead of *"a juror's vote should reflect her own opinion,"* you can say *"a juror's vote should reflect that juror's own opinion."*

Alternate between masculine and feminine pronouns: For example, if you use *she* to refer to judges in one paragraph, use *he* to refer to lawyers in the next paragraph. Be aware that this device may look artificial, and that if you are careless you may perform a sex change on somebody in the middle of paragraph.

Use the passive voice: * * * use this device only in desperation.[28]

C. CRITICS OF GENDER–NEUTRAL LANGUAGE

The formerly favored view of "man" and masculine pronouns as generic terms for both sexes persists among some critics,[29] some of whom use sarcasm to express their position.

Mankind means *humankind; womankind* has a place in the language only when a limitation is intended. *Mankind* is the inclusive word, and everyone knows it; not even the nuttiest word-fixer has suggested its replacement by *personkind.* Nor is anyone offended, much less misled, by Darwin's title "The Descent Of Man" or by thousands of similar constructions.[30]

Some critics are merely reluctant to innovate.

If you can avoid using "he" to refer to people in general without contorting your sentences, that is all to the good. Do not forget, though, that as a draftsman your overriding objective is to express an idea as clearly and simply as you can, not to pursue a social ideology, no matter how lofty.

* * * Throughout this book I have referred to the "draftsman". I would be pleased to refer instead to the "drafter", except that a drafter is a horse. In a few years from now all new dictionaries may well include "draftsman" among the meanings of "drafter". Then I will use "drafter" instead of "draftsman". * * * [I]nnovation in devising new meanings for words is a flaw, not an asset in a draftsman. The analogy is to the "creative" clerk who finds hitherto unthought of locations in which to file documents. Certainty of meaning largely depends upon the draftsman's unbendingly conservative use of language.[31]

A year after that commentary was written, *Webster's New Collegiate Dictionary* listed "drafter" as the noun form of the verb "draft," one of the meanings of which is "to practice draftsmanship." [32]   The

---

28. Plain English for Lawyers 65–67 (2d ed. 1985) (footnotes omitted, headings supplied). Copyright © 1985 by Richard Wydick; published by Carolina Academic Press. Reprinted by permission of the author.

29. E.g., Strunk and White, above note 1, at 60–61.

30. Friendly, Language and the Wopersons' Movement, Washington Post, May 2,

1978, at A19; see also Younger, The English Language Is Sex–Neutral, 72 ABA J. 89 (June 1, 1986).

31. D. Hirsch, Drafting Federal Law 31 (1980) (Dept. of Health & Human Services publication).

32. At 341–42 (1981).

language does change. The drafter's function may not be to innovate, but neither is it to lag behind.

——————

VI. PUNCTUATION

A. TREND TOWARDS LESS PUNCTUATION

In American writing generally, the trend is to use less punctuation, which chiefly means fewer commas. The saying goes, "When in doubt, leave it out." This trend has particular significance in legal drafting. Whenever someone's artless drafting leaves a provision ambiguous or misleading because of a missing or misplaced comma, a legal action may result.

Formerly, legislative bodies voted on legislation as it was read aloud to them. After the vote, a clerk wrote down the legislation and put punctuation marks into it. The punctuation marks were thought not to be part of the law, and the law was to be construed without reference to them.

Although legislative bodies now base their votes on written versions of bills, fully punctuated, the former practice suggests a good idea for a drafter. You do not want what you draft to end up in court because you depended on a comma or the absence of a comma to govern how a provision should be read. A sensible goal is to arrange the words so carefully that if a typist or printer inadvertently leaves out or puts in or moves a comma, the sense of what was intended will be so clear that no one will easily deny it. In short, it is wise to use as little punctuation as possible and to rely on it as little as possible to indicate meaning.

B. COMMA BEFORE LAST ITEM IN SERIES

In spite of the general trend toward less punctuation, it is a good idea to put a comma before the last item in a series—even though many people do not do so. The following sentence illustrates the point.

Ambiguous Sentence Without the Comma

Counsel of record are from the following firms: Smith, Jones, Randall and Perez and Lenberg.

Without a comma after "Randall" or after "Perez," it is impossible to know how many firms there are or who are in the same firm. One possibility is as follows:

(a) Smith,

(b) Jones,

(c) Randall and

(d) Perez and Lenberg.

The following reading is equally possible:

(a) Smith,

(b) Jones,

(c) Randall and Perez and

(d) Lenberg.

So is the following reading:

(a) Smith, Jones, Randall and Perez and

(b) Lenberg.

A comma after "Randall" would eliminate the ambiguity and clarify the firms as follows:

(a) Smith, Jones, Randall, and Perez and

(b) Lenberg.

A comma after "Perez" instead of after "Randall" would eliminate the ambiguity and clarify the firms as follows:

(a) Smith,

(b) Jones,

(c) Randall and Perez, and

(d) Lenberg.

Some drafters put a comma before the last item in a series only when there is a potential ambiguity; however, this approach requires stopping to assess every series you write and making a deliberate choice each time whether to punctuate. It is far easier—and safer—to make a habit of putting the comma before the last item in *every* series.

VII. GRAPHICS

A. GRAPHICS AND READABILITY

A reader responds to a document first in terms of how it looks on the page, regardless of what it says. Anyone who has encountered a page of solid small print knows that graphics have a great deal to do with readability. Several elements are worth attention for a readable style.

B. GRAPHIC ELEMENTS OF STYLE

1. *White Space*

White space makes the page easy on the reader's eye and so makes the reader more receptive to what the writing says. To have enough white space to make a page appealing to the eye, you need:

- Margins of at least one inch on all four sides.
- At least one or two paragraph breaks.
- The first line of each paragraph indented.

Some people rely on starting a new line to signal the beginning of a new paragraph. This reliance is a mistake because it leaves to chance whether a paragraph will end far enough from the right margin to make the paragraph break noticeable. The following two versions of two paragraphs demonstrate the point.

Hard-to-Read Paragraph Style Without Indenting

Some people mistakenly rely on starting a new line to signal a new paragraph. This sentence ends this paragraph.

This system leaves to chance whether a paragraph will end far enough from the right margin to make the paragraph break noticeable.

Safer Paragraph Style Using Indenting

Some people mistakenly rely on starting a new line to signal a new paragraph. This sentence ends this paragraph.

The indenting system does not leave to chance whether the end of each paragraph produces a noticeable paragraph break.

2. Headings

Headings do more than give information about the content of sections. They draw the reader's eye and signal divisions of the material. To function well graphically, headings need to be easily distinguishable both from the text and from each other. White space before and after headings helps. It also helps to use different placement, type size, and type style for different levels.

A system of distinctions helps readers almost subliminally. When we turn a page and encounter a heading somewhere in the middle of the next page, the type size and style help us get our bearings and know whether what follows the heading is a section, a subsection, or some smaller division of material.

Computers provide us more variety for heading styles than typewriters do, but underlining serves well enough in place of italics. To make headings function well graphically, you need:

- A clear distinction between all headings and text.

- A clear distinction among all levels of headings.

- A system of distinctions simple enough to keep the page from looking "busy."

3. Readable Type

Everybody knows the horror of trying to read the "small print." But it is not enough to have type large enough. Most typewriters and computers accommodate the eye with 10 or 12 point type, which are easy point sizes to read. In addition, for easily readable type, you need:

- Lines of a reasonable length.

- All-capital letters used sparingly.

- Serif rather than sans serif type. (This sentence is in sans serif type.)

Also, a ragged right margin may produce more readable type than a justified right margin if your computer justifies by varying greatly the spaces between words or between letters within words.[33]

Finally, of course, "draft" quality printing on a dot matrix printer or typing on a worn-out typewriter ribbon can discourage a reader as thoroughly as a solid block of small print.

VIII. THE PLAIN LANGUAGE MOVEMENT: SOME HISTORICAL NOTES

A. LEGISLATION: THE FIRST WAVE

The plain language movement grew out of the widespread public disenchantment with lawyers' pompous and often unintelligible style. Some people credit President Jimmy Carter with founding the movement in his famous executive order directing federal agencies to produce "simple and clear" regulations "understandable to those who must comply." [34]

However, earlier the plain language movement had focused on consumer contracts, not government documents. The leading federal legislation included the Truth in Lending Act of 1968 and the Magnuson–Moss Warranty Act of 1975. By the end of the 1970's, the first plain language legislation began to make its way through several state legislatures, beginning with New York's Sullivan Law.[35]

In general, plain language statutes that apply to consumer contracts, especially insurance contracts, regulate both language and format. The statutes are of three types: (1) those that prescribe subjective standards of audience understanding; (2) those that prescribe objective tests of the documents themselves; and (3) those that prescribe subjective standards with objective guidelines.

New York's law, for example, prescribes that every contract it monitors must be:

---

33. For further discussion of graphic design, see M. Mathewson, Verbatim, Nov. 1989 Student Lawyer 8; B. Felker, F. Pickering, V. Charrow, V. Holland, and J. Redish, Guidelines for Document Designers (1981).

34. Exec. Order No. 12,044, 43 Fed.Reg. 12,661 (1978).

35. N.Y. McKinney's Gen.Oblig.Law § 5–702 (1987).

1. Written in a clear and coherent manner using words with common and every day meanings;

2. Appropriately divided and captioned by its various sections.

At the other extreme are laws that present detailed tests by which to determine whether a given document meets the general standards. For objective tests, the lawmakers sometimes turn to readability tests, such as the Flesch Test,[36] that compute the average number of syllables per word and words per sentence.

B. CRITIQUES OF THE PLAIN LANGUAGE MOVEMENT

1. Critique by Affected Parties and Their Lawyers

When the first states began to pass plain language legislation, lawyers were critical, as were the corporations that were suddenly required to redraft all of their form contracts. Corporations complained that there was no way to ensure that a redrafted contract would be in compliance with the laws before the corporation put it into use. Some also expressed the fear that converting to plain language would make documents longer and thus actually discourage consumers from reading them.[37]

Lawyers feared the elimination of legal terms of art. They anticipated a mountain of litigation, although it did not materialize.[38]

2. Critique by Linguists

a. Readability Formulas

Linguist Veda Charrow criticizes readability formulas for not actually measuring comprehensibility.[39] In particular, she disapproves of Flesch's assumption that shorter words and sentences are more readable. She demonstrates her point with the following sentences:

Ten–Word Sentence With Nominalization

The happening of the accident creates a presumption of defendant's negligence.

Sixteen–Word Sentence With Strong Verbs

The very fact that the accident happened allows us to presume that the defendant was negligent.[40]

---

36. See R. Flesch, How to Write Plain English 24 (1979).

37. Browne, Development of the FNMA/FHLMC Plain Language Mortgage Documents—Some Useful Techniques, 14 Real Prop.Prob. & Tr.J. 696, 702–04 (1979).

38. See Block, Plain Language Laws: Promise v Performance, 62 Mich.B.J. 950, 950–51 (1983). Neither has broadly accepted plain language drafting in Canada led to litigation, according to R. Dick, Clear Language Drafting (Speech before the Canadian Institute for the Administration of Justice, Nov. 16, 1989), quoting Interim Report of the Joint Committee [of Can.Bar Assn. and Can.Bankers' Assn.] on Plain Language 11 (Can.Bar, Aug. 1989).

39. Let the Rewriter Beware 2–4 (1979) (Document Design Center pamphlet).

40. Id. at 5.

Although the Flesch Test would rate the first sentence more readable by virtue of its fewer words, it is probably less readable because it relies heavily on abstract nominalizations rather than strong verbs.

b. Mechanical Revisions

Charrow is critical of the mechanical revisions that Flesch and some other plain language proponents recommend. For example, she maintains that research shows that passive verbs make comprehension no more difficult than active verbs.[41]

She criticizes the plain language phenomenon known as "whiz deletion,"[42] which refers to removing relative pronouns and thus turning subordinate clauses into phrases. Removing the bracketed words in the following sentences would be "whiz" (for "wh___ is") deletion:

Deletion of "who is"

The tenant, [who is] planning to arrive at noon, called ahead.

Deletion of "which is"

This rule, [which is] explained in detail on page 2, takes effect immediately.

According to Charrow, the deletion makes sentences harder rather than easier to process.

c. Personalization

The other characteristic of plain language that has engendered considerable criticism is "personalization," which means using the personal pronouns "I" and "you" instead of referring to parties by their legal status, such as "mortgagor" and "mortgagee" or "lessor" and "lessee."

Professor Stephen Ross uses a prepayment clause to demonstrate the silly results that personalization can produce. It reads as follows:

> If I pay this loan off in full, ahead of schedule, I will not have to pay the full finance charge. I will pay a finance charge on the amount I have borrowed only for the number of days I have had the loan—from the day I received the loan until the day I pay off the loan.[43]

Professor Ross comments:

> * * * The consumer is referred to as "I" as if he were telling the Bank about rebates. Presumably it is the Bank that understands how rebates are computed. * * * The resulting tone is self-serving, like an advertisement in which a smiling consumer tells the bank how grateful he is that he will "not have to pay the full finance charge." This pretense that the consumer is writing to the bank may even be

---

41. V. Charrow, What Is "Plain English," Anyway? 4 (1979) (Document Design Center pamphlet).

42. Id. at 5.

43. On Legalities and Linguistics: Plain Language Legislation, 30 Buffalo L.Rev. 317, 347 (1981) (quoting National Bank of Washington form, quoted in Washington Post, Aug. 24, 1977, § D, at 1, col. 2).

deceptive, implying a comprehension on the consumer's part that he does not in fact possess.[44]

3. Critique by Reformers of Consumer Law

A different sort of criticism has come from those who seek to reform consumer law. They point out that a form may be simplified without offering any meaningful alternatives to a consumer who does not have bargaining power. Moreover, according to one critic, a major impediment to understanding contracts is that they overload consumers with information that consumers do not need at the point of entering a contract.[45] If this is true, then the way to make contracts more readable is not merely to simplify and explain concepts but to excise nonessentials altogether.[46]

4. Critique by Critical Legal Scholars

Critical legal scholars go a step further to argue that supposedly plain language only misleads nonlawyers into believing they understand a document even though they do not begin to understand its ramifications.[47] More broadly this is a critique of the plain language movement for its "apolitical quality." [48]

C. PUTTING THE CRITIQUES IN PERSPECTIVE

The main proposition of most of the critics is that readability, while valuable, should never be allowed to take priority over clarity and accuracy. Likewise, there has been general agreement that terms of art with legal consequences should not be eliminated, although in consumer documents extra effort should go into defining these terms.

Most critics take care to distinguish between the unworkable extremes advocated by some plain language proponents and the sensible reforms advocated by the movement generally. The scathing criticisms generally do not maintain this distinction and instead tar the whole movement with the same brush. For instance, one critic concludes that "much of the thinking behind the Plain English movement is naive, both about the complexities of language and about the extent to which linguistic reform can change sociolegal realities." [49] "The Underground Grammarian" criticizes with an even sharper tongue.

> There is, of course, an alternative to the plain English fad * * *. We could simply decide to educate all Americans to such a degree that they could read and understand even the OSHA definition of an exit * * *. Just think what happens in the mind of the person who

44. Id. at 348. Copyright © 1981 by Buffalo Law Review. Reprinted by permission of the Publisher.

45. Davis, Protecting Consumers from Overdisclosure and Gobbledygook: An Empirical Look at the Simplification of Consumer–Credit Contracts, 63 Va.L.Rev. 841, 855 (1977).

46. Id.

47. See Leskovac, Legal Writing and Plain English: Does Voice Matter? 38 Syracuse L.Rev. 1193, 1208–11 and sources cited (1987).

48. Id. at 1217.

49. Danet, Language in the Legal Process, 14 Law & Soc. 445, 490 (1980).

knows the difference between restrictive and nonrestrictive clauses. Anyone who understands that distinction is on the brink of seeing the difference between simple fact and elaborative detail and may well begin to make judgments about the logic of such relationships * * *. From that, it's not a long way to detecting non sequiturs and unstated premises and even false analogies.[50]

Doubtless there will always be those who suspect that all plain language advocates ultimately intend to produce legal documents readable by first graders.

D. EXPANDING REFORM

In spite of the critiques, the plain language movement has expanded. In fact, one explanation for the decline in introduction of new plain language legislation is the widespread voluntary reform,[51] including self-policing by industries,[52] organizations,[53] and individuals [54] has become widespread. The legal system has also gradually introduced more plain language, such as in model jury instructions [55] and required statements of clients' rights.[56]

Reform may be increasingly pervasive because plain language in large measure means writing well, and that means writing to be understood, which is not an especially controversial idea after all.

---

50. R. Mitchell, Less Than Words Can Say 153–54 (1979).

51. Felsenfeld, The Future of Plain English, 62 Mich.B.J. 942, 943 (1983) (article introducing symposium on plain language, including articles that survey its progress in consumer contracts, lawsuit papers, judicial opinions, legislative drafting, and legal education).

52. E.g., as early as 1979, 25 states had taken some action to achieve readable insurance policies. R. Pressman, Legislative and Regulatory Progress on the Readability of Insurance Policies 14 (1979) (Document Design Center pamphlet, crediting the strong unifying influence of the Nat. Assn. of Ins. Comm'rs for the remarkable speed and breadth of plain language reform in the insurance industry).

53. E.g., The Practising Law Institute sponsored seminars on plain language in 1979 and 1981, each with a course manual entitled Drafting Documents in Plain Lan-

guage; in 1983, the NLRB adopted a Style Manual encouraging plain language; the Economics of Law Practice Sec. of the ABA published an article to show lawyers how to draft bills in plain language (Morgan, How to Draft Bills Clients Rush to Pay, July/Aug. 1985 Legal Economics 22).

54. E.g., Carl Felsenfeld began his advocacy of plain language as a Vice President of Citibank. It was his voluntary conversion of the Citibank forms into plain language in 1975 that inspired N.Y.'s Sullivan Law. See Figure 1 at p. 139 and Figure 2 at p. 140, a loan note before and after conversion.

55. See, e.g., Committee on Model Jury Instructions, Ninth Circuit, Manual of Model Jury Instructions for the Ninth Circuit (1985 ed.).

56. See, e.g., Statement of Client's Rights, Rules Regulating the Fla. Bar, 494 S.2d 977, 1030–32 (1986).

IX. CHECKLIST FOR DRAFTING IN PLAIN LANGUAGE

Word Choice

1. Do you use words in common use as much as possible and legal terms of art only when necessary? In a consumer document, do you define terms of art that you use?

2. Do you avoid archaic terms such as "aforesaid," "hereinbefore," and "witnesseth?

3. Do you avoid "said" and "such" as articles?

4. Do you use "the" and other articles in common use rather than leaving out articles, saying, for example, "for *the* benefit of *the* beneficiary" rather than "for benefit of beneficiary"?

5. Do you avoid nominalizations (nouns constructed from verbs, usually ending in "tion" or "ment")?

6. Do you prefer active verbs and use passives only when on purpose you want focus on the object rather than the subject of the action?

7. Do you always use the same word to refer to the same thing and different words to refer to different things?

8. Do you prefer stating things positively? Do you especially avoid multiple negatives in the same sentence?

9. Do you avoid needless synonyms and other word strings?

10. Do you avoid needless detail that only gives the impression of precision?

Sentence Structure

11. Do you avoid convoluted sentence structure (though not necessarily avoiding long sentences as such)?

12. Do you take advantage of tabulated sentence structure to make a long sentence with complex material easier to follow?

13. Do you express parallel material in parallel structures?

Form of the Document

14. Do you aid a reader's access to a document through introductory material and through a table of contents for a long document?

15. Do you use enough division into sections and subsections, each with a heading, to make material easy to find?

16. Are your headings informative?

17. Do you number or letter all sections and subsections for easy reference?

18. Do you avoid excessive cross-references? When you do cross-reference, do you refer to substance as well as section number or letter?

19. Do you use a consistent scheme for treating matters of style such as numbers, punctuation, capitalizing (for example, in reference to "the plaintiff" and "the defendant" or "Plaintiff" and "Defendant"), and gender-neutral language?

Graphics

20. Do you use some variation in type size or style to make clear distinctions between headings and text, and between different levels of headings?

21. Is there enough white space on every page to make it easy on the eye?

22. Is the type big enough and dark enough to be easily readable? Is it serif rather than sans serif?

23. Do you avoid large blocks of all-capital letters?

Exercise 11.2

To review the principles of drafting style, compare the two documents below.

Note 1 is a Federal National Mortgage Association (FNMA, sometimes called Fannie Mae)/Federal Home Loan Mortgage Corporation (FHLMC, sometimes called Freddie Mac) Uniform Note adapted for use in New York in 1975. The original form was in type so small that it was nearly impossible to read.

Note 2 is the FNMA/FHLMC Uniform Multistate Fixed Rate Note dated 1983. The results of this conversion to plain language were so successful that the converted FNMA/FHLMC documents have been used as models by many other lenders.[57]

Note 1

US $_____   _____ New York
                                            City

_____, 19__

FOR VALUE RECEIVED, the undersigned ("Borrower") promise(s) to pay _____, or order, the principal sum of _____ Dollars, with interest on the unpaid principal balance from the date of this Note, until paid, at the rate of _____ percent per annum. Principal and interest shall be payable at _____, or such other place as the Note holder may designate, in consecutive monthly installments of _____ Dollars (US $_____), on the _____ day of each month beginning

---

57. See Browne, above note 39, at 698–704.

————, 19—. Such monthly installments shall continue until the entire indebtedness evidenced by this Note is fully paid, except that any remaining indebtedness, if not sooner paid, shall be due and payable on ————.

If any monthly installment under this Note is not paid when due and remains unpaid after a date specified by a notice to Borrower, the entire principal amount outstanding and accrued interest thereon shall at once become due and payable at the option of the Note holder. The date specified shall not be less than thirty days from the date such notice is mailed. The Note holder may exercise this option to accelerate during any default by Borrower regardless of any prior forbearance. If suit is brought to collect this Note, the Note holder shall be entitled to collect all reasonable costs and expenses of suit, including, but not limited to, reasonable attorney's fees.

Borrower shall pay to the Note holder a late charge of ———— percent of any monthly installment not received by the Note holder within ———— days after the installment is due.

Borrower may prepay the principal amount outstanding in whole or in part. The Note holder may require that any partial prepayments (i) be made on the date monthly installments are due and (ii) be in the amount of that part of one or more monthly installments which would be applicable to principal. Any partial prepayment shall be applied against the principal amount outstanding and shall not postpone the due date of any subsequent monthly installments or change the amount of such installments, unless the Note holder shall otherwise agree in writing. If, within twelve months from the date of this Note, Borrower make(s) any prepayments with money lent to Borrower by a lender other than the Note holder, Borrower shall pay the Note holder ———— percent of the amount by which the sum of prepayments made in such twelve month period exceeds twenty percent of the original principal amount of this Note.

Presentment, notice of dishonor, and protest are hereby waived by all makers, sureties, guarantors and endorsers, and shall be binding upon them and their successors and assigns.

Any notice to Borrower provided for in this Note shall be given by mailing such notice by certified mail addressed to Borrower at the Property Address stated below, or to such other address as Borrower may designate by notice to the Note holder. Any notice to the Note holder shall be given by mailing such notice by certified mail, return receipt requested, to the Note holder at the address stated in the first paragraph of this Note, or at such other address as may have been designated by notice to Borrower.

The indebtedness evidenced by this Note is secured by a Mortgage, dated ————, and reference is made to the Mortgage for rights as to acceleration of the indebtedness evidenced by this Note.

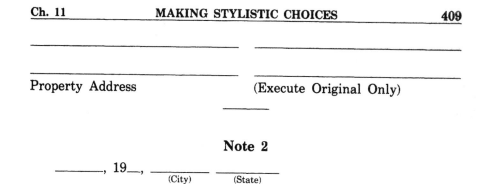

Property Address   (Execute Original Only)

Note 2

————, 19—, ————
            (City)   (State)

[Property Address]

1. BORROWER'S PROMISE TO PAY

In return for a loan that I have received, I promise to pay U.S. $————— (this amount is called "principal"), to the order of the Lender. The Lender is ————. I understand that the Lender may transfer this Note. The Lender or anyone who takes this Note by transfer and who is entitled to receive payments under this Note is called the "Note Holder."

2. INTEREST

Interest will be charged on unpaid principal until the full amount of principal has been paid. I will pay interest at a yearly rate of —————%.

The interest rate required by this Section 2 is the rate I will pay both before and after any default described in Section 6(B) of this Note.

3. PAYMENTS

(A) Time and Place of Payments

I will pay principal and interest by making payments every month.

I will make my monthly payments on the ——————— day of each month beginning on ————, 19—. I will make these payments every month until I have paid all of the principal and interest and any other charges described below that I may owe under this Note. My monthly payments will be applied to interest before principal. If, on ———————, ———————, I still owe amounts under this Note, I will pay those amounts in full on that date, which is called the "maturity date."

I will make my monthly payments at ——————— or at a different place if required by the Note Holder.

(B) Amount of Monthly Payments

My monthly payment will be in the amount of U.S. $———————

4. BORROWER'S RIGHT TO PREPAY

I have the right to make payments of principal at any time before they are due. A payment of principal only is known as a "prepayment." When I make a prepayment, I will tell the Note Holder in writing that I am doing so.

I may make a full prepayment or partial prepayments without paying any prepayment charge. The Note Holder will use all of my prepayments to reduce the amount of principal that I owe under this Note. If I make a partial prepayment, there will be no changes in the due date or in the amount of my monthly payment unless the Note Holder agrees in writing to those changes.

5. LOAN CHARGES

If a law, which applies to this loan and which sets maximum loan charges, is finally interpreted so that the interest or other loan charges collected or to be collected in connection with this loan exceed the permitted limits, then: (i) any such loan charge shall be reduced by the amount necessary to reduce the charge to the permitted limit; and (ii) any sums already collected from me which exceeded permitted limits will be refunded to me. The Note Holder may choose to make this refund by reducing the principal I owe under this Note or by making a direct payment to me. If a refund reduces principal, the reduction will be treated as a partial prepayment.

6. BORROWER'S FAILURE TO PAY AS REQUIRED

(A) Late Charge for Overdue Payments

If the Note Holder has not received the full amount of any monthly payment by the end of _____ calendar days after the date it is due, I will pay a late charge to the Note Holder. The amount of the charge will be _____% of my overdue payment of principal and interest. I will pay this late charge promptly but only once on each late payment.

(B) Default

If I do not pay the full amount of each monthly payment on the date it is due, I will be in default.

(C) Notice of Default

If I am in default, the Note Holder may send me a written notice telling me that if I do not pay the overdue amount by a certain date, the Note Holder may require me to pay immediately the full amount of principal which has not been paid and all the interest that I owe on that amount. That date must be at least 30 days after the date on which the notice is delivered or mailed to me.

(D) No Waiver By Note Holder

Even if, at a time when I am in default, the Note Holder does not require me to pay immediately in full as described above, the Note Holder will still have the right to do so if I am in default at a later time.

(E) Payment of Note Holder's Costs and Expenses

If the Note Holder has required me to pay immediately in full as described above, the Note Holder will have the right to be paid back by me for all of its costs and expenses in enforcing this Note to the extent not prohibited by applicable law. Those expenses include, for example, reasonable attorneys' fees.

7. GIVING OF NOTICES

Unless applicable law requires a different method, any notice that must be given to me under this Note will be given by delivering it or by mailing it by first class mail to me at the Property Address above or at a different address if I give the Note Holder a notice of my different address.

Any notice that must be given to the Note Holder under this Note will be given by mailing it by first class mail to the Note Holder at the address stated in Section 3(A) above or at a different address if I am given a notice of that different address.

8. OBLIGATIONS OF PERSONS UNDER THIS NOTE

If more than one person signs this Note, each person is fully and personally obligated to keep all of the promises made in this Note, including the promise to pay the full amount owed. Any person who is a guarantor, surety or endorser of this Note is also obligated to do these things. Any person who takes over these obligations, including the obligations of a guarantor, surety or endorser of this Note, is also obligated to keep all of the promises made in this Note. The Note Holder may enforce its rights under this Note against each person individually or against all of us together. This means that any one of us may be required to pay all of the amounts owed under this Note.

9. WAIVERS

I and any other person who has obligations under this Note waive the rights of presentment and notice of dishonor. "Presentment" means the right to require the Note Holder to demand payment of amounts due. "Notice of dishonor" means the right to require the Note Holder to give notice to other persons that amounts due have not been paid.

10. UNIFORM SECURED NOTE

This Note is a uniform instrument with limited variations in some jurisdictions. In addition to the protections given to the Note Holder under this Note, a Mortgage, Deed of Trust or Security Deed (the "Security Instrument"), dated the same date as this Note, protects the Note Holder from possible losses which might result if I do not keep the promises which I make in this Note. That Security Instrument describes how and under what conditions I may be required to make

immediate payment in full of all amounts I owe under this Note. Some
of those conditions are described as follows:

Transfer of the Property or a Beneficial Interest in Borrower.
If all or any part of the Property or any interest in it is sold or
transferred (or if a beneficial interest in Borrower is sold or transferred
and Borrower is not a natural person) without Lender's prior written
consent, Lender may, at its option, require immediate payment in full
of all sums secured by this Security Instrument. However, this option
shall not be exercised by Lender if exercise is prohibited by federal law
as of the date of this Security Instrument.

If Lender exercises this option, Lender shall give Borrower notice
of acceleration. The notice shall provide a period of not less than 30
days from the date the notice is delivered or mailed within which
Borrower must pay all sums secured by this Security Instrument. If
Borrower fails to pay these sums prior to the expiration of this period,
Lender may invoke any remedies permitted by this Security Instrument without further notice or demand on Borrower.

WITNESS THE HAND(S) AND SEAL(S) OF THE UNDER-
SIGNED.

————————————————— (Seal)
Borrower

————————————————— (Seal)
Borrower

————————————————— (Seal)
Borrower

————————————————— (Seal)
Borrower

[*Sign Original Only*]

—————

Exercise 11.3

Below are two Truth in Lending statements drafted by creditors to
comply with federal and state law. How readable is each one? Does
either go so far in the interest of readable style that it sacrifices
accuracy or completeness of substance? What features of plain language do you find in these statements that are worth using in legal
drafting generally? What features, if any, would you avoid?

Statement 1

YOUR BILLING RIGHTS
KEEP THIS NOTICE FOR FUTURE USE

This notice contains important information about your rights and our responsibilities
under the Fair Credit Billing Act.

Notify Us in Case of Errors or Questions About Your Bill:

If you think your bill is wrong, or if you need more information about a transaction on your bill, write us on a separate sheet at the address listed on the front of your bill. Write to us as soon as possible. We must hear from you no later than 60 days after we sent you the first bill on which the error or problem appeared. You can telephone us, but doing so will not preserve your rights.

In your letter, give us the following information:

- Your name and account number.
- The dollar amount of the suspected error.
- Describe the error and explain, if you can, why you believe there is an error.
  - (A) Do not send in your copy of a sales or credit slip unless you have a duplicate copy for your records.
  - (B) However, if additional information is needed, describe the item in question. The Bank may impose a charge of up to $5 for each copy of a sales slip, requested by you for your records, to help defray cost to the Bank for providing the copy(s).

If you have authorized us to pay your credit card bill automatically from your savings or checking account, you can stop the payment on any amount you think is wrong. To stop the payment your letter must reach us three business days before the automatic payment is scheduled to occur.

Your Rights and Our Responsibilities After We Receive Your Written Notice:

We must acknowledge your letter within 30 days, unless we have corrected the error by then. Within 90 days, we must either correct the error or explain why we believe the bill was correct.

After we receive your letter, we cannot try to collect any amount you question, or report you as delinquent. We can continue to bill you for the amount you question, including finance charges, and we can apply any unpaid amount against your credit limit. You do not have to pay any questioned amount while we are investigating, but you are still obligated to pay the parts of your bill that are not in question.

If we find that we made a mistake on your bill, you will not have to pay any finance charges related to any questioned amount. If we didn't make a mistake, you may have to pay finance charges, and you will have to make up any missed payments on the questioned amount. In either case, we will send you a statement of the amount you owe and the date that it is due.

If you fail to pay the amount that we think you owe, we may report you as delinquent. However, if our explanation does not satisfy you and you write to us within ten days telling us that you still refuse to pay, we must tell anyone we report you to that you have a question about your bill. And, we must tell you the name of anyone we reported you to. We must tell anyone we report you to that the matter has been settled between us when it finally is.

If we don't follow these rules, we can't collect the first $50 of the questioned amount, even if your bill was correct.

Special Rule for Credit Card Purchases:

If you have a problem with the quality of property or services that you purchased with a credit card, and you have tried in good faith to correct the problem with the merchant, you may have the right not to pay the remaining amount due on the property or services. There are two limitations on this right:

(a) You must have made the purchase in your home state or, if not within your home state, within 100 miles of your current mailing address; and

(b) The purchase price must have been more than $50.

These limitations do not apply if we own or operate the merchant, or if we mailed you the advertisement for the property or services.

Statement 2

In Case of Errors or Inquiries About Your Bill

The Federal Truth in Lending Act, the _____ Truth-in-Lending Act and the _____ Uniform Consumer Credit Code requires prompt correction of billing mistakes.

1. If you want to preserve your rights under the Act, here's what to do if you think your bill is wrong or if you need more information about an item on your bill:

   a. Do not write on the bill. On a separate sheet of paper write (you may telephone your inquiry but doing so will not preserve your rights under this law) the following:

      i. Your name and account number.

      ii. A description of the error and an explanation (to the extent you can explain) why you believe it is an error.

      If you only need more information, explain the item you are not sure about and, if you wish, ask for evidence of the charge such as a copy of the charge slip. Do not send in your copy of a sales slip or other document unless you have a duplicate copy for your records.

      iii. The dollar amount of the suspected error.

      iv. Any other information (such as your address) which you think will help the creditor to identify you or the reason for your complaint or inquiry.

   b. Send your billing error notice to:

      Mail it as soon as you can, but in any case, early enough to reach the creditor within 60 days after the bill was mailed to you. If you have authorized your bank to automatically pay from your checking or savings account any credit card bills from that bank, you can stop or reverse payment on any amount you think is wrong by mailing your notice so the creditor receives it within 16 days after the bill was sent to you. However, you do not have to meet this 16–day deadline to get the creditor to investigate your billing error claim.

2. The creditor must acknowledge all letters pointing out possible errors within 30 days of receipt, unless the creditor is able to correct your bill during that 30 days. Within 90 days after receiving your letter, the creditor must either correct the error or explain why the creditor believes the bill was correct. Once the creditor has explained the bill, the creditor has no further obligation to you even though you still believe that there is an error, except as provided in paragraph 5 below.

3. After the creditor has been notified, neither the creditor nor an attorney nor a collection agency may send you collection letters or take other collection action with respect to the amount in dispute; but periodic statements may be sent to you, and the disputed amount can be applied against your credit limit.

You cannot be threatened with damage to your credit rating or sued for the amount in question, nor can the disputed amount be reported to a credit bureau or to other creditors as delinquent until the creditor has answered your inquiry. However, you remain obligated to pay the parts of your bill not in dispute.

NOTICE: See reverse side for important information regarding your rights to dispute billing errors.

Appendix

BIBLIOGRAPHY

I. BOOKS

There are many books on legal writing in general. The few listed below are especially helpful on legal drafting in particular.

J.K. Aitken, ed., E.L. Piesse's The Elements of Drafting, The Law Book Co., Sydney, Australia (7th ed. 1987). This book is a reworking of a series of articles originally written as addresses for tutorial classes in drafting at The University of Melbourne. It focuses primarily on using arrangement and form to make a document clear enough that rules of interpretation need not be applied to it.

Irwin Alterman, Plain and Accurate Style in Court Papers, American Law Institute—American Bar Association Committee on Continuing Professional Education, Philadelphia, Pa. (1987). This is a plain language style manual for pleadings, motion practice, discovery, briefs, and other litigation documents.

Gertrude Block, Effective Legal Writing, Foundation Press, Mineola, N.Y. (3d ed. 1986). This book includes both practical advice on a wide range of stylistic matters and a useful review of grammar and punctuation.

Alexander A. Bove, Jr., The Complete Book of Wills and Estates, Henry Holt and Co., New York, N.Y. (1989). This is an informal treatise on wills written with the testator as the intended audience, including a chapter on "dealing with lawyers."

Scott J. Burnham, Drafting Contracts, The Michie Co., Charlottesville, Va. (1987). This book has two parts: one on how the principles of contract law are exemplified in drafting, and the other on how the principles of drafting are exemplified in contracts. It is a textbook with exercises that invite the student to apply knowledge of contract law to drafting agreements.

Charles R. Calleros, Legal Method and Writing, Little, Brown and Co., Boston, Mass. (1990). This is a textbook for an entire law school legal writing program. It includes a chapter on each of the following:

416

pleadings, motion for summary judgment, motion to exclude evidence before trial, contracts, and advice and demand letters.

Frank E. Cooper, Writing in Law Practice, Bobbs–Merril Co., Indianapolis, Ind. (1963). This book includes separate chapters on drafting each of the following: letters, pleadings, contracts, statutes, and wills.

Jack Davies, Legislative Law and Process in a Nutshell, West Publishing Company, St. Paul, Minn. (2d ed. 1986). This book by a veteran legislator presents the legislative process as an "intellectual journey" and includes a detailed chapter on bill drafting, which covers drafting techniques, mandatory provisions, sometimes useful provisions, definitions, common drafting errors, tactical drafting, and packaging bills.

Robert Dick, Legal Drafting, Carswell Co., Toronto, Canada (2d ed. 1985). This book includes detailed discussion of ambiguity, definitions, and style.

Reed Dickerson, The Fundamentals of Legal Drafting, Little, Brown and Co., Boston, Mass. (2d ed. 1985). In its first edition (1965), this was the first book to bring together the body of knowledge that is now known as "legal drafting." The second edition includes and updates most of the materials from Professor Dickerson's earlier book, Legislative Drafting (1954).

Elmer A. Driedger, A Manual of Instructions for Legislative and Legal Writing, Department of Justice, Ottawa, Canada, 6 vols. (1982). This is an exercise manual containing the substance of seminars conducted at the University of Ottawa. Its method is to comment in detail on students' redrafts of sections from ordinances and statutes.

William N. Eskridge, Jr. and Philip P. Frickey, Cases and Materials on Legislation: Statutes and the Creation of Public Policy, West Publishing Co., St. Paul, Minn. (1988). This is a textbook for a course on the public lawmaking processes, addressing law creation, interpretation, and evolution. It includes drafting problems and exercises throughout and a chapter expressly on drafting.

Carl Felsenfeld and Alan Siegel, Writing Contracts in Plain English, West Publishing Co., St. Paul, Minn. (1981). This is a definitive study of the Plain Language Movement and how to apply its principles to drafting contracts.

Francine Wattman Frank and Paula A. Treichler, Language, Gender, and Professional Writing: Theoretical Approaches and Guidelines for Nonsexist Usage, Modern Language Assn., New York, N.Y. (1989). This book is a full-length study of linguistic sexism, with suggestions about nondiscriminatory usage.

Bryan A. Garner, A Dictionary of Modern Legal Usage, Oxford University Press, New York, N.Y. (1987). This book is more than a dictionary; it is a guide to style and usage. In one alphabetical list, it provides entries on specific points of word usage and grammar and includes short essays on special topics such as Latinisms and sexism.

Bryan A. Garner, The Elements of Legal Style, Oxford University Press, New York, N.Y. (1991). In this style manual, the author includes rules of usage on punctuation, word choice, and grammar and syntax.

Hollis T. Hurd, Writing for Lawyers, Journal Broadcasting and Communications, Pittsburgh, Pa. (1982). This book is not as scholarly as the others in this bibliography. It is written in an informal, often humorous style, with chapter headings that begin with "rules, tips and hints." Two chapters are loaded with practical drafting advice in terms not found in the more scholarly texts. One of these chapters is on style; the other is on drafting as such.

Leonard Levin, A Student's Guide to Will Drafting, Matthew Bender & Co., New York, N.Y., Oakland, Cal., and Albany, N.Y. (1987). This book is designed as a supplement for a course in wills and trusts, or in tax planning. It surveys writing skills, summarizes probate law from the planning point of view, and includes in appendixes both brief exercises and longer drafting projects, each with discussion of the problems involved and possible or proposed solutions.

Robert J. Martineau, Drafting Legislation and Rules in Plain English, West Publishing Co., St. Paul, Minn. (1991). This is a book for anyone who drafts any type of legislation or rule, combining the principles of legislative drafting with those of the plain language movement. It is intended as a textbook and also for use in the "real world."

David Mellinkoff, Legal Writing: Sense and Nonsense, West Publishing Co., St. Paul, Minn. (1982). This book combines the legal scholar's knowledge and insight with informal style and brusk tone. The author shouts rules like "Beware the Twofer" and "Thou Shalt Not Never." This is not a convenient reference book in which to look up some particular drafting principle or kind of document. However, the person who reads it through can learn much from it about how to draft clearly, precisely, and concisely.

Mary Barnard Ray and Barbara J. Cox, Beyond the Basics: A Text for Advanced Legal Writing, West Publishing Co., St. Paul, Minn. (1991). This textbook includes a chapter on each of the following: statutes, jury instructions, contracts, pleadings, motions, interrogatories, opinion letters, and wills and trusts.

William W. Schwarzer and Lynn H. Pasahow, Civil Discovery: A Guide to Efficient Practice, Prentice Hall Law & Business, Englewood Cliffs, N.J. (1988, 1989 Supplement). This book does not purport to be a treatise on discovery law; instead its authors intend to give practical advice about efficient discovery practice in federal courts. In addition to text and case citations, it includes sample forms.

Thomas L. Shaffer and Carol Ann Mooney, The Planning and Drafting of Wills and Trusts, The Foundation Press, Westbury, N.Y. (3d ed. 1991). This is a textbook on wills, trusts, future interests, and taxes, with focus on the law-office planning context. In addition to chapters on the documents—wills and trusts—it devotes two chapters to language, focusing on drafting in plain language.

Shepard's Motions in Federal Court, 3 vols., Colorado Springs, Col. (2d ed. 1991). This set of books fully treats motion practice in federal courts, including local district court rules and cases cited by circuit.

William P. Statsky, Legislative Analysis and Drafting, West Publishing Co., St. Paul, Minn. (2d ed. 1975). This book is as much about reading and construing statutes as about drafting them. However, it incorporates considerable detail on statute drafting and advice about style that is useful for any legal drafting.

Jule E. Stocker, Stocker on Drawing Wills, Practising Law Institute, New York, N.Y. (10th ed. 1987). This book focuses on drafting a typical will, discussing legacies, devises, trusts, and powers of appointment. It analyzes tax considerations, including estate tax under the Tax Reform Act of 1986. It also provides a sample will with trust provisions, selected alternative clauses, and codicil.

George Vetter, Successful Civil Litigation: How to Win Your Case Before You Enter the Courtroom, Prentice Hall, Englewood Cliffs, N.J. (1977). This book includes chapters on winning strategies for using pleadings to achieve long-range goals, using motions to gain tactical advantages, and using discovery tools in combination.

Richard C. Wydick, Plain English for Lawyers, Carolina Academic Press, Durham, N.C. (2d ed. 1985). This book uses copious examples to show how to achieve the major goals of writing in plain language: omitting surplus words; using familiar, concrete words; using short sentences; using base verbs and the active voice; arranging words with care; and avoiding language quirks. The book also contains exercises on each of these matters and suggested answers to all of the exercises.

II. ARTICLES

A great deal of helpful material about drafting is in periodicals. The list of sources below is not intended to be exhaustive but includes a broad sample of the kind of coverage available.

ABA Committee on Estate Planning and Drafting, A Sample Will, 27 Practical Lawyer 21 (No. 2, Mar. 1, 1981).

Abrahamson and Hughes, Shall We Dance? Steps for Legislators and Judges in Statutory Interpretation, 75 Minn.L.Rev. 1045 (1991).

Allen, Symbolic Logic: A Razor–Edged Tool for Drafting and Interpreting Legal Documents, 66 Yale L.J. 833 (1957).

Allen and Engholm, The Need for Clear Structure in "Plain Language" Legal Drafting, 13 J.L. Reform 455 (1980).

Allen and Engholm, Normalized Legal Drafting and the Query Method, 29 J. Legal Educ. 380 (1978).

Alterman, Plain and Accurate Style in Lawsuit Papers, 62 Mich. B.J. 964 (1983).

Benson, The End of Legalese: The Game Is Over, 13 N.Y.U.Rev.L. & Soc. Change 519 (1984–85).

Benson, Plain English Comes to Court, 13 Litigation No. 1, 21 (1986).

Benson, Up a Statute with Gun and Camera: Isolating Linguistic and Logical Structures in the Analysis of Legislative Language, 8 Seton Hall Legis.J. 279 (1984).

Beyer, Statutory Will Methodologies—Incorporated Forms vs. Fill–In Forms: Rivalry or Peaceful Coexistence? 94 Dickenson L.Rev. 231 (1990).

Block, Plain Language Laws: Promise v Performance, 62 Mich.B.J. 950 (1983).

Browne, Development of the FNMA/FHLMC Plain Language Mortgage Documents—Some Useful Techniques, 14 Real Prop.Prob. & Tr.J. 696 (1979).

Bruno and Rosenfeld, Wither [sic] Whereas—The Legal Implications of Recitals, July 1988 Mich.B.J. 634.

Christie, Vagueness and Legal Language, 48 Minn.L.Rev. 885 (1964).

Conard, New Ways to Write Laws, 56 Yale L.J. 458 (1947).

Cusack, The Blue–Pencilled Will, August 1979 Tr. & Est. 33.

Cusack, The Plain English Will Revisited, July 1980 Tr. & Est. 42.

Davis, Protecting Consumers from Overdisclosure and Gobbledygook: An Empirical Look at the Simplification of Consumer–Credit Contracts, 63 Va.L.Rev. 841 (1977).

Dickerson, Legal Drafting: Writing as Thinking, or, Talk-back from Your Draft and How To Exploit It, 29 J.Legal Educ. 373 (1978).

Dickerson, Obscene Telephone Calls: An Introduction to the Reading of Statutes, 22 Harv.J. on Legis. 173 (1985).

Dickerson, Toward a Legal Dialectic, 61 Ind.L.J. 315 (1986).

Drafting Manual for the Army and Air Force Codes, 11 Fed.B.J. 240 (1950).

Driedger, The Preparation of Legislation, 31 Can.B.Rev. 33 (1953).

Felsenfeld, The Future of Plain English, 62 Mich.B.J. 942 (1983).

Fitzgerald and Spratt, Rule Drafting—I, 119 (Part 2) New L.J. 991 (1969).

Fitzgerald and Spratt, Rule Drafting—III, 119 (Part 2) New L.J. 1052 (1969).

Gray, Reducing Unintended Ambiguity in Statutes: An Introduction to Normalization of Statutory Drafting, 54 Tenn.L.Rev. 433 (1987).

Haynsworth, How To Draft Clear and Concise Legal Documents, 31 Practical Lawyer 41 (1985).

Jones, Some Reflections on a Draftsman's Time Sheet, 35 ABA J. 941 (1949).

Kirk, Legal Drafting: Curing Unexpressive Language, 3 Tex.Tech L.Rev. 23 (1971).

Kirk, Legal Drafting: How Should a Document Begin? 3 Tex.Tech L.Rev. 233 (1972).

Kirk, Legal Drafting: Some Elements of Technique, 4 Tex.Tech L.Rev. 297 (1973).

Leskovac, Legal Writing and Plain English: Does Voice Matter? 38 Syracuse L.Rev. 1193 (1987).

Lesser, The "No Damage for Delay" Clause: Avoiding Delay Claims in Construction, Oct. 12, 1987 Ohio State B.Assn. Report 1578.

Llewellyn, Remarks on the Theory of Appellate Decision and the Rules or Canons About How Statutes Are To Be Construed, 3 Vand.L. Rev. 395 (1950).

McCarty, That Hybrid "and/or," 39 Mich.St.B.J. 9 (No. 5, May 1960).

McElhaney, A Style Sheet for *Litigation*, 1 Scribes J. of Legal Writing 63 (1990).

Robinson, Drafting—Its Substance and Teaching, 25 J. Legal Educ. 514 (1973).

Ross, On Legalities and Linguistics: Plain Language Legislation, 30 Buffalo L.Rev. 317 (1981).

Slawson, The New Meaning of Contract: The Transformation of Contracts Law by Standard Forms, 46 U.Pa.L.Rev. 21 (1984).

Symposium: Making Jury Instructions Comprehensible, 8 Bridgeport L.Rev. (No. 2, 1987).

Trawick, Form as Well as Substance, 49 Fla.B.J. 437 (1975).

Wason, The Drafting of Rules, 118 (Part 1) New L.J. 548 (1968).

Word, A Brief for Plain English Wills and Trusts, 14 U.Rich.L.Rev. 471 (1980).

Wydick, Plain English for Lawyers, 66 Calif.L.Rev. 727 (1978).

Younger, The Definitive Word on Definitions, 72 ABA J. 98 (1986).

III. COMMENTS

Comment, Attorney Malpractice in California: The Liability of a Lawyer Who Drafts an Imprecise Contract or Will, 24 U.C.L.A.L.Rev. 422 (1976).

Comment, Sexism in the Statutes: Identifying and Solving the Problem of Ambiguous Gender Bias in Legal Writing, 32 Buffalo L.Rev. 559 (1983).

*

Index of Subjects

References are to pages.
Page numbers followed by "a" refer to annotations.
Page numbers followed by "n" refer to footnotes.
See also, Index of Documents.

See also, Index of Documents.

See also, Index of Documents.

See also, Index of Documents.

See also, Index of Documents.

Index of Documents

References are to pages.
See also Index of Subjects.

†